COULDN'T KEEP IT TO MYSELF

∎ ∎ ∎ ∎ ∎ ∎ ∎ ∎ ∎ ∎ ∎ ∎ ∎ ∎

COULDN'T KEEP IT TO MYSELF

WALLY LAMB
AND THE WOMEN OF YORK
CORRECTIONAL INSTITUTION
TESTIMONIES FROM OUR IMPRISONED SISTERS

HARPER ⬤ PERENNIAL

NEW YORK • LONDON • TORONTO • SYDNEY

A continuation of the copyright page appears on page 352.

COULDN'T KEEP IT TO MYSELF. Collection copyright © 2003 by Wally Lamb. All rights reserved. Printed in the United States of America. No part of this book may be used or reproduced in any manner whatsoever without written permission except in the case of brief quotations embodied in critical articles and reviews. For information, address HarperCollins Publishers, 195 Broadway, New York, NY 10007.

HarperCollins books may be purchased for educational, business, or sales promotional use. For information, please e-mail the Special Markets Department at SPsales@harpercollin.com.

First paperback edition published 2004.

Designed by Kelly Hitt

The Library of Congress has cataloged the hardcover edition as follows:

Couldn't keep it to myself: testimonies from our imprisoned sisters/Wally Lamb and the Women of York Correctional Institution.
    p. cm.
  ISBN 0-06-053429-X
    1. Prisoners' writings, American—Connecticut. 2. Women prisoners—Connecticut. I. Lamb, Wally. II. Women of York Correctional Institution.

PS548.C8 C68 2003
810.8'09287'086927—dc21

2002036869

ISBN 0-06-059537-X (pbk.)

20 21 22   WB/LSC   30 29 28 27 26 25 24 23

For Diane Bartholomew, who left behind a legacy of words

CONTENTS

ACKNOWLEDGMENTS

The editor and contributors wish to thank the following individuals for their time, talents, and assistance in the birthing of this book: George Allen, William Barber, Aaron Bremyer, Paul Brown, Angelica Canales, Lynn Castelli, Debbie Cauley, Linda Chester, Bruce Cohen, Marge Cohen, Evva Donn, Kassie Evashevski, James Fox, Dee Gibbs, Dorthula Green, Brenden Hitt, Kelly Hitt, Doris Janhsen, Leslie Johnson, Terese Karmel, Ann Koletsky, Christine Lamb, Pam Lewis, Ethel Mantzaris, Kay Miller, Kenneth Norwick, Paul Olsewski, Pam Pfeifer, Carl Raymond, Warden Pam Richards, Rick Roselle, Barbara Sanders, Beth Neelman Silfin, Dan Taylor, Pedro Valentin, Robert Youdelman, Ellen Zahl, and Gale Zucker.

Special thanks to publisher Judith Regan, editor Aliza Fogelson, and literary agent Leigh Feldman, and to the administrative, custodial, and educational staffs of York Correctional Institution.

NOTES TO THE READER

||||||||||||||||||||

ABOUT THE COVER The front cover art for *Couldn't Keep It to Myself* is an assemblage made by York School students who participated in an extension course in art appreciation taught by Pedro Valentin through Three Rivers Community College of Norwich, Connecticut.

ABOUT CONTENT When David Berkowitz, the infamous "Son of Sam" serial killer, signed a book deal to tell the story of his murderous spree, there was public outcry. To prevent high-profile criminals from profiting from heinous deeds, the New York legislature enacted the "Son of Sam" law in 1977. The statute allowed victims of a person convicted of a crime to access profits made from that crime. In a later case involving a book by a well-known organized crime figure, "Sammy the Bull" Gravano, the Son of Sam law was challenged and declared unconstitutional because of its overly broad restriction of First Amendment rights. A second Son of Sam statute, enacted in 1992, narrowed the scope of the earlier law. If an author made only incidental or indirect reference to a crime he or she had committed, then profits from the writing could presumably fall outside of the "profits made from a crime" definition. Following New York's lead, the U.S. government and some forty states, including Connecticut, passed their own versions of Son of Sam statutes.

Out of respect for Connecticut's Son of Sam law, the contributors to this anthology have not written directly about the crimes for which they were convicted. References to these crimes are incidental or tangential to the stories the writers have chosen to tell.

ABOUT EDITING While they were developing their works in progress, the contributors to this volume gathered and used critical responses from their peers, workshop co-facilitator Dale Griffith, and me. Most wrote numerous drafts and received written as well as verbal editorial feedback on each revision. There was, in addition, classroom instruction about various aspects of craft: the use of past versus present tense in writing memoir, how to recast memories as dramatic scenes with the help of fictional techniques, how to balance narrative with exposition, how to write successful segues. When the submission deadline arrived, I took off my teaching hat and put on my editor's cap. It was not a comfortable fit.

"What *is* editing?" I finally asked my German publisher, Dr. Doris Janhsen of List-Verlag, midway through the editing of this collection. "How much editorial intervention is too much? How little is too little? How do I balance the author's right to tell a story on her own terms with the reader's right to a smooth, logical, and interesting read?" Dr. Janhsen said she edited prose for clarity, pace, and dramaturgy. I went back to work on the manuscript, guided by those three principles. In the end, each of the selections in this book dictated its own editorial needs. "Fat" writing was made more lean. Flat phrasing was enlivened. Paragraphs and episodes were cut and pasted. Shorter, self-contained pieces were seamed together when theme or motif invited the fusion. Consequently, there is a range of editorial involvement, from minimal nip-and-tuck to a level of activity approaching "as written with." Most fell somewhere in the middle of the continuum. In all cases, the writers had final approval over their edited works.

ABOUT THE CONTRIBUTORS Nine of the eleven contributors in this collection wrote their pieces while incarcerated at York Correctional Institution, a maximum-security facility located on the Connecticut shoreline in Niantic. The two exceptions are Dale Griffith ("Bad Girls"), a State of Connecticut–certified teacher at York School and the workshop's co-facilitator, and Nancy Birkla ("Three Steps Past the Monkeys"), a Connecticut native and recovering addict who was imprisoned in the Kentucky State Penitentiary for Women. Birkla is a private writing student and my first cousin. The grandmother who appears prominently in her essay was my grandmother, too.

ABOUT COMMUNITY Founded in 1977, Interval House of Hartford, Connecticut, is the state's largest and most comprehensive service provider to battered women and their children. Says a representative:

"Every single day, story after story, the determined advocates of Interval House stand with abused women in their struggle for survival and justice." The contributors of *Couldn't Keep It to Myself* have made Interval House an equal partner in the sharing of revenues from this anthology.

—WL

COULDN'T KEEP IT TO OURSELVES

||||||||||||||||||||||||

WALLY LAMB

HE TOY DEPARTMENT AT THE DURABLE STORE SOLD two blackboards. The modest two-by-three-foot model came with wall brackets and a three-piece starter box of chalk. Its deluxe cousin was framed in wood, had legs and feet, and came "loaded": a pair of erasers, a pointer, a twelve-stick chalk set, and a bonus box of colored chalk. I was a third-grader when I spotted that blackboard. Good-bye to Lincoln Logs and Louisville Sluggers. From the age of eight, I wanted to teach.

My first students were my older sisters. As preteenagers, Gail and Vita were more interested in imitating the dance steps of the *American Bandstand* "regulars" than in playing school, but a direct order from our mother sent them trudging upstairs to my classroom. I'd prepared for their arrival: work sheets, white shirt and clip-on tie, alarm clock hidden under my bed for the surprise fire drill. If my sisters had to play, then they would play*act*. Vita cast herself as hip-swiveling Cookie Crane, as smoldering a third-grader as there ever was. Gail was Rippy Van Snoot, the class incorrigible. I was launching into opening exercises when Rippy reached past me, grabbed a blackboard eraser, and bounced it off my forehead. Cookie shrieked with delight and lit an imaginary cigarette. I forget which reprobate flung my flash cards into the air and made the room rain arithmetic.

Fourteen years later I was a high school English teacher with my first *actual* students. Paula Plunkett and Seth Jinks were the two I remember most vividly from my rookie year. Paula had pretty eyes and graceful penmanship, but she was encased in a fortress of fat. Sad and isolated, she sat at a special table in back because she didn't fit the desks. She never spoke; no one ever spoke to her. In my first-year-teacher naïveté, I sought to draw Paula into the dynamic, thinking group work and class discussion would save her. My plan failed miserably.

Seth Jinks was in the twelfth-grade class I'd been assigned because I had no seniority. "The sweathogs," these kids dubbed themselves. I was twenty-one, and so were three or four of my sweathogs. We honeymooned for a couple of weeks. Then one morning I walked up the aisle and tapped Seth Jinks on the shoulder. I needed to wake him up so I could exchange the paperback he hadn't read for the new one he wasn't going to read. "Seth, get your head off the desk," I said. "Here's the new book." No response. I poked him. He looked up at me with little-boy-lost eyes. "Go fuck yourself," he said. The room went quiet. The sweathogs, Seth, and I held our collective breath and waited for my response. And in that uneasy silence, and the days, and months, and decades that followed, teaching became for me not just a job but a calling. I have found special meaning in working with hard nuts, tough cookies, and hurtin' buckaroos—those children among us who are the walking wounded.

That said, I did *not* want to go to York Correctional Institution, Connecticut's maximum-security prison for women, on that warm August afternoon in 1999. I was keeping a promise I'd made to Marge Cohen, the prison school librarian. Marge had called three months earlier, as I was preparing for a twelve-city book tour in support of my second novel, *I Know This Much Is True*. Several suicides and suicide attempts had triggered an epidemic of despair at the prison, Marge had explained; the school staff, groping to find help, was canvasing the community. They thought writing might prove useful to the women as a coping tool. Would I come and speak? Because I'm frequently asked to support good causes and have a hard time saying no, I keep an index card taped to my phone—a scripted refusal that allows me to preserve family and writing time. That day, though, I couldn't find my card. I told Marge I'd visit when I got back from my book tour.

I would never have predicted an author's life for myself, but when I was thirty, while on summer hiatus from teaching, I'd sat down and written a short story on a whim. I liked doing it and wrote another. For my third story, I fused a sarcastic voice to the visual memory of the mute, isolated Paula Plunkett. For years I had worried and wondered about my former student. What had become of her? What had all that weight meant? Who had she been as a child? In the absence of actual knowledge, the life I invented around her remembered image became my first novel, *She's Come Undone*. It took me nine years to figure out the story of that bruised fictional soul whom I'd fathered and then grown to love and worry over. I loved and stewed over the flawed identical twins of my second novel, too—one of whom had a generous measure of Seth Jinks's anger. What I did *not* see coming was that the world would embrace these characters also. "Hello, Wally? Guess what?" The caller on the other end of the phone line was Oprah Winfrey. She called twice, once for each novel. The result: best-seller lists, limo rides, movie deals, and foreign translations. Oprah's Book Club had taken my life by the seat of the pants and sent me on the road.

Rock stars on tour bust up their hotel rooms. They get drunk or high, trash the furniture with their bandmates, party with groupies. But authors on tour are quieter, more solitary souls. Between appointments, we sit by ourselves in our rooms, nibbling like prairie dogs on room service sandwiches, or ironing our clothes for the next reading, or watching *Judge Judy*. Perhaps the most surreal moment during my book tour that summer occurred in a hotel room in Dayton, Ohio. While channel-surfing, I came upon the quiz show *Jeopardy!* at the exact moment my name surfaced. "He wrote the novel *She's Come Undone*," Alex Trebek stated. In the long and torturous pause that followed, the three contestants stood there, lockjawed and mute, itching but unable to press their thumbs to their buzzers. And sitting on the edge of the bed in room 417 of the Westin Hotel, I uttered in a sheepish voice, "Who is Wally Lamb?"

I'm a family man, a fiction writer, a teacher, and a guy who can't say no without the index card. On that nervous first drive to York Correctional Institution, I sought to calm myself with music. I was fumbling with CD cases and radio buttons when suddenly, over the airwaves, a piano pounded and the car shook with the vocal thunder of Newark, New Jersey's Abyssinian Baptist Choir. The unfamiliar song so overpowered me that I pulled to the shoulder to listen. When it ended, I looked up at the highway sign in front of which I'd landed. CORRECTIONAL FACILITY AREA, it said. DO NOT STOP. The inexplicable emotional wallop of that moment fills me with wonder to this day.

To gain access to the women of York prison, you check in with the guard at the main gate, hang your laminated badge on your shirt pocket, walk through a metal detector, then pass through a series of ten doors, some of which slide open mysteriously after you stand and wait.

You don't see who's flipping the switches, so it's an Orwellian entrance. At the prison school, I met my liaison, Dale Griffith, a warm and exuberant English teacher. Dale and I arranged the chairs in a circle, a uniformed corrections officer bellowed orders from the corridor, and thirty inmates entered the room.

Dressed identically in cranberry T-shirts and pocketless jeans, the women came in all colors, shapes, sizes, and degrees of gender identification. Their attitudes ranged from hangdog to Queen of Sheba. Most had shown up not to write but to check out "that guy who was on *Oprah*." I spoke. We tried some exercises. I asked if anyone had questions about writing. Several hands shot into the air. "You *met* Oprah?" "What's Oprah like?" "Oprah's cool, you know what I'm sayin'?" Uh, was that a question?

At the end of my talk, one of the women stood, thanked me for coming, and pitched me a curveball. "You coming back?" she asked. Thirty pairs of wary eyes were upon me and my index card was back in my office. "Uh, well . . . okay," I said. "Write something and I'll see you in two weeks. Any subject, two pages minimum. Your drafts will be your tickets into the workshop."

At session two, fifteen of the thirty chairs were empty. Stacie wanted praise, not feedback. Manhattan said she'd *meant* to be vague and non-specific—that *her* business wasn't necessarily the *reader's* business. Ruth must have thought she was a guest on *Oprah;* she'd written only a paragraph, but man oh man, did she want to *talk.* At age fifty-five Diane was the senior member of the group. For ninety minutes she hunched forward, fists clenched on her desktop. Her suspicious eyes followed my every move. Diane had written under the pseudonym Natasha and had exacted a promise before class that her work would never, ever be read aloud. I predicted she'd be gone by session three.

But it was *during* session three that Diane Bartholomew ("Snapshots of My Early Life") couldn't keep her writing to herself. Her shaky hand went up and she asked if she could share what she'd written. In a barely audible voice, she read a disjointed, two-page summary of her horrific life story: incest, savage abuse, spousal homicide, lawyerly indifference, and, in prison, parallel battles against breast cancer and deep, dark depression. When she stopped, there was silence, a communal intake of breath. Then, applause—a single pair of hands at first, joined by another pair, and then by everyone. Bartholomew had sledgehammered the dam of distrust, and the women's writing began to flow.

That was three years ago. I stopped counting sessions somewhere around number fifty. Writers have come and gone: the narcotics-addicted nurse who wrote a moving apologia to a deceased aunt whose support had never wavered; the high school athlete who, a month after graduation, brandished her softball bat during a convenience store robbery and wrote to figure out why; the young alcoholic mother who time-traveled, penning a personal letter to one of the prison's original 1917 inmates, also an alcoholic. The workshop sessions have been a journey rich with laughter, tears, heart-stopping leaps of faith, and miraculous personal victories. There have been bumps in the road, too. Addicts are elusive; they tend to begin promising drafts, take them to some interesting midway point, then give up on themselves and stop coming. There have been trust issues. Prison is not a place where trust is given easily, and a writer who shares her work in progress risks exposure. That risk taking must be honored. Only the writer should decide when, and if, her work is ready for the eyes and ears of nongroup members—ready, in other words, to go public. If another group member breaches that trust, she has to leave. Similarly, a few con artists and drama queens have been handed their walking papers. A functional writing community cannot accommodate the needs of would-be superstars or instigators of the guess-what-she-said-about-you variety. But those have been the exceptions. The brave writers whose work is represented in this volume have acted in good faith, faced their demons, stayed the course, and revised relentlessly. And in taking on the subject of themselves—making themselves vulnerable to the unseen reader—they have exchanged powerlessness for the power that comes with self-awareness.

"I started writing because of a terrible feeling of powerlessness," the novelist Anita Brookner has said. The National Book Award winner Alice McDermott noted that the most difficult thing about becoming a writer was convincing herself that she had anything to say that people would *want* to read. "There's nothing to writing," the columnist Red Smith once commented. "All you do is sit down at a typewriter and open a vein."

Michelle Jessamy ("Motherlove") was fourteen when she became pregnant by her teenage boyfriend. Despite the challenges, Jessamy's impending motherhood helped her get closer to her own emotionally distant mother. As she drafted her memory piece, that mother-daughter epiphany emerged as the centerpiece. Then, mid-draft, Jessamy hit a snag. She began writing a flashback to an earlier instance of sexual abuse—a hallway molestation by a friend of the family when she was eleven. The painful incident was integral to the story she needed to tell, but disclosing her long-kept secret made Jessamy feel uncomfortable. She stopped writing. But self-censorship felt uncomfortable, too. Jessamy had worked hard on her essay and wanted to see it through. The solution? A change of genre. On paper, Jessamy became Mo'Shay Shambly, and the pronoun *I* became *she*. Mo'Shay had the same hazel eyes as Michelle, the same experiences. But now Jessamy was writing autobiographical fiction. That little bit of distance unblocked her and she finished her piece.

Brenda Medina ("Hell, and How I Got Here") was self-censoring like Michelle Jessamy, but for a very different reason. For months after she joined our group, she labored on the same short essay about the death of her uncle Carlos—draft after draft after draft. One day I suggested to Medina that, God bless him, I didn't think I had the strength to attend to poor Uncle Carlos's death one more time. "There's something else I *want* to write about, but I can't," she told me. That "something" was what had landed her in prison ten years earlier at age seventeen: her affiliation with a violent street gang.

York Correctional Institution is vigilant in its efforts to eliminate gang influence within the compound. Incarcerated gang members who choose to uphold their allegiance to "the family" pay a steep price in the form of punitive segregation, loss of privileges, and loss of the "good time" that can shorten their stay on the inside. A self-described punk when she arrived at York, Brenda Medina had traveled a long and difficult road as an inmate, freeing herself from the psychological grip of her "family" and undertaking the rigorous step-by-step process by which an inmate repudiates her gang affiliation and begins rehabilitation in earnest. Even mentioning the name of a gang can cast suspicion that the inmate has reneged on her disaffiliation. Medina's very real fear was that, if she wrote about her past life, her work might be seized, taken out of context, and misconstrued as gang-friendly. If that happened, she could lose much of what she had worked so hard to achieve. My collaborator, Dale Griffith, dealt with the problem directly. She sought and received permission from prison officials for Medina to take up her gang experience as subject matter. With that hurdle cleared, the writer was on her way to a personal essay that, far from glorifying gangs, depicts their insidious hold on young people's lives and the cancerous destruction of their futures.

In her much-loved book on writing, *Bird by Bird: Some Instructions on Writing and Life,* Anne Lamott observes: "We write to expose the unexposed. If there is one door in the castle you have been told not to go through, you must." The writer's job, Lamott instructs, is "to turn the unspeakable into words—not just into any words, but if we can, into rhythm and blues." Bonnie Foreshaw ("Faith, Power, and Pants") is a woman of stately bearing, strong faith, and rhythm-and-blues diction, the latter a reflection of her Jamaican birth and South Florida upbringing. In Foreshaw's vernacular, her cousin is "my old cous'" and her problems are "botherations." She does not converse with friends; she "conversates." One day a while back, Foreshaw entered the workshop looking weary. "How you feeling today, Miss Bonnie?" I asked. "I'm feeling botheration and sufferation inside *this* place," she replied. Another day I rushed to the prison from a speaking engagement. I'm usually in jeans but that afternoon I was wearing jacket, tie, and dress pants that had fit me better before I'd lost some weight. "How's the writing going, Bonnie?" I asked. Ignoring the question, she gave me a frowning once-over instead. "Those *your* pants?" she wanted to know.

The problem was this: Foreshaw's speech was colorful and cut-to-the-chase direct, but her writing "voice" was ponderous and deadly dull—the result, I suspect, of her having tried too hard to please grade school teachers more interested in grammatical correctness than in voice. In an early draft, Foreshaw wrote of a disciplinary measure taken against her: "There I was, already in prison. Yet, I was being persecuted even further into the bowels of hell. However, I was willing and able to endure whatever punishment was going to be inflicted on me because of the grace of God's spiritual influence, guidance, and protection. I would make it through this ordeal."

"Bonnie!" we'd advise her during workshop discussions. "Stop preaching and *conversate*!" When she did, Foreshaw's writing came alive.

A writer's voice, says the author and teacher Donald Murray, is

forged from family background, ethnic heritage, childhood neighborhood, present neighborhood, and the writer's roles in life. "And ironically," Murray says, "the more personal, the more individual you
become, the more universally you will be read." The fiction writer Sandra Cisneros says she tries to write in the voice she would use with a
friend sitting across her kitchen table while she's wearing her pajamas.
Her stories are read the world over.

Invoking one's natural voice on paper is easier for some writers than
for others. Robin Cullen ("Christmas in Prison") is a wry ironist in person *and* on paper. Nancy Whiteley ("Orbiting Izzy," "The True Face of
Earth") deports herself with a world-weary toughness and a little girl's
vulnerability. Her writing voice captures those qualities exactly. Con-
versely, Brenda Medina, who comes from a large Latino family and is
bilingual, had to be coaxed into introducing a little Spanish "music"
into her prose. Bonnie Foreshaw had to let us know she came from
South Florida and had not sprung whole from the pages of the Old Testament. Nancy Birkla ("Three Steps Past the Monkeys") credits her
twelve-step recovery with saving her life, but her writing soared when
she stopped sounding like the manual.

The trick, says Donald Murray, is to avoid imitating some "literary"
voice you might admire and to accept your own voice—flawed and
human as you might be. Many of the inmates with whom I work are
avid readers of romance novels. Their first autobiographical efforts are
apt to be florid accounts in which they star as tragic Victorian heroines.
Gently, we coax our fellow writers away from sentimentality and purple
prose. Listen to how Carolyn Adams ("Thefts") first wrote about her
arrest for embezzlement: "The detective handcuffed me to a metal fold-
ing chair like a mental patient and I was crying, crying, crying. Through
my tears, I could see the stares of police officers and arrested people as
they shuffled past, all of them glancing hatefully at me. When I was led
down the hallway to have my picture taken, I responded robotically to
the detective's commands due to my ordeal." Now listen to a passage
from one of Adams's later drafts. Locked in the holding room on her
first day in prison, she is looking out an escape-proof window when,
illogically, a goose wanders into her field of vision: "Oblivious to the
humans locked inside, it waddled along, doing what geese do: eating,
shitting, and looking stupid. I stood there, envying that son-of-a-bitchin'

goose as it passed by on its way to greener pastures." In revision, Adams discards the voice of the self-consciously suffering heroine in favor of her own, angrier voice. In doing so, she better communicates the pain and humiliation of her experience.

To imprison a woman is to remove her voice from the world, but many female inmates have been silenced by life long before the transport van carries them from the courthouse to the correctional facility. "If you tell anyone about this, I'll make big trouble for you," the pedophile warns her when she is a frightened little girl. (Because the molester is her father, grandfather, cousin, or stepdad, he's in a good position to deliver on the threat.) "What goes on in this house *stays* in this house!" her violent parent screams after she's just taken a punch or witnessed a sibling's beating. "Shut your fucking mouth or I'll shut it with my fist!" her abusive husband promises. She knows he means it; the last time, he dislocated her jaw. Because incest and domestic violence cut across the economic divide, women of all means are schooled in silence. Of the eleven contributors to this volume, eight have been battered and nine have been sexually abused, a statistic that reflects the norm for incarcerated women. Their essays, then, are victories against voicelessness—miracles in print.

For her audition piece, Barbara Lane ("Puzzle Pieces") submitted an idyllic dreamscape: released from prison, she reunites with her children and grandchildren at a country cottage with beautiful gardens. The family is poised on the brink of happily-ever-after. Lane attached a note to her sample, stating that she wanted to write about her life to better understand it. A hardworking middle-class mom with no prior criminal past, Lane alleges that she shot and killed her emotionally abusive husband in a moment of frenzy when he taunted her with the knowledge that he had sexually abused her granddaughter. Disoriented and debilitated by post-traumatic stress disorder, Lane was put on a suicide watch when she entered York prison. Convicted of manslaughter, she had served two years of her twenty-five-year sentence when she learned that her twenty-one-year-old son, a father of two, had been killed in a highway accident. In the company of uniformed corrections officers, she attended his wake alone in shackles after her family had been evacuated from the funeral parlor by order of prison officials.

Not long after joining our group, Lane put aside her pastoral fantasy and got to the tough stuff. She wrote prolifically and was eager for feedback from the group, but she could not read her memoir aloud without breaking down. One of the other writers or I would read it for her, and she would sit there, weeping silently and drawing Kleenex after Kleenex from the box on her lap. Yet if Lane's story was harrowing, her prose was flat and dispassionate. One day I commented that she must do a lot of crying *as* she wrote. No, Lane said. She relived her memories dry-eyed, recording details and bits of dialogue in an emotionless state. "It's my post-traumatic stress," she explained. "Up to the point when I snapped, that was how I survived—by detaching. I thought I was all right. I thought I was handling things and keeping everyone safe."

In the two years Barbara Lane has participated in the writers' group, both her writing and her demeanor have changed. More assertive, less debilitated by grief, she now reads her own drafts without breaking down. Concurrently, her writing voice has become less devoid of emotion and far more moving. Lane has hitched her sorrow, fear, despair, and anger to vivid remembered detail and transferred her emotions to the page. She has gone about the difficult work of confronting her chaotic history head-on rather than being confronted, over and over, by it; and the process has empowered her to express emotions that had long been locked away. The operative emotion that drives her later pieces is righteous anger. "My eyes are wide open," she asserted recently in a piece about her daily life in prison. "And I don't like much of what I see around me."

Soon after Diane Bartholomew dropped the pseudonym Natasha, she discovered a writing voice as plainspoken and unvarnished as she. Bartholomew dedicated herself to the purpose of recording her life with a fury the likes of which I had never witnessed. She wrote so much that she began to understand how writing works and, because of that, she became an astute and generous critic of the other writers. She hungered for critical feedback from her peers but deflected praise with a shrug and a breaking of eye contact. "I don't know if it's any good or not," she'd mumble. "But at least it's honest."

Bartholomew's writing transformed her. "I always used to tell people that someday I was going to write my story, but I never really believed it would happen," she told me once. Now that it *was* happening, she couldn't stop. On alternate Thursdays when I visited, the unassuming Bartholomew would ambush me on my way to class, eager to swap her latest installments for the text I'd taken home and critiqued for her. She began to color-code her printed revisions so that I could focus on what was new in the piece—what she'd added, cut, switched around, or clarified. She was a ravenous consumer of whatever I could teach her. "I don't want to hog your time, Wally," she'd whisper before class. "But if you could give me a few extra minutes afterward." As soon as class was over, Diane would jump from her seat and fan her work across the long tables, picking my brain about form and narrative flow. "Now, do you think my hunting piece should go before or after the one about our trip to the beach?" she'd ask. "Oh, and Wally, I've been thinking about what you said last time—how the car seems to be my main symbol. But I don't think it's the car. I think it's the open road." She'd nod at the fourteen or fifteen pieces she'd spread across the table, shoulder to shoulder like a line of Rockettes. "Yup, it's the road, Wally, not the car."

She could be impatient. She couldn't help it. The more her writing came to matter to her, the more unbearable those two-week turnarounds became. With the warden's permission, Dale Griffith began faxing Diane's work to my office. I'd be in one room, writing my novel in progress, one hard-won sentence after the next. The phone would ring in the adjacent room. The fax machine would whir. Fifteen minutes later, I'd have one more measly sentence written and there'd be a new ten-page draft waiting for me from Bartholomew.

"Good God, Diane, Joyce Carol Oates doesn't write *this* fast," I'd tease her. "What are you doing? Writing a full-length book?"

"Maybe I am," she told me once. "And if so, I'm going to dedicate it to my dead mother. Her whole life, everyone kept telling her how stupid she was, same as they did me. I'll hold up that book and tell her, wherever she is, 'Look, Ma. Look what your daughter did. I guess we weren't so stupid after all.'" Bartholomew's productivity was daunting, her mission to get her life down on paper nearly monomaniacal. I did not understand the timetable under which she was laboring.

Because York C.I. is a maximum-security prison, volunteers are forbidden to give gifts to inmates. Contraband goods entering the facility can become a serious security and safety risk. So on a pre-Christmas 2000 visit to the compound, I arrived empty-handed. Diane Bartholomew, however, had a gift for me—a simple card. The message she'd written inside said, "So many times, I wanted to throw in the towel and give up, but you, more than anyone, know my character by now. I wasn't a pest all my life for nothing. Wally, we all look forward to Thursday afternoon like little children waiting for a treat. The treat is the opportunity to share our stories and to get the feedback that makes our work worthwhile. To say thanks sounds so hollow, and you always say, 'Show it, don't tell it.' So let me put it this way. You have become the umbilicord for a rebirth of hope in me. Please thank your wife and boys for sharing you with us women here at the prison."

That December day there was far more peace and goodwill *inside* the prison than outside. When I left the compound, I stopped by the mall to do some holiday shopping and ran into an acquaintance. "It's been a while," she said. "Catch me up." As I described the prison workshops, a distasteful smirk took hold of this woman's face. "Gee, maybe I should go rob a bank or kill someone," she said. "Then *I* could go down there and join all the fun."

If I have learned anything these past three years, it is that prison is *not* fun—not at all the coddling Club Med that some describe. At York C.I., a woman is told when to rise, what to wear, when to shower, when to eat, when to use the phone, and when to go to bed. She may share her eight-by-ten-foot cell with someone who is violent, vindictive, or mentally unstable. That cell may be searched by officers at any time for an unstated reason, the inmate's personal belongings dumped onto the floor or seized. Her mail can be read, censored, or confiscated. An institutional lockdown can abort her classes, her workday, or a planned visit with her children. If the visit goes on as planned, her interactions with her kids are monitored by corrections officers and surveillance cameras. After her visitors leave, she is obliged to submit to a strip search, during which her vaginal and anal cavities are examined for contraband. There are justifiable reasons for all of the above. A maximum-security prison must be safeguarded for the good of inmates, staff, and the general public. But it is *not* fun to be there, and the person who likens it to a country club is either ignorant or cynical.

"Mr. Wally, look what we made," Tabatha Rowley said one afternoon as the workshop convened. She held up a collage of uncommon beauty, a disjointed patchwork replica of the *Mona Lisa*. A few weeks earlier, the students explained, their art appreciation teacher, Pedro Valentin, had divided a copy of da Vinci's masterpiece into twenty-four squares. Each of twenty-four women was given a square and invited to make a replica. The assignment called for ingenuity, though; the art class was operating on a shoestring budget and had no paint or supplies. The women had improvised, painting with instant coffee mixed with creamer and composing squares from pine needles, magazine clippings, and eggshells. "Kinda funny that I got Mona Lisa's cleavage," Diane Bartholomew quipped. "Me, with my mastectomies." The assemblage—simultaneously fractured and united, chaotic and ordered—struck me immediately as a metaphor for our group. "If we ever turned your stories into a book," I said, "this would be the perfect cover."

"Hey, why *don't* we make a book?" Dale Griffith asked. The women looked at one another and nodded. And there it was: the genesis of the volume you hold in your hand.

My intent was to edit and finance the printing of a modest collection of the women's work. I'd distribute four or five copies to each participant and a batch to the prison library. Back in my office, I put my assistant, Lynn Castelli, to the task of mastering a desktop-publishing program. We priced the job with a local printer and made decisions about paper stock and binding. I decided to spring for the full-color cover of the fractured *Mona Lisa*.

"What are we going to call our book?" one of the women asked during the next workshop session. None of the suggestions we tossed around seemed right. "Wally, what are you going to call the new novel *you're* working on?" someone asked. I explained that I'd taken as my working title a line from a gospel song I'd heard on my very first drive to York prison.

"Couldn't Keep It to Myself?" Tabatha exclaimed. "I know that song!"

"Sing it," Carolyn suggested. And Tabbi obliged, treating us to a spontaneous a cappella rendition of "Said I Wasn't Gonna Tell Nobody" that lacked none of the joyful thunder of the Abyssinian Baptist Choir.

Said I wasn't gonna tell nobody
But I couldn't keep it to myself
What the Lord has done for me

So I gave my title to the gals. How could I *not* have? "I knew that once we got you here, you'd keep coming back," Dale Griffith said, a mischievous twinkle in her eye. "You were called."

A few months later, I was in New York on book business, seated at a conference table with my publisher, Judith Regan. I was describing my work at the prison—how these latest students of mine had changed my life. "I'd like to read their work sometime," Judith said. I knew that she was just being courteous—that her schedule was packed and her time limited. I seized the opportunity, nevertheless. Two or three of the women's pieces were in the attaché case that sat on the floor beside me; I'd been editing them on the train ride into the city. I pulled out Nancy Whiteley's essay "Orbiting Izzy" and began reading aloud. I kept looking up from the text to Judith's face. Somewhere between pages one and two, her expression changed from polite to genuinely engaged. Ten pages later, I was done. Judith wiped her eyes. "Shall we do a book?" she asked.

By January 2001, Diane Bartholomew's cancer had returned and spread to her lymph nodes. Misdiagnoses delayed her treatment for several months. Each time I visited the compound, Bartholomew seemed weaker, her energy at a lower ebb, her voice more thin and whispery. She came late to some sessions, left early during others. Once her chemotherapy treatments began, she was too sick to come at all.

By special permission, I visited Bartholomew in the medical unit. Was there anything I could do for her? I asked. Two things, she said. First, she needed badly during this crisis to talk to her sister, Katie, who lived in Pennsylvania, but Katie got by on a modest income that couldn't easily accommodate the 33 percent "cost of incarceration" surcharge the state of Connecticut tacked on to the phone bills of inmates' relatives. There was legislation coming up for a vote that would eliminate the service charge. Would I write to my state representative? "Done," I said. "What's the other thing?"

Diane's second request was trickier. "I'm planning to beat this thing, because I have so much more of my story left to write," she said. "But in case I don't make it, Wally, would you finish it for me?" I told her I didn't think I could promise that—all the more reason for her to get well and write it herself.

One afternoon in May, York School vice principal Mary Greaney wheeled Bartholomew unexpectedly into a workshop meeting. Diane was bald and kerchiefed by then, ravaged by her treatments. She had reclaimed some of her Natasha-like secrecy, too. While the other women worked at their word-processing stations, she passed me a private note. It said: "I may be getting out of here. The parole board's going to meet to discuss my case."

"Diane, that's great," I whispered. "Maybe they're finally going to show you a little mercy." That made her chuckle. It had nothing to do with mercy, she whispered back; it had to do with the cost of cancer treatments.

Bartholomew was released from prison the following month, halfway through her twenty-five-year sentence. She returned without fanfare to the house where, thirteen years earlier, she had killed her husband.

I made a half-dozen visits to Diane's home, the first few times with Dale Griffith, the others by myself. I brought flowers, lunches, good wishes from the writing group members. I located and installed a used computer for her so that she might continue her story. She used it, instead, to compose thank-you letters to the people who'd supported her while she was in prison. It was strange, she said; as much as she'd hated that place, she missed it. Missed the people. She wondered how this one was doing, and that one. She hadn't realized freedom would feel so lonely.

In October 2001, I spoke at a fund-raiser for a shelter for battered women held in Hartford at the governor's mansion. Security was tight in the wake of the September 11 attacks and the anthrax scares, but the mansion had been decked out for Halloween and the event was crowded. During my presentation, I described the writing workshops at York C.I. and read a portion of Diane Bartholomew's autobiography. When I finished, the applause was extended and genuine. Many people, including Connecticut's first lady, Patty Rowland, approached me to say they'd been moved by Bartholomew's words. Several asked me to relay their good wishes and prayerful intentions.

I drove to Diane's later that week, on a beautiful Indian summer day. We sat in the sun on the tiny upstairs porch outside her bedroom, and I filed my report on the fund-raising event. "So what do you think of that, Miss Big Shot?" I said. "Everyone at the governor's mansion getting off their butts to stand and cheer your writing?"

Diane shrugged. "I don't know if it's any good or not, but at least it's honest." Then she held out her hands, palms up, and I took them in mine, my fingers curling around hers. For the rest of that visit, neither of us said much. Diane dozed, her face to the warm breeze. She was done, now, with words. But having in the last two years of her life written 30,000 of them—roughly a third of her life story—she had left behind her legacy. Her sister Katie called me Thanksgiving evening. She was succinct. "Diane died," she said.

Dale Griffith and I drove together to the funeral home. More than once during the workshops, Diane had seen fit to inform us that, as a young woman, she'd been "quite a looker." At her wake the snapshots and framed pictures arranged around her coffin proved she'd been right. I shook hands with her family—daughters, siblings, and in-laws I'd never met but knew through Diane's writing. After paying our respects, Dale and I retreated to the back of the room, where we were joined by Robin Cullen, a workshop member who'd been released from York Prison the year before. Between the family up front and the three of us in back were dozens of empty chairs. "Look at that," Robin whispered. "Diane saved seats for all the women who would have come if they were free."

Years and years ago, my sister, in the role of troublemaker Rippy Van Snoot, beaned me on the head with a blackboard eraser. "Go fuck yourself," Seth Jinks said. Paula Plunkett never spoke at all. Each of these jolts, and others that followed, made me, first, a teacher and, later, a writer. I have come to know my current students not merely as the substance abusers, gang members, thieves, and killers they *have been* but also as the complex and creative works in progress they *are*. They are "tough cookies" not because of their crimes but because they will be neither defeated nor silenced. Each contributor whose work you will read has discovered the intertwined power of the written word and the power that resides within her. The good news is that she couldn't keep it to herself.

In the months since Diane Bartholomew's death, I've continued my Thursday visits to York C.I. as I've labored to prepare this manuscript for publication. I have a single reader in mind: the woman I ran into while Christmas shopping at the Crystal Mall. I plan to hand-deliver a copy to her and ask her to read it. There are things she needs to know about prison and prisoners. There are misconceptions to be abandoned, biases to be dropped. There are a heart and a mind that need opening. There are many.

We are a paradoxical nation, enormously charitable and stubbornly unforgiving. We have called into existence the prisons we wanted. I am less and less convinced they are the prisons we need.

THE TRUE FACE
OF EARTH

||||||||||||||||||||||||

NANCY WHITELEY

Born: 1968
Conviction: Conspiracy to commit
credit card fraud
Sentence: 27 months
Entered prison: 2000
Status: Released

ADDY! WAKE UP!" I SAID, LANDING *PLOP* ON MY father's belly. I rubbed his sandpaper cheek against my smooth one and breathed in the sweet scent of Bryll Cream. "You promised to take me flying today if the weather was nice, and *look*!" Dad's sleepy eyes followed my pointing finger out the window to the fluffy farm animal clouds in an Easter egg blue sky. I was six.

"Okay, Peanut," he mumbled. "Go see what Mommy's doing and I'll get ready." I jumped off the bed, waiting at the doorway until his feet hit the floor.

In the kitchen, Mom was cracking eggs into a navy blue bowl. "Morning, honey," she said. "Scrambled, right?" I told her scrambled eggs were for babies and ordered Daddy's favorite, the kind you flip. Mom lifted an eyebrow and grabbed her spatula.

Kathy, my oldest sister, was working at Friendly's that morning, and my middle sister, Janet, had a horseback riding lesson. So it was just Daddy and me, the way I liked it. After breakfast, we were off to the airport, Dad driving and me fiddling with the radio in search of a song I liked. I stopped on Blood, Sweat, and Tears. *What goes up must come down . . .* I sang along, snapping my fingers. Mommy always hollered when I turned the music loud enough to shake the dashboard, but Daddy never did.

At the airport, Dad took his sweet time, drinking coffee from a cardboard cup and chatting with his friends—men in plaid shorts, Mr. Rogers sweaters, and clip-on sunglasses that flipped up in the shade. We watched the flight school pilots practice their landings, take off, then circle back and land again. When that got boring, I sat in the dirt and hunted for pretty rocks, pocketing a beautiful pink diamond that Janet later dismissed as "boring old rose quartz."

"C'mon, Peanut. You're getting filthy," Dad said. And with that, he waved so long to his pals. We headed, hand in hand, toward the gleaming six-seater Beechcraft Bonanza.

Dad lifted me up onto the wing, and I found the cockpit step and climbed inside. A few minutes later, the engine roared and we rolled onto the tarmac. Dad drove us faster and faster around the runway until, as if by the giant hand of God, we were lifted off the ground and into the air.

*   *   *

He honked for me at around eight. I climbed into his primer-gray Grand Torino, settled my ass into the bucket seat, and planted my bare feet on the dashboard. I lit his last Marlboro and crumpled the crush-proof box one-handed, tossing it out the window.

We stopped at Food Bag for the essentials: potato chips, beef jerky, more cigarettes, and strawberry Hubba Bubba, my favorite gum. His older brother had already purchased the liquid refreshment, a case of Bud. It sat warming on the car floor beneath my knees.

At fifteen, I was blond, blue-eyed, and long-legged—but scrawny from the back. Instead of a nicely rounded butt, I had a bone—evidence that we had indeed evolved from monkeys. I flipped down the visor mirror and checked my makeup. Most people considered me pretty, but I couldn't see it. Reaching up, I yanked my tube top lower. Better that he look at my chest than my face.

His named happened to be Jason, but that wasn't important. He wore the uniform of all teenage boys of that era: white tank top, ripped Levis, high-top Converse sneakers. That evening, he'd tied a blue bandanna across his brow, pirate-style.

Jason lit a joint and its sweet smoke filled the air. We drove without destination, content to toke and drink and listen to Led Zeppelin screaming about winding down the road, their shadows taller than their souls. On the main drags, we slowed down so that everyone else out cruising that night would notice us. On the back roads, we sped.

I knew boys only gave their dates a few chances to put out before they moved on. I'd seen dozens of girls left sobbing after evenings with guys who pawed and pleaded but kept hearing no. The year before, Ricky Craig had dumped me three dates in a row for not letting him put his hand inside my pants, and two weekends ago, my friend Jill had been abandoned at Burger King because she wouldn't let Dave Rosemont take off her bra.

I glanced over at Jason, applied another coat of watermelon lip gloss, and smiled. I would *not* be getting dumped tonight.

My father, Lars Hiasson Johansson, was a corporate man. He traveled the country, often the world, as a top sales executive for a major company. Slicked back, toned down, wheeling and dealing, Dad was proud of his ascension in the firm. "You want to get ahead in life, Peanut? Always do your job a little better than the guy standing next to you," he'd told me more than once. Dad dispensed corporate wisdom for whatever crisis I was facing.

On summer evenings, it was common for my father and me to take after-dinner walks—"constitutionals," he called them. We reserved this time to discuss *serious* issues. "Daddy, this boy in school, Alan Bain, keeps bothering me. Today he knocked me down on the playground and I *hate* him!"

"Well, Peanut, always look people right in the eye," Dad advised. "That's what you do in the business world. And if they happen to have a glass eye or some other defect, then look at the bridge of their nose instead. They'll never even know the difference." From those long-ago days to these, my father's tried-and-truisms have remained with me, popping into my head at odd moments like explanatory footnotes. But at the time, I couldn't fathom how staring at the bridge of Alan Bain's nose would stop him from bugging me.

When Daddy smiled, the wrinkles at the corners of his pale blue eyes looked like birdie footprints. "Listen, Peanut, I've been thinking," he began, during one of our walks. "You know Mommy's a good mom, right? And that she loves you very much?"

I nodded, waiting.

"Everyone loses their temper *sometimes,* right?"

"Right."

The day before, the art teacher had shown us how to make 3-D pictures using construction paper, dried macaroni, and Elmer's glue. I'd returned home from school bent on making myself a macaroni horse. After assembling my supplies, I'd sat at the kitchen table and gone to work. But midway through, I'd accidentally knocked over the macaroni box, scattering a hundred million pasta pieces on Mom's clean floor. I was on my hands and knees, sobbing and scooping macaroni, when Mom came in and caught me. I cowered, scrunching into a tight ball, but as she came for me, a miracle happened. Dad arrived home early from work. He looked from Mom to me, then back again. "No problem, Peanut," he said. "We'll have this cleaned up in a jiffy." And with that, he dropped to his knees in his smoky gray business suit and helped me.

"Just try not to get her mad, okay?" Dad said now, midway through our after-dinner constitutional. "Especially when I'm not home."

I looked up, into his eyes. At six feet, Dad was a giant back then. Although I doubted it was possible to prevent Mom's anger, I promised him I'd try. Then I changed the subject. "Hey, Daddy, guess what I want?"

"An ice-cold martini and a good cigar? Oh, no, that's what *I* want."

I giggled and told him I wanted bubble gum ice cream in a waffle cone. "Okay, kiddo, we can manage that. Just remember one thing, will you? Daddy loves you, no matter what happens. Think you can remember that for me?" As usual, I had no idea what he was talking about, but I agreed just the same. There was ice cream to eat. And anyway, what could happen?

At bedtime, someone always read to me—Mom, or Kathy, or Dad if he was home. Of the three, I preferred Dad because he always chose my favorite book, *The Little Prince,* reading, again and again, the fox's warning to the Little Prince: that he was responsible for whichever rose he tamed. After he finished, Dad always left the door open just a crack to let in the hallway light. Under the covers, I'd imagine my father as the Little Prince, who'd come out of the sky to protect me, his rose, from whatever in life was scary.

I don't know. Maybe Dad should have read me Saint-Exupéry's fable a few *more* times, especially the part where the fox advises the Little Prince that what is essential is invisible to the eye. Jason had transportation and eye appeal, but not much else. "So what do you feel like doing tonight?" he asked. "Hey, open me a beer, will you?"

I reached down to the seat well and grabbed two of the warmish cans. "I don't know. What do *you* want to do?" Pulling off the pop-tops, I bent a nail. "Damn!" I muttered, whacking my beer can against the dashboard in protest.

"Careful, baby," he warned. "This car's almost a classic."

On we drove, headed nowhere. Steering with his right hand, Jason reached over, took my hand, and guided it beneath his to the head of the stick shift between us. Hand over hand, we shifted gears. "This is second," he said. "And here's third up here. You stick with me and next year, when you go to the DMV, you'll pass with a perfect score. And, hey, maybe I'll even let you drive my car for the test." Turning his eyes from the road to me, he smiled.

I smiled back, trying to look grateful, but I was nervous. I knew what all this shifting meant and where it was headed. I puffed my cigarette, sipped my beer. Crossed my legs, uncrossed them. I touched my throat, my necklace—the tiny gold cross I'd gotten years before for my First Communion.

"Hey," I said. "Let's go to the airport."

He turned to me with a puzzled smile. "The airport? Why?"

"I don't know. I just like to watch the planes."

One night when I was seven, a loud crash from downstairs made me bolt up in bed. The door opened, the light went on. Kathy rushed into the big bedroom I shared with Janet.

She was still in her Friendly's uniform, a little gray mini-dress with a frilly white apron that was clean whenever Kathy left for work and stained with ice cream when she came home. She sat down on my bed, straightened my twisted-up Holly Hobby nightgown, and put her arm around me. At thirteen, Janet was resentful of *everything*, so I was surprised when she got out of bed and walked across the room toward us. Her face was scowling. Her hair was crazy from sleep. She sat on my bed and leaned against our big sister.

"You fat stupid bitch!" Dad screamed. "Can't you do *anything* right?"

"How would *you* know what I do?" Mom sobbed. "You're always out with that girlfriend of yours—that *slut*!" What was she talking about, I wondered. Daddy didn't have a girlfriend. He had us. Me.

Our cat, Also, a huge gray tiger, meandered into the room and joined us on my bed, nestling on my lap and tucking his paws neatly beneath himself. I had named him Also because he was the only striped kitten born in a litter of Siamese. We were soulmates, Also and me. Two odd-balls who never seemed to fit in anywhere.

"Well, maybe you should think about *why* I'm gone so much! Keep this up and pretty soon I won't bother coming home at all!"

The front door slammed. Daddy drove off. There was clattering down in the kitchen for a while, the sound of Mom sobbing. When it was quiet again, Kathy tucked us in and went off to her own room. I lay

awake for a long, long time, dozing only when, at last, I heard Dad's car
pull into the driveway.

We pulled into the dirt parking lot across from the airstrip. I figured
maybe Dad was in there, cleaning his plane or having a drink at the Flying Squire. But the thought of visiting him, or even getting a glimpse,
was useless. The dad from my childhood was long gone by then.

Jason's idea of mood music was Blue Oyster Cult. He slipped a cassette into the player and jacked the volume. *Don't fear the Reaper, we'll
be able to fly, baby, I'm your mannn . . .* I looked out at the straight lines
of green, red, and blue runway lights and, beyond that, the dark. Maybe
God was up there, drawing pictures with some cosmic Lite Brite set,
sending a message just for me.

Without a word, Jason reached past me and pulled the seat back
release lever. I flopped back, frightened. I felt like a biology class frog
about to be dissected. When he pulled off my top, I swallowed and
smiled, willing myself not to cover my bare breasts. He pulled down my
shorts and panties, shimmying them off my left leg. They dangled
around my right ankle.

He drowned my face with sloppy, slobbering kisses as he groped
clumsily, stroking my thighs with his callused hands. One hand moved
up, between my legs. I liked the feel of his stubbly beard scraping
against my face the way Dad's did when he came home from work, or
from a business trip. I wasn't too fond of the rest of it.

"Goddammit, Joan! I wrote the checks, I put them in the envelopes, I
even stamped and addressed them for you!"

"So I forgot!" Mom blubbered. "So what?"

"So the phone company called and threatened to cut off service, same
as the electric!" Dad screamed back. "You told me you mailed them two
weeks ago and here they are, still in your purse. What the hell is *wrong*
with you?"

Listening to the downstairs fighting was a nightly ritual now—a
scarier version of taking my bath or brushing my teeth. But if there was
terror and confusion, there was also Kathy to keep me safe. "I'm your
protector," she promised me during one of our parents' battles. "Always
and forever."

"Go ahead! Crucify me because I made one small mistake!" We heard a slap, a crash, a sharp howl of pain from Mom.

"That's it," Kathy said. "We're out of here." Janet, who had trained herself to sleep through our parents' fights, was shaken awake and told to get on her coat and shoes. "Hurry up, *both* of you," Kathy ordered, then ran down the hall to get dressed herself.

Janet rolled out of bed. I watched her button her coat over her PJs and slip on her sneakers. When she caught me looking, she glared back, disgusted with my helplessness as I sat on the floor in my nightgown, struggling with my coat's impossible zipper.

"I suppose you need help, right?" she seethed. "C'mere then, brat." I got up and went over to her. Sighing disgustedly, she zipped me up, lickety split.

Kathy came back dressed, purse slung over her shoulder, car keys in hand. I shoved my Kermit the Frog doll in my coat pocket for company and exited behind them. Outside, Janet and I tumbled, wide-eyed and blinking, into Kathy's VW Bug and were driven across town to the Blue Colony Diner.

We spent hours there, poking at soggy pancakes and cold, congealed eggs. We talked about school, friends, Kathy's job—anything except our parents' battles, our father's clobbering of our mother. We skirted *that* topic as gingerly as our cat, Also, tiptoed along the knickknack shelf.

The next morning, I woke up tired and tense. I dreaded walking downstairs—seeing Mom. But when I entered the kitchen, everything was back to normal. It was as if I'd only *dreamt* the previous night. I opened my mouth to ask Mom if she was all right, then stopped myself, afraid the question might set her off. Instead, I ate in silence, grabbed my book bag, and headed for school.

At the bus stop, I stood apart from the other kids, afraid they might somehow know about what had gone on at our house the night before. I knew my fear was unfounded—that they'd all been asleep in their beds while my sisters and I were waiting it out at the Blue Colony Diner—but still, I kept my distance. "It was nothing," I whispered to myself, my eyes on the approaching school bus. "Nothing at all." It came out like a prayer.

Sex was turning out to be nothing like what they promised in the movies. For one thing, my legs were so cramped that I finally had to

stick my feet out the window. I was embarrassed by my backseat nakedness and bugged by Jason's groping and grinding against me. "Sweetie,
relax," he hissed, his breath wet against my cheek. And then I felt the
hot, searing pain of his entering me. I bit my lip to stop myself from
screaming. Tears fell into my tousled hair.

To ease his banging against me, I wrapped my legs around his back
and closed my eyes, praying for it to be over. When I opened them again,
I noticed the white plastic rosary hanging from his rearview mirror. The
beads rocked back and forth from our motion. I shut my eyes again,
hoping against hope that God was busy with other things—that He
wasn't watching me.

He finished with a grunt, pulled out, and rolled off of me. For a few
seconds, I just lay there, feeling raw and stunned. Jason zipped, sat up. I
hurried to get myself dressed.

I had never given much thought to that space inside of me that Jason
had just filled, but as soon as he pulled out, I felt a strange emptiness the
likes of which I had never experienced before. Sex made me feel lonelier
than ever and, heaven knew, I already felt more alone than I could bear.

I found some McDonald's napkins in the glove compartment and
cleaned myself off as best I could. I flipped down the visor and looked at
my face in the mirror. This time, though, I wasn't checking my makeup.
I was looking for some visible sign of what I'd just done. Did I look
older? More mature? Dirtier? All I saw was myself, my face chafed from
nose to jawbone, burned by Jason's rough kisses.

I'd been out by the pond, harvesting treasure, so my sneakers were
soggy that afternoon when I entered the house. My hands were wearing gloves of muck. The cracked robin's egg I had found was hidden in
my fist.

Passing by the living room, I stopped cold. Why was our minister
here? Pastor Fortin belonged at our church, Prince of Peace Lutheran,
not here on Torrey Lane. Whatever the reason for his visit, my instinct
was to push him out the door before he discovered who we really were.

"Look at those hands of yours," my mother snapped. "For God's sake,
go wash up. Oops. Sorry, Pastor." Her orders chased me up the staircase.
"And use soap! And throw out that filthy egg!" Her X-ray vision was one
of the things that spooked me about Mom. I had never even opened my fist.

On my way to the bathroom, I bumped into Dad. He'd been gone a week and his sudden reappearance was as confusing as his abrupt exit had been. Was everything going to be okay now? Was Pastor Fortin here to help my parents stop fighting? I scrubbed my hands clean but defied Mom and kept the egg, wrapping it in Kleenex and easing it into my shorts pocket. When I returned to the living room, I moved instinctively toward Daddy, who was seated on the loveseat opposite the minister.

Pastor Fortin and Dad did most of the talking. As their voices rose and fell, I studied my mother and sister for clues. Janet sat slumped on the couch, inspecting her long hair for split ends and rolling her eyes at phrases like "the will of God" and "visitation rights." Mom had positioned herself in the easy chair at the edge of the room. Her eyes shifted back and forth between the minister and Dad. When I gazed up at my father, he looked back, but his eyes seemed to be staring at the bridge of my nose.

That's when I got it. Dad was moving out and my parents were getting a divorce. The fat lady—my mother—had sung. Later, back in my room, I unwrapped the fragile egg and squeezed, pulverizing its paper-thin shell.

Jason's Torino became Jimmy's Mustang. Frank had a Chevelle and a crooked smile. John walked with a limp. Joey sported a goatee and a straggly rat's tail braid. Larry liked to beat me up as a prelude to passion. Billy was the jealous type, accusing me of sleeping with everyone from my thirteen-year-old next-door neighbor to one of my teachers. (He was wrong about the neighbor.) Mickey broke my arm but not my stride. I even managed to seduce my father's airplane mechanic. Was his name Chris? Rob? It was hard to keep them straight—that neverending line of boys who fucked me at the airport.

Girls at school began to snicker. "Nancy the slut," they'd whisper from behind as I slumped to class. The angry ones met me face-to-face. "Come here, you bitch! Were you with my boyfriend last weekend?"

Sometimes I'd respond in bad-girl fashion—"I never kiss and tell, but go ahead and dust me for fingerprints"—but, more often, I'd hold my books a little tighter to my chest and keep walking. What did I care what those girls thought? I didn't need *their* friendship. I was popular enough with the boys.

"Look 'em right in the eye," my father had advised. I developed a slouch from staring at my classmates' shoes instead.

At first I thought it was *my* fault that Dad left home. I searched my mind for something really, really bad I'd done, but I couldn't come up with much. Had he ditched us because I crabbed about dumping the kitty litter?

I missed him every single day—the walks we'd take, the books we'd read. At breakfast, it made Mom pout if I asked for "Daddy eggs." I went back to eating scrambled instead.

I kept picturing it like a scene from a movie: the moment when Dad would realize his terrible mistake—his assumption that it was even *possible* to live without us—and throw open the front door, announcing he was home to stay. I don't remember when, exactly, I stopped listening for his car in the driveway at dinnertime. Over time, my expectations eroded away.

Unable to face the truth in public, I lied to my friends, insisting that Daddy was on a long, long business trip. One day, Alice Andrews, a freckly blonde with a turned-up nose, lowered the boom in front of a dozen or so of our fellow second-graders. "He's not on any trip," she said. "Your parents got a *divorce*." The others waited, wide-eyed, for my confirmation or denial. I burst into tears and ran. From that day on, the subject of Dad stayed dropped.

Sundays were visiting days. For a while, Dad picked us up after church, but because our time together was so short, Mom began giving Janet and me the option of skipping Sunday services and going off with Dad early. I was secretly thrilled to get out of boring old Sunday school.

He'd pull up in his big company car and toot. We'd climb in and be driven someplace for lunch, or to some park. More often than not, we headed for the airport. But Daddy became busier and busier. Often, he'd be "out of town" on visiting days. After a few tearful Sunday morning stand-ups, I learned not to wait by the window. Instead, I'd watch *Wonderama,* eating fistfuls of Kix cereal out of the box, something we weren't allowed to do, especially in the living room. Janet would sit in her room and sulk.

"Ma, I got suspended again," I called out one day after school. I shut the front door, dropped my books onto the brown velour sectional sofa, and headed for the kitchen. Mom was working by then, but it was her day off. She sat at the table, eating an Entenmann's crumb cake and a half-gallon carton of Sealtest vanilla fudge.

"Oh, honey," Mom sighed. "What did you do now?"

I loved my mother: her curly hair and rosy cheeks, her Avon face cream aroma, the way her skin always felt cool to the touch, even in the hottest weather. I adored even Mom's doughy, enfolding obesity. By then, I was a long-legged fifteen-year-old who fucked boys at the airport, but each morning I staggered into the kitchen, yawned, and sat on Mom's lap, curling my body to hers like a baby. Yes, she hit me. Scolded me. Scared me to death sometimes. I was riding the bucking bronco of Mom's mood swings even *before* Dad left. But if she had instilled fear, she had also instilled in me a love of music, art, and the English language. When I was little, Mom had gardened, canned, baked, and hand-sewn our clothes. She'd raised purebred puppies and cats and had taken hundreds of photos of my sisters and me, which she developed and printed herself. For every slap or scream or humiliating remark she delivered, she did ten wonderful things in counterbalance. Growing up, I had confided in her as if she were my best friend, which, I guess, she was. And as best friends do, my mother took my side against outsiders, even when I was wrong.

"Well, this girl in my algebra class was calling me names, so I slapped her across the face." I didn't tell Mom *which* names I'd been called— tramp, whore, used goods. Mom still had delusions of my virginity. Who was I to pop her balloon?

"Ladies do not fight, Nancy," she reminded me for the hundredth time. I nodded in agreement and she promised to take me shopping.

That was the pattern: whenever I was sent home from school for a mandatory "vacation," Mom would drive me to the mall and buy me things to keep me busy. During my last suspension, I'd scored two kinds of blush and Pink Floyd's *The Wall.* While my classmates sat in school, listening to the teachers drone, I sat sprawled on my bedroom rug, reading fashion magazines and listening to Roger Waters declare, *Mother's gonna keep you right under her wing. She won't let you fly, but she might let you sing. . . .*

Poor Mom. If men were my solace, Sara Lee was hers. She must have been trying to fill an emptiness as deep as mine.

*   *   *

After Dad's escape, the family more or less fell apart. Kathy's "always and forever" protection expired when she went away to secretarial school. Mom went from stay-at-home mother to working mother. By default and against her will, Janet became my caretaker.

"No way am I eating *that*. What is it anyway? Doggie diarrhea?"

"It's Hamburger Helper and Mom said to cook it. So *you're* eating it."

"You're not my mother. You can't tell me what to do." I crossed my arms, stuck out my tongue, and blew Janet a raspberry cheer.

"You rotten little brat!" Grabbing me by the shirtfront, she pulled me an inch away from her face. "You think I *want* to stay home every day watching you? I'm missing absolutely *everything*! So just sit there and shut up, or else go somewhere and play." She let me go and grabbed the skillet lid, banging it repeatedly, her face turned away so that I wouldn't see her tears.

Mom had gone to work at the Berkeley Knitwear factory. All day long, she sewed Berkeley Knitwear labels onto the insides of clothing. At night she sat at the kitchen table and studied for her real estate license. For about two years, I wore cheap, double-knit outfits complete with the Berkeley label: two tiny hands, facing forward, palms out, like the sign you'd make for "Halt! Stay away!" In Fairfield County—the land of Izod shirts, argyle socks, and six-figure incomes—this fashion statement was, of course, social suicide.

Because we weren't allowed to talk about THE DIVORCE, it loomed over our domestic lives. Mom worked and went to school. Then she came home and wept, screamed, hit us—harder now, and more often, and for longer durations. Dad's and Kathy's defections had left us short on rescuers. Life on Torrey Lane became bleaker, sadder, and scarier than ever. Mom wasn't quite Mom anymore. She was herself, but worse.

Back to the airport I rode, again and again, leading a parade of horny boys and men. It became an obsession for me: to crook my finger and get the cutest guys in school to screw me at the airport. I always had them park in the exact same spot so that I could lie there, watching the lights from the planes while they went at me. Always a single encounter, always a quickie. I didn't want romance or phone numbers or conversation afterward. All I ever wanted was a ride home, which was fine with them, once they'd flown the friendly skies of Nancy. Satisfaction guaranteed—for them. All that screwing never did shit for me.

By the time I was sixteen, I'd had enough of high school and hallway ridicule. My brilliant plan was to quit school and get pregnant. So on a hot June afternoon the week before exams, I went from classroom to classroom, teacher to teacher, surrendering my textbooks.

"Nancy, why are you doing this?" my science teacher, Mrs. Kingsley, wanted to know. "Your grades are among the highest in the class. Take the final. Even if you only got a C, you'd still pass the course."

Mrs. Kingsley was the one teacher I actually liked, and I felt bad disappointing her. "But, Mrs. K., all I want to do with my life is get married and have babies. There's scientific proof you don't need a diploma to get pregnant—fifteen girls at our school this year are the data."

"Not funny, Nancy," she said, doing her best to stifle a grin.

"I'll have a dozen kids, Mrs. K. I'll be happy as a clam."

"And how happy do you think a mollusk ever gets?"

Mrs. Kingsley said she'd be there if I ever needed her, and although she sounded sincere, I never put her to the test. I walked out of Newtown High and never looked back.

As for my plan, the marriage part didn't quite pan out. I'd have taken the first offer that came along, but none did. I discovered that the boys who wanted me so badly at the airport weren't nearly as interested afterward.

I was confused about the baby part, too. I wanted one for the companionship but was less sure about the responsibility side of the equation. In my ninth-grade health class two years earlier, boys and girls had been coupled and given a raw egg—supposedly their "baby." You could name it, decorate it. Some suck-ups had even made little cribs and clothes for theirs. The assignment—which was supposed to show how difficult it was to be a parent—was to carry the stupid egg for two weeks without breaking it. My egg's father was Chuckie Dowd, a total geek, so it was easy for me to get *him* to carry it around for the first week and a half. The day I got custody, I put the egg in my purse and totally forgot about it. I got home from school that afternoon, tossed my purse onto a kitchen chair, and went to get a snack. I was standing at the open refrigerator door when I began to smell my mistake.

Short of both a boyfriend and a baby, I took a job at a small mom-and-pop lighting store, selling fixtures and dusting chandeliers. Naturally, I met a guy there. Shane was twenty-six. He drove around in a van, delivering and installing fixtures. He had one of those white stripes running through his black hair. He worked for one of our suppliers.

"Hey, cutie. Wanna go to a movie with me this Friday night? Monty Python double feature at the Danbury drive-in?" He placed a case of sixty-watt CFC candelabra bulbs on the counter. We'd run out.

"*This* Friday night? Gee, I was going to stay home and watch *Love Boat. TV Guide* says Gopher's finally going to get laid. But I *guess* I could skip it." Although I was going for wise-ass nonchalance, I'd been hoping Shane would ask me out from the first time I'd spotted that stripy head. I liked the idea of adding "Skunk Man" to my collection of conquests.

"Great," he said. "I'll pick you up here after work. You close at six, right?" I nodded, walked him out to his van. "How about you wear that little pink skirt I saw you in last week?" he said. His smile revealed white, even teeth.

The year after Dad left, Mom announced we were moving from the big house on Torrey Lane to a small, three-bedroom ranch across town. I fought the move with everything I had, screaming, wailing, stomping, throwing my toys. I had already lost Daddy. Now I'd lose flashlight tag with the neighbors, the tire swing hanging from the ash tree, the pond behind the church. But Mom was determined. A thirteen-room house and six acres of land were more than she could handle by herself, she said. "Please, honey. Don't make this any harder than it already is."

I didn't relent. For weeks, I alternated threats with temper tantrums and pathetic sobbing. None of it worked. And then my cat ran away. Also and I had been best friends. Even through the worst times, he had remained cool and composed, his ears pricked forward, listening to my problems. A big old tomcat, he had taken off plenty of times before, but unlike Dad, Also always returned within a week. If we moved, he wouldn't know where to find us.

Because of all the trouble I'd caused, moving day was a covert operation. I'd been dropped off at my friend Lisa's house for a sleepover the night before, and when I went home the next day, it was to a different house.

Along with our new address, Mom instituted a new way of eating—
the first of her many doomed dieting attempts. "Eww, what are those
brown wormy things?" I asked one night, staring into the boiling pot on
the stove and whatever was wiggling around in there.

"Whole wheat spaghetti," Mom said. "It's healthy."

"I hate it."

"You can't hate it if you've never tasted it."

"Oh, yes, I can."

When the phone rang, I lunged to answer it, but Mom was faster. And
from the tone of her voice, I knew it was Dad. "No, I'm tired of doing
your dirty work for you. *You* tell them. . . . What? Don't you even *want*
to see them? . . . Well, screw you, you piece of ———!" She slammed
down the receiver and pressed her hands to her face. "Dammit," she
whispered. "Dammit, dammit, dammit."

"Was that my daddy?" I asked.

"Get out!" she screamed. "Go to your room! Now! Now! Now!"
Each "now" was accompanied by a hard whack on the fanny.

In my room, I fell to the floor, grabbed fistfuls of my hair, and yanked
hard. I banged my head repeatedly against the wall—the more violently
the better. Once my anger subsided, I felt a warm wetness and looked
down. My jeans were soaked, crotch to knees. In my blind rage, I'd
managed to pee myself. Cold, wet, and humiliated, I got into bed and
pulled the covers over my head. I sat there, rocking back and forth, for
a very long time.

Shane Fitzpatrick was a tall, angular ex-jock from a big Irish family.
He was ruggedly handsome, with his pale blue eyes and great build, but
what I liked best about Shane was the things he *wasn't*: ugly, stupid,
abusive, dirty. He wasn't addicted to drugs, gambling, or alcohol. Looking back on it, Shane wasn't much of anything at all.

I loved the money he had to spend on me, and the fact that he called
me "baby" and "sweetheart." Sometimes he'd arrive at my house with a
single red rose wrapped in plastic from the gas station down the road.
None of the airport boys had ever gone to the trouble.

Shane's best friend was Richie, a short, clownish redhead with
corkscrew curls. Richie made more money than Shane but could never

find himself a date. Instead, he tagged along on ours and often paid for the three of us.

I was the reluctant member of this trio, resentful of Richie's constant presence. Most nights, Shane only left his side for the fifteen minutes or so it took us to have sex, and I half-expected him to invite his best bud along for that, too. I didn't quite get *why* they were friends. Behind his back, Shane called Richie a nerd, a dork, "fag boy." I giggled at these names but began to feel sorry for Rich. I mean, there's no such thing as a *mean* nerd.

Since my fairy-tale marriage to the handsome prince was slow in coming, I began attending GED classes at night. I enjoyed the freedom of completing assignments at my own pace and the luxury of not being ridiculed by the snooty Newtown girls. The girls in GED class had problems as big or bigger than mine. The teachers kept telling me how bright I was. I took a bunch of aptitude tests—oral, written, manual dexterity—and the results came with a printout of about two hundred job options: doctor, lawyer, accountant, actress, teacher. According to that computer, there wasn't much I couldn't do.

At the alternative school, I became close to a classmate named Paula. Tall and slender with long, straight hair the color of coffee with a dash of cream, Paula was eighteen, a year older than me. Two years earlier, she'd gotten pregnant by a boy who had promised to love her forever but dropped her for a freshman girl as soon as she began to show. The girls at Paula's school were no less forgiving of "loose chicks" than the ones at mine. She quit during her third trimester, gave birth to a plump baby girl, and handed her over for adoption.

Like my cat Also, Paula was a soulmate of sorts—a fellow oddball who understood things about me that others didn't. We daydreamed about going off to college together, or getting jobs somewhere far away—a place where the labels people had stuck on us fell away like wet Band-Aids.

One night when Paula was sleeping over, we were looking at bikinis in the latest issue of *Vogue*. "Well, *my* bikini days are over," she sighed. "I have stretch marks *everywhere*."

"There you go, exaggerating again," I said. "You're probably the only one who can see them."

"Oh, yeah? Look." She pulled up her nightgown, exposing the welt-like lines that ran from her belly button to her panty line.

"Uh, well . . . look at this cute one-piece," I said, holding up the magazine. "You'd knock 'em dead in this."

It wasn't the stretch marks that bothered her so much, Paula confessed; it was the lost daughter they represented. "I only knew her for three days," she said. "But for nine months before that, she was a part of me. I miss her. I hate not knowing where she is." Paula stubbed out her cigarette and began to cry.

I put my arms around her and held her close to me, the way my sister Kathy had done for me. It felt awkward to dispense comfort like this, but it felt good, too. I thought about those stretch marks all night long, understanding now *why* we were soulmates. Paula understood emptiness, too.

I never did eat Mom's whole wheat spaghetti that night. When I was sure everyone else was asleep, I stripped off my soggy jeans and underwear, washed myself, and changed into clean clothes. The next morning, when Mom did my pigtails, the lumps from my head-banging hurt like hell.

Mom's new realities—divorce, downsizing, tedious factory work—stoked the anger that burned inside her. And while my sister and I both suffered, it was Janet who bore the brunt of our mother's misplaced rages. Our responses to Mom were different. Pissed off at the injustice of my mother's irrational firestorms, I fought back—shielding myself from her blows, answering her insults with taunts of my own. But Janet was too terrified to defend herself. Instead, she absorbed the blows, the humiliating verbal assaults.

One afternoon in the car on the way to our piano lesson, Janet was in trouble for having forgotten to defrost meat for supper. "Can't rely on you to do one simple thing! You're worthless! Isn't she, Nancy? We can always count on Janet to be the stupid one in the family."

It wasn't true. Late out of the womb, slower to walk and talk than Kathy and me, Janet was pensive and methodical, but far from stupid. The As on her report card proved it; Janet had more of them than Kathy and me combined.

"I'm sorry, Mom. I just forgot to take it out of the freezer."

"Oh, you 'just forgot'? Well, I notice you didn't 'just forget' to dig into the new ice cream carton when we weren't finished with the old one yet!"

Janet shot me a desperate look. "I *didn't* open the ice cream, Mom."

"So you're accusing your little sister of something you did? You're pathetic!" Guilty now of having tapped into the new ice cream *and* being the world's worst sister, I sat in survival-of-the-fittest silence.

By the time we reached the piano teacher's house, Janet's eyes were bloodshot and her nose was a faucet. Her face looked like an overripe tomato. "You have exactly five seconds to pull yourself together!" Mom warned. "Now get in there and act normal! And don't you dare say a thing!"

Sweet Mrs. Shaffner swung open the door of her big, pretty house and welcomed us in. "My stars, Jan, what happened?" she asked. Maybe *she* could be our mother, I thought. Maybe Mom would forget to pick us up forever.

"Nothing's wrong," Janet said, lowered her head. "I'm fine. *Really*."

Like junior meteorologists, Janet and I became experts at detecting the slightest barometric fluctuations of Storm Mom. We could tell what kind of a night it was going to be by listening to the way our mother slammed the car door after work, by the sound of her footsteps on the front stairs. On the worst nights, we hurried into our rooms, pulled the covers to our chins, and pretended to be asleep.

As Mom's tirades increased, Dad's visits grew more sporadic. On the Sundays he did show up, he seemed distracted. We'd sit in his house watching football, bored senseless, our conversations confined to the station breaks. "So, Peanut," he'd say. "How are things at home?"

"Fine."

"Great. How's school?"

"School's fine." Was he reading from some manual for divorced fathers?

"You like the new house?"

"It's fine, Dad."

He must have known, on some level, that we *weren't* fine. Either that or he'd managed to convince himself that his volatile ex-wife had woken up sane one day and his girls were happy and safe.

After these visits, Mom would give us the third degree. *What did you do today? What did he say? Did he talk about me? Was anyone else with him?* To tell her we'd had fun was a deadly mistake. "Of course, it was fun!" she'd snap. "*I* get to clothe, feed, and discipline you. *He* gets to spend all *his* money on fun!"

Gradually, we learned safer responses. "We had a rotten time, Mom," we'd assure her. "We watched football. We drove out to the airport and watched the planes. Then we ate. Then we came home." Pleading fatigue, we'd retire to bed before she could pick a fight, even if it was only seven o'clock.

I missed my period. I bought one of those drugstore tests and peed into the little cup. The paper strip turned bright pink.

I wasn't shocked. Shane and I had been having unprotected sex for almost a year. A part of me had been wondering what was taking so long.

Up in the attic, I found a blue baby sweater. Amazed by its tiny size, I took it downstairs, washed and dried it, and hid it in my sock drawer. I took it out and looked at it about twenty times a day.

Worried about how to break the news to Shane, I practiced different techniques in the mirror. Sometimes I'd pretend it was happy news, sometimes I'd say it with a sad face. But these exercises never showed Shane's reaction. Why hadn't I done anything to prevent this? Had I done it on purpose? The year before, I had quit school intent on getting married and having babies ASAP. Did I still want that life? What about the plans I'd made with Paula? What about college—that list of careers the aptitude tests had spat out?

We were in the car outside McDonald's when I told him. After all that practice, I opted for the direct approach as he bit into his Big Mac. "Shane? Guess what? I'm pregnant."

I told him about my missed period, the test kit, the nausea. I looked out the side window as I spoke, concentrating on a brown dog that was sniffing around the Dumpster for scraps. When I looked back at Shane, he was sitting there with his mouth full, not chewing. His eyes bulged, his neck stretched forward. Until then, I'd never realized how turtlelike he looked.

Was he choking? Should I review the steps of the Heimlich maneuver? Finally, he blinked and swallowed. "Are you sure?" he asked.

I said I was.

"Okay, then. We'll go to a doctor. Don't worry."

"Okay," I said. He started the car and backed out of our space. I rolled down the window and threw my burger to the dog.

We had planned to go to the movies, but Shane drove me home instead. He said he needed time to think. Which meant, I suspected, that he was going to go someplace and get hammered with Richie.

"Don't worry": easy for *him* to say. He wasn't the one walking around with a person inside of him. I was in a kind of tug-of-war with myself—the part of me that kept thinking about the little blue baby sweater versus the part of me that kept thinking about poor Sigourney Weaver in that movie *Alien*—the hostess of an unwanted guest. And I kept trying *not* to think about that stupid ninth-grade parenting experiment. As soon as Chuckie Dowd had handed over our "kid," I'd accidentally converted it to scrambled egg.

The doctor's office was a walk-in clinic with chrome chairs and dusty fake plants. Shane and I waited an hour before a nurse with fat ankles and glasses on a chain invited me inside.

Dr. Cusamano had poofy hair and a mouth full of perfect game-show host teeth. "Nancy Johansson, come on down!" I half-expected him to say. "You're the lucky winner of a BRAND-NEW PREGNANCY!"

It wasn't really like that, of course. Noticing our ages or the looks on our faces, he was somber and sensitive when he gave us the news. Had we made any decisions? We shook our heads. He reviewed our list of options. When he mentioned abortion, I burst into tears.

"Well, there's no sense pruning the branches if it's going to kill the tree," Dr. Cusamano noted cryptically. "If just the *idea* of abortion hurts this much, maybe you should explore other avenues."

Avenues? Trees? What was I, some freakin' landscape project? Between us, Shane and I split the cost of the appointment, exiting the clinic with forty dollars less in our pockets and a lot more on our minds.

When I was nine, Dad remarried. Gwendolyn was tall and sophisticated and she smoked Virginia Slims. She was the anti-Mom, really, although the two women had been friends before the divorce. Now they hated each other. I understood where Mom was coming from, but Gwendolyn's antipathy confused me. Sore loser, sure, but sore *winner*?

Our visits with Dad dwindled to almost nothing, which was fine with me, since I hated Gwendolyn's guts. She didn't care for me either. There was always something wrong with my hair, my clothes, the way I held my fork.

Around this time I began to have serious sleeping problems. I'd lie awake in bed for hours, watching shadows on the wall, re-counting the ceiling cracks. The longer I stayed awake, the more panic-stricken I'd become. One night I held out as long as I could until, finally, the loneliness overwhelmed me. I gave up and tiptoed to my mother's room. It had happened once before and Mom had let me curl up and sleep with her. But this time . . .

"Can't sleep? Well, let *me* help! Go get me a wooden spoon!"

Shaking and crying, I went out to the kitchen, grabbed a spoon from the big jar on the counter, and handed it over to Mom. *Whack!* across my shoulders. "Maybe *this'll* make you sleepy!" *Whack, whack, whack!* against my bare legs. Shielding myself made her madder. "Don't you *dare* block me!" Back in bed, I touched the angry red welts, the blood that seeped from the worst ones, and I prayed. For sleep. For Kathy or Dad or God to come back and save me. But no one came—not that night or ever.

The next day, while Mom was still at work, I pulled every one of the wooden spoons out of the kitchen jar and took them outside. I leaned each one diagonally against the porch steps and stomped. I buried the broken pieces in the flower garden. Mom never once mentioned their disappearance.

Shane and I went to the Blue Colony Diner to discuss our "situation." We ordered Cokes and Swiss cheese omelets from the ancient waitress, and I fed a quarter into the tableside jukebox. I selected "Peacefrog"—the Doors' anti-abortion tune. *Indians lay on the desert highway bleeding, ghosts crowd the child's fragile eggshell mind . . .* I was hoping Shane might pick up on the subliminal message.

He lit a Marlboro. I wanted a cigarette, too, but refrained from shaking one out for myself. I didn't want to hurt the baby.

"You know I love you," he said. "But right now I can't handle the responsibility. I think you should have an abortion. But don't worry. I know where we can go and I'll pay for it. Nowadays, it's as easy as one, two, three." He snapped his fingers to demonstrate.

Shane's cool, take-charge attitude was nothing like his initial reaction in the McDonald's parking lot. I figured he'd probably been coached by one or more of his five handsome brothers. No doubt unwanted pregnancies had surfaced before as a Fitzpatrick-family dilemma.

When our eggs came, I pushed mine away, but Shane dug in. "We wouldn't have to get married or anything," I said. "I don't even *want* to."

"Listen, kitten, I never mentioned this before, but . . ." Between mouthfuls, he told me about some girl named Sheila or Sherry whom he'd *also* impregnated. She'd kept the baby, he said, and moved to upstate New York. He sent money every month. He just couldn't afford to pay for another mistake, he said. "And besides, sweetie, the baby thing ruined our relationship. We hate each other now. You don't want that to happen to *us,* do you?"

I still couldn't sleep. After months of trying to cure my insomnia by alternating kindness with beatings, Mom began giving me "sleepy pills." They were tiny and white, bitter to the taste. Her doctor had prescribed them for her. I liked the way they took away my worries and let me drift off. Before long, I was forcing myself to stay awake nights so that I could take another of Mom's magic pills. The only catch was, they left me feeling dopey the next day—groggy enough for my fourth-period teacher, Mr. Izbicki, to notice.

"Nancy, come over here and sit down for a minute," he said. "Why haven't you handed in your Harriet Tubman report yet? And what's happened to all those As you had at the beginning of the year? What's wrong?"

"Nothing, Mr. Izbicki. I'll do my report tonight. I promise."

"You look tired. Are you eating okay? What did you have for breakfast?"

"Kix, some cinnamon toast. Oh, and orange juice." I longed to get away from him, but he held me in his gaze. "I'm fine, Mr. Izbicki. Everything's fine."

Back at my desk, I began to work on my vocabulary sentences, but I found it impossible to concentrate. When the dismissal bell rang, I was surprised by the doodles in my notebook. I'd filled up several pages.

The doctor told me I was too early along to feel fluttering in my stomach. "It's your imagination," he said.

I opted for twilight amnesia. "You might feel a little pressure, but nothing severe," the nurse assured me. "It's like a vacuum cleaner going into your cervix and cleaning things out. Now put your feet up here."

The stirrups sent a chill through my body, but she was right. I didn't feel much at all. No one had warned me about the pain that came afterward. Back in Shane's car, I could barely breathe from the cramping. "You okay?" Shane asked. He reached over and patted me on the head like a puppy.

"Mm-hmm," I said, weathering another cramp.

Shane swung into Pathmark Pharmacy and grabbed my prescriptions. "You just sit tight now, and I'll get these. You want anything else?"

I nodded. "Smokes. And Hubba Bubba—strawberry."

Alone in the car, I wondered when it would hit me—when I'd start sobbing over what I had done. If God was really up there keeping score, Nancy Johansson, Human Being #2431986573545, must have just gotten some major penalty points. I tried to make myself feel guilty by imagining what the baby might have grown up and done. Discovered a cure for cancer? Helped feed the poor? I even tried giving the suctioned tissue a name. But nothing worked. I wanted to cry, but I couldn't.

I told my mother I had a stomach flu and went to bed. The next day, I snuck the baby sweater back to the attic. The day after that, it was as if the pregnancy had never happened.

When I was twelve, Janet went off to college in Massachusetts, a three-hour drive away. After all the separations I'd already suffered, you'd think I'd have been a pro by then, but no, my sister's absence hit me almost like a physical blow. As much as Janet and I fought, she was one of my only friends, and an ally in the war with Mom.

I was sprawled on the couch one afternoon, watching my soaps and ignoring the pile of textbooks on the coffee table, when the screen door slammed back against the wall and Mom stormed in with a look on her face to scare the devil. She was waving a sheet of paper.

"This thing says you haven't been to school in twelve days! I go to work and slave all day while you sit here and play hooky? HOW DARE YOU!"

I wanted to tell her the truth: that I hated school—the way the girls picked on me because of my cheap clothes and because I'd sprouted boobs before any of them had, the way the boys followed me down the hall, howling like wolves and pinching my behind. "Mom, I'm sorry," I said. "Let me—"

"Skip the lip service, you rotten, ungrateful little liar!" She reared back and smacked me hard across the mouth.

For a second or two, we stood facing each other, two frozen statues in a garden of cheap brown velour and beige shag carpet. When I poked my tongue against my bottom lip, I tasted blood. I tasted something else, too. Righteous indignation. I knew if I didn't put an end to this, I would not survive Janet's absence. Mom leaned back to deliver another slap. I grabbed her wrist, stopping her hand in midair.

I addressed her quietly, through clenched teeth. "Don't hit me again, Mom. Because from now on, I'll hit you back when you do. And it will hurt."

The expression on her face turned from anger to confusion. Her arm went limp. When I let go, it flopped to her side. "Look at you," she whispered. "I hit you and you don't even cry. You're no more capable of feelings than he was." Her face searched mine for a reaction I refused to give. Then, to my surprise, she turned and walked out of the room without another word.

I stood there, twelve years old, alone but powerful.

I didn't know if Shane had told Richie about the abortion, and I didn't ask. The three of us continued to go out together to diners, movies, and bars—the kind of crappy saloons that didn't card minors like me. We were at the Bushwhacker for "Two for Tuesday Night" when Shane, shit-faced on half-priced drinks, tried to bum twenty dollars from his buddy. "I'm a little short," he said. To demonstrate, he stood and pulled his jean pockets inside out like bunny ears.

Something was bothering Richie that night. He was irritable, not his usual walk-all-over-me self. "Don't got it," he said. "And just so you'll know, I'm not your personal ATM machine."

Shane had a temper even when he *wasn't* drunk—even when he *hadn't* just been embarrassed in front of his girl. My hands began to shake in anticipation of the ugly scene I knew was coming. "No? Well, fuck you, you fuckin' clown," Shane said. "You fuckin' Ronald McDonald redhead. What'd you spend all your money on? A hooker, because you can't get laid without paying for it?"

"No, asshole," Richie replied. "I spent it on Nancy's abortion. Oh, and just a reminder, you still haven't paid me back for the last two."

I froze, a bottle of Bud halfway to my lips. I felt a coldness in my groin.

Shane's face glowed with anger. He took a drunken swing at Richie that did little more than push the air around. A big hairball of a bouncer approached, grabbed him in a bear hug, and walked him out the door. A minute later, I heard Shane's car rev up and drive away.

Richie and I sipped our beers in silence, staring at the inaudible TV perched in a cobwebby corner above the bar. We were both too dazed to speak at first, and when we *did* start talking, neither of us said much. I kept waiting for Shane to come back and drive me home.

The bartender announced last call and the hairy bouncer began lifting stools one-handed and placing them legs-up on the bar. "Oh, great," I said. "We're stranded."

"No, we're not," Richie said. "Hey, Bony Joe!" he called across the bar. "What do you say you loan me your pickup?"

A tall skeleton in a leather jacket and waist-length white hair stood up and smiled toothlessly. "Got five bucks?" he asked. Rich fished in his jeans pocket for the money. Keys flew above the bar and Richie caught them midair in his small, smooth hand.

I got my bearings and walked tipsily toward the door with Rich. "Where'd you say you know this guy from?" I asked.

"I didn't," Richie said. "He and my dad were in 'Nam together. He's a waste case now, though. Shell shock or traumatic stress or whatever they're calling it these days. Come on. I'll get you home safe." He grabbed me awkwardly by the elbow and ushered me outside.

Had my threat to hit back made my mother afraid of me, or was she just scared I would go away and leave her, too? Whatever the reason, Mom's reign of terror was abruptly over. She was a new woman.

Or rather, an older and more recognizable woman—the loving, overindulgent mom I remembered from early childhood. Little by little, home began to feel like a safe haven again and, of course, I took full advantage.

By the time I turned thirteen, I was smoking openly in the living room, skipping school whenever I felt like it, and staying out as late as I wanted. Mom never told me what to do anymore, at least not with any conviction. Whenever she did try to put her foot down, I ignored her.

The Lutheran summer camp I had been attending since I was seven was a disaster that year. I swore, spat, smoked, kissed nearly all the boys (campers and counselors alike) and several of the girls. Desperate not to return home from college for a summer with Mom, Janet had taken a counselor's job. In the interest of getting me to behave, she yelled, reasoned, rolled her giant gray eyes, and, finally, begged. In response, I laughed and plotted my next outrageous act.

When school started again, Mom did the unthinkable. She ratted me out to Dad. I was relaxing with a Coke and a soap opera when he barged in. I leapt to my feet, spilling soda on the living room carpet.

"Who the *hell* do you think you are?" he began.

I missed him so much. I had been waiting for him to come home for years. "Who do I think *I* am?" I shouted back. "Who do you think *you* are?" Palms out, arms extended, I kept pushing against his chest, shoving him backward as I ticked off his failures. "You weren't here when I came home with As on my report card. You weren't at the field when I was named first string in soccer, or at any of the meetings when I got all my Girl Scout badges. Didn't see you at parents' night or any of the school plays. So beat it, buddy! Get away from me! Just get the fuck out!"

And he did. Got in his car, backed down the driveway, and drove away. Good riddance, I thought. Those Sunday afternoon visits were corny anyway.

That was about it for Dad.

The inside of Bony Joe's rickety truck was littered with beer cans and fast-food crap. When Richie turned the key in the ignition, Ozzy Osbourne screamed from the speakers. *If you could see inside my head, you'd see that black and white is red. . . .* Rich moved quickly, ejecting the tape. Then he did something totally unexpected. He actually *talked* to me.

"I didn't mean to hurt you with what I said about the abortions," he said. "It just came out. You okay?" I shrugged. Nodded. "You've gotta watch out for Shane, Nancy. He's careless with girls and their feelings. He's going to hurt you, too, when the next chick comes along. He won't miss a beat. It's how his father was, how his brothers are. It's all he knows." I said nothing to refute him. I knew it was true. "I don't know, Nance. You know what I wish? That just once, *I* could meet a girl like you. And if I did? You better believe I wouldn't waste the opportunity."

From any other guy, it would have been a come-on. But Richie had none of the bravado that guys like Shane hid behind. None of the bullshit lines they used to get what they wanted. There was a sweetness to Richie's naive openness, his lack of finesse.

And there was something else about Rich. He actually *listened*. "After the abortion?" I said. "All I felt was . . . nothingness. I mean, I had cramps, but that was physical. I'm talking about emotionally. Shouldn't I have cried? Felt *something*? What am I, a monster?"

"You did the best thing, Nancy. You're still just a kid, and Shane would've been a lousy daddy. You're not a bad person at all."

I didn't buy it, but it was a relief to hear it anyway—and, at long last, to confide to someone how I felt. I rested my head in the crook of his surprisingly strong arm. His clean white T-shirt smelled like Ivory soap. Belatedly, I began to cry for the pregnancy I'd ended.

So, naturally, Richie and I wound up in bed.

Sex was different this time, though. For one thing, going to bed with Richie meant we actually *were* in a bed. But it was about more than a mattress, a box spring, and clean sheets. At first, I couldn't figure out if Rich had no clue about what to do with me, or if he knew *exactly* what he was doing. He traced the outline of my body with his hands, his fingertips, his tongue. Unhurried, he seemed awed, almost mesmerized, by plain old me. I felt safe. For the first time ever, I relaxed into the feelings he was producing in me, the sensations his touch was awakening. I had deflowered many a horny sixteen-year-old at the Danbury airport, but in many ways, I was, until Richie, a virgin myself. I'd never given myself to any of those other boys. They only thought I had.

When I got back to my house the next morning, the phone was ringing. I stared at it, hoping it would stop, then snatched it from its cradle. "Hiya, sweetie," Shane said. "Sorry about last night. Did you get home okay?"

"Yeah, I did. I'm fine." Had he just heard the tremor in my voice?

"Hey, can you come down to the Blue Colony, meet me for breakfast? I'll ask Richie, too. My treat. Make up for last night." I said I'd have my mom drop me off on her way to work.

A scalding shower and thirty minutes later, I walked into the diner. Shane was already seated, sipping on a Coke. He looked tired and unshaven, not a good sign. A hangover meant a bad mood. Tensing up, I slid into the booth beside him. When I smiled, he looked away.

When Richie arrived, he sat across from Shane and me. Amid the clatter of coffee cups and silverware, we were as silent as three stones.

Shane was the first to speak, in a voice so low I had to strain to hear him. "I always knew you were a whore, Nancy," he began. "But, Jesus Christ, *this* geek?" He kept staring into his soda, stirring and stirring with his straw. "Bartender said you left with Monkey Boy here, and I knew you didn't go home. I waited down the road from your house so I could apologize. Waited until fuckin' five o'clock. Fuckin' Richie, man. My best friend and my girl."

My explanation came out sounding like pure shit: we were upset, we were both drunk, we hadn't meant for it to happen. Shane grabbed my arm and twisted it. He talked a few inches from my face. "I've just got one thing to say to you, bitch. Steer clear of me from now on. Stay out of my fucking sight." He tightened his grip, digging his fingernails into my arm.

"Let her go, asshole," Richie said. He jabbed his finger in Shane's face and stood up so abruptly, our coffee spilled. "Let her go *now!*" A restaurant full of egg-eaters stopped their jaws and stared.

Shane released me with a shove. "For the record," he said, "the only reason I don't smack you both is because I'm afraid I might catch whatever freaky disease you both have."

"The only disease she and I ever had was *you*," Richie countered. "And now, thank God, we're cured. Come on, Nancy."

I stood, gathering my purse, my cigarettes, and whatever shred of dignity I had left. Richie took me by the hand and guided me toward the exit. "You're a dog, Shane!" he called back. "You got exactly what you deserved!"

Outside in the bright sunshine, Richie looked a whole lot taller. He was strutting like the chicken farm's only rooster.

During my sophomore year in high school, my father was promoted to vice president of his corporation. He and Gwendolyn built a huge house in Southbury, just one town away. Several people reported sightings of Dad. He was pretty hard *not* to notice, I guess, driving around in that new Mercedes.

If my father could afford the good life, I wondered, why were my mother and I doomed to count every nickel? We bought generic, discount, store brand, closeout. I'd stopped wearing Berkeley knitwear by then; instead, I went to school in my sisters' hand-me-downs and outfits borrowed from a shrinking pool of girlfriends. I was ashamed to dress so cheaply. At least when I was naked in some guy's backseat, it didn't matter.

Often, I caught myself still looking up when I heard a plane overhead. I told myself I'd been an idiot to believe all that crap about princes and saviors. Little by little, I trained myself not to look up.

Okay, maybe Richie *did* still dress like imitation Keith Partridge. Maybe he *wasn't* ever going to win the Iron Man competition or the Tom Cruise look-alike contest. But he was a welcome change from the boorish jocks and handsome hoodlums I was used to. He was affectionate and sweet—the kind of guy Mom just loved. "Richie, I'm sooo glad you could come for dinner again," she'd gush. "More pie?" I told myself I was in love.

We were happy enough. He bought me clothes, music, a sterling silver ring with a turquoise butterfly. He took me to restaurants—cloth-napkin-on-your-lap places instead of the Blue Colony Diner, the scene of so many of my bad memories. We never argued. How could you pick a fight with someone who treated you like a priceless Fabergé egg?

That spring, I passed the GED test with flying colors and drove with Paula to Mohegan Community College, an hour away. Mohegan accepted us on a one-semester probationary basis. To matriculate officially, Paula and I would have to take a four-course load and get Bs or better in each. It wouldn't be easy, I figured; my high school absenteeism had created some Grand Canyon–sized gaps in my education, and besides that, I'd have to balance school with work. Paula was in the same boat. We decided we'd give it a shot.

We found a small apartment in New London, two blocks away from Ocean Beach. It was ugly but affordable—a fixer-upper, a start. More than that, it was, at last, a leg out of Newtown. We shopped for curtains and rummaged through our families' attics and garages for dishes, lamps, and silverware. All summer long, I anticipated my new beginning with mixed feelings of exhilaration and dread.

On a cold, rainy morning in late August, Richie and I said our good-byes in his soft, cushy bed. "I'll miss you, honey," he whispered, breathing against my neck in that way of his that had become semiannoying. "I'll wait until you're settled before I come visit. Just give me the word. But write to me, okay? And call me every day. Collect."

When Rich dropped me back at Mom's so that I could pack, I picked the newspaper off the stoop on my way inside. Dad's latest promotion—to CEO, this time—was front-page news. I stood there, studying his picture, surprised at how little all that success had aged him. Even if I'd wanted to send him a congratulatory card—which I didn't—I couldn't have done it. Dad had never passed on his new address.

I took the newspaper to my room, snipped out Dad's picture with my manicure scissors, and placed it at the bottom of my suitcase. Then I went out to the backyard and stuffed the rest of the paper in the trash can.

The rain had stopped by then; the sky was dazzling blue. I couldn't help it: the habit of looking up had been a hard one to break. I flopped down on the wet grass and squinted up at the heavens. In spite of everything that had happened, all the years that had gone by, I wondered if somehow, somewhere, just maybe, Dad remembered about foxes and little princes—about how a person was responsible for whichever rose he tamed.

Later, when Mom asked if I'd seen the newspaper, I told her the carrier had probably forgotten to deliver it. "Or maybe someone stole it," I added.

"Damn thieves," Mom muttered, biting into her cheese Danish.

The weather that fall was spectacular, summer holding its own through late September. Paula and I settled into the semester and took jobs as cocktail waitresses at the Heartthrob Café, a fifties bar down the road from our apartment. Our outfits were black stretch pants and pumps with pink button-down shirts, knotted at the waist. Having calculated that maintaining our tans increased our tip potential, we were sipping wine coolers and sunbathing on our front porch in our bathing suits when Richie's blue Honda pulled unexpectedly into the driveway.

"Hey, baby!" he called up to me.

"Oh, God," I mumbled, slipping on my cutoffs and shirt. "Oh, shit."

Paula said a polite hello and went inside. Richie folded me in his arms and squeezed. When was the last time I'd called him? A week ago? Longer? Feeling both guilty and peeved, I invited him in.

He told me how much he missed me, and how great my tan looked. I said I missed him, too. I wanted him to get in his boring car and drive back to the dark, dreary town I'd finally managed to escape. Richie didn't belong in this place of sunlight and sea breezes. His hair looked more orange here, his face more plump and pale. I imagined him escorting me across campus or hanging out at the Heartthrob, people looking at us and laughing.

He could read the signs; Richie was an expert on getting screwed over. Half an hour after he'd arrived, he shook his head and told me I could call him if I wanted to, but he doubted I would. Watching him drive away, I felt sad. And mean. And wretched. Maybe Mom was right. Maybe I *was* as cold as Dad.

But as the sun went down and the wine cooler bottles emptied, my self-recrimination evaporated like fog. By nightfall, Richie's visit took on a dreamlike quality: something I'd only imagined and not really lived.

Maybe that was how Dad had done it—how he lived inside the shame of having abandoned us. Maybe Dad had turned us into dreams.

Months later, I was seated in the student common at Mohegan Community College, trying my best to get through a reading assignment for my literature class and to ignore the seductive gaze of a tall, well-muscled jock across the room.

I was reading *Wind, Sand, and Stars* by Antoine de Saint-Exupéry, which I'd selected from my professor's list of suggestions because of my fondness for the author's other work, *The Little Prince*. I had assumed both books would be similar, but boy, had I been wrong. I stifled a yawn, looked over at the jock, looked down again, read on. For all I knew, Antoine was a poof.

The aeroplane has unveiled for us the true face of earth. The sentence transported me back to those Saturday mornings when I'd sat on Dad's lap inside the shiny Beechcraft, zooming across the sky and looking down upon those perfect squares of earth. *The aeroplane has unveiled for us the true face of earth. . . .*

No way, I decided. I hadn't learned the truth about the face of earth or anything else during those plane rides. Everything I'd believed back then had turned out to be a big, fat, stinking rotten egg of a lie.

I slapped my book shut and looked up. He smiled. I twirled a piece of my hair. Smiled back. He rose and came to me. Up close, his eyes were the impossible blue of Easter eggs and summer skies.

His name was Kevin, but that didn't matter. There was an airport nearby. He knew the way.

ORBITING IZZY

NANCY WHITELEY

ERVOUS ABOUT MY HAIR, I HAD SETTLED ON A SLICKED-back French twist. I put on a stolen Liz Claiborne suit, stockings, matching maroon pumps. "Be brave," I muttered, and faced the mirror. Bleached blond hair, green eyes, long legs, huge breasts: I'm one of those girls who looks slutty no matter what I wear. My sister Janet once bought me a workout outfit for my birthday. She's about my size, but smaller-chested. When I modeled it for her, she said, "Hey! I tried this on before I bought it. I looked slender, kind of athletic. You look like a hooker." I decided my trampy look would have to do on this particular day, however; it was the first day of my first temp job, postprison, and we straight-and-narrow types don't like to be late for work. At twenty-nine, I'd been out of jail for about a month; I had served just under three years for doing things like stealing Liz Claiborne suits. I smoothed down my skirt and headed for the door.

Driving through the slushy roads toward the one-man accounting firm to which I'd been assigned, I recalled the last time I had worked legally, eight years earlier. I was tending bar at the Brickyard Café, shaking someone's vodka martini, when trouble sauntered through the door. Aldo: tall, dark, Italian, and gorgeous. I was so distracted that I removed the top of the cocktail shaker, poured, and realized I'd missed the glass.

Aldo straddled a bar stool as I sopped up spilt vermouth and vodka. "As Dr. Carl Sagan has proven, the universe is just a baby," he said. "It's still expanding. And the center of the cosmos is right here."

"Right where?" I asked.

He pointed to my lips, leaned forward, and left his kiss. I'd never heard pickup lines laced with astronomy before. I was starstruck.

Everyone who knew Aldo warned me that he was morally bankrupt and emotionally vacant, the most deplorable guy I'd ever hooked up with—and, believe me, there were *already* some major assholes in Nancy Whiteley's Hall of Shame. Soon enough, I realized that Aldo deserved every bit of his reputation as a criminal and a ladies' man. So I promptly married him.

For five years, we lived like rock stars. We drank, sniffed cocaine, shopped till we dropped, and flew the friendly skies on other people's credit. For our encore, we did three years in prison. After our release, Aldo wanted to resume our life together, but I'd said no. It would have been the easier choice in the short run, but it was also a guaranteed passport back to prison—the *last* place I wanted to be. This temp job was my first shaky attempt at reentering the nine-to-five orbit and managing on my own.

When I arrived at Isadore Weintraub's accounting firm, he called me into his backroom office. There sat my new employer: a nervous, shifty-eyed man with thin, mousy hair and horn-rimmed glasses.

"Where are you from?" he asked, studying me suspiciously.

"Hartford," I said. I omitted the prison part.

"How are you at spelling? And, you know, *filing*?"

"Well, pretty good, I think," I said. Isadore looked relieved.

"Good, good. Because the last gal your service sent me said that she 'wasn't too good with her alphabet.' Jeepers, can you imagine that?"

Jeepers, I couldn't, and told him so.

"Did you bring your lunch?"

I held up my lunch box. He led me to a tiny refrigerator in an office across the hall from his. Although the desk was all set up and ready to go, I sniffed the dank, musty aroma of abandonment. "This was my father's office," Isadore explained. "He passed away five years ago."

I nodded, smiled respectfully, and reviewed the escape routes. What kind of a man kept an office shrine to his dead father?

Mr. Weintraub dismissed me to my receptionist's desk out front, where I sat, task-free, chewing on pencils for about three hours. During hour number four, he called me into his office. Flustered, he sat surrounded by instruction manuals, pamphlets, and computer parts. He peered at me from over the rims of his bifocals. "What do you know about installing modems?" he asked.

"Only enough not to try it," I answered politely.

"I did what the instructions *said* to do," he whined. "But nothing's working. It better not be broken. This system cost me three thousand dollars."

"Not to be rude, sir," I said, "but if you don't know anything about computers, why would you attempt to customize a three-thousand-dollar machine by yourself?"

That got me tossed out of his office, back to my pencil-chewing station. I was pretty sure that, by the end of the day, I'd be following in the footsteps of my predecessor, the temp who'd been alphabet-challenged.

But at five o'clock, Isadore wished me a good night and told me he'd see me in the morning. Somehow, against the odds, my candor had launched the beginning of a beautiful relationship.

Isadore Weintraub, CPA, PC, suffered from a condition which caused the skin on and around his nose to flake and peel. He was an Orthodox Jew with horrendous stomach problems. Food couldn't be hot, sweet, fatty, or milky, and it had to be kosher. Consequently, there was almost nothing in this galaxy that Isadore could eat, except canned corn and matzo. Yet he was plump around the middle. That always made me pause: how could someone on such a limited diet be overweight?

I guess you could liken me to a meteor that had crashed head-on into Planet Isadore. For every eight-hour day, he assigned me only about one hour's work. Bored and restless, I took to wandering into his office at regular intervals, asking for things to do. Slowly, we began to talk about our lives. Izzy confessed that he had always been uptight, nervous, and discontented, even though, materially, he had everything a man could want. Poring over the month's credit card bills, fat with his wife's purchases, he would sigh. "Men are from Mars, women are from Filene's." His marriage had been one long, comfortable yawn, he said—an exact replica of his parents' marriage.

Before I knew it, I was talking about *my* marriage, too. "He still loves me, Izzy, and I know he needs me, but he scares me, too. Getting sucked back into Aldo's lifestyle is the *last* thing I need. But it's just so hard being on my own."

"Nothing awful has ever happened to me." He sighed. "But nothing wonderful has ever happened either." I told him I'd had more than my share of both awful *and* wonderful.

"I'm unhappy," he confessed. I admitted I was miserable, too.

One afternoon shortly after my arrival, *Mrs.* Isadore Weintraub bustled into the office to check me out. Plump, pear-shaped, and politically correct, Carol Weintraub wore her drab brown hair in the shape of a football helmet. I was certain she didn't even own a pair of *un*sensible shoes. I could have been kinder, I guess. After she appeared one afternoon in an unflattering purple sweat suit, I began to call her Barney. Izzy laughed guiltily at the nickname. Occasionally, he'd ask me to call his wife by her proper name.

Whenever Carol visited, we groped and strained for conversation. We had nothing in common, except for our love of shopping, and I was pretty sure *her* purchases were made with credit cards that bore her actual name. Although I sensed from the start that Izzy's wife hated me, she began giving me gifts—edible offerings mostly. Maybe she thought of me as a charity case. "Gee, thanks," I'd say, as she handed me stuff like nacho cheese–flavored corkscrew pasta chips. In my old life with Aldo, I had washed down oysters and caviar with hundred-dollar bottles of champagne. But, apparently, minimum-wage temps weren't supposed to have a sense of taste.

One Friday morning I arrived at work to find a bouquet of long-stemmed red roses on my desk. "Remembering the good times," the card read. Even Aldo's handwriting seemed sexy. I put the card in my desk drawer. Took it out. Put it back again. Took it out. The bouquet looked out of place next to the bologna sandwich I'd brought for lunch—my fifth that week. I resisted the urge to call and thank him.

Just as the roses began to wilt, a series of other thoughtful gifts appeared: candles, perfume, an engraved name plaque for my desk. Aldo must not have realized how tight my working woman's budget was. If he had, he'd have sent me *useful* stuff like toothpaste and dish detergent. But Aldo knew what he was doing. Occasionally, he enclosed money in a mushy greeting card. I knew that to keep the cash was to take a bribe from the devil himself, but I was too poor and too weak to refuse. Lusting for a trip to the hairstylist, a fancy restaurant meal, an upscale department store purchase, I'd snatch the crisp fifty-dollar bills from the card, crumpling them into my purse. I will always wonder if things would have turned out differently for me had I returned Aldo's gifts and cards, unopened.

As the weather warmed and the birds flew back from parts unknown, Izzy and I began to argue about who should walk to the bank and make the daily deposits. I wanted to go so that I could smoke a cigarette; Izzy felt he needed the exercise. I usually got my way—it was a secretary's job, after all, and there was never enough for me to do in the first place. But Izzy fell into the habit of pulling on his Keds and accompanying me.

The bank, two blocks away, was a tiny local branch. The tellers were all heavy, middle-aged, divorced women who took turns winking at Izzy and giggling behind their Ring Dings and powdered doughnuts. Until *I* came along, that is. They were overtly hostile to me, rude and unforgiving of my short skirts and high heels. The curse of the trashy broad is that she's an easy target for "decent" women.

Soon enough, gossip began to circulate around town about Isadore's new secretary. "Izzy, who cares?" I shrugged. "Those rumors began at the Little Bank of Frustrated Women and we both know it. They're jealous." Izzy responded with a funny look, a creepy smile that stayed in my mind for days. I had imagined the gossip would upset him, but he seemed proud of it. It was the first sign of trouble ahead.

I stayed at work later and later that spring, as I had nothing to rush home to. I was living in a dreary little low-rent apartment in downtown Hartford. I had few friends and, after rent, heat, electric, and phone bills, barely enough money left to feed myself and the roaches. I had never experienced living within my means before, and I hated every second of it.

Sometimes I longed for the days when I had been at the center of the shopping world—when I would only stop buying once the piles of purchases blocked the car's back window. I missed traveling, too: zooming through the sky, feet up, in those roomy, leather-upholstered first-class seats, balancing a watery Bloody Mary on my knee, lemon wedge instead of celery, thanks, and can we get more cashews here? I missed five-star hotels, famous restaurants, and the mink coat the cops had confiscated. I'd sit in my pathetic apartment, recalling the words of the seductive warning Aldo had whispered to me one night, under our three-hundred-dollar Laura Ashley comforter. "You know you're ruined now, don't you? You can't ever go back to being Janie Punch Clock or Suzy Lunch Pail. From now on, you're *always* going to want the best, babe. And with me, you'll always have it."

In fact, without Aldo, my lunch pail *was* pretty empty. Izzy noticed that some days I hadn't even brought bologna and began sharing his bland food with me. I felt embarrassed to take these handouts, but my growling stomach usually drowned out whatever objections my pride was voicing. We'd sit huddled together, chomping away, Izzy amazed at the mess I made when I ate—the crumbs I left everywhere. A detective couldn't have told where *he* had eaten.

After lunch, we began kicking around a soccer ball. We didn't go outside, like normal people, but kicked the ball up and down the office corridor. The doorway to the backroom was my goal; the one to the front office was his. On the days I didn't feel like playing, Izzy would beg me for a game. He was like a schoolkid. How could I refuse?

One of our clients, Elaine, was a mystery to me. She was the pretty young widow of an older man, an Asian American physician named Dr. Yup, who had died the previous spring. Elaine's grief didn't seem convincing; I suspected foul play. After I shared my theory with Izzy, we began the game of inventing scenarios by which Elaine had done in Dr. Yup so that she could collect the insurance money. It became an obsession of ours. Izzy would buy pizzas and sodas and we'd head to the cemetery, climbing the hill to Dr. Yup's grave. There, we would sit and picnic, me devouring the onion, pepperoni, and pepper-laden pizzas while Izzy nibbled on the crusts. Sometimes we'd call below to poor Dr. Yup, asking for clues. But he never responded.

For a time, Izzy was my best friend. We were side by side every day for months. He tiptoed; I crashed into things. He beat around the bushes; I chopped them down. Our worlds were so far apart that we couldn't get enough of investigating each other's differences. Like an earthling and a space alien meeting face-to-face, we were fascinated by each other.

Gradually, I became a reluctant student in Izzy Weintraub's School of Responsibility. He taught me things I had never imagined could have anything to do with me. Getting an oil change for my car every three thousand miles? It seemed so anal. "Izzy, why do you obsess over every little detail? I hate this car stuff. That's why girls get married." I could picture Aldo under my car, biceps bulging, draining the thick black liquid.

But Izzy was a patient professor and, eventually, the concept of responsibility began to make sense to me. He put me on his family's health insurance and insisted I have a complete physical. He made me a member of his corporation and named me vice president. He even gave me a company credit card with a $250 limit and his name on it so that I could get myself out of emergencies.

"Ms. Whiteley, would you please explain this forty-dollar charge to me?" he asked one day, waving in my face a bill from the bar at the Hartford Sheraton.

"Hey, Izzy, everyone's definition of 'emergency' is a little different," I explained. He sputtered and shook his head, but I paid him back and he got over it and we moved on.

Izzy taught me how to do simple tax returns. I taught him how to drink.

"Wanna have a drink?" I asked him near quitting time one afternoon. He looked confused. "Oh my God, Izzy, don't you *drink*?" I was incredulous.

"Well, I sip a little wine sometimes," he said. "But it makes me queasy. I had a mudslide once."

"C'mon, let's go to the liquor store," I said, rummaging around for my keys. "We'll take my car. I just had the oil changed."

Twenty minutes later, we were back in the office with premixed mudslides for Izzy, a bottle of Absolut and a jar of green olives for me. I poured our drinks over ice and plunked a few olives into mine. We sipped, talked, got tipsy. It felt slightly wicked to be enjoying cocktails in the office "after hours."

But if "after hours" was a novelty, nine-to-five became more and more of a drag. Not having enough to do left me too much time to think—and, often, I thought of Aldo. Word got back that he'd bought a new Saturn sports coupe and had moved into an apartment in nearby Bristol. I'd think of the fun he was no doubt having and feel jealous of his freedom, while I, Suzy Punch Clock, sat imprisoned in an office forty hours a week. On the worst days, my mind would drift to the row of filing cabinets lining the office adjacent to Izzy's. Every single file held a wealthy person's birth date and Social Security number, just the information with which Aldo and I could forge someone's identity and steal his credit. Aldo would love those files, I'd think. Then I'd think about his letters promising me, over and over, that he had changed—that he was committed to the straight-and-narrow and could make it, too, if only he had me to lean on.

Whenever the urge to dial Aldo's number overwhelmed me, I would pick up the phone and call my big sister, Janet, instead. Janet possessed all the common sense I lacked. I complained to her about my plight. "I don't even know how I'm going to make my insurance payment this month. I'm sick of this shit. Poverty *sucks*."

"You *know* you have to forget that guy," Janet countered. I could tell from ten towns away that she had her hands on her hips. "Aldo's a speeding train and you're the dumb cow on the track. No matter how much we holler 'Move! Move!' you just *stand* there. If you call him, you'll be dead meat."

"I know, I know," I'd agree. But I kept wondering if just maybe things *might* be different this time.

Meanwhile, back at the office, Izzy had a plan. His mother, a wealthy widow, lived right up the road from our office. When he first suggested that we go there for lunch while she was away, I was a nervous wreck. Izzy's and my relationship was strictly platonic, but I imagined him trying to kiss me and ruining everything. After all, there were *bedrooms* up there. But God bless Izzy; he was a docile gentleman who simply wanted to show me his childhood home.

The house was clean, neat, and perfectly decorated. The bedrooms had been left as if they still housed the now-middle-aged children who had lived in them decades before. One room, pink and frilly with baby dolls and a canopy bed, had belonged to his sister, Brenda. Another displayed the pennants and polished trophies of Izzy's brother, Mort, the family jock. But math whizzes don't get trophies. Groomed to be the son who would follow in his father's footsteps, Izzy had slept in a room as bland and spartan as his adult life.

It was out in the garage that I discovered the centerpiece of the Weintraub home. According to Izzy, his mother had purchased the fiery red Porsche 944 convertible to console herself after her husband died. Sports car therapy must not have worked for her, though. The tires showed no sign of wear; the odometer registered a whopping four hundred miles. Well, whether or not this sweet vehicle had failed to cure Mrs. Weintraub's blues, I was certain it would make *me* feel better. It was a humanitarian gesture, really. That poor Porsche looked like it was dying to be driven. And so I made a silent vow to get behind the wheel and go.

The more I understood about Izzy and me, the more I realized that we operated from different philosophies: Eat, drink, and be merry versus Prepare for a rainy day. Take our spouses, for instance. I had married Risk; he had married Safety. Or take our attitude toward finances. I spent my money as soon as I got it; he saved every single dollar to ward off impending doom.

"Izzy, what are you saving *for*?" I groaned one day.

"Well, umm, a rainy—"

"Izzy, you're forty-five years old! Your health stinks, your job's a bore, and your wife's a nag. It's raining *now*! It's *pouring*!"

"Yes, but—"

"Don't you ever just want to say 'fuck it'? Grab an umbrella and get out there in the storm?"

Next thing Izzy knew, he was riding shotgun, hooting like a high school kid while I put the pedal to the metal of his mother's Porsche, rag top down. Eighty miles an hour, ninety, a hundred. I may not have understood the ins and outs of retirement planning, but I practically had a *degree* in risk.

It didn't stop there. We downloaded "Donkey Kong" and "Space Invaders" on the company computer, Izzy swearing that the hard drive would break. We took long walks, blasted rap music, rented go-carts, closed the office as the desire struck us. Sometimes I'd sneak outside and pop up at Izzy's office window—pretend it was the drive-thru.

"I'll have a large fries, a chocolate shake, and a double cheeseburger."

"Did you want that on a bun or a matzo?"

That summer, Izzy got to enjoy his first real childhood, and I almost grew up. And then, as suddenly as it had begun, it was ruined.

One day I found a note on my desk thanking me for a wonderful time. The next day, another note. The correspondences kept coming, growing more and more amorous, evolving into love letters. Izzy always asked me if I had read what he had written—if I had a response. "Oh, yeah, well, I guess I must have accidentally lost that last one," I'd lie. To my dismay, he'd run to his computer and print me another copy.

I *had* to quit. What had once been easy became awkward, even painful. He had mistaken my gift to him—affection—for romance. And God knows, he deserved better than me, the trashy temp who would love him only as long as she could shock him. "You're ruined now," Aldo had whispered that night under our plush, stolen designer quilt. I had neither the heart nor the stomach to ruin Izzy.

Or maybe I'm *not* that kindhearted. Maybe my abrupt exit from the Weintraub accounting firm was just an excuse to go back to my ex-husband and all those creature comforts. Maybe I'll never know.

Too ashamed to face Izzy, I resigned over the phone one stormy July morning. I went back to Aldo and my old, scary life. I kept expecting I might hear from Izzy—receive a note telling me about some silly new thing he'd tried, or get a call from him telling me he forgave me for having introduced him to risk. But once I left the firm, Izzy offered no clues about how he had gotten on with his life. In that respect, he was as silent as poor, dead Dr. Yup.

Not long after I quit my job, I was back in prison: conspiracy to commit credit card fraud. This bid, I had a cell mate who suffered from sadness, something I knew about all too well. One late night, in the dark, her disembodied voice said, "Nancy? Do you think that people can just come into our lives for a moment and love us, and we love them back, and they change our whole lives, and then they just disappear?"

I groped for the joke, some sarcastic quip to lighten the moment, but nothing came to me. "That's all that ever happens," I said. I rolled over, trying to gather a little warmth from my tattered prison linens. A few hours later, I fell into a dreamless sleep.

———

With a stolen credit card, Nancy Whiteley and her husband embarked on an extended first-class travel and shopping spree that took them to Jamaica, DisneyWorld, and the Mall of America. The couple were apprehended in Florida, and Whiteley was flown back to Connecticut, where she entered York Correctional Institution. Because hers was an interstate crime, she was transferred to a federal facility the following year. She was later released to the custody of a halfway house. After a period of "home confinement" at the residence of her sister Kathy, she regained her freedom during the summer of 2002. Since her release, Whiteley has maintained full-time employment and rigorous commitment to a twelve-step program that addresses her addiction to alcohol and drugs. Halfway to a bachelor's degree, she hopes to enter Western Connecticut State University as a full-time student in 2003.

Of her participation in the writers' workshop, Whiteley says, "For some reason, I can put down on paper the things I can't say aloud. Writing's hard, but I feel a strong compulsion to do it. I wish I felt that way about exercising."

THEFTS

||||||||||||||||||||||||||||

CAROLYN ANN ADAMS

Born: 1950
Conviction: Larceny by embezzlement
Sentence: 5 years
Entered prison: 1998
Status: Released

1. THE RIGHT TO REMAIN SILENT

Seated on a bench in the busy corridor outside courtroom A, I fidgeted and waited for my lawyer, whose fee had cost me my 1996 Dodge Spirit. It was the morning of my arraignment. The noise level rose and fell with the chatter of criminal lawyers and their clients. I exchanged quick glances with several of the others who'd be facing the Superior Court judge that day. We all looked guilty of something.

I *smelled* Ned in the crowd that morning before I spotted him. It was Ned, all right: tan fishing hat, tattered trench coat over a bulk of layered clothing. Grateful to see a familiar face, I smiled and opened my mouth to speak, but Ned averted his eyes and passed without a word.

Ned had been one of the people I'd assisted in my position as executive director of a mental health advocacy board. A former high school science teacher who'd earned a double master's degree before the onset of paranoid schizophrenia, he had spent thirty of his fifty-six years as a resident of Norwich State Hospital. He'd been released into the community when Connecticut began the systematic closing of its psychiatric facilities, but Ned missed his former "home." Each morning, he made the five-mile trek from his drug-infested neighborhood up Route 12 to the single hospital building still open. He'd make his rounds through the offices, telling jokes, mooching coffee and small change, or conning some secretary into typing his latest letter of protest to the governor or the mental health commissioner or the CEO of R. J. Reynolds Tobacco Company. (It was Ned's contention that, since cigarettes helped him cope with his schizophrenia, they should be provided for him free of charge.) He always visited my office last, chatting until the urge for a smoke overtook him. Then he'd leave, meandering back down Route 12, oblivious to the honking horns of drivers rushing to get to the Indian casinos. When the weather turned warm, Ned sometimes brought along his saxophone. After visiting, he'd spend the day out on the dilapidated bleachers of the abandoned softball field, playing to the ghosts of patients past.

Prior to my suspension and arrest, my job had been to evaluate state-funded agencies that provide psychosocial services for patients discharged from the hospital. As a high-functioning person with psychiatric demons of my own, I felt an affinity with Ned and other fellow consumers of mental health services. But, once again, I'd blown it—had failed myself and the people for whom I'd advocated. After my arrest, one of the board members had made it her business to let me know that Ned and some of the other clients were the ones judging me most harshly. They'd trusted me to be their voice and I had betrayed them.

I'd been embezzling advocacy board money over a four-year period, gambling most of it away at area casinos. When I started stealing, I informed the agency's auditor that we'd hired another CPA firm and were no longer in need of his services. To hide the missing funds, I handled the computerized audits myself, thinking I would win big at the casino, replace what I'd stolen, and resign my job. But that big win never came, and one morning, during a routine call to my office, my secretary asked me about a missing financial report. The chairperson and treasurer of our board were on their way in to help her look for it, she said; they'd instructed her to tell me to get to the office immediately. I promised I'd be right in to straighten things out. Instead, I drove to the casino and gambled for two days straight. My disappearance further aroused the board's suspicions, and I was suspended without pay and medical benefits while an investigation was launched.

During the six months that I was under investigation, I sold my car to help pay my legal expenses and took a stopgap job managing a condominium complex to support myself and my fifteen-year-old son. I'd been hired by a group of elderly condo residents, and then befriended by them. They dropped by the office frequently, to chat about their families and bring me homemade cookies.

I was at my desk in the condo office that day when the door opened. A man and a woman stood in the entranceway. "May I help you?" I asked.

The woman, a petite blonde, wore a red skirt and a tartan plaid sweater. The man was balding, in his fifties. "We're from the Chief State's Attorney's Office," he said. "We've come to arrest you."

My hands began to shake. My mouth went sour with the taste of yesterday's booze. Having lost my prescription benefit, I'd been off my psychiatric medicines for months, medicating myself instead with a daily pint of Seagram's Seven. For half a year, I'd been trying to convince myself that I'd be able to handle this moment when it came, but I was wrong.

As the detectives approached, I reached across my desk, grabbed a scissors, and drew the blade across my wrist. They rushed me, one detective twisting my arm behind my back until I dropped the scissors, the other handcuffing me, tightening the left band over my bleeding wrist.

Outside, three police cruisers waited, their blue lights flashing. They'd attracted the attention of the elderly condo residents. Some stood on the sidewalk, staring openly. Others peeked from behind curtains. I looked away from their disbelieving faces.

At the station, I emptied money, keys, wallet, and lipstick from my purse onto a table. A detective ordered me to remove my jewelry, which she placed in a brown envelope. She listed items piece by piece, then pushed a form in front of me to sign. "Fingerprints!" she shouted.

My arresting detective walked me to the fingerprinting room. Since it was already full, he handcuffed me to a metal chair in the hallway amid people reeking of booze and looking stoned on crack. My eyes and throat burned from crying. After I was fingerprinted, I was led down another hallway to be photographed. "Shoes off! Stand against the measuring tape!" the detective behind the camera barked. "Hold your hair back! Look at the camera! Turn right! Turn left! Face front! Okay, I'm through. Take her to lockup."

The barred cell they led me to was one of several lining both sides of a narrow corridor. "In here," the sheriff said. As the door slammed shut behind me, the stink of urine, vomit, and sweat hit my nostrils. The cell was small and grim: cinder-block walls, a metal toilet with a drinking fountain on top, a metal bench along the back wall. Three women were seated there. A fourth lay on the floor without benefit of blanket or pillow. Instinct told me it would be safer to stand at the front of the cell than to sit with the others. So I stood there in my yellow Chanel suit and matching heels, staring out.

The woman on the floor popped her head up. "Is you my public defender?" she asked. I told her no—that I'd been arrested, too. This made the others stir. "Well, sister, you look like a lawyer or something. I knows you don't get high. What'd you do?"

I didn't want to answer her or to see the abscesses and needle tracks on her arms and neck. When I tried to speak, I began to cry instead.

"Ah, honey, Niantic ain't like they show in the movies," one of the others said. "It ain't about nothing. Niantic's more like going to camp."

"That's right," another agreed. "Three hots and a cot. Good ole Camp Ni-Ni." They all laughed at that one.

Minutes before my arraignment, my attorney approached me outside courtroom A. "Bad news, Carolyn," he said. "Have a seat." His law firm represented the savings bank from which I'd drawn the forged advocacy board checks, he explained. The bank had made good on the money and reimbursed the board, but my lawyer had just learned they intended to file a civil suit against me. The conflict of interest meant he could not defend me after all. "But don't worry," he said. "I've gotten you another attorney. Same caliber as me."

My new lawyer wouldn't look me in the eye, and his impatience during our initial meeting made me nervous. "This part of it will be over in a flash," he said, rechecking his watch. "All you have to do is stand before the judge and plead not guilty." I was right to be concerned. For nine long months of court appearances, my attorney's attitude communicated loudly and clearly that he didn't give a fiddler's fart about my case or me. I was convicted.

"I acknowledge that you have psychiatric things going on," the judge told me during my sentencing. "But I'm not a psychiatrist, and I don't profess to know anything about these issues. I've agonized over this decision all week, deciding finally that any mental-illness defense you may have had was forfeited when you accepted a plea bargain with the state. Therefore, I remand you into the custody of the Department of Correction for a period of five years."

The holding cell to which I was led looked like the one I'd been in when first arrested. This time there was only one other occupant, a woman in her sixties with long yellowy gray hair. Seated on the bench in back, she picked nervously at her fingers and did not look up when I entered the cell.

I sat on the opposite end of the cold metal bench. After several minutes, the woman abruptly spoke. "Going to York?" When I nodded, she began to laugh and cough. "You're going to hell then, plain and simple," she said. "Not me. I'm going to Whiting" (by which she meant the state's facility for the criminally insane). "Food's better at Whiting. I killed Jimmy, you know. Had to 'cause the spies were gonna take him straight to hell. Jimmy's my boy. He had to be free from the powers of the devil. I done the right thing."

Her chaotic muttering continued for what seemed like hours, her voice rising and falling with her level of agitation. Then, down the corridor, I heard someone say, "Open Adams."

The holding room where I waited to be processed into the Department of Corrections system had white floor tiles and metal benches bolted to white concrete walls. I made my way to the back and looked out the thick safety-glass window. The view was bleak: a concrete building, a patch of grass. I don't know how long I'd been staring out at nothing when I saw it: the goose.

I thought I was hallucinating. But no, it was real. Oblivious to the humans locked inside, it waddled along, doing what geese do: eating, shitting, and looking stupid. I stood there, envying that son-of-a-bitchin' goose as it passed by on its way to greener pastures.

All afternoon, the holding room filled up with new arrivals from around the state, the majority from Connecticut's inner cities. Several of the women called to each other by nickname—Pom Pom, Manhattan, Rebel, Snooks. Many acted as if they were at a class reunion instead of a prison.

"Hey, Bridgeport!"

"Whassup, Hartford? You back here, too?"

A fat woman with a gold front tooth, her hair done in neat cornrows, entertained the others by bothering the corrections officer whose desk was positioned just outside the locked room. The officer ignored the woman's taunting and window-tapping as best he could, but she persisted and he finally looked up. "Hey, baby, you old trick," she called, grabbing her crotch and swaying. "Want some of this?" The officer told her to sit down and shut up.

"Aw, you know you like it. Come let Mama suck that big old dick of yours." The others laughed and hooted.

"I told you to shut up, you worn-out piece of shit!" the officer shouted. "One more word out of that mouth is a ticket!"

The woman's taunts continued, but at a volume just lower than what the officer could hear. He must have heard her appreciative audience, though. I stuck my fingers in my ears to block out the laughter bouncing off the walls.

"Ever had any affiliation with a gang?" my interviewer asked.

I checked the officer's face to see if he was joking, but he was dead serious. "Of course not!" I said. He handed me a tattered book of prison rules and warned me that if I lost it, I'd be charged five dollars. "Step over to the wall," he said. He took my picture with a digital scanner. A few minutes later, I was handed a plastic photo ID that contained my vitals: name, inmate number, age, weight, height, hair and eye color. If I lost my badge, the officer warned, I'd be charged for the replacement and possibly get a discipline ticket for tampering with prison safety and security.

The officer who escorted me to the showers had spiked hair thick with gel, gold posts up the sides of her ears, and uniform pants tucked into her boots, Nazi-style. "Take everything off," she ordered.

"Even my bra and panties?"

"What did I just *say,* you stupid bitch?"

I undressed and stood naked before her.

"Now, turn around, bend over, spread your butt cheeks, and cough." There I stood, a woman who had been too inhibited to appear naked before her husband unless it was in the dark, now facing this hostile stranger under the glare of fluorescent lights. Ashamed, I obeyed her because I had no choice.

"Okay," she said. "Now hold out your hands, palms up." She poured a thick yellow liquid into my cupped hands. "Rub this stuff in you pubic hair and the hair on your head," she commanded.

I made the mistake of asking her what it was. "Delousing shampoo!" she snapped. "And now, because you had to be a smartass and let it drip out of your hands, *I'm* going to put it on you!" With that, she dumped the rest of the bottle over my head and scrubbed hard.

Midway through my delousing shower, an inmate entered the room and picked my clothes off the floor. "Where are you going with those?" I asked.

"Laundry," she said.

When I told her my suit had to be dry-cleaned, she smirked. "Aw, too late," she said. "I already washed it."

The supervising officer handed me what looked like a pile of rags. These were the clothes I'd be wearing for the next five years, she explained: two pairs of frayed jeans, three nubby maroon T-shirts, a cheap pair of black sneakers, and a gray sweatshirt with a hole under the arm. "What bra size are you?"

"Thirty-six B."

"Too bad. All's I have are forty-four Ds. And here, put these on."

She handed me a thin cotton nightgown and a pinstriped robe. Both bore the stamped logo: *Property of YCI.* I put them on, grateful to cover myself.

"Follow me," she said.

The room we entered next had wooden benches and walls the color of runny baby shit. The three other women in there had wet hair and night-clothes identical to mine. "Wait for the nurse," the officer said. "She has to pull your urine. I gotta go now." Oblivious to the trauma she'd just inflicted on me, she was suddenly addressing me as if we were friends.

I sat, hugging my pile of prison clothes. A woman at the back of the room bent over a metal toilet and vomited.

"Don't worry about her," someone said. "She's just dope sick. She'll be okay." The woman who'd just spoken was birdlike, so skinny that her facial bones were visible. Her arms were dotted with needle marks.

"What are *you* in for?" she asked me.

"Embezzlement from a state agency," I said.

"Yeah? How much time they give ya?"

"Five years."

She whistled and shook her head. "You woulda gotten less time if you murdered someone. This state don't want *nobody* messing with *their* money!"

2. THE RIGHT TO SPEAK

Like many people in the criminal justice system, my crime and imprisonment are directly related to my mental illness. Currently, I am working with a diagnosis of major depression, bipolar disorder, and post-traumatic stress, anxiety, and dissociative disorders. Related to these, I must also manage my addiction to money, a compulsion that took root in my childhood. As an adult, I have stolen and paid the price. As a child, I was stolen from, by a thief who went free.

It's 1954. My brother Bobby and I are walking on the railroad tracks near the Thames River. We never tell Mommy when we go to the tracks because she says hobos will steal me. Bobby's eleven and I'm almost four. "Climb on piggyback and we'll cross the trestle to the other side," he says. I do what he tells me. Bobby jumps over the spaces, and I can see the river below us where there are no tracks.

Across the river, there's a long redbrick building. I ask Bobby who lives there. "That's the poorhouse," he says. "That's where they take people who don't pay their bills. Once you're there, you never get out. And when you die, they take your body and pitch it in the river for the crabs to eat."

I don't want to hear any more but Bobby continues.

"One time I saw the firemen drag the river for a drowned man. When they found him, they pulled up his body with a giant hook. He was an old man from the poorhouse. He was all swollen and purple and instead of eyes, there were just two big crabs in the sockets."

Mommy and I huddle together under the rickety porch. Mommy's trying to peek through the broken wood latticework. It's summertime. I'll be four in September. I'm hunched in the black dirt, writing my name with a twig. The harder I press the twig, the more I bother the ants. I watch them run in different directions. Some of the ants carry little white balls of bread. Mommy says the ants have a king and a queen and the rest are workers. Mommy says ants' work is very hard. There's a small mound of dirt with a hole in the middle and Mommy says that's where they live. I watch them hurry up and down the hill.

My legs are falling asleep. They tingle as I try to shift positions. "Sssh," Mommy says. "Be quiet. We don't want him to hear us."

I suck in my breath so that he won't hear me, but I can't keep holding it in my puffed-out cheeks. It come out in a loud WHOOSH. Mommy leans toward me and whispers in my ear, "I said be quiet!"

I hear him walking above us on the porch. He bangs on the door. "Anybody home?" he hollers. "Anybody home?"

The pounding stops and everything is quiet until I hear crinkling paper. This is a good sign because it means he will leave a note in the screen door and go away. Finally, we hear footsteps stomping down the stairs. I can see the bottom of his pants and his black shiny shoes as he walks away from the porch and down the driveway.

"I think he's gone, Mommy," I say.

"Let's wait a few more minutes, Pickle Puss," she answers. "I want to be sure."

We hear the start of a car engine, but Mommy makes us wait some more. One time we thought he was gone, but he was only circling the block to try and catch us. When he saw us, he started chasing Mommy. "You'd better have my money by this Thursday or else!" he shouted. This really scared me. I don't want Mommy to be sent to the poorhouse.

We wait a little while longer under the porch. It's so quiet that I'm getting sleepy from the singing birds. I can smell the ripe summer afternoon—our neighbor's new-mown grass and honeysuckle vines. I lay my head in Mommy's lap. I like doing this. Every time she speaks, I can hear the sounds inside of her and it comforts me. I am beginning to doze when Mommy says, "C'mon, Pickle Puss. I think we can get out of here now."

Together we crawl on our hands and knees to the broken lattice. Mommy removes the slat and puts it back in place after we crawl out so that no one will guess this is our hiding place. I'm always afraid someone is going to bend down one day and catch us, but so far no one has.

When I stand up, I have pins and needles in my legs. It takes a minute for the tingling to go away.

Mommy and I were always hiding from someone: the milk man, the bread man, the light company. Sometimes we hid from the landlord and, often, from my daddy. That day we were hiding from Shorty, who was, as Mommy always said, the peskiest. Shorty was a door-to-door salesman who sold people cheap household goods on credit. He'd come around every Thursday, the day Mommy got paid. He'd collect a dollar from her, take out an account card, and mark in red, "Paid $1.00." Mommy bought Melmac dishes, a percolator, and dishcloths from Shorty. I always begged her to buy the lamp with the grass-skirted hula girl or one of the little dolls Shorty sold from every country around the world, but Mommy never bought me these.

As soon as my mother settled her account with Shorty, she would buy something else on credit. Mommy looked pretty whenever she got something new from Shorty. Her eyes would shine. But Mommy always looked sad, even when she was smiling. She worried all the time—about how she was going to pay the rent, the light bill, the grocery bill. Mommy used to say that if she didn't have anything to worry about, then she'd worry about *that*. When I'd see her looking so sad and scared, I would climb onto her lap. "Please don't worry, Mommy," I'd say. She would look at me with those sad puppy dog eyes and say, "I'm not worried, Pickle Puss. Someday our ship will come in."

One time I asked my mother how much longer it would be before the ship came in, and she said, "I guess it sunk."

My mother is seven or eight years old in one of the most memorable photographs I have ever seen of her—a sepia-colored class picture, circa 1918. Young Harriet stands in the front row, her strained smile and slightly turned stance suggesting shyness. She's wearing a lace-collared sailor dress with pleats that kiss the tops of her high-button shoes. Her hair, in long ringlets, is crowned with an oversized bow. Harriet's sad eyes haunt the photo. They seem already to see the difficult life in store.

My mother's family was prominent. Her maternal grandfather, George Weaver Rouse, was a city sheriff and state legislator who, as an army officer, had been one of the guards who'd surrounded the city of Washington the night President Lincoln was assassinated. Harriet's father, Arthur William Pierce, was one of the Pierces of New Hampshire and a direct descendant of President Franklin Pierce. Harriet's parents were straitlaced, religious, and keenly aware of social class. My mother once told me that her mother had slapped her across the mouth for saying hello in public to a woman of questionable background.

Harriet was a bookworm who obeyed the fourth commandment, serving her parents willingly and well. Intelligent, reserved, and well-mannered, she was the epitome of the perfect daughter of that era—until she met Larry May.

My mother's sister, Nellie, once told me that it was difficult *not* to take notice of Larry May when he cruised through the village of Voluntown in his shiny black Ford. The young women of the town trained their eyes on Larry's dark, brooding good looks as well as his car. Larry could have had his pick of Voluntown's single girls, so most people were surprised when he took a liking to shy, mousy Harriet.

My parents met in 1929. Harriet was a clerk in her grandfather's general store and Larry was a customer who began visiting the store several times a day. One afternoon, he invited Harriet for a ride in his car. On a summer's evening, the young couple took that drive. Harriet's mother chaperoned from the rumble seat. My grandmother forbade further contact between Harriet and this French Canadian Catholic, who was clearly beneath her daughter, fancy car or not. But Mother had fallen in love. Later that summer, with Nellie's help, she climbed out the bedroom window and drove away with Larry.

My parents' elopement was the talk of the town for a while, but soon enough, the couple settled into conventional small-town life. Larry was promoted to a superviser's position at the plastic wire and cable factory. They bought a home and began a family. Over the next eighteen years, Harriet bore seven children. I was the youngest.

My father was a hard worker and a hard drinker. He'd receive his wage each Friday and head for the Jungle, a local tavern, remaining there until he'd drunk and gambled away the weekly income, or until his wife appeared by herself or with one of the older children to beg for grocery money. On those nights, Larry would come home drunk and mean as hell, ordering Harriet to get her nose out of her goddamned book and *do* something! Fix him something to eat! Shut those kids up, and their goddamned crying!

One Friday night in 1953, Daddy returned home meaner than ever. He stormed through the house, picking up whatever wasn't bolted down and smashing it. Lamps, dishes, framed pictures: all were converted to wreckage. Fearful that her children might be hurt, Mother told us to hide in the dark in one of the upstairs rooms. Daddy climbed the stairs, kicked in the door, and grabbed Bobby, his youngest son. My brother was nine at the time. When Daddy punched him in the mouth, teeth flew and blood spurted. Mommy charged up the stairs. With a strength she had never shown before, she pushed her husband away from the children and out of the room. Caught off guard by Mother's attack, Daddy staggered backward and tumbled down the stairs, striking his head against the radiator and landing askew at the bottom step.

I'm peeking down at Daddy from behind Mommy's skirt. He's sitting on the floor, holding an unbroken brown beer bottle. Blood's dripping

from his forehead into his eyes. When he catches me looking, he says,
"Carolyn, come here and help your daddy up." My brothers and sisters
huddle with me, all of us looking down at Daddy. Except Bobby.
Bobby's face is buried against Mommy and his skinny arms are wrapped
around her waist. Mommy's apron is soaked with blood.

Later, the policeman taps the bottoms of my bare feet with his night-
stick. "Don't cry, Curly Top," he says. "We're just going to take your
daddy somewhere and have a talk."

The source of my father's rage that night was a gambling loss. He had
bet our house in a card game and come up short. We were homeless.

Having reached her limit, Mother decided to leave Daddy. But where
would she and her seven children go? Reluctantly, she swallowed her
pride and went to see her mother. "I don't have room for that brood of
yours," Grammy told her. "You never should have married that no-good
bum in the first place." On her way out, Harriet spotted her father in the
garden. She approached and explained her dilemma. He agreed to lend
her fifty dollars, on the condition that she would never tell her mother.

Harriet's plan was to leave Voluntown and find work and lodging in
the nearby factory town of Norwich. Whatever belongings she and the
older children could carry were gathered up, and the eight of us began
our fifteen-mile journey. We trudged along the side of the road for
hours, my older siblings carrying me piggyback on their shoulders while
Mother did her best to distract us with lengthy versions of songs like
"Found a Peanut." At Pachaug cemetery, we stopped for drink from the
iron pump beside the caretaker's cottage and rested in the soft grass
around the graves of my mother's grandparents.

By the time we arrived in Norwich, we were dirty, hungry, and bone
tired. Mother bought a newspaper, then sat on the sidewalk curb and
read the classifieds. Calling from a pay phone, she rented us an apartment. The next morning, she walked to Werman's Shoe Factory and got
herself a job.

Mother never asked my father for financial support and he never
offered any. Her take-home pay at Werman's Shoe was forty-two dollars
per week. We did without a telephone and television. During the months
when we couldn't swing the utility bill, we did without electricity, too.
Yet, despite our deficits, we had the luxury of music. The previous occu-

pant of our apartment had left behind a piano. Each morning before she left for work, Mother would bang out "Reveille" to wake us up for school.

We moved often, from one tenement to the next, one section of town to another. When I was six, we moved to Norwich's West Side, an ethnically diverse neighborhood within walking distance of Werman's Shoe. "You people move around like a pack of gypsies," Grammy scolded Mother. "How do you think *I* feel with everyone knowing my daughter lives and works with all those West Side Polacks and West Side Jews and West Side wops? Well, that's fine and dandy for you, but don't expect *me* to visit you!"

The del Vecchios, a big Italian family, lived just down the street from us. Mrs. del Vecchio had twelve kids, a no-good husband who was dying of cancer, and more unpaid bills than us. To get by, she'd make sheet pizzas and peddle them in the neighborhood for a dollar apiece. Mommy bought Mrs. del Vecchio's pizzas because she felt sorry for her. One time I went with my mother to pick up a pizza for our supper and got a peek inside the del Vecchios' apartment. Small red candles burned everywhere, but the drawn shades made it dark and gloomy. On the walls were crucifixes and pictures of Jesus with His bleeding heart. Old Man del Vecchio lay on the parlor sofa, covered with blankets. When his head popped up, I shrieked and jumped back out the door.

"Who's screaming?" Mrs. del Vecchio yelled.

"It's that bratty Carolyn," one of the del Vecchio kids said.

I thought *they* were the brats. Mommy said they were always in trouble and forbade us to play with them. My older sister Patty used to sneak out to see Sonny del Vecchio. She ended up pregnant at sixteen. In those days, there were few options: for the most part, if a girl got pregnant, the boy had to marry her. So Patty married useless Sonny del Vecchio and ended up having seven kids by the time she was twenty-seven. "God's punishing you for running off with that good-for-nothing you married," Grammy told Mother. "Now *you* know what it feels like to be disgraced by a daughter."

On the West Side, we lived on the top floor of a six-story tenement. The hallways were lit by dim yellow bulbs that cast an eerie light on the dark wooden stairs. There were different cooking smells on each landing, depending on which nationality lived in which apartment. The railing on our landing had two missing posts. Once, I looked through the gap and down. My knees went watery as I imagined myself slipping through the space and falling.

The tenement's backyard was little more than the bank of the Thames River. "Bobby, you make sure you keep an eye on Carolyn," Mommy would warn my brother when we went out to play, and Bobby would look about as enthusiastic as *any* thirteen-year-old boy who'd just been given the assignment of a tagalong little sister. Outside, we were met by a large group of neighborhood kids: the Thayers, the Fatones, the Maruzzos, the Perrys.

Often, we kids played cowboys and Indians. Because Mommy fixed my hair in braids, I was always the Indian princess, riding the broken broomstick I'd made my palomino pony. One day while we were playing, a pretty new girl named Linda joined us. She had blond, curly hair like Baby Sally in *Fun with Dick and Jane*. I galloped up to her side. "Me Tonto," I said.

Linda stared at me for several seconds, then asked in a serious voice if I knew where the Lone Ranger took his garbage. I said I didn't. "To the dump, to the dump, to the dump, dump, dump," she replied. Now Linda was not only the prettiest girl I had ever seen, but also the funniest.

Linda lived upstairs from the gas station her father owned. One afternoon she invited me home for supper. This was the first time I had ever eaten over at someone's house, and I was dazzled by how bright and pretty everything looked. Linda's mother, Goldy, was a plump, cheerful woman who wore a flowered apron and had the same blond hair as Linda. I had never seen TV before I was a guest at Linda's. Her mom set up trays for us, and we watched *The Mickey Mouse Club* and ate hot dogs, beans, and corn. We washed it down with grape Kool-Aid in aluminum glasses and had red Jell-O for dessert. Convinced that Linda's parents were the richest people in the world, I assured her we had hot dogs, beans, corn, and Kool-Aid every night at our house, too. "Next time," I said, "you can come home and eat with me."

Linda kept asking when she could come over. Then one afternoon when I thought no one else was home, I announced, "Today's the day!"

It was a humid August afternoon. As we entered the tenement, the stink of cabbage hung in the dim hallway. Linda followed me, wide-eyed, up the stairs. "Shsssh!" I called as we neared the top landing. The month before, Mommy had let Daddy come back to live with us. I'd begun to tiptoe up the final landing so that, if my father was home, I could walk in undetected.

Outside our apartment door, flies buzzed over the steel cans overflowing with smelly garbage. Mommy had hung fly paper to the ceiling, and the long, sticky strip was covered with dead flies and live ones still struggling to escape their gooey grave. "Wait here," I whispered.

I went inside to make sure Daddy wasn't home, and drunk. When the coast was clear, I returned to get my friend. She was gone. Ashamed, I stood in the doorway and saw where we lived through Linda's eyes.

Thursday was payday at Werman's Shoe. Every Thursday, Bobby and I would walk to the factory yard and wait for the screech of the noon whistle. A few minutes later, high up in the brick building, a window would open and Mommy would appear. Smiling, she'd release her signed paycheck to us and I would watch that piece of paper fall, end over end, to the ground. Bobby and I would both try to guess where the check would land so that we'd be the one to catch it. Once we had the check in hand, we'd dance in a circle and sing: *A treat! A treat! We eat! We eat!* I'd look up at Mommy, tiny in the big mill window, and catch the kiss she blew down before the window closed.

Some Thursdays, with Mommy's permission, we brought her paycheck to Cip's Grinder Shop. There were "grinder wars" in Norwich—D'Elia's versus Cip's versus Romano's—and Cip's was the best. Bobby and I would enter the store, inhaling the fragrance of meats, cheeses, and olive oil. Mrs. Cipriani would cash Mommy's check, cautioning us as she counted the bills into Bobby's hand not to lose the money our mother had worked so hard to earn. We'd buy grinders and Orange Crush soda for supper, and if Bobby had any extra money from his paper route, he'd buy a *Superman* comic for himself and a *Casper the Ghost* for me.

I was at my happiest and hungriest at those moments, the new, unread comic book gripped tightly in my fist and my mouth salivating in anticipation of a Cip's meatball grinder washed down with Orange Crush.

I'm sitting on the steps out front, sucking a grape Popsicle. It's melting fast, the sticky juice running between my fingers. I take a bite, letting the cold sweetness thaw on my tongue.

I'm playing this game I play when I wait for Mommy to come home

*from work. It goes like this: every third car coming around the corner
will be my car when I grow up. I play until one of my cars is a junky
blue pickup truck with a homemade wooden bed.*

*Thunder rumbles and I think about a story Mommy read to me. Rip
Van Winkle must be up there, bowling. I look all the way down the
street. When's Mommy coming home? No one's up in the apartment
except Daddy.*

*Big fat raindrops begin to fall, slowly at first, smacking the hot
cement sidewalk. Then rain pours out of the sky, drenching me. I know
I have to go in, but I hate it in there. Where's Mommy?*

*Inside, I start slowly up the stairs, then hurry past the second landing
where the fat Polish man lives. One time, I left my dolly in the downstairs foyer. A few days later, I was coming up the stairs and the Polish
man handed me my dolly. She was naked. The man had drawn hair
between her legs. I took it back and ran upstairs. Now, whenever he sees
me, the Polish man gives me a sly look as if he and I share a secret.*

*I count stairs as I climb, stopping at each landing to peek through the
railings to see if Mommy's coming. I reach the top landing. Our two
cans are heaped with garbage. The front door's open and I can hear
Daddy's footsteps inside the apartment.*

"Carolyn, is that you?"

The way Daddy pronounces my name, it sounds like CAH-lyn.

"Cah-lyn? Cah-lyn, wanna pean'?"

*Daddy always offers me a peanut when he's drunk so that I'll go to
him. But today, before he sees me, I duck behind the cans. I hold my
hand over my nose and mouth because the garbage smells. I hunch
down when I see him at the door. "Cah-lyn? That you?"*

*I have to pee so bad and I can't hold it much longer. Then I hear foot-
steps on the stairs. Mommy! It's Mommy! She's home!*

*I'm happy now, and I don't even care about the spanking I'll get for
wetting my pants. The warm urine streams down my legs and splashes
my shoes, soaks my socks. Mommy's home. I'm safe.*

*Mommy draws my bedroom curtains. She says if you get sunlight in
your eyes when you have the measles, you might go blind. I'm staying
home from school today, but Mommy has to go to work.*

Mommy places a Sears catalog—a "wish book" she calls it—on the bed. She hands me some scissors. "It's the old one," Mommy says. "You can cut out paper dolls if you want to. I wish I could stay home with you, Pickle Puss, but I can't afford to miss work." When she bends down and kisses me, I wrap my arms around her neck. Her pincurled hair smells like Pond's talcum powder and shoe factory leather. I love Mommy's smell. "I'll come check on you at noontime," she says on her way out the door. I know without seeing it that there's a bright red stain on my cheek from Mommy's kiss.

I go through the catalog, page by page. So many pretty things dazzle me. I cut out a perfect Mommy and Daddy and find their children, a blond boy with a crewcut and a pretty, dark-haired girl with a Tonette permanent. I cut out beds, nightstands, curtains. Soon I have set up the rooms of the paper doll family's house. I cut a small slit where the pillow joins the bedspread, just wide enough for the paper dolls to slip through. I cut out pajamas, sticking them on the dolls with my spit. Now I'm tired of playing paper dolls. Tired and sleepy. . . .

I'm awakened by a heavy weight on top of me. I smell stale beer. When Daddy moves, I can hear my paper dolls tearing. "Now just lay still and let's rest a minute," he says. He keeps rubbing a lump against my underpants. I try to turn away, but the heaviness of his body makes it impossible to move. Daddy reaches down with one hand to the top of my underpants. It's hard to breathe. I'm afraid. I feel myself being split in two.

I close my eyes and picture Dick, Jane, and Spot. Someday I will have a puppy just like Spot. I can feel myself rising out of my body, floating above my bed. I look down at what is happening below me, far away. I feel nothing. I'm not even there.

In Mrs. Wilcox's seventh-grade science class, we were doing an experiment with a boiled egg and a milk bottle that had a candle lit inside. We were waiting for the heat from the flame to suck the egg inside the bottle. Mrs. Wilcox asked me to read aloud from our textbook about why this was going to happen. When I looked at the page, the words seemed like a jigsaw puzzle. I couldn't read. Nausea rumbled through me and I began to gag.

"Maybe the smell of the egg made you sick," the school nurse suggested. "Why don't you go home and lie down and see if you feel better?"

No one was home when I arrived, but my mother's friend Marlene was out in her yard. "You okay, Carolyn?" she asked. "Why don't you come in and lie down at my house?"

Marlene put me in her daughter Rita's room. I was still queasy and my head ached so badly, I could hardly hold it up. Marlene said she had to go to the doctor's on Friday and asked me if I wanted to go with her. She could pick me up at school, she said, and the doctor could take a look at me.

The sign outside the ladies' clinic said, "Emmons, Carter & Clark, OB/GYN." When I asked Marlene what OB/GYN meant, she said these were doctors for women who were going to have babies.

I sat in the waiting room when Marlene went in. A few minutes later, the doctor came out and asked me to follow him into his office. Marlene sat in a chair. The doctor told me my mother had given permission for him to examine me. "I won't get a shot, will I?" I asked. He shook his head.

I followed a nurse into an examining room and got ready. Then the doctor came in and felt my stomach. He gave me a funny look. A few minutes later, he called me back into his office. "You're going to have a baby in about four more months," he said. "There's a home called Woodfield where you can go to have it and no one will have to know."

A baby? What did he mean? What was he talking about?

Woodfield was a main brick house and four separate cottages: Oak, Cedar, Maple, and Elm. Sandra and I lived in Oak. Sandra was Jewish and her family owned a furniture store in Danbury. Her mother, a small woman with unruly black hair and a deep tan, visited often, pulling up to the main house in her big black Cadillac and honking her horn to announce her arrival. She was always sending Sandra the cutest "I love you" and "I miss you" cards, complete with small gifts and poems she'd write herself:

I got some sun, alas, alack,
My olive skin is now jet black!

I envied Sandra's casual relationship with her mom and wondered what it would be like to have a joking, lighthearted mother. Mommy was always so sad and serious, and she couldn't afford the cute cards and things Sandra's mother sent.

Sometimes, after staff was asleep, we girls of Oak Cottage would remove the window screen, climb out, and enter a different cottage. We'd pull the covers off the sleeping girls and, giggling, run back to our own cottage before anyone caught us. The next morning, we'd get a lecture about our bad behavior from old Miss Day—"Prune Face" we called her. Wasn't this the very same kind of impulsive bad conduct that had gotten us all into our present pickle to begin with? Well, a few bad apples spoiled the bunch, Miss Day would remind us. Now *everyone* had to suffer by doing such extra chores as toilet-scrubbing and silverware-polishing. So there.

Often, the girls at Oak Cottage congregated on the screen porch to relax and talk. One night, Jane began to list all the places where she and her boyfriend had had sex, a beach and a bathhouse included. Others joined in about their boyfriends, describing how they'd gone "all the way" and how their parents now hated the boys they loved. Sheila wondered aloud if our being at Woodfield was God's way of punishing us for what we'd done. Scared of being found out, I changed the subject to that night's planned raid on Cedar Cottage.

My job at Woodfield was to assist Cook in the kitchen. Overworked and impatient, Cook never had a kind word for me. If she explained how to do something and I couldn't quite remember it, I was afraid to ask her again because she'd holler about how useless I was.

One day, Cook demonstrated how to cut radishes into rosebuds and then set me to the task. Although I'd just watched her do it, I couldn't figure it out. I began to cry, softly at first and then harder. Cook yelled and threw the radishes at me and I became hysterical.

I was taken to see the social worker, Mrs. Shea. Although she was only about forty, Mrs. Shea had salt and pepper hair and walked with a cane. She'd had polio as a child and it had left her with one leg shorter than the other. Mrs. Shea peered over her glasses and gave me that pitying look. She said the doctor was going to give me something to calm me down and that I no longer had to work with Cook.

I liked the faraway feeling the liquid phenobarbital gave me. Whenever I sipped it, the constant noises of Woodfield would recede into the background and everything would turn quiet and peaceful. The medicine made me so sleepy, I was not assigned another cottage job and so had more free time than the other girls. Mr. Lewis, the chief administrator, gave me permission to walk outside and stroll the yard, where beautiful gardens bloomed and brown bunnies hopped in the grass. The cottages at Woodfield were hidden from the road by a row of thick trees, and it was hard to believe that a busy main street ran just in front of them. The phenobarbital made me feel more relaxed than I'd ever felt before, and I would recline on a lawn chair, smile, and sleep.

Bridgeport Hospital, Bridgeport, Connecticut, August 20, 1962
"The Lord is my shepherd. I shall not want." Between the titanic waves of pain, I am trying to say the Twenty-third Psalm. "He maketh . . . He maketh me lie down in green pastures." I clutch the rail of the hospital bed and scream, "Please, God! Please, help me!" I am answered by another wave of pain. "He leadeth me beside still waters. He restoreth my soul." I'm certain my body is being torn in two. This is worse than what Daddy does. "Yea, though I walk through the valley of the shadow of death, I will fear no evil, for Thou art with me."

I feel an explosion between my legs. Something pops. Water gushes out of me and I scream and scream and scream.

"What's all this noise in here?" the angry Chinese woman asks. She's dressed in a white lab coat and has a stethoscope around her neck. "Maybe you'll remember this the next time you feel like spreading your legs."

She scares me but this pain scares me more. I'll do anything to stop it. I stick my arm through the bed rail and grab a fistful of the Chinese lady's lab coat. "Please help me," I beg.

"I am helping you! Quiet down!" Prying my fingers loose, she orders me to lie down. A man comes in and looks at me. The woman places my feet in the metal stirrups at the sides of the bed. She gropes between my legs. "She's crowning. Let's get her into delivery!"

I'm being wheeled fast down a hallway. My bed pushes open two doors. Bright lights hurt my eyes. Someone holds a mask to my face. . . .

When I wake up, I'm in a dimly lit room. On a large chalkboard, someone's written, "Baby Boy May, 1:52 A.M., 7 lbs." Vague memories of the pain and terror return. I place my hand on my stomach, amazed that it's flat. Suddenly, it dawns on me: I've had the baby.

I wake up in a hospital room, my bed beside the window. Turning on my side, I watch the rain dribble down the glass. "So what did you have? A boy or a girl?" a cheery voice asks. I turn to see a smiling woman in the other bed. She looks like Betty Crocker on the cake mix box. "A boy," I say.

"Well, you'd better get ready," she says. "They're bringing in the babies soon." She holds up a mirror and pats down her short, curly hair. Her breasts strain the thin pink nylon of her gown. "I had a boy, too," she says. "Isn't that great? I'm naming him Peter after his daddy. What are you naming yours?"

I've looked in a book of names back at Woodfield, considering this question myself. "Daniel," I say. "It means 'loved by God.'"

The nurse comes in and rolls Betty Crocker's bed to a sitting position. "Good morning, Mrs. Winters. How are we feeling today? Little Petey can't wait to see Mommy."

I ask the nurse if she's going to bring me my baby, too. She shakes her head and yanks on the curtain surrounding my bed. "Since your baby is being given over to the child and family agency, we feel it's in your best interest not to see it. Now Mrs. Winters needs some privacy. Don't disturb her."

From behind the drawn curtain, I listen to the arrival of Betty Crocker's baby, all of the oohs and aahs. I reach down and touch my flat stomach. Now I'll be able to fit into normal clothes again.

"Carolyn? Carolyn, wake up. You have visitors."

A different nurse pulls back the curtain. Mommy steps forward, a sad smile on her face. I haven't seen Mommy since last June when she and Marlene drove me to Woodfield. She holds out a bag. "I've brought you some presents to make you feel better," she says. As I reach for the bag, she comes closer and gathers me in her arms. She's crying, holding me tight.

"Look, Mommy," I say. "Look how flat my tummy is!"

Inside the bag there's a pretty pink and white dotted Swiss dress and a pair of white patent leather flats. "I picked them out for you from Popular Club to make you feel better." At the bottom of the bag is a small, gift-wrapped package. I open it and look inside. It's a pretty teardrop pearl necklace. "That one's from Marlene," Mommy says.

I'm so proud of my new things. I thank Mommy and she hands me some Archie comic books. One issue is extra thick and it's all about Betty, who I like much better than Veronica. There are Betty paper dolls near the back of the book. I'm surprised and happy because Mommy doesn't like me to read comics. She pulls up a chair and sits beside my bed.

"Can I go home today?" I ask.

"No, Pickle Puss. You have to go back to Woodfield for a couple more weeks. But you'll be back home in time to start eighth grade. You can wear your new dress for the first day of school. Okay?"

I feel tears in my eyes, a lump in my throat. "Did you see it?"

Mommy shakes her head. "There's no need. The adoption agency's picking up the baby tomorrow. The quicker this is over, the better. . . . You know we can't tell anyone about this, right? Not even your brothers and sisters. They think you're still at church camp. No one needs to know, Carolyn. I don't ever want to talk about it again. Not ever."

I'm used to not talking about things, especially things that have to do with Daddy. "What happens in this house stays in this house," Mommy always says. "We don't air our dirty laundry in public." So I know not to ask any more questions about the "it" neither of us has seen.

Mommy stands and tells me she has to go now. "Marlene's waiting downstairs to give me a ride back. She says she'll see you when you get home." Before I came here, Marlene told me all this was killing my mother—that she didn't know how much more Mommy could stand. After that, I kept checking on Mommy while she was sleeping to make sure her chest was still moving. I felt scared Mommy was going to die.

"Carolyn, I've brought you a sanitary belt and maternity napkins. The doctor says you're doing fine so it's okay to take a shower." The nurse hands me a bottle and tells me to sit on the toilet and pour the

liquid over my stitches "down there." With this new equipment, I walk to the shower room, one hand holding the back of my johnny closed.

I enjoy the shower, the first one I've had since I gave birth. Again, I'm amazed that I can look past my flat stomach and see my feet. I dry myself, take the bottle the nurse gave me, and sit on the toilet. Slowly, I pour the iodine mixture between my legs, watching the deep orange droplets hit the toilet water below and spread. The sanitary belt is a stretch of elastic with hooks on both ends to secure the maternity pad. The pad's so big and bulky, I feel like I'm wearing a baby diaper. I douse myself with hospital powder, then pick up my hairbrush. I'm amazed at how much my long, curly dark hair has grown over the summer. In the mirror, I study my face. It's an ordinary face, not much different from most twelve- and thirteen-year-old girls. Why do I feel so old?

Back in my room, I look at the pretty pink and white dress Mommy has brought me, a simple A-line style. Soon, Mr. Lewis from Woodfield will be here to pick me up. I pull the dress over my head. It fits perfectly. I slip my feet into the new white patent leather flats. I pack my nightgown, slippers, and the free Cepacol mouthwash into my round overnight bag with the one-strap handle. I like this bag because it reminds me of the ones models carry in Seventeen *magazine. I pack the boxed necklace from Marlene, my comics, and the* True Story *and* True Confessions *magazines Betty Crocker gave me after she was through with them. Mommy would be upset to know I have magazines like these, but I want to bring them back to Woodfield because Sandra likes to read them, too.*

It's 8:15 A.M. Mr. Lewis is due at 9:00. I feel that nervous feeling in my stomach and my hands are clammy. I look out in the hallway. No one's around.

Down the hall, there's a door with a red exit sign above it. I walk to it. Open it. Head down the stairwell. I've heard Betty Crocker tell her visitors that the baby nursery is on the next floor down from ours. At the second landing, I open the door and look both ways. There's a sign marked NURSERY *with an arrow pointing straight ahead. I follow it. My heart is racing. I approach a long window. On the other side are the babies.*

I find the one that says "Baby Boy May." His face is pink and wrinkled and he's sucking on his tiny fist, eyes shut. He has the May square

jaw. I stare at him for a long time, memorizing each part: his perfect
miniature feet, his tuft of blond hair, his tightly shut eyes. I can't connect
the child lying here to the "it" I carried inside my body. This baby was
the secret. He doesn't seem real.

Just as he opens one dark blue eye, a hand clamps onto my shoulder.
"Young lady, didn't you see that sign? Children aren't allowed on the
nursery ward. Now scoot before you get in trouble."

I break free and run, even though it hurts. Down the hallway to the
door, back inside the stairwell. I run up the stairs and back onto the
maternity ward. "Hey, you!" a nurse shouts from down the corridor.
"You're not supposed to be here." She's hurrying my way.

I run back to my room, the nurse chasing me. Standing beside my bed
are Mr. Lewis and Nurse Webb, stiff smiles on both their faces. "We've
been waiting for you, Carolyn," Mr. Lewis says. "It's time to go back."
The nurse who's been chasing me looks from me to them. Understand-
ing passes across her face. Oh. I'm one of those Woodfield *girls.*

It was drizzling; I was cold in my new dress. I sat in the backseat of
Mr. Lewis's car, and he and Nurse Webb rode up front. Having a baby
hadn't been one bit like Nurse Webb described in our child-birthing
classes, but I decided I wouldn't tell Sandra when I got back. She'd get
too scared. I thought about the other girls that summer who'd gone off
to the hospital to deliver their babies. They'd come back to Woodfield
visibly changed. Nurse Webb always put them in a separate room.
Sometimes I'd walk past and look in at them, their bent knees holding
up a blanket, a faint light passing through the cover from the sun lamp
used to dry their stitches. Now I was one of those girls.

Nurse Webb turned back toward me. "You did really well, Carolyn,"
she said. "I'm proud of you." They treated me differently now. Their
speech, the way they looked at me: for some reason, I was now more
mature in their eyes. I couldn't quite figure out why, but I knew it had
something to do with the baby. For the rest of the drive back to Woodfield, the three of us said nothing.

Mr. Lewis parked the car and we walked slowly across the gravel
driveway to the main cottage. The other girls saw me, called to me. "She
has to rest now, girls," Nurse Webb called back. She led me by the
elbow inside.

In the hallway, Cook approached. I looked away from her and then looked back. In her eyes was a kindness I'd never seen before. "Glad you're back," she muttered and walked past me.

Nurse Webb took me to the recovery room. "I think you should lie down before supper," she said. "I'm going to set up the sun lamp."

After supper, Sandra and I walked to the side porch and sat opposite each other in the wooden glider. I told Sandra there wasn't much to it—it hurt for a little while, then you went to sleep and woke up with a flat belly.

"Just look at you!" Sandra exclaimed. "You're so tiny. No one would ever even know you had a baby!"

All I've done since I left the hospital three days ago is daydream about Daniel. I know the new parents will rename him, but to me he is Daniel. I dream about snatching him from the social worker's arms and running as fast as I can until we are safe in the deep, deep woods. I see the two of us alone in a log cabin, far away from other people. No lights, no telephone. I catch fish and we live on berries and nuts. We have a puppy, too. I make all of Daniel's toys myself. No one finds us, not ever.

I decide to tell Sandra my plan. "I can't stay here for two more weeks," I say. "I have to get home and tell my mother I want to keep him. Isn't Woodfield on the bus line?"

Sandra shrugs but retrieves Anita, a skinny black girl from Bridgeport who's trustworthy and can tell me how to get to the bus station. Anita was attacked and raped by a gang of boys. She has a somewhat nasty attitude, but I don't care about that if she can help me. "It's a stupid idea," Anita says. "They never gonna let you have that baby. How much money you got? I'll lend you fifty cents but you better send it back." Pooling my own money with Sandra's and Anita's, I have enough for bus fare back to Norwich. If I slip out after supper, they won't notice me missing until 9:00 P.M. bed check.

After supper, I pack my few belongings in my round hatbox. I give Sandra the arts and crafts things I've made that summer, and she hugs me and makes me promise I'll write to her as soon as I'm home. Anita reminds me to put the fifty cents I owe her in the first letter I write. I climb out the window and they lower my bag down to me.

It's almost dusk. I make my way through the woods and find myself standing on a stone wall, cars rushing past me at a four-way intersection. I'm confused and scared by all the traffic, the people rushing past on foot. Remembering Anita's directions, I head toward the intersection of Main and Fairfield. I see a sign marked BUS STOP *and walk up to it, stand there with other people. What if they catch me before the bus comes? Before I can board the connecting bus that will take me home?*

The bus chugs to a stop. I pay my fare and make my way to the back. It's August 23. The weather's hot and humid. As I sit in my seat, I feel a sudden rush of blood between my legs. My head feels light. Everyone seems to be talking from far away. Hovering near the roof, I look down at all the passengers. I see a girl in a pink and white dress with a round suitcase. Tears stream down her cheeks. I hate this girl for ruining my life.

"Carolyn! Where have you been?" my mother wants to know. "Mr. Lewis called and said you'd run away. Everyone's been worried sick." I am calling from the bus depot in New London. Norwich is still another twenty minutes away.

"Can someone come get me?" I ask. My throat's choked up. I can barely speak.

"I'll see if I can find someone."

I hang up. Sit down on a stone wall. There's blood on my dress, my legs and socks. Everything seems far away. Later, my sister Janice and her boyfriend, Paul, pull into the bus station parking lot. I manage to crawl into the backseat of the car.

"You look awful!" Janice says. The rest of the ride is a blur.

When we get home, I'm unable to get out of the car unassisted. Paul and my sister prop me up by placing their hands under my arms and walking me toward the house. My mother, at the top of the stairs, asks me what's wrong. She seems a million miles away.

When I wake up, my whole body aches and there's a roaring in my head. I feel a loud pop. Blood spurts from my nose and mouth.

I was sick for the next several weeks. Slowly, my body began to heal, but I sank into a deep depression and would not come out of my room. Mommy took care of me but said little about Woodfield or the baby.

Then one day she told me it had been six weeks since the birth—time to call Mrs. Shea, the social worker, make an appointment, and sign the adoption papers.

I kept stalling until the afternoon my sister Janice came into my room. "You have to quit being selfish and do what you need to do!" she said. "Mother isn't getting any younger and what you've put her through has been too much of a strain. Don't you realize what this has been like for her?" What I realized was that Mother had broken our secret and confided to her oldest daughter that I'd given birth to our father's child.

The next day, I got up, got dressed. My mother and I took the bus to New London. Inside the social service building, Mrs. Shea took us to a room that looked like a library. Another woman was seated at a desk, legal papers spread all around her.

When the papers were placed in front of me, I began to cry. My eyes met stony Mrs. Shea's, and she nodded as if to say I was doing the right thing. My mother's face was stoic. I signed the documents and watched the hands of the woman behind the desk as she dented the page with her seal. Then, for some reason, I looked up from her hands to her face. The tears running down her cheeks took me by surprise.

—➤●◄—

In 1971, Carolyn Adams wed a Vietnam veteran and law enforcement officer and relocated to Mobile, Alabama. She enrolled in the University of South Alabama, later graduating with a bachelor's degree in accounting. Before the onset of her mental illness, Adams worked for many years in municipal government and served as city clerk for the town of Fairhope, Alabama. Following her divorce and return to Connecticut, she was employed as an accountant at the U.S. Coast Guard Academy and later served as executive director of a state-funded mental health advisory board, the position she held at the time of her arrest.

Carolyn Adams has been both an advocate for the mentally ill and a long-term consumer of mental health services. Diagnosed with a number of serious psychological disorders, she maintains that her crime and incarceration are directly related to her mental illness.

Released from prison in 2001, Carolyn Adams currently volunteers at a wellness center for battered women, CRIS Radio for the Blind, and Care Connection, a service for the elderly. She plans to continue to ply the craft of writing and resume her advocacy on behalf of the mentally ill. Her goals are to educate the public, to reduce the social stigma of mental illness, and to assist people with mental disorders who have become enmeshed in the criminal justice system.

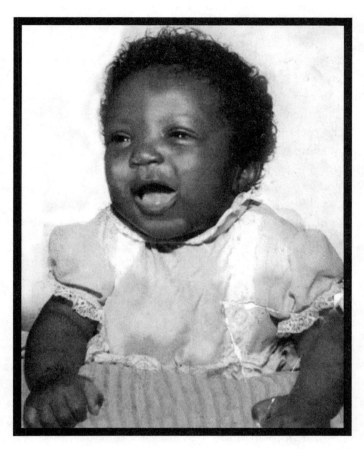

H A I R   C H R O N I C L E S
||||||||||||||||||||
T A B A T H A   R O W L E Y

Born: 1973
Conviction: Assault in the first degree
Sentence: 7 years
Entered prison: 1996
Status: Released

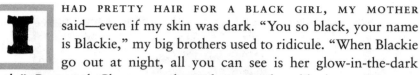HAD PRETTY HAIR FOR A BLACK GIRL, MY MOTHER said—even if my skin was dark. "You so black, your name is Blackie," my big brothers used to ridicule. "When Blackie go out at night, all you can see is her glow-in-the-dark *teeth*." Pete and Choo teased me because they liked me, Mommy explained. When she pounded me, she did it out of love. Grandma drank to help her blood flow, and Auntie smoked weed so she could sleep. Uncle stuck needles in his arms to make his muscles big. "Uncle K, why you burn up Mommy's spoons?"

"Sometimes when I cook, the spoon slips into the fire."

"Why you cookin' in the bathroom?"

Uncle Wesley wasn't really our uncle; he was my neighbor's boyfriend's brother. He baby-sat for us while Ma went to work cleaning Mrs. Lewis's roach-infested house. I never saw Mrs. Lewis, but Ma described her as old, white, and nasty, scratching all day at her privates like she was digging for gold.

Did my brothers know what Uncle Wesley was doing when he'd drape that big tan blanket over his back and pull me down onto the floor and under? Did they look away from their cartoons and see their confused four-year-old sister lying there, letting it happen? Until now, I never told anyone the scariest part: what Uncle Wesley did made me feel loved.

The attic room reeks of reefer, and the stink of spilt beer rides its back. The raggedy linoleum floor's littered with cigarette butts, candy wrappers, and Kool-Aid stains that stick to your sneakers. Pete cracks open the 64-ouncer, lifts it, and chugs. His throat muscles flex like a snake forcing rats down his gullet. At fourteen, my brother sure knows how to guzzle down the grog. At twelve, I'm just a rookie.

Pete's thunderclap of a belch makes us laugh. "Okay, watch," he says, and lights the joint that's plastered to the pink inside of his bottom lip. The monstrous pull he takes burns the weed halfway down. "Here, sis," he says, passing it. "Toke like a troopa."

Copying Pete, I inhale deeply and try to hold it in. No go. I choke so long and hard, it feels like my internal organs are heading up my throat. Pete pounds me on the back, knocking me to my knees. He laughs his head off, having a ball. I laugh, too, but damn, my ribs hurt from all that coughing.

A few minutes later, I don't feel like me. Pete's thick glasses have always made his eyes look oversized, but now they're bigger than headlights. His lips, naturally full, have become BODACIOUS. "You fired up, huh, sis?"

"I don't know. Am I?" The corners of the attic walls are shifting.

"Hell, yeah. We just smoked some blazin'-ass weed. You *toasted*."

I stare out the window, watching the tree branches rock in the breeze. I'm on land but seasick. Flying headfirst to the open window, I hurl beer, pureed bologna, and Cap'n Crunch onto the roof. Pete's laughing so hard, he can't even speak. I slip down onto that filthy linoleum and groan. . . .

It's the bass from a Run DMC tune that shakes me awake. Seeds from the weed Pete is smoking pop and fall like shooting stars. "Get up and help me smoke the rest of this shit," he says, pulling me off the floor. My vision's blurry and my head weighs a hundred pounds. I vow I'll never drink or smoke again.

Uh-huh.

We were close, Pete and me. In his own way, he was my protector, beating up any boy who looked twice at me. He didn't want me getting treated the way he treated *his* girls. Pete took it upon himself to make me tough and streetwise. "So that you'll survive," he said. For Pete, survival meant trust no one. Get or get got. Take or be taken. He taught me how to cop, bag-up, and sell cocaine and weed. How to load and shoot sawed-offs, thirty-eights, and nine-millimeter clips. How to rob. "Schooling you to the game," he called it, when he invited me along on stickups. During one, he shot up a Chinese food delivery truck, nearly scaring the poor driver to death. "Run!" he shouted, clutching the money bag with one hand and my wrist with the other. Back home, he was furious with our lousy thirty-five-dollar take. "Here," he said, tossing me the money. "Take this and buy yourself something. I'm gonna go get some *real* loot." I never pulled a stickup on my own, but I helped my brothers and their friends rob a candy store once and, another time, a freight train car full of granola bars.

Did I know Pete was bad news? Sure. But I told myself I knew his secret, too: that, beneath his thugged-out exterior, he was hiding a good heart.

Did I know the difference between right and wrong? I did. But back then, I was more interested in scoring junk food than wrestling with the ethics of my behavior. After you smoked a couple of blunts, those munchies would kick in full force.

Live by the gun, die by the gun, the saying goes. A bullet wound to the head killed Pete when he was twenty. Another gun put me in prison at the age of twenty-three. My ex-boyfriend had shoved me to the ground one time too many and I thought I was going to die. Using reasoning clouded by alcohol, angel dust, and weed, my only thought was: *Get before you get got.* I was lucky; my victim didn't die from the wound I inflicted. But my self-defense argument didn't cut it with the judge. I was convicted of Assault I and ordered to serve seven years.

Prison is not a nice place. There's depression here, and danger, and disease. You resign yourself to being ripped off and jerked around. You settle for substandard health care. You smile pretty for the staff and watch your back. But being locked up is better than being dead. I thank my god and my good luck that the Duracell battery stuck up my butt hasn't conked out yet.

In prison, I detoxed from a ten-year binge, entered recovery, and, little by little, began to understand who I was beneath all those bad habits and bad decisions. My art helped me do that—I rediscovered myself in memoir, in songwriting and performance, and in drawing. "You've got pretty hair for a black girl," my mother used to say. One day not long ago, I took pen and paper and sketched out the story of my life: Tabbi in pigtails, in plaits, in a fried blond buzz-up, a Nubian "natural." That picture got me to thinking about the connection between my styles and my self-esteem, my locks and my life. So call what you're reading "The Hair Chronicles of Tabatha Rowley."

At the time I was incarcerated, I sported my hair in long bronze dreadlocks with honey blond highlights. For some, dreads are worn as a political statement against oppression, but mine were about style, not substance. They completed my wild, thuggish look: baggy jeans, hoodie, combat boots. Almost everyone on my block rocked dreads.

New "admits" at York must scour their scalps with bug shampoo. That humiliated me. *Do I look like I'm carrying cooties in here?* I wanted to ask the officer. But what does someone with lice look like? My perception told me it was someone mangy-looking and sleep-deprived—a stinking, dirty Caucasian.

Mommy taught me that. "Only white people get lice," she assured me the day a girl in my fourth-grade class—Mary, with her orange freckles and rose red lips—got sent home to get deloused. Once Mary's secret was out, the whole class got itchy. I was "bugging out" to the point where it

Tabatha Rowley's graphic autobiography: a life recalled in hairstyles.

felt like my whole body was crawling with insects. "Relax. Black people don't even get lice," my mother said. "If one jumped on you, it would die instantly because of the grease." I'm not sure if this was something my mother believed or if she was just saying it to calm me down, but whoever had made Quelling a part of the York C.I. admission policy apparently didn't buy into the myth of black immunity. White, black, yellow, and red—we were all doused and deloused.

Having my hair Quelled turned it dry and brittle. Strands stood up like porcupine quills and the prison commissary didn't sell the right products to calm it down again. I felt angry, bitter, and confused. And true to a pattern that I have since come to recognize and understand, I made my hair a convenient scapegoat. I decided to chop off my dreadlocks.

It took an eon to hack off my thick hair with a nail clipper. By the time I'd finished, my fingers were cramped and my arms were as heavy as lead. Religious leaders often condemn superstitious ritual as a distortion of true faith. But like many children, I was raised on beliefs which, most likely, echo back to ancient history: *If your hand itches, you're going to get money; if your ears are ringing, someone's talking about you; if your feet get swept, you're going to jail.* Whenever I combed or cut my hair, it was my habit to burn it for protection against evil—to send it back from whence it had come. Smoke rises and ash falls back down to earth. So my intent was to send my hacked-off dreads home to be burned. I'd be damned if anyone at this place was going to place a voodoo spell on *me*!

Until I got to jail, I never imagined there'd be a time when I'd lose control over where my hair went or who got ahold of it. I put my dreads in a brown paper bag and packed them into my bunk drawer until I could figure out how to send them home. The next night, my roommate and I were told to step out of our cell. From the cold, narrow corridor, I watched as two corrections officers dumped out and defiled my personal property. Alarmed, I told myself I had nothing to worry about because I'd done nothing wrong.

"What's *this*?" one of the officers asked. He was holding up my locks.

Why was that officer staring at me so hatefully? And why on earth was he confiscating my hair? Whatever the reason, I was *really* scared now. If he threw away my hair, I would wind up wherever it had gone.

I began to feel as if I'd done something terribly wrong. But what? Had my hair been contaminated with some chemical foreign to jail?

Was it because I was black? Some of my peers had warned me that many of the staff members were prejudiced and targeted blacks for harassment and ridicule. My cellmate was white. Why hadn't *her* property been searched? Had something *possessed* the officer—compelled him to seize my hair so that he could make a doll of me and stick it with pins? The day after the confiscation, the sharp pains I experienced seemed to prove the latter theory. It felt as though someone were prodding my sides and abdomen with a sharp metal rod. I went to see the nurse, whose main goal was to get me out of her office.

"It's probably gas," she said. "Either that or you're using muscles you're not used to using." She shook her head, sending frizzy blond hairs into the air.

"What do you mean?" I asked.

"You know. When you people are out there, you tend to neglect your bodies. Just sit around and get high all day."

I believe her assumption was that I was one of the junkies that pass daily through her revolving door, dope sick, detoxing, and telling her the same old stories: *I didn't do it; my urine got switched and they packed me back in; I shouldn't even be here.* In a sense, that nurse *did* know an aspect of me; alcohol and weed aren't exactly *good* for you. A drug is a drug and addiction is addiction. But I had never smoked crack, sniffed 'caine, shot heroin, or prostituted myself as she seemed to have concluded. And anyway, no one deserves to be talked down to and assumed valueless—no matter what their poisons.

Shortly after my room was searched, a class A disciplinary ticket came flying under my cell door. I jumped up and looked out to see who had dropped it off, but no one was in sight. Had it been a ghost? Tickets are no joke. Could this one affect my eventual parole? It read: *Contraband braids found in Inmate Rowley's (#245187) bunk drawer, concealed in a paper bag. Potential escape item. Attempt to alter appearance.*

Escape item? Was I going to tie my dreads together and climb less than a foot down from the window ledge to the ground, then leap like Wonder Woman over the electric fence? Alter my appearance with *what*? The locks I'd just cut off my head? Did they think I had smuggled them in the way some women sneak contraband into prison—tucked firmly (or, in some cases, not so firmly) in their vaginas?

Three days later, I headed to the Disciplinary Reports Board to have my ticket heard. I was terrified I'd be put in the hole. The only thing I knew about the hole was what I'd seen on television: that it was a dark, damp, cramped place; that you went days without food or water; that you were released days or weeks later, dirty, dehydrated, and emotionally beaten. Along the walkway to the hearing, officers stared at me sympathetically. Many times since my arrival at York, I had wanted to cry but resisted. Now, my tears ran freely.

As I waited to be seen, one of our unit's officers walked by and said, loudly enough for the disciplinary officer to hear, "Rowley? What in the world did *you* get a ticket for?"

"My hair," I said. "I cut my dreadlocks."

"That's stupid," he said. "You don't get in any trouble around here."

As I explained to the hearing officer what had happened, his eyes seemed to say, *I've been working here too long, Toots. Don't even try it.* After I finished, he said he'd give me a break if I pled guilty. At the time, I didn't know that a prisoner has the right to challenge a disciplinary ticket, possibly prove her innocence, and have the infraction removed from her record. So I agreed to the guilty plea. Since this was my first ticket, it was dropped to a class B offense and my only sanction was a thirty-day loss of commissary privileges. Little did that officer realize the favor he was doing me by handing out that punishment. During the time I was banned from the prison store, I stopped eating the overpriced Honeybuns, Slim Jims, and cookies I would regularly buy. I became more health-conscious—as health-conscious as you can be in a place where you're deprived of proper nutrition—and I managed to save $4.25 a week, enough to buy myself a Walkman.

Dreadlocks date back to the beginning of time when there were no combs or hair relaxers—when your only choice was to cut your hair or not. But today, dreads can make a statement in favor of nonconformity to the ways and looks of Caucasians who, historically, have oppressed black people. Bonnie Foreshaw, a fellow prisoner here at York, is a wise, strong-minded, and steady-willed Rastafarian woman who is over six feet tall and whose locks reach well past the back of her thighs. "Girl, dreadlocks send a message that there is no higher power than Jah Rastafari," Bonnie told me. "The hair on your head affects people and is a testament to the world about who you are."

As Bonnie spoke, I thought about how my white lawyer had reacted to me the day he visited prison and saw that I'd cut off my locks. "Wow, what a difference," he'd said, flashing a smile of approval. "Your hair looks great!"

"Having dreadlocks can bring you trials and tribulations, persecution and prosecution by the system," Bonnie warned me. "Locks can cause you to know the full understanding of black rage."

"Look at those old lady shoes!" Solomon, the class bully, announced. We were on the playground before school, Solomon guffawing and pointing. "Tabatha the witch got on her mama's wig and her grandma's shoes!"

In grade school, I was often teased about being a sorceress because I shared the name of Samantha's daughter on the TV show *Bewitched*. There were times when I claimed to *be* a witch, threatening to cast spells on people unless they left me alone. I'd twitch my nose or circle my finger in the air and warn my tormenters that if they didn't stop, I would turn them into boogers. But my magical powers, real or imagined, had deserted me on one of the most miserable days of my childhood: second-grade picture day.

A blue-plaid jumper, a matching tie, and the plain white dress shirt of your choice: our Catholic school uniforms made things easier when it came to dressing for school on normal days. On gym days, we could wear casual clothes—which, for me and a few of the others, meant the exact *same* clothes from week to week. My hair was also predictable: the usual three plaits tied with ribbons by my mother, which I would change to two twists on the sides of my head as soon as I got on the bus. In the school bathroom before leaving for home, I'd put back my hair the way Ma had fixed it, but the parts were never straight. "Tabbi?" Ma would say, eyeing me suspiciously. "You been messin' in your hair?" And, of course, I'd deny that I had.

When the professional photographer was due at school, the dress rules were cast aside and our mothers could get as creative as they wanted with our 'dos. The night before second-grade picture day, Ma pressed and filled my hair with sponge rollers, resulting in a Diana Ross Afro like the one she wore in *The Wiz*—except mine was much larger and curlier: Dorothy from Kansas meets Angela Davis from Berkeley. Ma parted my "big 'do" and snapped white butterfly barrettes on each side. "Barrettes are for kindergarteners," I groaned. The look wasn't helped any by the outfit my mother had chosen for me: violet skirt and jacket, sleeves trimmed with fake purple fur, brown-and-white-plaid-blouse with collar points sharp enough to slice an orange. And the shoes? Patent leathers with ankle straps and a cork platform two inches high.

In the schoolyard that morning, a few of the others jumped on Solomon's bandwagon and started teasing me. They stood *behind* him, of course. Without Solomon, they were nothing. My eyes narrowed, my fists tightened, and the world turned silent. I was staring at their moving mouths when the school bell woke me from my rage. It was time to get to class.

I was too angry to fake a smile for my picture—bottom lip poked out, I met the enemy's eye and the shutter clicked, capturing the memory of my horrible day. (In the picture that resulted, my hair fills the entire background, except for two tiny blue specks that show through, thanks to those stupid barrettes. I'm surprised my hair didn't push right past the frame.)

At dismissal time, the pouring rain drenched my hair as I ran toward the bus. I was glad to be rid of the big 'do, but now my long, wet, greasy hair hung past my shoulders and covered most of my face. I may have shared a name with Samantha's TV daughter, but that afternoon I looked more like the Addams family's Cousin It!

On the ride home, Solomon settled into the seat across from me. I turned to look at him as he curled his lip to say whatever he was going to say about my hair. Before he finished the first syllable, his nose caught my right hook. His head slammed into the back of his seat and his big buckwheat eyes widened in surprise as he cupped his gushing nose.

You'd think, after my picture-day experience, that I'd want to leave my hair alone, but no. As I grew, I became fond of experiments of all kinds and my head was the perfect laboratory. One time my brother Choo talked me into letting *him* style my hair. I was going for a one-side-long-one-side-short-like-Salt-n-Peppa style. Instead, I got Elvis Presley side-burns and a receding hairline—the edge-up from hell! Another time a girlfriend introduced me to home perms, peroxide, and W-2 solution. Ever see a dark-skinned black girl with fried platinum hair? I may have looked like a *Star Trek* extra, but Oswaldo, the owner of Caribe's Mini-Grocery, sure approved. Usually when I walked the aisles at Caribe's, he'd sit in his bulletproof glass booth and focus on my ass. But when I

became a high-fried blonde, it was my head that he was checking out.
"What are *you* starin' at?" I snapped.

"Staring at you, blondie."

"Yeah? Well, first you better cut down that bushy black mess of yours
and trim those scary-ass eyebrows and *then* you can look!"

In an effort to figure out who I am, I have sported some pretty big
styles and some pretty wild cuts. By the age of thirteen, the wildness was
in me, tangled up in my hair, my clothes, and my need to rebel against
my mother's harsh rule. And all of the above was tangled up in my
growing love affair with the spotlight and the stage. . . .

It was two A.M. and there I was, stuck outside up on the roof. I'd broken the lock on the attic window for quick and easy reentry, but my little sister Sonia had jammed a stick, a metal hanger, and a stereo speaker
in front to prevent me from sneaking back into the house. Sonia was
mad because I'd run off for the night after promising her I wouldn't
leave her alone anymore while Ma was working at the bar. But at thirteen years, I was eager to explore and experiment. Baby-sitting my
eight-year-old sister just wasn't my thing.

I'd snuck out that night to meet Tara and Abby, my fellow performers
in a rap group we called TAT. We were the opening act for the rap con-
cert at the Rafola Taylor Center, a neighborhood meeting place for basketball games, talent shows, and concerts. As planned, we'd met in front
of the center at nine P.M. and we were looking slick. Tara and I wore
black sweatshirts with yellow iron-on letters that spelled out our first
names. Abby's sweatshirt had the same colors in reverse because she was
the middle performer. We wore tight black jeans and yellow-on-black
Puma sneakers. Originally white-on-black, we'd colored the shoes yellow with markers to match our outfits.

Hair was key for TAT. Abby wore her usual ponytail, and Tara and I
rocked our hair in a bob style, one side short and one side long. I'd dyed
my hair light brown and shaved lines into my sidebuns. Tara wasn't
allowed to dye her hair. Neither was I, but I did it anyway. The first time
Ma saw me with brown hair, she beat me with an extension cord. It
became a kind of ritual between my mother and me. I'd dye it, get
beaten, and dye it again. Eventually Ma realized she had less control
over me than she'd assumed.

As the time approached for us to open the show, my throat was dry and my muscles were tense. I'd drunk two beers before I left the house and smoked a joint in the parking lot outside the center. These, I reasoned, would give me the courage to perform. So as we took the stage, I was pretty high. My heart raced as I looked down at the hundreds of people filling the auditorium.

We're TAT from B-P-T
To make your head bop is our responsibility

Tara rapped, I sang, and Abby performed the beat box, making music with her mouth by blowing through her cupped hands into the microphone.

I'm Tabbi T. and I'm on the go
I rap so fast that I can't rap slow

The audience was loving us and I was loving them right back!

I'm Tara T., yeah, you know who I am
When the fellas see me, they scream out "Damn!"

When Tara rapped her lines, all the guys cheered. Then I sang the close: *We're TAT in the place to beeee!* The approval of the roaring crowd was a better rush than weed or brew. This big, colorful, moving blur was in *my* control.

But what goes up must come down. As soon as we were off the stage, my feeling of failure returned. Tara picked up on it and said, "Tab, chill out. You were fresh and smooth as always." But no matter what anyone said, I was inconsolable.

At 1:30 A.M., the show was over. Tara was hanging and Abby had left with some blazing-looking guy in a black-on-white MGM suit and glittery Gazelle glasses. I ached to hang out in the parking lot with the rest of the crowd, drinking alcohol and smoking weed while hip-hop blasted from car stereos, but the bar where Ma worked closed at two A.M. I had to get home *fast*. I ran down alleys and through backyards, taking every shortcut I knew and a few I invented on the spot.

This was the drill: scale the house to the attic window, climb inside, remove the forbidden eyeliner and lipstick, and get undressed and into bed as if I hadn't been anywhere. If my little sister was awake on those nights of escape and return, I'd have to bribe her not to tell. Usually, Sonia would be up and waiting, her green eyes wide open, arms crossed, mouth twisted to the side, her cocoa skin red with anger. She'd tap her foot the same way Ma did when she waited for me to answer one of her *you're in trouble now* questions. In the past, I'd always been able to bribe Sonia. But because I'd betrayed her trust time after time, my little sis had grown weary. Offering her a dollar no longer worked. Neither did threatening her. She just didn't want to be home alone.

Today I remember how, when I was Sonia's age, those moving shadows and mysterious noises did me in. I was scared of the dark, and people were *home* with me. I realize now that my little sister must have been terrified. But during my "rap diva" stage, I was mainly focused on myself.

Right hand on the door frame, left foot on the knob, left hand gripping the big outdoor light, I climbed up the house and onto the roof. But when I got to the attic window, it was barricaded shut!

I banged, called desperately. Sonia appeared, glaring. "I'm not letting you in!" she yelled.

"Come on, Sonia! Ma's gonna be here any minute!"

It was cold outside and I had to pee. I imagined myself frozen stiff at the window in a knocking stance, pee-cicles hanging from my crotch. "Sonia, you open this window right now or I'll—"

"You'll what? Tell Mommy? Why'd you lie to me, Tabbi?"

I shivered, gave her one of those *please feel sorry for me because it's cold out here and Mommy's gonna be home soon* looks. "I'm sorry, Sonia. I won't do it again."

"You always lyin' and thinkin' I'm stupid. I'm not lettin' you in."

And she was right. I was in the business of making promises I never meant to keep. I did it time after time without guilt or regard for Sonia's feelings or her fears of the dark. (And dark was Ma's law: conserve electricity to keep the bill down, or else!)

Sonia walked away from the window, leaving me out in the cold and about to burst my bladder. I decided I'd have to climb back down, enter through the front door, and risk a pounding from Ma if I ran into her. But first things first. As I squatted, peeing on the roof, Sonia came back to the window and dismantled her barricade. "You lucky I love you, girl," she said. "I should've let you stay out there. Ick, you peed on yourself."

"No, I didn't."

"Yes, you *did*. I'm telling Mommy you peed on the roof."

Downstairs, a door shut. Ma was home!

Knowing she'd be drunk, we hoped she'd go straight to bed. If not, this was going to be one of *those* nights: fist, broom, cable cord, iron, or whatever else she might use to vent her rage at her defiant daughter. Sonia knew what would go down, too, and changed instantly from adversary to co-conspirator. We sat at the bottom of the attic stairs for half an hour, whispering and calculating our mother's movements through the house. We heard a crash. Silverware hit the floor. She'd knocked over a dish rack on her way to the bathroom. Well, I thought, at least she made it to the bathroom, unlike a certain would-be rap superstar.

We were just about to make a dodge for our room when the toilet flushed. I thought my heart would burst through my chest. There was silence. Poor Sonia. All she had to do was tell the truth about why she'd been up in the attic. It was me who'd have to explain why I'd been using the window up there as a late-night entrance and why I was fully dressed and made up like a diva.

Ma's door closed. We held our breath and tiptoed out of the attic.

On our way to our own room, we peeked through Ma's keyhole. She was stretched across her bed, fully dressed, coat and all. She'd managed to get one shoe off before passing out. "Let's undress her and put her to bed," I told Sonia. The danger had passed. Once Ma was asleep, she was asleep.

Ma's nightstand was littered with papers, candy wrappers, old chicken bones, a plate of dried mashed potatoes. To the right, a bureau was covered with beer bottles with butts floating inside. Clothes, shoes, garbage, and lottery tickets covered the floor. In the midst of it all was Ma, spread-eagle. She was snoring with her mouth wide open, her eyes half-shut.

Sometimes when I think of the things I pulled back then, my eyes water and I get a tight feeling in my chest. That night, I got lucky. The barricade had come down and my bratty burden of a little sister—the one I constantly fought with and betrayed—had let me back inside and spared me a pounding.

In the bathroom, I washed off my makeup and took off my rap star clothes. When I got in bed, I thought about the night just ended: the adrenaline high of being on stage, the performance, the hoots and cheers of the packed house. But the crowd's roar was overtaken by those other, more familiar voices: *You're no good. You can't sing. You so black and ugly, ain't no one gonna love you.*

From that time on, whenever I got mad enough, I would run away from home. And when I reached my destination—an aunt's house, a friend's—I would cut my hair and dye it a different color. My hair would keep the cops from recognizing me, I figured, in case Ma put out a missing person report.

She never did.

After I turned fifteen, my mother got tired of the chase—indifferent about whether or not I came home. So, for longer and longer stretches of time, I stayed away. I exchanged my first abusive boyfriend for my second, and number two for number three. My mother had taught me how to take a punch, and so I tolerated my men's fists until that night when it became intolerable.

A year after I entered prison, I decided to let my hair go natural. I refrained from my usual processor treatment and the result was an Afro—a style I had once boycotted for being too corny, too "seventies."

But now, Angela Davis's fro had nothin' on *mine*. Early Michael Jackson's? Well, maybe. Sometimes when I passed by the officers with my new look, they'd mock me by singing those old Jackson Five tunes: *A B C, it's easy, Simple as 1, 2, 3* . . . and *Buh buh buh buh buh buh buh.* Yup, I was still getting teased about my "big hair," although unlike my past dealings in elementary school, a right hook now would get me cuffed—get me time in "seg" and an extra six months tacked on to my sentence. So instead of letting my fist fly, I would stop on the walkway and play along, do a Michael Jackson dance for my tormenters—right leg behind the left, vice versa, and a 360-degree spin with a bounce back. I'd add a short Charleston chew step for good measure. Mockery had lost some of its power over me. I'd come to like my Afro and was learning to like myself.

Because wearing my hair in its natural state contrasted with everyone else's processed styles, some of the other inmates nicknamed me the Last Nubian Queen. "You have the most beautiful jet-black hair," Ately said, passing me on the walkway. "Don't perm it." She said she wished *she* had the patience to go natural. It *took* patience, all right, to keep six inches of hair maintained in an even circle—spraying it with sheen, picking out the loose curls, patting it down to near-perfect roundness. Commissary didn't carry hair spray, but with a pick and a pat every now and then, my thick hair held up fairly well against the wind.

The only thing I didn't like about my Afro was the fact that it shed. Curly black hairs, long and short, would fall into the sink when I combed it—the same kind of hairs Uncle K used to leave all over the bathroom when I was a kid. Uncle K's natural was full of Ax hair dressing, and so, harder to remove from the sink *I* was supposed to keep clean. I remember thinking my uncle's Afro was so corny. He even wore a part in the middle, for crying out loud, which made him look like a cartoon character whose hair had been shot through by a speeding bullet. Lord, I'd think, let the seventies be *over*!

And, of course, they are. It's 2001 now; I've been in prison for five years. I do the best I can with my hair, keeping it pretty and tamed with limited supplies. I've forsaken my 'fro. But ever since the day I hacked off my golden bronze dreadlocks, I have worn my hair in its natural, jet-black color. It's a lot healthier without all those chemicals, and so am I. I had never realized how beautiful black looks on me.

I still cut and restyle my hair as I change. And when I do, I flush the loose hairs down the toilet. In spite of everything, I remain semi-superstitious, a burden I am trying to shed. However, I am still not fond of my hair going into the garbage can or even the sewer system and being spread all over the world. No part of us is valueless.

Since coming to prison, I have taken advantage of the opportunity to get in tune with who I am, who I was, who I am becoming, and why. Those "whys" of my journey have become clearer as I've discovered and dug up the roots of my low self-esteem and the self-destructive habits that contributed to my rage and my incarceration. Today, I am a woman with better decision-making skills and control over my actions. Physically, mentally, and spiritually, I am strong. My hair charts the history of how I got this way. As my friend Bonnie pointed out to me, hair is a faith, a testament for all the world to see.

Tabatha Rowley was raised in "the ghettos of Connecticut"—
mainly Bridgeport. Through Project Concern, a school integration
program, she attended Assumption Catholic School and, later, Paul Lau-
rence Dunbar Middle School. Dropping out of high school in the tenth
grade, Rowley subsequently earned her general equivalency diploma as a
participant in the Grafton Job Corps. Prior to her incarceration, she supported herself and her young son as a fast-food clerk, a nurse's aide, a
drug dealer, and a musical performer.

Rowley entered York Correctional Institution in 1996. A gifted singer-
songwriter and a popular inmate with both fellow prisoners and staff,
she was a featured performer at talent shows and assemblies held at the
prison. Rowley was released to a halfway house in the summer of 2001,
during which time her surviving brother, Choo, was shot and killed. He
was thirty-one. Tabatha Rowley was paroled in 2002 and currently
works at a Friendly's restaurant. She has reunited with her son, Kevin,
now ten, and has returned to the recording studio. Her song "In This
Together," which explores the difficulty of parenting from prison, is featured on the compilation CD *Keep It Real* (Terrelonge Records).

Of her life and writing Tabatha Rowley says, "I sometimes marvel at
the contrast between the confused, miseducated kid I was and the positive, steady-minded woman I am today. I hope my story will help wake
up other misguided young people and prevent them from having to experience the degradation, dehumanization, and isolation of prison."

THREE STEPS PAST THE MONKEYS

NANCY BIRKLA

Born: 1952

Conviction: Drug trafficking

Sentence: 7 years

Entered prison: 1990

Status: Released

I WAS FOUR YEARS OLD WHEN I SAT IN FRONT OF OUR television set watching *The Wizard of Oz*. My monkey nightmares began shortly after. Each night, sometimes two or three *times* a night, my father would climb out of bed and carry me from room to room, inspecting closets and cabinets and checking under the beds. Dad was moving up the corporate ladder back then, so we relocated often. Wherever we went, the monkeys hid in our suitcases and moved along with us.

The Wizard of Oz is everywhere, of course, but by guile and good luck, I managed to avoid the Wicked Witch and her fleet of flying monkeys most of my life. My luck ran out one autumn day in 1995 when my Intro to Film professor turned off the lights and screened an excerpt for our class. I was forty-three at the time, in my third semester at Jefferson Community College in northern Kentucky. I'd been drug-free for six years and out of prison for five, but I was still pretty much in the dark about why I was the way I was. As I sat there watching Dorothy's airborne abduction to the witch's lair, a sense of dread overtook me and I was a child again, transported on a rush of resurfacing memories not to Oz but to Allentown, Pennsylvania.

Besides my film class, I was taking a creative writing course at Jefferson that semester, and the day after *The Wizard of Oz* sent me reeling, a poetry assignment was due. In my agitated state, I scrawled a verse effort that was more riddle than poem—a string of nightmare images that made sense only to me. I titled it "The Death of My Childhood." The poem resurfaced this past summer atop a disheveled pile of papers stuffed in a faded blue folder marked "Prison Journal."

Those daily scrawls—some detailed reports from the front, others rage-filled rants—had been crucial to my survival at the Kentucky State Penitentiary for Women. Released in June 1990, I promised myself I would someday write a prison memoir based on what I'd recorded. But having moved forward, I was reluctant to go back. I dodged my own assignment for over a decade.

I'm ready now. Traveling cautiously in reverse, I hold hands with two of the people I have been: the addled inmate in prison issue and the four-year-old girl whose pretty white dress is fanned out with crinolines. We three are looking under the beds and in the dark recesses of memory. We're determined to confront the monkeys.

* * *

When I was a kid, I went through a phase in which I was afraid to have my hair washed. Shutting my eyes to the soap and steam made my breathing stop, and nothing my mother said or did could convince me that shampooing was safe. Finally, we devised a system. I'd lie on my back on the kitchen counter and slowly inch my head under the faucet, inhaling and exhaling deeply. As Mom scrubbed, I'd stare, eyes open, at the same spot on the ceiling and count the little grooves in the spackle design. By the time I reached one hundred, the ordeal was usually over.

On October 4, 1989, the day they came to arrest me, I hadn't showered or shampooed in days. I'd wanted to clean up but couldn't. The thought of being enclosed in the shower stall, encased in steam, made me wheeze and grab for my inhaler. Still, the worst effects of my withdrawal had finally begun to subside. I'd stopped using drugs two weeks earlier, detoxing cold turkey because I had no health insurance to cover the cost of treatment. My nostrils still burned from the daily cocaine binges of the preceding months, but the nosebleeds had finally let up. And after fourteen days of nausea and nonstop diarrhea, I could finally get through an entire day without battling the hourly urge to give up, get dressed, and go out and cop some dope.

"Come in!" I called. I had turned the living room into an infirmary and was sprawled on the couch, surrounded by Kleenex, paper towels, cans of warm ginger ale, a bottle of Pepto Bismol, my asthma medication, and a large soup pot, in case I couldn't make it to the bathroom in time. The door opened and Roadie and Hubble, my black chow chows, greeted the arresting officers. I recognized one. He'd moonlighted as a security guy at some of the rock shows my husband and I had worked. I was pretty sure he recognized me, too.

They were nice enough. They told me I was part of a sweep of barroom drug traffickers. They opened the cruiser door for me. En route to the police van waiting down on Preston Highway, they pulled into a Burger King drive-thru and offered me a Coke. From their staticky police radio, I kept hearing the words "Operation Barfly."

The officer I recognized helped me into the van. "Look, you're our first pickup, so there's going to be a long wait," he said. "I won't cuff you, but remember to hold your hands behind your back whenever the back door of this van opens." He jumped back down onto the pavement and smiled. "Sorry about this, kiddo," he muttered. "Just doing my job. Good luck."

This wasn't so bad, I reasoned. If they drug-tested me, my urine wouldn't be "dirty." Since I had no previous arrests, they'd probably release me under my own recognizance. And if worse came to worst, there was five hundred dollars hidden inside a Pink Floyd album cover back home for emergencies like this. Everything was going to be okay. But damn, *Oprah* would probably be over by the time I got home. I hated missing *Oprah*.

It was unusually hot in Kentucky that October, I remember—the temperature still in the eighties. As the afternoon dragged on, the heat rose and the van filled to capacity and beyond. The later arrivals, squeezed together on the floor, brought news with them. "Operation Barfly," which had resulted in eighty-two indictments, was the lead story on the five o'clock news. Turns out Chip Trainer, lead singer for the rock band Dead on Arrival, was really a narc planted in the local bar scene by the Drug Enforcement Agency. In silence, I worried that Chip might have reported back to DEA that I'd tried trading him speaker cabinets for drugs.

By dusk, fourteen of us had been crammed into the back of the transport van. Everyone except me had been "cuffed" with nylon wire, but cigarettes had not been confiscated, and even with their wrists tied together, my fellow arrestees had managed to light up. The sweltering, smoky air, the claustrophobic quarters, my parched throat and pounding heart: I knew I was in trouble. Desperate for a drop or two of moisture, I eyed the Plexiglas window that separated the van's air-conditioned cab from the rear quarters. Fogged with condensation, the cool, moist glass might offer some relief. I inched closer and tried poking my tongue between the grids of the metal grate that protected the window. No luck. No relief.

Four hours after I had climbed into the van, we arrived inside the garage at police headquarters. We waited for the doors to open. And waited. And waited. The coughing I'd been suppressing turned to wheezing, then to gasps for breath. Drop to the floor, I told myself— there'll be less smoke near the floor. The others began pounding on my behalf. "Open up!" a man yelled.

"No one promised you jokers a picnic!" a female officer yelled back. "We'll let you out when we're damn good and ready!"

"A woman's having an asthma attack back here," the man screamed. "She's in serious trouble. *Please!*"

The van's back door slammed open. "You!" the officer said. "Get out here NOW!" I knew she was speaking to me, but I could barely breathe, let alone stand and climb down from the van. Several sets of hands pulled and dragged me up and out. I landed in a heap on the garage floor.

"My inhaler's in my purse," I croaked. "If I can just get my asthma—"

"No drugs without an order from the docs, *honey,*" the officer said. "Hey, where's your cuffs?" From the way she yanked and tied the wire around my wrists, I was pretty sure that a doctor's order for asthma medicine wasn't going to be a priority. Resorting to old survival techniques, I stared up, trying to catch my breath by counting ceiling tiles. Midcount, a light blinded me. I squinted into the eye of a channel 11 TV camera. Shielding my face with my hands, I jerked away. The rest of the booking process remains a blur.

"We'll help you," my father told me over the phone. "But it's probably not going to be tomorrow, and maybe not the day after that." Poor Mom and Dad: over the years, they'd answered calls about car wrecks, emergency room visits, and endless financial crises. Dad would show up at some place hundreds of miles away from home to move me out of a bad living situation "one last time." Mom would fly to Chicago or some other meeting point to take me home and help me recover from my latest breakdown. But a drug arrest was untraveled territory. "Your mother and I need time to think," my father told me now, his voice icy and unfamiliar. "And apparently, so do you."

And so I waited, a prisoner of both the commonwealth of Kentucky and of some internal terror of unknown origin. I spent the next four days pacing the perimeter of my tiny cell, begging for drinks of water that never came, and trying as best I could to head off the panic attacks fueled by . . . what were they? Hallucinations? Memories? Whatever these visions of fires and churning waters and malevolent monkeys were, they seemed to have escaped from some guarded chamber deep within my chest.

A good lawyer and a full ten-thousand-dollar cash bond was what it took my parents to get me sprung from Jefferson County Jail. I have never felt a deeper shame than when I was released and taken to them. Still, I assumed our familiar pattern was in place. First, a good chewing out. Then, a softening. Finally, an invitation to return to their home so I could be cared for and helped back on my feet. But I'd miscalculated. This time, Mom and Dad had another plan.

The cab took us directly from jail to the substance abuse treatment center at Our Lady of Peace Hospital. The contract I signed stated that if I left the hospital within the following thirty days, my bond would be revoked and I'd go back to jail, probably for a very long time. As soon as I was checked in, Mom and Dad took the next plane out of Louisville.

Holding tight to my self-delusion, I felt furious over my parents' new "tough love" approach and their inability to understand my situation. I was strong enough to stay clean on my own. Hadn't I just gone cold turkey and remained drug-free for two whole weeks? Hadn't I been through enough of an ordeal without being imprisoned in a treatment center? If they insisted on counseling, I could enroll in some outpatient program. And I did *not* have an alcohol problem. Why was I being asked never to *drink* again?

Because I'd arrived at Our Lady of Peace without a packed bag, I was given permission to leave a message for my husband to bring me some clothes and personal items. When Bobby failed to show, the nurses gave me a toothbrush, toothpaste, and a comb. Each day I waited for my things to arrive, and each night I was handed a pair of hospital scrubs to change into so that my one set of clothes could be washed while I slept. Because the scrubs were like the ones I'd worn in jail, putting them on was a nightly refresher course in anger, shame, and panic. "Look, you just don't *understand*!" I whined. "I *have* to talk to my husband. Just let me go home and grab some clothes. I'll come right back. I *promise*." In response, they revoked my phone privileges and forbade communication of any kind with Bobby.

"Addiction is a disease of compulsion and obsession, not only with drugs but also with people, places, and things," I was told. "Put the focus on yourself, not on what's happening back home." I focused on myself by hosting a daily "poor, poor, pitiful me" party.

Nights were the worst, but at least at Our Lady of Peace, I could look out a window, or get myself a drink of water when I was thirsty, or pace the long corridor when my anxiety descended. My hyperactivity subsided a little earlier each night. Within a week, I was able to sleep for several hours at a time.

Fortunately, access to my mental assessments from those early months in recovery did not become available to me until years later. *Major depression . . . suicidal ideation . . . impaired judgment . . . expansive personality . . . symptoms consistent with post-traumatic stress disorder, but denies any specific associated trauma . . . Prognosis for successful treatment: marginal.* Had I understood how sick I was when I began my recovery journey, I might never have started.

And if my psyche was in rough shape, my body was as bad or worse. At 235 pounds, I was the fattest woman in the program—"morbidly obese" in the language of assessment. The other women on the unit wore makeup and stylish haircuts, cute jeans and tops, little matching sweat suits. I was still in the same clothes I'd been wearing the day I was arrested. Why hadn't I thrown away a shirt this faded and stained? How could I have let my hair get so ratty-looking? The woman staring back at me in the mirror looked pathetic and old. When had this happened to me? And *why?*

When I addressed the issue of my appearance in group therapy, pinning the blame on my husband's having failed to bring me my things, the others remarked that Bobby hadn't delivered my bag because he was indifferent to me. The observation was a stinging slap in the face, as the truth often is. What I had worried about for a long time was finally on the table.

Bobby and I had met in LaCrosse, Wisconsin, seven years earlier. He'd been touring the Midwest as lighting technician for a rock and roll band, and I was a fixture in the local nightclub scene. I'd been working in bars for years, befriending and hanging with members of the bands that passed through, nursing crushes on many of them. But by my late twenties, I'd faced the fact that I was probably not going to "hook up" with any of these guys in the same way my girlfriends had. I was always their "good buddy" instead. So when Bobby paid attention to me in a different way, I was immediately interested.

Well, interested and annoyed. It was the summer of 1983. Video games were just catching on, and I was at the Surf Club, riding a tabletop game called Centipede. My goal was to beat the game and program my name into the machine as high scorer. So I was miffed when, during my best run of the night, a hand in my peripheral vision slammed down a quarter, challenging me. I'd have much preferred to play unopposed, but I knew I had to adhere to the "accept all challenges" rule. Bobby was terrible, but while playing against him, I obtained my goal. Thrilled, I began programming my name into the game's "hall of fame" when, suddenly, the monitor went black. There was Bobby, towering over me, the unplugged end of the game's cable in his hand. My score was gone, and with it my bid for Centipede immortality. Bobby was laughing hysterically.

I was furious, of course, but flattered, too, by this cocktail of aggression and attention, directed exclusively at me. A few days after Bobby's band moved on, I received a letter. "I'll call you sometime soon," he wrote. Yeah, sure you will, I thought. I was astonished when he did.

I loved the highs of my life with Bobby—the traveling, the music, the parties, the drugs—but the lows were brutal. Bobby's temperament ran from white hot to ice cold. One minute he'd be all over me, planning our happily-ever-after future; the next, he'd push me away or disappear for a day or two. We broke up, reunited, called it quits again, got back together. Five years after we'd begun our up-and-down, long-distance relationship, we were married.

Bobby's dream was to build a state-of-the-art lighting and sound company. The problem was that he assigned me his dream, too, insisting that I dedicate my life to the business he'd chosen for himself. And I *did* work hard, handling the phones, balancing the books, lugging heavy sound equipment, but balking all the way. Resentful of Bobby's control over me, I began to think of myself as "marital victim," a role I remained unwilling to relinquish for many years. In my diseased perception, being my husband's whipping girl justified my self-destructive impulses. It was *Bobby* who caused my problems, I reasoned; if only he treated me better, I wouldn't feel so depressed all the time—wouldn't *need* to numb my pain with alcohol, drugs, and food.

Ours was an abusive relationship. Too afraid to defend myself physically when Bobby lashed out, I used my mouth as an assault rifle instead. "Asshole!" and "ignorant motherfucker!" worked in the clutch, but my most effective verbal jabs were the ones I laced with words I was sure he wouldn't know. Because Bobby was defensive about his intelligence level, I tried hard to make him feel stupid. My self-assigned role as victim came in handy at these times. *He* was the abuser, I reasoned; I was the helplessly abused.

Ultimately, it was my marriage, not my drug abuse, that took center stage during my thirty days at the treatment center. Each time I attempted to justify my bad behavior by blaming Bobby, I was asked to examine my own actions instead. I resisted vigorously at first, but by my second week, I found myself facing hard personal truths about my home life, my work, and myself.

Anyone who works with substance abusers will tell you that the success rate is low. One evening, a man from our group slashed his veins with a pair of nail clippers and departed abruptly. Others were discharged for dirty urine tests or discovery of drugs during room inspections. Some left in a huff, of their own accord. Others were pressured into premature exits by family members and co-dependents. Because the alternative plan was for me to go back to jail, I stuck it out, dropping some of my defenses along the way and gaining insight. Much to my surprise, I began to feel better.

I experienced one major incident during treatment. It happened one evening shortly before my discharge. Reading the journal entry I scrawled that night brings back the pain and anger of the moment.

11/27/89

I've been poked fun of many times in my life, but to be mocked by a room full of treatment center crazies tops all the other times put together.

About a dozen of us were in the lounge watching TV tonight when one of the nurses suggested we might want to take a look at a channel 11 news special, "Cracking Down on Drugs in Kentuckiana." I'm not sure why I didn't see it coming, especially since I'd already seen myself on the channel 11 news the night I was arrested. This time I was part of a two-hour special, so I'm pretty sure everybody who knows me now also knows about my drug bust. I cringe when I think of going home and facing people.

> The hardest part tonight wasn't the fact that those most humiliat-
> ing moments of my life were being broadcast on TV. Much worse
> than that was the ridicule from my supposed "support group."
> After "cheering" the image of me being arrested, everyone began
> taunting me about the way I looked—swollen face, filthy hair, and
> that same old stupid dirty shirt that I finally got to throw away.
> Mostly it was the guys who got to me; their loud hooting and hol-
> lering, their puckered lips and smooching noises. Well, I couldn't
> help it. I exploded, crying and screamed, calling them a bunch of
> "psycho asshole losers." Now I've been sequestered in my room
> for a "time out." A roomful of adults act like five-year-olds, and
> *I'm* the one who gets sent to my room. This is a bunch of shit!

But I survived that night and faced my fear that, without the hospital's safety net, I would falter in my recovery. Before I left Our Lady of
Peace, I located a home group where I could attend regular support
meetings, and a sponsor, a woman further along in her recovery who
would guide me through the twelve steps recovering addicts must take.
When I entered the treatment hospital, my doctor had pegged my
chances for success as "marginal," but in signing the release papers, I
noticed the words "prognosis: good" written next to his signature. I felt
proud of myself for the first time in years.

For the next several months, my life centered around recovery
and waiting. I attended meetings daily, sometimes twice a day, and
remained loyal to my once-a-week after-care program. With my sponsor's help, I started writing on the twelve steps. Many aspects of my life
remained difficult—my return to my home and the business, the
rebuilding of my parents' trust—but I remained faithful to my goal of
staying clean. Through it all, I dreaded my appearance before the sentencing judge.

On that warm morning in May, a group of recovering friends met me
at the courthouse, circled me, and prayed the "Serenity Prayer." Inside,
I took my assigned seat next to Bobby and faced the judge. My attorney
was optimistic. The presentencing investigation report had been positive, and the prosecutor had agreed to a recommendation of five years'
probation. I was more than ready to embrace good news, but I was
equally prepared for bad. I'd called the prison that morning to see what

an inmate could pack and bring along with her. At my feet was a paper grocery bag filled with extra socks and underwear.

Bobby went first, pleading guilty to charges of complicity. He was sentenced to five years' probation. As the judge ran through the stipulations of Bobby's supervision, I tried to calm my shaking by telling myself that I'd receive probation, too. It had been my first offense. My recovery was on course. Even the prosecutor had recommended supervision over incarceration.

The judge shuffled his papers in silence, then stared over the straight dark line of his reading glasses and into my eyes. "Selling drugs is a serious offense," he said. "I hope you realize how fortunate you are that nobody died as a result of your actions. I hereby sentence you to seven years for each of four counts of trafficking in a controlled substance, to be served concurrently for a total of seven years in the Kentucky State Correctional Institute for Women."

Because the state penitentiary was at full capacity, my admittance there was preceded by a two-week return to Jefferson County Jail. In my first few days there, the outside temperatures reached the nineties, the building's air-conditioning went down, and the floor fan they dragged in buzzed loudly as it pushed around the hot, stagnant air. No towels or washcloths were provided, so I used the underwear and socks I'd brought instead. I gave away two sets to other women and ran out on the third day. My panic attacks returned with a vengeance. With only seventy-two hours of my seven-year sentence served, I didn't know how I was going to do it.

Mostly, I worried about how I'd manage progressing in the twelve steps. The first step—admitting that I was powerless over my addiction and that my life had become unmanageable—had been the easiest. I'd faced *that* grim reality before recovery was even a thought. The second step—coming to believe that a Power greater than myself could restore me to sanity—had been more challenging. No problem agreeing with the second part; my life definitely had taken an insane turn and needed an about-face. My problem was with the Higher Power. I believed in God but had serious doubts that God believed in me. I'd answered all the second-step questions in my recovery guide and had prayed and prayed. Still, my sponsor had advised that I couldn't move to the third step—turning my will and my life over to God's care—until I could honestly state that I knew God had faith in me. "In God's time" was the answer I heard whenever I expressed my doubts to recovering people. "Just keep coming back." But how was I supposed to keep returning to meetings when I was locked back up in Jefferson County Jail?

5/30/90

My first night at the state penitentiary. It's surreal, as though I'm looking in from the outside at someone else's life. I'm sitting in the darkness again, gazing out a window from what could feel like a college dormitory lounge if it weren't for the fence, the barbed wire, and the guard up in the tower. He's standing out on a small porch, smoking a cigarette with one hand and holding his rifle with the other. No matter how hard I try to accept my situation, I'm dying inside. Seven years sounds like the rest of my life.

I'm afraid to go to sleep. Last night I had a horrible nightmare. Bobby was standing over me, holding my arms down and screaming that I was a fat bitch. He was force-feeding me Hershey bars, shoving them into my mouth faster than I could chew or swallow.

Then came the worst part of the dream. I left the house so that Bobby could cool off and I was walking back in the neighborhood. Suddenly, I heard a deafening screech and a big red monkey jumped down on me from a tree overhead. He had sharp claws and long, jagged teeth, which he sunk into my upper arm. I tried to push him off, but he kept biting me, slashing at me with those claws, until I used the trick I had taught myself when I was a kid, opening and closing my eyes hard, forcing myself awake.

I've been dreaming some really crazy shit these past few weeks—crazy shit that somehow seems normal, too.

Crazy stuff had felt normal to me for as far back as I could remember, although my life had begun conventionally enough. Of all the places I'd lived during my childhood years, the one I recalled most fondly and vividly was my birthplace: Norwich, Connecticut.

Born into a large, close-knit Italian clan on my dad's side and a not-so-close French-Swedish bunch on my mom's, I adored my family. Downstairs in our house on McKinley Avenue lived Aunt Bea, Uncle Cal, and my cousins, Sandy and April. A few doors up the street lived Dad's sister, Aunt Anna, her husband, Walter, and three more cousins, Vita, Gail, and Wally. The "McKinley Avenue Kids" is what the rest of the family dubbed us. Our parents took turns visiting and baby-sitting, hauling playpens and rolling strollers up or down the street, depending upon who was going where. We cousins played together, ate meals together, and visited our grandmother together, too. Nonna Pileggi's two-story stucco house on Norwich's East Side was as pink as a Shirley Temple cocktail. Tiny pebbles embedded in the sidewalk out front spelled the initials B.P., for my Italian immigrant grandfather, Bruno Pileggi. Four of Dad's other siblings lived in Nonna's house, and two more lived a block away.

The youngest of Vita and Bruno's eleven children, my father became the first and only one to leave Norwich. In search of the best life he could give his young and growing family, Dad climbed the corporate ladder, eventually becoming executive vice president of a major corporation in the Midwest.

I was four when we moved to Allentown, Pennsylvania. We spent about three years there, I think, although establishing time lines for my childhood remains difficult for me. Mostly, I have to think about what town we lived in when something happened and then do the math, approximating my age or grade in school to the geographical location.

In Allentown, we lived in "garden apartments"—long rows of two-story dwellings that stretched across several acres of grassy hills. I recall the layout of our apartment in Allentown but can remember only two of our neighbors: Holly, the little girl my age who lived next door, and the woman down the hill from us, whom I believed was a witch. There was nothing particularly witchlike about this woman. No wart on the end of her nose, no black cat or broomstick. Young and attractive with long dark hair, she wore skirts and shorts like everybody else. Scared to death, I went nowhere near her.

After Allentown, many other moves followed. I remember little about the schools I attended, or specific teachers, or the usual kid-centered events most of my adult friends recall. I remember the nightmares, though—the terrifying dreams that eventually seeped into my waking hours as well.

The monkey nightmares began in Allentown. The cannibal dreams, too. I don't remember any of the cannibals ever "getting me," or even revealing themselves. Mostly these nightmares were about feelings of anxiety and fears of confinement. In the middle of a normal, run-of-the-mill dream, I'd hear distant drum-beating, singsongy chanting. My heart would race. Sometimes I'd be able to run and hide with everyone else, but more often I'd stand there, frozen with fear as the drumming grew louder and the cannibals got closer and closer.

Fire and water figured into other nightmares. I'd be drowning, or standing outside our house, watching helplessly as my parents, trapped inside, went up in flames. More than once, I dreamed about a moat of dark water surrounding our home, creating a barrier between my parents and me. Trapped, drowning, smothering, and however the hell it was those monkeys made me feel, before long I lost my ability to distinguish between the terror of my dreams and the safety of my actual life. It was back in Allentown that my panic attacks began and, with them, the techniques I used to relax these illogical and unspecified fears.

My drug addiction took root in me long before I took my first "hit" of any controlled substance. My first drug was not alcohol, or weed, or speed, or blow. It was candy. I found my way to drug abuse through food.

6/4/90

They're calling me and Mary Ann, the other woman who was processed in with me, "Humpty" and "Dumpty." I guess we look like two big, round blue beach balls in our too-tight prison scrubs. When I entered this place, showering with that nasty neon yellow cootie soap, I prayed to God for a uniform that would fit. Seemed like the most important thing to pray for at the time, after weighing in at a shocking 255 lbs.

Out of the three sets of pants and tops issued to me, only one set fits. The other two pairs of pants might do, if they have to, but I can't possibly squeeze myself into the 1X tops. The 2X shirt barely fits and the others are useless.

Mary Ann got one 2X shirt and two 3Xs. I begged her for the other 2X, which I don't believe fits her anyhow, but she refused. I smiled secretly when, soon after her refusal to help me, she realized none of her pants fit, not a single pair. She had to remove the draw-string even to get a pair pulled up beneath her belly. Those pants don't stand a chance against *her* wide ass; I give the material half a day, at best. She's definitely fatter than I am.

Damn, where did that come from? I don't feel good rejoicing over somebody else's humiliation. I've only been locked up for a few weeks, but my recovery self is slipping away.

By the time I was in third grade, my parents were already worried about my eating habits. I might not remember much about the houses we lived in, or the schools I attended, but I do remember the food. I recall that gorging myself with mashed potatoes calmed the distur-bances that now lived inside of me, night and day. Stuffing myself on candy caused the monsters to lie down and sleep. Chocolate worked best. Each time my family took me shopping, I campaigned for Hershey bars until I got them.

Because I knew my consumption was being monitored, I began sneaking food. Sometimes I ate entire suppers at other people's houses and then went home, complaining to my mom, "I'm starving." My mouth still waters thinking about the macaroni and cheese my friend Janice's mom made. Loaded with several kinds of cheese, it was starchy enough to calm me the way mashed potatoes did. Sometimes Janice's mother mixed ham and peas in with the macaroni and cheese, and sometimes she served it plain with fish sticks and peas on the side. No matter how she prepared it, I managed to manipulate my way to their dinner table whenever macaroni and cheese was on the menu.

On and on, city after city, new school after new school, the one ele-ment of constancy in my life was food. Eventually, the consequences of my ravenous appetite caught up with me. By the time I was in fifth grade, Mom was shopping for me in the "chubbette" department of Montgomery Ward's. In sixth grade, the kids began teasing me. We lived in Smithtown, New York, then. A boy at school altered my last name from Pileggi to Pigface. Until we moved, he and some of the other boys taunted me daily with the playground chant, "Here comes Pigface! Pig-face Pileggi!"

Smithtown is where another addictive manifestation surfaced. I think I was about nine when I figured out, by accident at first, that if I hurt myself, some of the pain inside would kind of "leak out." What started out as a private double dare to stick a safety pin through the tippy top of my thumb evolved into an oddly soothing habit. I'd stick my arms and legs with pins, pens, sharpened pencils. I recall my mother becoming upset with me when she discovered that I'd poked holes up and down the pleats of my red-and-navy-blue-plaid dress. Mom's assumption—that I had willfully ruined a perfectly good out-fit—was off the mark. How could she have known that it calmed me to jab and stab away, later lying in the dark and tracing the gouges and scabs with my fingertips? Wounding myself quieted whatever had felt unquiet inside of me that day. When I touched the wounds, I could relax and sleep.

6/13/90

I like seeing my own blood. When blood was being drawn for var-ious tests a few days back, I felt almost high watching it. I have lots of mosquito bites, and today I felt almost hypnotized as I ripped off a scab and squeezed blood from the fresh hole I'd gouged. By picking at all my bites, I've created fields of red scabs all over my legs and arms. I actually sat for about half an hour today, visualiz-ing the pictures I might create if I were to take a pen and draw lines between them, like a little kid with a new connect-a-dot book.

Yesterday, I took the safety pin that came with my monthly ration of sanitary napkins and stuck it through the corner tip of my thumb. I'm not sure why. I guess I just had to see if I could still do it. Right now I'm fighting an urge to stab myself with this pen. I'd love to watch the ink bleed below my skin. I have no idea why I do some of the things I do. All I know is, when I do them, the pain inside recedes a little. I feel calm again, able to rest.

God, I really am crazy!

When I was eleven, Dad received another big promotion. As my family prepared for a major relocation to South Bend, Indiana, I was permitted to travel back to Norwich all by myself to visit my relatives. I remember that trip as one of the happiest weeks of my childhood.

Usually on our visits back to Norwich, I had to share my grandmother with my family. But this time, I got to stay overnight at Nonna's and have her all to myself. We talked, watched TV, rocked together on the front porch. I was a normal, happy kid, spending time with my grandmother. At Nonna's, I didn't even feel fat.

Happy as I felt that week, Nonna seemed able to read my deeper sadness—to understand something about the turmoil that churned inside of me. One night, tucking me into the blankets on her living room sofa, she bent and kissed my forehead. In her thick Italian accent, she said, "Nancy Ann, you're a smart, talented, beautiful girl. God has blessed you and He loves you very much."

The lights went out and I lay in the dark, puzzled. God *loved* me? Weren't my nightmares and other miseries His answer to my bad behavior? Proof that He *didn't* care for me? The last thing I heard that night was the chiming of Nonna's parlor clock, lulling me to a peaceful sleep.

Call that trip back to Norwich the calm before the storm, however, because the move to South Bend was a killer. Indiana kids started school later, so my junior high classmates were a year or two older and a rougher breed than I was used to. Miserable, I cried, manipulated, misbehaved. And I ate. A conference was held, a decision made to transfer me to Holy Family parochial school and have me repeat the second half of sixth grade.

Unhappy about the demotion, I nevertheless liked my new school from the moment Sister Callista introduced me to the class. "She's cute," I heard one girl whisper to another. In the half-dozen schools I had already attended, I'd never heard a classmate say anything remotely like that.

Despite the compliment, neither my academic performance nor my behavior improved significantly at Holy Family, but my craving for chocolate hit the moon. I was up to a half-dozen Reese's peanut butter cups a day when I began scavenging for discarded soda bottles in a field between school and Kroger's supermarket. At Kroger's, I'd move from the bottle return to the candy aisle. That was where I discovered economy-size bags and launched myself into the world of business. I'd canvass the neighborhood, adding other kids' nickels and dimes to my cache of bottle money. With my enhanced purchasing power, I invested in eight-packs of Reese's, Milky Ways, and Three Musketeers. The other kids got their candy for a few cents cheaper, and I scored a couple of extras for myself. It was, I figured, a win-win situation.

Today, it amazes me to ponder the parallels between my childhood behaviors and my subsequent methods of "feeding the beast." But addiction is addiction and the user is always financing the next fix. Over the years, chocolate bars and peanut butter cups became alcohol, cocaine, and quaaludes, but if the poisons changed, the modus operandi did not.

South Bend was also the place where my fear of dentists surfaced. Prior to this move, my uncle Bruno, a dentist back in Norwich, had always worked on my teeth. With visits home less frequent, that was no longer practical. But sitting in a new dentist's chair filled me with inexplicable dread. Although nothing or no one held me down, I felt as if I was being restrained against my will and could only endure checkups by resorting to my old trick of staring trancelike at the ceiling. Later, I would not remember the drilling or filling.

6/15/90

Okay, today I had the freakiest anxiety attack yet. They're wearing me down, these bouts of panic. They'd be bad enough to deal with outside of prison, but they're unbearable in here. I want drugs. I really do. I need something to help me feel less trapped and confined all the time, even when I'm not in a confining situation.

This morning I was called out of my job at the prison school to go see the dentist. Immediately, I felt my chest caving in. Because of my dental phobia, I haven't been to a dentist in years. So today, when my anxiety became full-blown, I told the doctor I just couldn't sit in his chair. He was kind. He told me lots of women experience anxiety about dental work and assured me he would only be examining and cleaning my teeth. He didn't understand. What I meant was, no matter what he was or wasn't going to do to my teeth, I couldn't bring myself to land my ass in his chair. So when he insisted, running from the room seemed like a reasonable alternative.

The guard who stopped me told me I had two choices: I could either submit to the exam willingly or be restrained for it. Jesus Christ, I thought, when will this end?

After three unsuccessful attempts to stay seated, the dentist's patience began wearing thin. The guard pulled his cuffs from his belt and I began to cry. Why am I so crazy? Why do such normal things feel so abnormally scary to me?

On my fourth attempt, I finally managed to remain seated by focusing on a spot on the ceiling. Then, just as my anxiety began diminishing, I had some strange hallucination or out-of-body experience. I don't even know *what* it was. Wide awake, I felt myself rising up toward the ceiling and looking down on two little girls and a grown man. Both girls were stripped down to their underwear and the man was naked. One of the girls—the one sitting where I'd been sitting—struggled to free herself. Her hands had been tied to the chair. She was wearing cotton underpants— blue flowered ones, with little bumps in the fabric, the kind I'd worn many years ago myself. The man was fondling the other little girl. A sick sensation swept over me. I struggled to see the man, but all three faces were a blur.

"Almost through," the dentist said, and his voice snapped me out of it. What the hell is going on with me? I've heard about stuff coming back to people—stuff they never remembered happening—and now I'm terrified of what I might find out. My insides are pulling and twisting. I keep trying to get some help, counseling or something, but so far all I'm told is the waiting list is long. I can't stand being here anymore. God, just help me to make it through this day. I want to go home. I want to wake up from this nightmare!

My first attempt at easing my inner turmoil with drugs happened when I was in eighth grade. Mom was under a doctor's care for several conditions at the time, and her medicine cabinet housed a row of prescription vials. I knew one of them contained tranquilizers, a pill that could calm you down. My problem was that none of the bottles *said* "tranquilizer." The solution? Try them all, one at a time, until I found the one that made me feel relaxed. Fortunately, I couldn't swallow pills and so had to chew them instead. Chomping down on what I now believe was one of Mom's iron pills, I grimaced, spat, and aborted my mission immediately.

On and on, year after year, I figured out new ways to buffer the unnamed fear that lived inside me. Surprisingly, though, in terms of alcohol consumption, I was a "late bloomer." I drank my first beer the night I graduated from high school. I liked the effect and drank another, and another, and another. By the time I started college in the fall, I was well acquainted with alcohol-fueled oblivion. For the next seventeen years, "using" was the most important element of my life.

6/19/90

Earlier today I thought about the vision I had of Nonna. The date was September 19 of last year, Bobby's and my second wedding anniversary. I'd been trying for a couple of months to stay "clean" but didn't realize that the prescription antidepressant I was taking, along with the Xanax and sleeping pills, continued feeding my addiction as powerfully as cocaine had. Alcohol wasn't working either, although I'd begun drinking daily, a habit I'd never adopted before. I woke up on that particular morning knowing I had to score—my choice *not* to use cocaine was gone.

Nothing about that day felt happy or right. Without acknowledging our anniversary, Bobby began barking orders at me. Mike and Mark arrived early to prep for a show that night. As usual, they told me with their eyes how sorry they felt about the way Bobby was treating me. Wiping away my tears, I admitted to the guys that it was our anniversary.

One of them must have said something to Bobby, because eventually he *did* acknowledge our wedding day. Glaring and breathing hard through flared nostrils, he spoke words that pounded me harder than any clenched fist. "I did *not* forget what day this is," he said. "I purposely didn't say anything, but if you want to hear it, here goes. You're a fat, lazy bitch and I'm sorry I ever met you. Marrying you was my biggest mistake."

Things went from bad to worse. I'd been anticipating an anniversary card from Mom and Dad, with their usual one-hundred-dollar check enclosed. Gotta go home and check the mail, I thought. Gotta cash that check, score, and get back to work. Gotta get with Missy, figure out how to split an eight ball with someone.

Under the guise of forgetting a briefcase, I made it home a little after noon. There in the mailbox was the envelope I'd been hoping for, the one with my father's handwriting on the front. But why was it addressed only to me? And why was there a note inside instead of a Hallmark card?

Dad got right to the point. He and Mom hadn't *forgotten* my wedding anniversary, but they no longer acknowledged my marriage or the way I'd chosen to live my life. It had taken me getting clobbered just that one time, eight months earlier, for my parents to reach zero tolerance concerning the abuse in my marriage. We had followed our familiar pattern: I'd called for help, they'd come, they'd taken me back home. But after only two days away from Bobby, I'd made the decision to go back to him. Despite the way he treated me, I loved my husband and believed things would get better. There was the house to consider, the dogs, the business. After a lifetime of relocation, I just couldn't start over again, so I had overruled my parents' objections and gone back. Things between the folks and me had been strained ever since. Still, there was the hundred-dollar check, payable to me. I wasn't sure why they'd sent it.

I never did score any coke that day—couldn't quite finance my fix with my parents' money. Instead, I went back to the club and began drinking as a way to "take the edge off." With each sip I took, my options seemed to shrink. I couldn't go back to my parents' home. Couldn't stay with Bobby. Couldn't live without drugs and could no longer live with them. Sometime between midafternoon and midnight, I decided to kill myself.

I took a cab home. Sitting in the dark in a drunken stupor, I planned my suicide. I'd climb into the bathtub, fill it up with water, and pull in a couple of plugged-in appliances. A curling iron and a radio would probably work, a hair dryer maybe. My dog Roadie watched me as I cried, then jumped up on the loveseat and nestled beside me, lapping at the tears that ran down my face and neck. This was it, I knew: the bottommost moment of my life.

And that was when Nonna came to me. Dead for twenty years, she entered the room and sat beside me on the loveseat. The darkened room filled with light. She took my hand. In her familiar Italian accent, she began to speak. "Nancy Ann, you're a valuable woman. God loves you and wants to create a miracle for you. Just tell Him you believe in Him and ask Him to do it."

Grandpa was with her. My grandfather had died shortly after I was born, and I couldn't remember ever having seen a picture of him. Still, I knew it was he who stood beside Nonna. The benevolence of their presence lifted the heaviness from both my body and my soul and filled me with a profound calm. Was I having a heart attack? A stroke? "God bless you, Nancy Ann," Nonna said, and the room faded back to darkness.

I fell to my knees and asked God to help me. "I'm not worthy of Your love," I said. "But I need You to come back to me. Please help me find a way out of my suffering." After I finished praying, I got up, went to bed, and fell into a deep, untroubled sleep. The next day, I began my sobriety.

6/27/90

The littlest things fuel the rage I feel inside. I don't know how to stop it from taking me over. Earlier this week I ran out of yellow legal paper, the kind that now feels like a friend I write with daily. When I went to the canteen to buy another pad, they said they were out, too. I borrowed a few sheets of paper from the woman across from me. But now she won't loan me any more, because she's running low, too.

I feel crazier than ever tonight, because getting a fucking piece of paper took me over an hour. I needed to write a response to the letter I received from Cheryl, so finally I stole some paper. I can't believe I stole paper so that I could write to the minister's wife.

I was "getting it" for a minute or so before my recovery was snatched from me. Now it's gone. I barely even remember what recovering feels like. I'm no different than anyone else here anymore; and now I'm a thief again, too. Why is this happening to me? Why am I here?

In the letter I'd received that day, Cheryl Linkletter had written about God's love for me. God always listens, she advised; I should talk to Him like I'd talk to her or anyone else. She said she had a strong feeling the Lord wanted to use me, if I would let him. All I needed to do was tell God how sorry I was about everything I'd done. If it came from my heart, He'd forgive me and help me understand His plan for me.

Fat chance. The fact that I was not going to be "shock probated" as I'd hoped and prayed had finally begun to sink in. A nonviolent first offender can sometimes get a second chance by petitioning the court for an early release date under the presumption that a short-term prison experience has "shocked" her back to good behavior. If the judge grants the petition, the remainder of the sentence is served outside of prison under strict guidelines and a long probationary period. My request had been presented to the judge, who had reviewed it but not acted. Too much time had elapsed since, so the best I could hope for was a transfer to a work-release halfway house.

6/27/90 CONTINUED

Cheryl's wrong. God's not listening to me. God's never listened to me and nobody else has either. I've tried. I've fucking tried for a long, long time, but I'm worn out. I'm just a stupid fucking loser and this is probably as good as my life will ever get.

I hate myself, I hate my husband, and right now, I hate God, too. Satan must own me. He must prevent my prayers from reaching God. I'm a stupid, fucking, flunkie loser who's probably possessed. After this life will come hell, or maybe this is hell already.

God, if you exist, please listen. Help me find some relief. I can't remember what hope feels like anymore.

On June 28, 1990, the day following that last journal entry, I awoke thinking about my grandparents. The rage I'd felt the night before had quieted, replaced now by a sadness bordering on despondency. I could see no further than my life in prison.

The woman for whom I was to proctor a test that morning was late. As I waited for her, my mind wandered back to Cheryl's letter and, once again, to the vision I'd had of Nonna on the night I'd planned to take my life. A twinge of hope began to tickle me and my mind filled with "what ifs."

What if my prison sentence had spared me from further batterings or a slide back into drugs? What if I'd been sent here to learn some important lesson? What if, while I was here, I took a few college classes. "Dropping out" is what I'd always called my failure to finish school, but flunking out is what it really was. Now I might be able to amend that mistake.

Suddenly, it struck me what was happening. For the first time since my arrest the previous fall, I was embracing my incarceration instead of thrashing against it. Having come the long way around to a belief that a Power greater than myself could restore me to sanity, I had just completed the unfinished second step of my recovery and was approaching the third. I was on the verge of turning my will and my life over to the care of God.

I asked to be excused. I walked to the bathroom, locked the door behind me, and dropped to my knees. I recognized the irony of all those other nights when, drunk or stoned, I'd knelt down before toilets in public rest rooms and grimy apartments. "Bowing down before the great white porcelain God," I'd called it. Gratitude swept over me. I didn't have to live that way anymore, even if where I needed to be was in prison.

6/28/90

When I woke up this morning, I never dreamed this would be the most amazing day of my life—the day I would finally work my third step.

I was at my job in the tech school when I just decided I could accept my life. I went to the bathroom, got down on my knees, and talked to God. I asked Him to pick me up and carry me until the time came when I could once again carry myself. I told God I was willing to accept the fact that everything has happened for good reasons which I can't yet understand.

When I finished praying, I got off my knees and returned to the classroom. Before I could even sit down, Mrs. Nicely told me I was wanted in the warden's office and that I was to take my stuff. I felt excited. Had that space in the halfway house opened up?

Trotting across the prison yard, I put on the headphones of my Walkman. An unfamiliar song was playing and something about the singer's voice grabbed my attention. When I realized the song was about grandparents protecting their loved ones, I nearly stumbled off the path. I'd been listening to the Judds' "Guardian Angel."

I've never believed much in the "signs" others claim God sends, but today I know in my heart that God sent me an undeniable message that my prayers had been heard and that my life is a miracle in progress. What happened next defies logic.

When I arrived at the administration building, the warden was waiting outside for me. A "shock probation" order had arrived belatedly from my judge, she said. She broke into a smile. "Nancy, how would you like to go home today?" the warden asked.

So here I am, writing this in my own living room, surrounded by my dogs and their new puppies. Hubble got so excited when he saw me, he peed on the floor and Roadie has been ignoring her pups to stay by my side. But Bobby is off working somewhere. I guess my release from prison isn't important enough for him to come home. For some strange reason, I don't even care.

I face many problems in my future, but at least now I can get back to my recovery. I'll pick up where I left off, go to meetings, work my recovery steps. Something is at the root of my sadness and anxiety, and I know in my heart that it's big. Maybe it's just not time yet to learn what it is. I don't expect my life to magically become better or easier overnight, but today I believe I can make it through anything with God's help.

Believing my life would not "magically become better" proved to be an accurate assessment. The battles between Bobby and me resumed. Although my craving for drugs had subsided, food had taken over once again as my closest friend. By the time I reached my fourth recovery anniversary, my weight had peaked at an all-time high of 275 pounds.

My panic attacks, triggered by my fear of confinement, continued as the greatest threat to my progress. Riding in a car was possible only if I was the driver and only if my window was rolled down. Even in winter, snow and cold wind rode with me inside the car. Entering an elevator was out of the question, as was an appointment with a dentist or any other professional who might put me in a room alone and make me submit to an examination.

My husband eventually figured out that restraining me terrified me more than pushing, hitting, and yelling. Holding me down against my will became his new power tool. No, things certainly did not become better at all overnight.

During the summer of 1993, Bobby and I traveled back to Norwich for a family reunion. It was a joy to reconnect with aunts, uncles, and cousins I hadn't seen in years, but the return trip to Louisville was hellish. Having boarded the plane for the final leg of our flight home, I was seized with sudden anxiety. I ran back up the aisle and off the plane. For five minutes or so, I experienced a panic so intense, I thought it would kill me. As two flight attendants hovered over me, reminding me that the pilot was ready for takeoff, I prayed as hard as I had the night before I'd put down the drugs and the day I'd been released from prison. This time I asked for nothing specific, only for God to give me what I needed, and to do it in a way which might help me begin to understand what those needs were. I stood, reboarded, and flew home.

By the following summer, I had lost a hundred pounds and faced the fact that my marriage was going to kill me if things didn't change. I filled out college applications and financial aid forms, and soon was fighting a new terror: telling Bobby about the full tuition scholarship I'd won as a result of an essay I had written. Regardless of his reaction, I had made the decision to resign from my position as his primary grunt and go back to college. It was non-negotiable.

"You never finish anything you start," Bobby reminded me. "Face it. You're a failure and you're going to fail at this thing, too." But by the end of my third semester, I'd earned As on every single assignment, even in math. Rather than inhibiting my progress, my husband's hurtful prediction became my greatest motivator. The panic attacks continued, but so did I.

So at the moment when my Intro to Film professor announced that we would, that day, be viewing and evaluating MGM's classic film *The Wizard of Oz*, my throat began closing up and the weight upon my chest made it difficult to breathe, but I remained seated anyway. *God, please don't let it be the monkeys,* I found myself pleading. *Please help me understand what's going on here, why I'm so terrified. . . .*

And suddenly, unexpectedly, God answered my plea. The locked door of that ancient chamber deep within my chest exploded open, the demons escaped from the shadows, and I finally understood. As I watched the monkeys carry Dorothy off to the witch's castle, I remembered.

Back in Allentown—the man who was our neighbor . . . *he* was the one I'd looked down upon from above the dentist's chair, back in prison. *He* was the swooping predator, the jailer, the cannibal. And oh, my God, the little girls whose innocence he'd eaten were my friend Holly and me. For a few dizzying moments, I was six again:

Daddy, help me! The monkeys are here again!

The man who lives next door to Holly gave us Hershey bars and said we should never tell the secret. If we tell, he says, the witch lady will set our house on fire and send the flying monkeys to snatch you and Mommy away. I didn't tell, Daddy! Why do the monkeys keep coming? The man says we're beautiful. He says he loves us and will protect us from the witch and the monkeys as long as we never tell the secret.

Make them go away, Daddy—the monkeys, and the fires, and the cannibals. Please, Daddy. Help me find a way to make them go away for good.

Postscript: February 2002

The only promise my twelve-step fellowship makes is that if I apply the principles of recovery to my life, I will continue experiencing freedom from active addiction. Anything beyond that freedom must be earned. For the past thirteen years, I have worked hard to create a better life for myself and the gifts resulting from those efforts have been plentiful.

Soon after regaining the missing pieces from my past, I left that former marriage and my old home—the one I'd felt too afraid to let go of. A few years later, an old and platonic friendship ignited unexpectedly into love. John and I live atop a wooded hill with the family we've gathered: our three canine boys, Boney, Buster, and Buddy; our horse, Slowpoke; and a pond full of goldfish and koi. Over time, my ex-husband and I have put our shared past peacefully to rest and my relationship with my parents has healed and grown.

An addict who wishes to hold true to the principles of her recovery must conquer her shame and regret over the past and, as much as possible, share her experiences with others. I try to carry a message of hope wherever I go because I know through experience that hope is a miracle that can become contagious.

Recently, I rented and watched a video of *The Wizard of Oz*. I had planned the exercise as a confrontation of my old fears, but I was in for a surprise. The characters who had once terrified me now seemed secondary, even irrelevant. What I followed now was the story of a lost little girl who traveled a strange and spooky landscape in search of courage, wisdom, and love—a girl who, guided by the compass of her inner strength, finally made her way back home.

Twelve-step recovery remains paramount in Nancy Birkla's life; she attends meetings faithfully and belongs to a "step study" group. In the spring of 2001, Birkla graduated from Jefferson Community College with an associate of science degree in human services, having maintained a 4.0 grade point average. Since then, she has worked as a coordinator for an Indiana agency that provides life-skills counseling, housing, and job opportunities to adults with developmental disabilities. Currently, she is employed as a tutor of college English for students with disabilities and international students for whom English is a second language.

Birkla states: "One day I figured out a dying little girl lived inside of me, so I threw her a lifeline in the form of paper and pen. With love, mutual respect, and help from God, we finally are able to call each other 'friend.' The world seems more beautiful because of it."

HELL, AND HOW
I GOT HERE

||||||||||||||||||||

BRENDA MEDINA

Born: 1975
Conviction: Homicide
Sentence: 25 years without parole
Entered prison: 1993
Status: Incarcerated

1. MY MOTHER'S SECRET

The year I was six, my older brother David decided to play a prank on two of my sisters and me. Mimi was fifteen at the time and Jeanette was twelve; we three shared a bedroom. In the middle of the night, David burst into our room, startling us from our sleep. He was shouting and waving a butcher knife. His face was covered in blood. When our screaming stopped and we realized that David's blood had come from the ketchup bottle, Jeanette and I began to laugh. But Mimi didn't find it funny. For months after, she refused to talk to David and would wake from sleep screaming and drenched in sweat.

Ours was a full house: two parents, nine kids. Nine years my senior, Mimi had assigned herself the role of caretaker for Jeanette and me. She looked out for our safety, scolded us whenever she felt we needed it, and supervised our regular Friday night Monopoly games. I loved Monopoly night with my sisters. We'd play long past our bedtime, sliding the board under the bed and faking sleep whenever we heard footsteps. When the coast was clear again, we'd return to the game. The danger of discovery was part of the fun.

Mimi, Jeanette, and I were playing Monopoly the night I discovered my mother's terrible secret. I rolled the dice and moved my token, counting incorrectly and landing on New York when I should have been on Chance. On an ordinary night, my sisters would have pounced on the error, but that night, neither even noticed. It was hard to concentrate because of the screaming.

Mimi left the Monopoly game, locked the door, and turned up the stereo. But even at maximum volume, Michael Jackson's *Wanna be starting something, wanna be starting something* . . . got drowned out by the trouble in the living room. I made a run for the door to see *why* Mom and Dad were screaming, but both my sisters grabbed me and held me back.

The voices escalated. There were slamming noises. Then we heard a third voice in the living room—our older sister Madeline. She was shouting at Mom. Glass shattered. There was a long and tortured scream. Then, silence.

Without saying a word, Mimi, Jeanette, and I rose together from the bed and approached the door. In the hallway, we saw David, standing in front of his bedroom in wrinkled pajamas, looking sleepy and scared. I clasped my sisters' hands and walked between them, David following behind.

At the entrance to the living room, Jeanette let go but Mimi tightened her grip on my hand. It took me a minute to register just *what* I was seeing. Madeline stood above our parents, her hands over her mouth. Daddy was bent over Mom, who was on the floor, thrashing like a fish out of water.

Yanking free from Mimi's hold, I moved toward my parents. I was just about to reach them when I felt a stabbing pain. I looked down at the broken glass around my bare feet. When I picked up my left foot, I saw the jagged piece lodged in my big toe and pulled it out. Wiping the blood with my hand, I looked back at my mother.

"Put the spoon in her mouth so she won't swallow her tongue!" Daddy shouted. Swallow her tongue? Why would Mom swallow her tongue? Was this even possible? *"Se va mori?"* Jeanette kept shouting. *"Se va mori?"* Her question became a terrifying chant.

"Of course she's not gonna die, stupid!" I screamed. "Shut up! Shut up!"

Mimi had been standing as still as Mom's statue of the Virgin Mary, but now she approached Daddy. In a shaky voice, she asked, "Why isn't the ambulance here yet? You called for an ambulance, right?"

Daddy shook his head.

"Por que?" Mimi cried. "If no one's called for an ambulance, then *I* will!"

"Mommy doesn't need an ambulance," Madeline said. Her eyes stayed fixed on our writhing mother. "If you want to help her, call a priest."

"Dios mio!" Jeanette started up again. "Mommy's dying!"

"No, she's *not*!" I yelled, my fists pounding against her. Jeanette didn't strike back or push me away. She just stood there, taking whatever blows I gave her. When I was too tired to deliver any more, I fell on top of her and sobbed.

I'm not sure how much time had gone by when Jeanette whispered, "Look!" Mom was sitting up, Daddy kneeling behind her to make sure she didn't fall back and hurt herself. Mimi knelt beside her, caressing her cheek.

Mom didn't look like herself. She was panting, staring hard at something on the wall: the black velvet painting she loved as much as I hated. The ancient Indian warrior in the portrait wore the big-feathered hat and fearless look of a tribal chief. Mom often said the Indian in that painting would protect our family from bad spirits. But whenever I looked at his cold, merciless stare, I wondered who would protect us from *him*. On that strange night, Mom seemed mesmerized by her Indian.

"Come on," Madeline said, lifting me off the floor. *"Vamonos."* I held tight to her neck and wrapped my legs around her waist. Jeanette and Mimi followed us back to the bedroom. "Was she really going to eat her tongue?" I whispered to Madeline as she tucked me in. She kissed my forehead and told me to go to sleep. When she went to leave, Mimi was waiting at the doorway.

In whispered tones, Mimi grilled Madeline about what had happened. Reluctant at first to answer her, Madeline suddenly sighed. "All right. I guess you're old enough to know."

They stepped outside, closing the door halfway. Jeanette and I snuck out of bed and inched toward them on hands and knees. I was closest to the door. Behind me, Jeanette kept tugging my nightgown and asking me what I heard. I turned back, raised my finger to my lips, and whispered, "Shhh!"

What Madeline was telling Mimi was unimaginable. Something controlled Mom, she said—made her talk in a strange voice, forced her to scream, throw things. It made her want to take her own life.

I couldn't believe my ears. My whole life I'd been told I was safe— that there were no such things as monsters. Now, suddenly, I was hearing that a monster, an evil force or vague "something," entered my mother's body and took her over. It didn't seem real, and yet, if it wasn't, what had I witnessed?

That night was the first time of many that I observed my mother's being overtaken by the mysterious "something." Each episode seemed weirder and scarier than the last. But if, at times, Mom appeared possessed by bad spirits, she was also a firm believer in the Father, the Son, and the Holy Ghost—and the Holy Trinity's ability to deliver her family to salvation. Mom often invited her gray-haired aunts and cousins to our home for prayer sessions, during which the women worked their way through a communal rosary. To safeguard against evil, Mom lit candles at the feet of the saints whose statues populated our house. And just in case flame and candle wax failed, Mom also consulted Aunt Rita, who knew the the chants and potions of Santeria.

In the wake of our family troubles, my sister Marizol rejected Catholicism and converted to the Pentecostal religion. Marizol's new church friends began to drop by to visit Mom. Whenever Mari would bring the church people home, they'd gather in the living room, Bibles in hand, and form a circle around my afflicted mother. That was my cue to grab my dog, Toby, and head for my room. I wanted no part of this holy voodoo. For hours, I'd sit in my room, clutching Toby and trying not to listen. Sometimes Mom would laugh louder than their prayers. At other times, she'd shriek. "Come on, Toby," I'd say, whenever the screaming started. The two of us would hide under my bed.

When I was old enough to go to school, my mother insisted that the family break from tradition and enroll me at Saint Margaret's, the Catholic school just down the street. Dad opposed the idea on the grounds that parochial school charged tuition and public school was free. But public school had turned my older siblings into troublemakers, Mom argued; they were always in the principal's office for something or another. It might be too late for them, but there was still time to save me. As usual, it was Mom who got her way.

Each morning, she'd kneel before me, buckle my black patent leather Mary Janes, and smooth the wrinkles out of my blue-and-gray-plaid uniform. Once I passed inspection, I was off to Ms. Foster's first grade.

Because Saint Margaret's was on the corner of our street, I usually walked to school by myself, dragging my feet all the way. Mom would stand out on the upstairs porch and watch me. I'd look back at her and wave before I entered the two-story white building and Mom would wave back. At the end of the day, she'd be stationed on the porch again as I exited school. I'd look at her and wait for her nod. Once she gave it, I knew it was okay to start home.

I hated Saint Margaret's. Most of my classmates were white kids from wealthy families and I was the skinny little Puerto Rican girl whose family was poor. The others were dropped off each morning in their expensive new shoes, their crisp white button-down shirts to match our plaid uniforms. I'd show up in a Kmart shirt with frayed cuffs and my sister's hand-me-down Mary Janes. "Nice shoes, Brenda," snobby Monica Bradley noted once, running past me at recess with her giggly friends. Everyone in my class knew as well as I that I didn't belong at Saint Margaret's—that I was the odd girl out.

One winter school morning, Mom didn't go out on the porch to send me off. Instead, she followed me down the stairs to the front hallway, put her own coat on, and picked at the lint on mine. Waving away my gripes, she wrapped my black scarf around my neck like a tourniquet and shoved my mittens onto my hands. When I'd been bundled to her satisfaction, she shouted back upstairs for Marizol to *hurry up, hurry up*! When Mari came down, the three of us trudged toward Saint Margaret's. "I'm in first grade," I protested. "I can walk to school by myself."

"Mommy's got an appointment with Father Robert," Marizol explained. "I have to translate." She flashed me her big, pretty smile. "Better confess if you did something bad and I'll try to help you."

Father Robert was the head priest at Saint Margaret's—a tall, dark-skinned man with Brillo-pad hair. Before that morning, he'd been my ally, reassuring my parents at open houses and school plays that I was a nice, quiet girl. So why did he suddenly want to talk to Mom? Had Father Robert somehow found out about my last confession? I'd knelt in the booth and listed all the sinful things I'd done the week before: fibbing, talking back, popping off the head of Jeanette's Barbie doll and hiding it at the bottom of her toy box. "Four Our Fathers and four Hail Marys," he'd said. I'd thought that penance too harsh and cut the numbers in half. Could Father Robert have somehow found out?

The only other thing I could think of was the Monica Bradley incident. The Friday before, Monica had called my friend Lynnette "Miss Piggy" and made her cry. Later that day, as Monica made her way to the easel with a cup of yellow paint, I'd stuck my leg into the aisle and tripped her. She'd landed face down on the floor, her uniform soaked in paint. Wearing my most innocent face, I'd convinced Ms. Foster that it had been an accident. Had Monica *un*convinced her? Was that why we were on our way to Father Robert's office?

We entered the school and climbed the stairs to the second floor. At the top, Ms. Foster gave my mother and sister a pleasant smile and shooed me into her classroom, business as usual. I looked back over my shoulder, watching Mom and Marizol disappear down the hall. I slumped to the coat area, removed my winter gear, stored my lunch box, and took my seat. We pledged allegiance, said morning prayers, did morning drills. I couldn't concentrate. What was going on in Father Robert's office? What had I done?

Midway through the morning, a horrifying thought crossed my mind. What if the meeting wasn't about me at all? What if the school had found out about my mother? Had someone tipped them off that Mom wasn't normal—that a "something" sometimes took her over and turned her into someone else? Maybe they even knew about *La Negra*. Had Father Robert summoned my religious mom to confront her about her demon doll?

Mom had a collection of pretty porcelain dolls, but *La Negra,* an ugly old rag doll, was her favorite. *La Negra* had been in Mom's collection forever. Her skin was charcoal gray. Her eyes were Xs stitched in white thread, her mouth a thin, single strand of red yarn. She wore a green flowered dress and matching bandanna. I hated that doll, not just because it was ugly and scary-looking, but also because I was jealous. At times, my mother seemed to love *La Negra* more than she loved me.

Mom knew I was terrified of *La Negra,* so sometimes when I was bad, she'd use the doll to punish me. One time I made Mom angry for a reason I cannot today recall. What I *do* remember is her round cheeks turning the color of fire as she screamed in my face, "Stay right here! I'll teach *you*!" A minute later she was back with her precious *La Negra*. She propped the doll in the corner of the utility closet, then grabbed me by the wrist and shoved me inside there, too. "No, Mommy! No!" I begged, screaming and kicking. It did no good. The door was slammed and locked. I sat in the pitch black in the presence of my worst nightmare, my mother's demon doll. I don't know how long I was in there before I heard the door handles turn and could squint past my mother's dark and blurry shadow to the light of day behind her.

"Brenda? Are you all right?" Ms. Foster asked. I nodded and forced a smile, hoping to deflect hers and the class's attention. All day long, I fought back tears and nausea, thinking about the possibility that they'd discovered the truth about our family, my mom's fits, my babyish fear of *La Negra*. The last thing I needed was for them to know who I really was. I had enough trouble fitting in at Saint Margaret's.

By the time the 3:00 P.M. dismissal bell sounded, I thought my head would explode. Any other day, I'd have run down the stairs and out to escape that place as fast as possible. But not this day. Not knowing what Mom had been told, I had no idea what to expect and I was afraid to go home.

Mom was up on the porch as usual. She nodded permission. I moved slowly toward her. When I got inside, Mom told me to change out of my uniform and start my homework, the same as usual. She went about her business, making no mention of her meeting with Father Robert. Marizol wasn't around, so I couldn't ask her. The big meeting remained a mystery until Daddy got home from work.

Mom had made me go to bed early, so I was already snuggled in bed with Flicker, my ivory-colored glowworm, whose face turned green when you clicked on the nightlight inside his head. If *La Negra* was the thing in our house I most hated, Flicker was the thing I most loved—a beacon against the dark. I heard Daddy's footsteps, his voice, the squeak of his and Mom's bedroom door. At first I couldn't make out what their muffled voices were saying. But a few minutes later, the shouting made their conversation loud and clear.

"Delia, we just don't *have* that kind of money!" Daddy yelled.

"Hector, *por favor, calma te.*"

But Daddy didn't seem interested in calming down. "I never wanted her to go to that school in the first place! Public school's good enough for all the other kids. Why does this one have to go to a damn Catholic school?"

It was suddenly clear to me what Mom's meeting with Father Robert had been about. This wasn't the first time Mom and Dad had had this argument. My parents were late, again, with my tuition.

"Why does she have to go there, Hector? Because we have to save her, that's why. Keep the devil away from her." My mother—who sometimes shrieked and laughed like the devil himself, who clutched to her breast the evil *La Negra* and believed in the power of Santeria and an Indian warrior painted on black velvet—was hell-bent on the idea that Jesus Christ would rescue her youngest daughter's soul.

"I don't *care* if he's giving us more time to pay!" Daddy screamed. "I want her *out* of there!"

"And I want her in!"

Whatever objections Daddy raised, Mom trumped them, her Spanish revving to a thousand words a minute. Tightening my grip on Flicker, I pushed my face into my pillow. The last words I heard Daddy say were, "*Esta bien,* Delia. Okay, okay. We'll find a way to get the money."

When the house was quiet, I pulled back the covers and got out of bed. Flicker and I walked to the window. I looked toward Saint Margaret's, staring at the tip of the icy steeple, the only part of the school visible above the rooftops. Standing there, I cursed my Catholic school, and cursed my mother, too, who had committed herself to locking me up each day in that holy, hellish place.

One afternoon I was on the front porch with Mom. She was seated on the chair facing the woods across from our house. Mom claimed that staring at the moving trees calmed her nerves. "Will you brush my hair?" I asked her.

She looked at me, surprised, then nodded and smiled. Mom was her normal self that day; everything was fine. I knelt between her legs, enjoying the rhythmic caress of her hands, the brush. I began singing the new song Mimi had taught me. "*I'm in love with a big blue frog—*"

From the sky came a loud crack of thunder.

I stopped singing. I *couldn't* sing. Couldn't breathe. . . .

When I opened my eyes again, my throat hurt. Mom's face was over mine and she was glaring at me with an expression both strange and familiar. Daddy stood behind her, struggling to pry her fingers from my neck.

When Dad got Mom away from me, Madeline grabbed me in her arms and rushed me off the porch. It was over so quickly, I had no idea what had just occurred. Later, Daddy hugged me and promised he'd always keep me safe.

Following the porch incident, my father acted as if everything was still the same, but he began watching me closely whenever Mom was near me. He never would say much about that strange day, or about Mom's situation. I remember asking him once if she was crazy. He shook his head and looked away. Sometimes at night when my father thought he was alone, I could hear him praying, pleading with God to keep us safe from evil. Those overheard prayers told me what Dad believed: that a dark force sometimes took possession of his wife, the mother of his children.

For years, I struggled with the question of what was *really* wrong with Mom. Had she been taken over by an evil spirit? Was she crazy? I wanted to believe that *nothing* was wrong with her—that she was as normal as anyone's mom. Unfortunately, that wasn't one of my choices.

The older I got, the more obvious it became to me that something was wrong with my mother's head, not her soul, but I was a minority of one. I could never understand why Marizol had brought her preacher home instead of a shrink—why everyone in my family but me was on board with the "evil spirit" thing. That was one boat I refused to step foot on. I don't know why. Maybe I was afraid to consider the possibility that monsters *can* exist—that uncontrollable "somethings" can enter you and take you over.

2. FAMILY VALUES

Addiction comes in many forms: drugs, dice, the bottle, the mall. Mine came in the form of a dangerous boy named Manny. From the time I was fourteen until I landed in prison three years later, Manny ran through my veins.

I met him one summer day while attending Adult Ed. I had hated Kennedy High School—not because I wasn't smart enough to do the work, but because the cheerleaders, the punk rockers, and even the "pocket protector" crowd heightened the feeling that always followed me—that I was the girl who didn't belong. Adult Ed was the compromise my parents and I had reached. To my surprise, it was where I found my place.

"Awright already, you look good enough. Let's go eat." Leaning against the bulletin board, fixing my lipstick, I looked up and saw "my boys" coming toward me—Bobby, Stitch, and Green Eyes. I was the only female in this little Adult Ed crew, which was the way I liked it. My older sisters were always telling sob stories about how this girlfriend had stabbed her in the back, how that one had "stolen" a boy she liked or bought an outfit she was saving up to buy. Girls competed, but guys were your buddies—which was why I preferred to hang with Green Eyes, Bobby, and Stitch.

But our group was about friendship, not romance. Oh, Bobby flirted with me and I flirted back. I couldn't help myself. With his caramel skin and dark hair, he was easy on the eyes. But I *knew* Bobby—his pattern of moving on to his next conquest after he'd gotten the girl into bed. Boys were more trustworthy than girls, but only if sex wasn't in the picture. I flirted with Bobby and the others—took their teasing and teased them back—but I wouldn't date them.

The four of us were at the food cart, waiting for our orders and laughing at a front-page *Weekly World News* story: "Woman Eats Carrots During Pregnancy, Gives Birth to Rabbit-Boy." When Green Eyes called to someone, I looked up from the paper. That was the first time I saw him.

He was wearing white jeans and a Tommy Hilfiger shirt that fit his powerful physique just right. Leaning his weight on a carved wooden cane, he approached with a swaggering limp—and an air of mystery.

"What's up?" Stitch said. "I didn't know you were coming here today." The mystery man and Stitch exchanged a strange handshake. He and Green Eyes, too. Bobby got a regular slap of the hand.

I stood by the pay phones a few feet away, sipping on my Pepsi and taking quick glimpses. Olive skin, sexy hazel eyes: it was hard *not* to look. The guys huddled together, talking in low voices and studying something that circulated among them. "You're stupid, Bobby," the new guy said. "If I had a girl like that, I'd make something happen." He turned to me and smiled. "You look *good* in these."

Blood rushed to my face as it dawned on me *what* was circulating: the pictures of me Bobby had snatched from my purse earlier as a joke. "Hey, Bren," Stitch said. "Come over here and meet my brother, Manny."

"Since when did *you* get a brother?" I said. Stitch just smiled.

Manny's eyes wandered up my body to my face. "Hope you don't mind me looking at your pictures," he said. I stared back, stone-faced. Laughing, he turned back to Bobby. "Got your hands full with this one, man. She's got a major attitude."

" 'This one' has a name," I informed him. "And 'this one's' leaving."

I didn't give Manny another thought until a few weeks later, when I ran into him at Louie's Pizzeria. He walked toward me as soon as he spotted me. "Hello, again," he said. "Hey, I'm sorry if I upset you that day at school."

I shrugged, pointed to his cane. "What happened to your leg?" I said.

"Someone shot me."

"Yeah? Who?"

He looked down, scuffed his shoe. "Just some guy. So, you're good friends with my brothers, huh?"

"Am I? Who are your brothers?"

"Green Eyes and Stitch."

I informed him that Green Eyes didn't have any brothers in Connecticut and Stitch didn't have any at all.

"Well, let's just say we're in a fraternity together," he said, laughing. "Except we don't go to college."

"Is that why you give each other that stupid handshake?"

The smile dropped off his face. "That handshake's sacred," he said.

We chatted for a few minutes more and I told him I had to go. Halfway to the door, he called to me. "What's the story, Brenda? Don't I get the digits?"

"Sure," I said. "My number's 1–800–YOU WISH."

Hey, I grew up in the neighborhood, not on Sesame Street. I *knew* what gangs were: their secret handshakes and special colors. I'd been warned to stay away from roughnecks, and done it. But meeting Manny and hearing this talk about my friends' mysterious "brotherhood" aroused my curiosity. I began questioning Stitch and Green Eyes at school but got answers that were annoyingly vague. About their "fraternity brother," Manny, they volunteered next to nothing.

One day, Bobby pulled me aside. "Why you keep asking those guys about Manny?" he said. "Leave it alone, Bren. That guy's no good for you."

I gave him a friendly poke. "And who *would* be good for me? You?"

"It's not like that. Manny's trouble. He runs with a gang." It was the first time any of my friends had used the word.

Bobby's warning excited me as much as it scared me, partly because of my mother. Gangs had been one of her chief excuses for keeping me under "house arrest" throughout my childhood. "Those hoods out there would love to get their hands on an innocent girl like you. You stay here in the house." But when I reached high school age, I declared myself liberated. I began to go where I wanted, when I wanted to. And if Mom objected, so much the better. Control of my own life was a fight I intended to win.

I didn't think of Manny as a battlefront at first. I was focused more on his sexy laugh, his "outlaw" aura. Manny was like a good suspense book: after a few pages, you're hooked. You need to know more, your mother be damned.

My fifteenth birthday was a rough one, sabotaged by my bully of a brother, David. Earlier that day, Madeline had stopped by with a treat for me, two Boston cream doughnuts, my favorite. Before I could eat them, David discovered them on my bedroom dresser. "Gimme one of these, you spoiled brat," he ordered. I didn't like him demanding instead of asking and said no. To retaliate, he squeezed a doughnut in each fist and smeared the mess across my dresser. "Happy birthday, *Brendita*," he said.

Hostility was common at our house, but David was small change next to Mom, Queen of the Bullies. My sisters had left home, one by one, to escape her iron-fisted control. What confused me was why most had run straight into the arms of controlling, iron-fisted men. It was going to be different for me.

I was still sulking about the ruined doughnuts when my friend Maritza called to wish me happy birthday. Maritza and I had drifted apart, so I was touched that she'd remembered. We made plans to go out that night. "I want you home by midnight," my mother warned. I informed her that what she wanted and what I wanted might be two different things.

Maritza and I played arcade games at Crazy Eight, then caught a late movie. We were heading up Willow Street when someone called Maritza's name. A group of guys was across the street, checking us out. "Oh, shit!" Maritza said. "My boyfriend's over there. He's gonna be pissed I'm out this late."

When we crossed the street, Jose grabbed Maritza's arm and took her aside for a little talk. "I knew you'd come to me," someone said. It was Manny.

Excited and a little scared, I tried for a look of indifference. "Is that what you think I'm doing?"

"I *know* that's what you're doing. I'm just not sure if *you* know it yet. Come on up, sit with me." He pointed to the stairs of the building in back of us. "It's okay. No one's gonna shoot at you. Me and my uncle live here."

Manny pulled the beer he was drinking from the bag and spread the paper on the step so I could sit. He sat down beside me. "Sip?" he asked. I shook my head. I looked over at Maritza and Jose, whose argument had turned to kissing. "Maritza's a good girl," Manny said. "I'm glad my brother has her."

The "brother" thing: I'd given up trying to pry information out of Stitch and Green Eyes, but if Manny was going to give me an opening, I'd take it. "So what's *that* about?" I asked, pointing to his necklace.

He fingered the beads. "It's what we wear. They represent our family." They looked like the beads I'd strung from a kit when I was a little girl.

"Stitch and Green Eyes wear those same white and mustard colors."

He paused, took a sip of his beer. "We all do," he said.

"Who's 'we'?"

"The Unidad. Don't ask me anything more, okay? That's all I can say because you're not one of us."

There it was again: that same old "left out" feeling of mine. "Okay," I said, snippily. "What *can* we talk about then?"

He was born in New York City, he said, and had moved to Connecticut when he was ten. "My parents died together in a car accident, so my uncle and grandmother came and got me. I was okay with it, though. It's not like they were *good* parents. My little brother lives up the street with my grandma. She couldn't take us both in, so I ended up here. But it's okay. My uncle lets me do whatever I want."

Manny described one painful setback after another, confiding in me like no one ever had before. I was both overwhelmed and flattered. "You don't even know me," I said. "Why have you told me all this?"

"Because I'm safe with you. I can see it in your eyes." He took my hand in his and placed it against his chest. "And you're safe here," he whispered. Beneath my palm, I felt his strong, rhythmic heartbeat.

Manny was nothing like Gabriel, the only other boy I had slept with. After Manny and I made love, he stayed. Each encounter drew us closer and closer together. I told myself Manny was exactly what I was looking for.

From the start, my mother distrusted Manny, but she didn't forbid me to see him until the afternoon her nosy old aunt Maria stopped by to stir up trouble. Manny was visiting that afternoon, too. He and I were talking out on the porch when Aunt Maria's scowling horse face appeared at the screen door. She inspected Manny from top to bottom and disappeared back inside.

"Go home, Manny," my mother ordered a few minutes later. "I don't want you coming around here anymore." Her old hag of an auntie cracked a victory smile.

Mom started screaming as soon as Manny had gone. "From now on, you stay away from that hooligan! Maria says he's in a gang."

"He is not!" I shouted back.

"I saw him myself," Aunt Maria butted in. "Hanging out with all the other roughnecks at the corner of Baldwin Street, wearing certain colors. You young kids assume a woman like me wouldn't know what it means. But I do!"

"You don't know anything," I said, inching closer to her face. "Except how to make people miserable!"

It happened so quickly, I didn't see it coming: the burning slap across my face. I put my hand to my cheek, glaring back at Mom and wishing I was my brother. Whenever Mom hit David, he hit her back. But no matter how hard or how often my mother struck me, I could never bring myself to raise a hand to her. Instead, I stared back, dry-eyed and defiant. Back in my room, I took out my anger on the wall that stood in the way of my fist. Mom may have taken round one, but I was going to win the fight. Manny would be my knockout punch.

I met him secretly each afternoon at Washington Park and faced the daily interrogation as soon as I got home. "You're late. Where have you been?" At Lily's house, I'd tell her. At the pizzeria with Lily. Lily and I were studying at the library. "You always hated the library," Mom would note. "Now we can't get you out of that damn building."

"Do you want me to get good grades or not? Make up your mind."

When Mom couldn't catch me red-handed, she resorted to threats. "If I catch you with that boy, I'm shipping you down to Florida to live with your aunt," she told me one afternoon. "And not for a nice little visit either. You'll stay there until you're eighteen." I didn't scare easily, but Mom got to me that time. Three years in exile with lonely old Aunt Luz would be like a death sentence. I could no longer risk my secret meetings with Manny.

Dressed in my usual disguise—baggy black jeans, oversized leather coat, floppy hat—I set out to meet Manny the next afternoon. I entered Washington Park through the gate at the far end of the playground, headed toward the benches, and took a seat at our usual spot. A minute later, he was there.

"Don't do this to me, Bren," he whispered. He reached out and took my hand, placed it against his heart.

"Manny, I have no choice. If I don't, she'll ship me off to—"

He put his finger to my lips. "Go home," he said. "Don't worry. I'm gonna take care of everything." He rose from the bench, kissed my forehead, and ran off down the path.

I'll take care of everything: what had he meant? I imagined him running up the stairs of our building, bursting into the apartment, putting a gun to my mother's head. I shook off the thought. Gang or no gang, Manny wasn't like that. For a minute there, I'd been thinking like Aunt Maria.

Still, I knew the company Manny kept. By then, I'd met many of his "brothers" at the meeting place on Baldwin Street. The Unidad had taken over an abandoned building and made it their hangout and place of business. It was pretty pathetic: peeling paint, boarded-up windows, no electricity. The inside was even worse, with its moldy smell, its furniture that looked like it belonged in the landfill. Manny and his brothers sold drugs from a downstairs window covered with a sheet of plastic. Their "patients," as they liked to call the addicts who bought from them, would come to the window to exchange money for "medicine."

The first time I went to the building, it was swarming with people of all ages, a few as old as my father. I'd never been in a hangout like this before—or anything like it. I felt a little wild, being at this place and with these guys I knew my mother would hate.

There were girls at the house, too—something I hadn't expected. Three of them stood aside, whispering to each other and staring me down. Then they approached, smiling and greeting Manny like I wasn't there, exchanging the handshake. "You have sisters, too?" I whispered after they left.

"Yeah. But that's all they are, Bren. My *sisters.*"

All afternoon, people came and went, sharing hugs and stories, laughter and beer. I felt both repulsed by and drawn to this filthy, friendly place.

Near the end of my visit, a group of guys came down the stairs, heading for the door. Each stopped to give Manny the handshake and the greeting, *Siembre Unidos!* When the last guy approached, I was shocked to see it was my brother, David, wearing the white and mustard yellow beads. He extended his hand to Manny and muttered the greeting. Then he turned to me. "Does Mommy know you're here?"

"Does she know *you're* here?" I said.

Suddenly, he looked panicky. "You won't tell on me. Will you?"

It was the perfect opportunity to pay David back for a thousand injustices. But I didn't enjoy seeing people squirm the way he did. "No, I won't tell her," I said. He nodded and walked away without another word.

"Why didn't you tell me David was part of the Unidad?" I asked Manny.

"Because it's my duty to keep a brother's secrets." I rolled my eyes. "I don't expect you to understand," he said. "You're not one of us."

After my breakup with Manny at Washington Park, I didn't hear from him for days. Stitch and Green Eyes said they hadn't heard from him either, but I didn't know whether to believe them or not. Secrecy was a Unidad specialty. One morning at school, I was complaining to Green Eyes and Lily. "My parents claim they made us break up because they love me. What do *those two* know about love? I hate them!"

Lily stood silent, her dark eyes glistening, her big, pretty smile turned down in a frown. "I know you love Manny, Brenda, but your parents have a point. They're scared for you. I'm scared for you, too, Bren. I know what gangs are all about."

"We're *not* a gang!" Green Eyes protested. I shut him up with a dirty look. Lily's older brother, Kevin, had run with a gang called the Latin Dreamers. Then he'd turned his life around. He was working a job he liked, making plans to go back to school. When he tried to leave the gang, his fellow Dreamers took him to an alley and shot him in the head.

"You don't have to worry about me," I assured Lily. "And neither do my parents. I know what Manny's in, but I also know *him*. He's good inside."

"I just hope he never hurts you," Lily said. Her smile reappeared. "Because if he does, he'll have to answer to me."

When school was over that day, I went straight home, dropped my books on the couch, and headed for my room. All I wanted to do was blast my music and be alone. "Brenda, is that you?" my mother called.

"Can you come in the living room, please?" I recognized her sweet, we-have-company voice. The last thing I wanted to do was to socialize.

"Later," I said.

"Brenda, you get in here *now* and don't make me ask you again!"

At the entrance to the living room, I stopped dead in my tracks. There, on the couch by the window, sat Manny.

He rose slowly, casually, and walked toward me, his hand extended in greeting. I looked at Mom. Her eyes moved from me to Manny. She gave him a little smile and left the room without a word.

At the private meeting Manny had arranged with my mother, he had told her I meant more to him than his group of friends did. He'd given them up, he said. Against all odds, my suspicious mother had believed him. He and I could see each other again, she had declared. She told Manny not to worry about my dad—she'd talk to him and make everything okay. True to his word, Manny had taken care of everything—had charmed my mother into believing he'd met her terms. Unaware that she'd just lost the first battle, Mom incorrectly assumed she had won the war.

As I suspected, Manny had not forsaken the Unidad. Quite the opposite. Whenever we arrived back at my house, he would take off his beads, kiss them, and slip them in his pocket before putting on the false halo he wore for my mother. I didn't really care that he'd lied. All I cared about was the fact that we could now be together, out in the open. With Manny, I had found my place in the world.

I was, of course, in denial. Having vowed I would never allow a man to run my life as my sisters had, I ignored the evidence that I was following in their footsteps. I ignored, too, the fact that Manny and Mom were not that different from each other. Both wanted to be in charge of things—me in particular. Both assumed I could be molded to their specifications.

"You should start hanging out with more girls," Manny informed me. "If you're around guys all the time, people will think you're easy." I disagreed but dropped some of my male friends.

Manny appointed himself my fashion adviser, too. "What's this?" he asked one night. We were at my sister's apartment, baby-sitting for my niece and nephew, and I was laying out my clothes for school the next morning because I was sleeping over.

"It's what I'm wearing tomorrow. Why?"

He picked up my black miniskirt and handed it to me. "Put it on."

"Why?"

"Because I wanna see how it looks on you."

"You'll see tomorrow."

"Don't fuck with me, Brenda. Put it on!"

"Fine!" Usually I changed in front of Manny, but this time I snatched the skirt from his hands and stormed into the bathroom. When I returned wearing the skirt, he was on the bed with his hands crossed in front of him. "Turn around," he said. I did. He motioned me closer.

He took my face in his hand and squeezed. With his other hand, he gripped the waistband of my skirt and yanked. When he'd gotten it off of me, he tore it to pieces. With a shove, he sent me thudding back against the wall.

"No girl of mine's gonna strut herself like a little slut!" he shouted. His fist flew past my face and into the wall.

Later, he undressed and slipped into bed beside me. My face was to the wall. "I'm sorry, Brenda," he whispered. He kissed my shoulder, the back of my neck. "I get crazy 'cuz I love you so much. You're so beautiful, Bren. So sexy. I can't handle other guys thinking of you that way."

I forgave him immediately. I loved hearing how much Manny loved me. I loved that he wanted me all to himself.

Like many guys, Manny believed in a double standard. I was his, exclusively, but he had roaming privileges. Late one night after he'd stood me up for our date, I heard pebbles clicking against my window. Pulling back the curtains, I saw him standing below, grinning and stoned out of his mind.

"Where the hell were you?" I hissed.

"Come down," he begged.

The clock on my bedstand said 1:00 A.M. If I went out through the front door, Dad, the light sleeper, would hear me and there'd be trouble. So I did what I often did in situations like this: crouched on the windowsill, sprang toward the billboard five feet away, grabbed on, and climbed down. At the bottom of the sign, I let go, landing on all fours like a cat.

"So, where the hell were *you*?" I said.

"I'm here now, aren't I? Nothing makes you happy." His words were slurry, the pupils of his bloodshot eyes as tiny as pinpoints.

"Keep your promises. Then I'll be happy. What's *this*?" In the billboard light, I'd spotted a lipstick smear on his jacket collar. Manny tried a kiss instead of a straight answer, but I yanked free and headed to the billboard. "Go back to your whore," I said. As he walked away, I picked up a rock and took aim. It flew past his head. Manny waved his middle finger in the air and kept going.

The next morning, Manny came calling with one of his cousins, a chubby twelve-year-old named Bubbles. "It was my fault," she said. "I got lipstick on him when I gave him a good-bye hug." Bubbles couldn't look at me. She spoke like she was reading lines in a play. I chose to believe her anyway.

It wasn't all bad—far from it. He gave me roses from the gas station bucket, stuffed animals from the carnival, passionate kisses. All couples had problems, I told myself. That was just life.

He would sometimes disappear for days without letting me know where he was. Quizzing Stitch and Green Eyes about his whereabouts was a waste of time. "You're lying to me!" I told Green Eyes one day at school, poking my finger against his chest. "I thought you were my friend."

"I *am* your friend, Brenda. But I'm his *brother*."

When Manny got back, he tracked me down at my sister Marizol's, where I was staying for a few days. Mari and her kids had gone off somewhere on that hot, sticky day and I was in the shower. I heard a noise and poked my head out. Manny grabbed me by the neck and shoved me to the bathroom floor. "You think I'm fuckin' stupid?" he screamed. "I know what you're doing."

"What am I doing?" I whispered.

"Washing off the stink of sex," he said.

Was it drugs? Was he crazy? After he stormed out, I struggled to my feet and locked the bathroom door. His false accusations made me feel dirty and cheap, and I eased back into the shower to scrub myself clean of what Manny imagined.

Manny had a gift for making me feel guilty when I'd done nothing wrong. His accusations kept me off balance and confused. But whenever I'd tell him I'd had enough—that I was ending our relationship—he'd cry, beg, remind me of how few breaks he'd had in life before I came along. "I'm never going to lay a finger on you again," he'd promise. Maybe it's true, I'd tell myself. Maybe he's learned his lesson. And what was waiting for me if I *did* leave him? The same world that had never accepted me—that had never made me feel special the way Manny sometimes did. So the cycle continued: explosions, promises, sweetness, new explosions.

One night, the phone rang. "Meet me at the building" was all Manny said. He'd returned the day before from a weeklong disappearance.

I took my time getting to the hangout. Let *him* wait for once, I figured. But as I climbed the hill on Baldwin Street, a cop car sped past, siren blaring. David was at the building, pacing out front. "Brenda, don't flip out," he said. "The cops arrested Manny. They been watching him. They know he sells."

I found Green Eyes at his regular corner. His girlfriend, Erika, was with him. Erika and I had been friends back in parochial school, but I hadn't seen her since. From the look of the white- and mustard-colored beads around her neck, she'd changed since our days with the nuns. "Manny's always telling me that if a member of the family falls, the rest are there to pick him up," I told Green Eyes. "All's I got for his bail is forty dollars. How about you?"

It had been a slow night, he said, but he'd make the rounds. He told Erika and me to wait for him at the police station.

The cops wouldn't tell us anything. As we waited for Green Eyes, I asked Erika what it was like being down with the Unidad. "I love it," she said. "For the first time in my life, I have a family." When Green Eyes showed up, he was empty-handed. The Unidad's Hartford chapter was having a party, he said, and most of the Waterbury brothers had driven up there. Manny would have to stay in jail until Monday morning when he went to court.

The three of us walked back to Baldwin Street. As we entered the abandoned building, Erika turned to me. "Hey, Brenda," she said. "Why don't you become one of us? You've got what it takes. I could bring you in."

Until then, I had always dismissed the idea of joining the Unidad, but suddenly it didn't seem like such a crazy idea. If I lost my "outsider" status, I could be let in on some of Manny's secrets. It might bring us closer. "Think about it," Erika said. "Hang out this weekend. I'll introduce you to the sisters."

All that weekend, I studied the members' interactions. They laughed, talked, joked around. They really *did* seem like a family—and not a hostile one like mine. One of the sisters Erika introduced me to had been in the group that stared me down that first day I'd gone to the building with Manny. Now she had a name—Liz—and she was friendly. "The Unidad's the best family," Liz assured me. "You should join."

On Sunday night, David and his girlfriend, Sandy, were at the building. I hadn't told David I was considering joining the family because I knew he'd disapprove. But in the middle of a conversation with Erika and Sandy, it was suddenly clear to me. I *wanted* their sense of belonging—this family of friends. Not much of a drinker, I grabbed Erika's beer bottle and took a swig. "Guess what?" I said. "I want to be your sister!"

Erika jumped up and hugged me, screaming. "Come on!" she said, taking my hand. "I'm taking you upstairs to see Carmen." Sandy told us to wait up—she wanted to join the Unidad, too.

Carmen, a squat, sloppy woman in her early thirties, was president of the Unidad girls. With an expression somewhere between contempt and indifference, she looked us over. "You think you got what it takes? Okay, I'll give you a choice. You can either get a beat-down or do something for the family."

Sandy looked at me, waiting for our answer. I wasn't afraid of a beat-down, but I figured Carmen was looking for the other answer. "I'll do something for the family," I said. Carmen cracked a smile and turned to Sandy.

"I'll do something for the family, too."

Carmen nodded. She checked her watch. "Follow me," she said.

As she led us down the stairs and outside, Carmen briefed us on the woman who lived in the gray house next door. This bitch didn't like the family, Carmen said. She'd sit on her porch sometimes, mimicking the sign and laughing. It was time she learned the Unidad was nothing to play with. "You two will be the ones to teach her that lesson," she said.

Carmen knew the woman's schedule. She'd be passing by any minute. "Use those on her," she said, pointing to a pile of two-by-fours. "She's a big bitch. You'll need 'em."

Sandy grabbed two pieces of wood and handed one to me. We crouched on either side of the gate to the front sidewalk. Carmen retreated and hid. A few minutes later, she called to us. "Okay, here she comes."

There was no way I could punk out at this point. I looked over at Sandy, crouched and ready to pounce. I watched our victim approach, focusing on her fat feet, squeezed into a pair of black sandals. "Now!" Carmen said.

"Hey!" I screamed, jumping up. The woman turned to face me. Her hair was pulled back in a ponytail. Her eyes were wide with shock. Sandy took the first swing, a loud whack to the back of the woman's head.

For a second, I just stood there, frozen. But when the woman started defending herself against Sandy, I jumped in. Raising my two-by-four above my head, I brought it down on her. She screamed. I pounded her again and again. Even after she fell to the ground, I kept hitting her.

Then everything went dark. My legs wouldn't work. It was like I was in a weird dream. "Brenda, get out of here *now*!" someone shouted. I blinked, looked around. I was slumped against the fence in front of the building, gripping a piece of two-by-four. I dropped it and ran for my life.

A few minutes later, I was in some alley, at the bottom of a flight of stairs. I was bent over, holding my stomach, gasping for air. "Bren? Are you okay?" I looked up at Erika. "You did it! We're sisters now."

She pushed in beside me on the step. "Carmen really liked what she saw tonight," she said. "You won't be on probation long. Here." She removed her beads, kissed them the way a Catholic kisses the cross on a rosary, and handed them to me. I slipped the beads over my head and let them drop around my neck. I felt a piece of my soul slip away.

The next day, I went to the courthouse for Manny's hearing. Although I was forbidden to talk to him, we exchanged loving looks, silent promises. When the judge sentenced Manny to two years in Little Cheshire, I burst into tears. I fingered the beads around my neck and Manny nodded in recognition. He gave me the Unidad sign as they led him away.

3. DANCING IN LEG CHAINS

I might have been a great actress
with awards up on my shelf.
I'd have been a big success,
if I hadn't lost myself.

Deep down, the real me exists.
When it's safe, she'll show her face.
While she's waiting for that day,
I am here to take her place.

"Brendita, que paso? Mercedes? Oh, my God, what's wrong?"

My arrest nine years ago is a blur of scary sounds, smells, and sights—the vomity stink of the holding cell, the bite of shackles against bone, the nonstop crying of one of my codefendants. The worst of these memories, by far, is the pain on my mother's face when the detectives arrived at 5:30 that morning to pick up Mercedes and me. Mom's face, and Daddy's confused desperation. I can still see him running down the hallway after us, shouting promises as he struggled to dress himself. "Don't worry, Brenda! I'll follow you down there! I'll be right behind you!" All the way to the station, I stared out the back window of the cop car to make sure my father was still there.

"Garbage!"

"Murderers!"

"Not so tough now, are you?"

Mercedes and I collected these and other comments on our way to the tiny holding cell inside the Hartford courthouse. An egg-shaped sheriff opened the door and hurried us in. Providencia and Brandy, our friends and codefendants, were already there. "Better get used to *that* sound, girls," Humpty Dumpty said as he slammed the door behind us. "You may be hearing it for a long time." A second sheriff, a white man in his thirties, addressed Brandy, the only white girl. "You're a disgrace to our race," he hissed. Brandy's sobbing continued for over an hour.

Although I was damned if I'd give that racist officer the satisfaction of *my* tears, his remark upset me, too. The assumption was typical. The three little Spics were *expected* to engage in criminal behavior; it was the all-American white girl who'd betrayed the code. Another officer passing by looked in and sneered. "Feel like a big woman now?" No, I wanted to tell him. I feel like a scared little girl. Instead, I stared back, stone-faced, and said nothing. Weakness was a tool they could use against me. I had to show them how hard I'd be to break.

As we waited for who knew what, Providencia paced, Brandy cried, and Mercedes sat and rocked, her knees to her chest. Trying to keep my mind off whatever was coming, I concentrated on the graffiti scrawled all over the cell's filthy walls: TINA AND DAVE 4-EVER. GET ME OUT OF HERE! JOSE WAS HERE '88, '90, & '91. But distracting myself didn't work. Plunking myself on the bench beside Mercedes, I hid my face in my hands and rocked, too.

I heard the jangle of chains before I saw the corrections officers in charge of our prison transport. "We'll take the others first," one of them told the sheriff. A female officer with a bad perm and a strictly business attitude interviewed us, asking several routine questions. Finally, she asked the one she'd been leading up to. "Are you gang members?" Provi, Brandy, Mercedes, and I shook our heads in unison. "Skip the pretense, ladies," the officer said. "We know all about your gang activities from the Waterbury police. You girls are all over the news."

A line of handcuffed, shackled women gawked at us as they passed by. "Hey, those are the ones did that murder down in Waterbury," someone said. "Look at 'em. They're *babies*." One woman stopped dead in her tracks to stare. "This ride's gonna be fun," she said. Dried puke decorated her shirtfront.

Once the "girls" were out of the building, it was our turn. Our cell was popped open and a CO entered and threw his armful of hardware on the floor. "Sit side by side on the bench," he said. One by one we were shackled, handcuffed, and belly-chained. My eyes were burning. My face felt hot. *Don't cry,* I kept telling myself. *Don't let him see you cry.*

Outside, we were led past the blue bus that held the other women and helped, one by one, into a smaller van. "Aw, come on, let 'em ride with us!" someone from the bus shouted. I was relieved not to be riding with these criminals but also curious. Did the officers assume they were too dangerous for us—or vice versa?

On the way to prison, I kept looking out the back window of the van, hoping against hope that I'd see my father's car. Halfway there, I gave up and closed my eyes. Not knowing if God would even bother to listen to me, I asked Him to be with my parents through this mess.

At Niantic, they gave me my new name—221437—and made me pose for a mug shot. In a back room, three female officers ordered me to take off my clothes. Their instructions mortified me: pick up your hair, stick out your tongue, lift up your breasts, bend over and cough. I was handed a bag of toiletries and ordered to the shower. With my head under the water, it was finally safe to cry.

"I'm your ride," the officer said. He had a booming voice and kind eyes.

"Where am I going?" I whispered.

"To your housing unit. First time here, right? How old are you?"

"Seventeen."

"Well, don't worry. You'll be okay."

I climbed into the back of the empty van. Where were Mercedes and the others? When would I see them again? The van stopped in front of an old wooden building. The officer unlocked the steel door and led me inside. "Guess they were expecting you," he said, grabbing the linens and a pillow from a metal chair by the entrance. The hallway he led me down reminded me of one of those psycho wards in a bad horror movie.

The room I'd been locked into smelled like mothballs. Dirty mattress, grungy toilet, white radiator, back wall window. I thought about my bedroom at home—the clean sheets on my queen-sized bed, the pictures of my friends. I made the bed, put on the nightgown they'd given me, and stared out the window. Hours later, I began to doze, my face still hot and wet with tears.

"Breakfast!" I opened my eyes. A heavyset woman stood at the door, holding a tray. I stared at her for several seconds. "I don't want any," I croaked.

She placed it on the floor anyway. "In case you change your mind."

After she'd gone, I got up and walked over to the tray. Juice, coffee, an apple, a piece of cake. I figured the bowl of tan paste was supposed to be oatmeal. I bent down, poked the cake. It was hard and stale. I drank the juice, bit into the apple. As I chewed, I noticed the paper on the floor. *Inmate Medina, Brendalis #221437 confined to seg pending investigation.* I had no idea what it meant.

Later that morning, I was escorted across the compound to the office of Deputy Warden Sackett. Women stared as I passed, made comments. "Which one? That one?" "If she's so tough, why did she have to *jump* that girl?" "Doesn't look like much of a murderer to me." *That's because I'm NOT a murderer, stupid!* I wanted to scream back. Instead,

I held my tongue and wore my couldn't-care-less-what-*you*-think mask. If I let them know they could get to me, prison would get a lot harder than it already was.

"I sent for you because I have to ask you a few questions," Deputy Warden Sackett said. His voice was soft. His office, with its plants and posters, was the first good place I'd seen at Niantic. "I need to know if your victim was a member of a rival gang."

"I don't think she was in a gang," I said. "But I didn't know her."

"If I let you out in population, are you going to cause trouble?"

I shrugged. "What's 'population'?"

"A regular housing unit," he said.

"Isn't the building I'm in already jail?"

My confusion made him smile. "You're in seg. Segregation. I had to put you there in case you were planning to cause trouble with members of other gangs. Tell you what. As long as you don't cause problems, I'll move you to Fenwick North. Keep you with your codefendants, okay?"

I nodded, relieved. But, of course, I tried hard to show the deputy warden that I didn't care much one way or the other.

That night, Mercedes, Provi, Brandy, and I were escorted to Fenwick North. Three officers were waiting for us at the front door. "The girls in the unit have been following your case on the news," one of them said. "They've been expecting you." Which would explain why they were huddled together inside, gawking at us.

"You four are high-profile right now," another CO warned. "We don't want you causing any commotion." Provi appointed herself our spokeswoman, promising that we'd be "good little girls." The officer told her a little bit of smart-mouth went a long way at Fenwick North.

My room was on the first floor. I noted with relief that my roommate, a young white girl named Sarah, kept things clean and neat like I did. When she introduced me to the family pictures on her wall, I tried to seem interested. "Where are the phones?" I asked.

My sister Nancy accepted the charges. The month before, my parents had put a block on long-distance calls because I'd run up their bill. Not being able to call them was a relief, in a way; I'd have been too ashamed to talk to them from this place. "What *happened*?" Nancy asked. I wanted to explain everything, but all I could manage was, "I go to court on Monday. Tell Mom and Dad I love them." My sister began to cry.

Later, Mercedes and I walked down to the TV room. Provi was already there, entertaining her new fan club with war stories about our glamorous gang life. "Another time we had to drag two girls down the street by their hair 'cuz they kept fuckin' with us," Provi said.

"Damn, I ain't fuckin' with you four," someone said. "Y'all are crazy!"

I rolled my eyes and leaned toward Mercedes. "Dragged two girls by their hair?" I whispered. "When did that happen?" Mercedes shrugged.

Later, awake in bed, I heard my roommate shift in the bunk below. "You awake?" she asked. I said I was. "I have a confession. When I first heard you were going to be assigned here, I was really scared."

"Why?"

"Because of the news. I thought you'd be mean. I'm glad you're not."

"Oh," I said. "Thanks." I didn't tell her I'd been afraid to meet her, too.

The next day, while I was eating lunch with Mercedes, an officer approached and told my friend she had a visitor. Mercedes smiled, jumped up, and left. A few minutes later, another officer came for me. "You have a visitor," he said. Were my parents here? My brothers and sisters?

I was taken to an office where a lieutenant was waiting. "We're transferring you back to seg," he said. "We think it would be safer." Safer for who, I asked. He wouldn't say.

In chains, I was escorted back to the room I had occupied the night I arrived. To my surprise, Brandy was locked in the adjacent room. "Bren, why are we here?" she called from under her door.

"I don't know. They wouldn't tell me anything."

"Provi and Mercedes are downstairs. We were just yelling out the windows to each other."

You'll only be sent back to seg if you break the rules, they'd said. Come with me. You have a visitor. But I had *broken* no rules. There had *been* no visitors. Why were they lying to me? Why was I here?

When I was released from seg fourteen days later, I found out why. Provi had threatened some girl, using "us" as her weapon. We had all received disciplinary tickets because of it. Provi was the only one of the four of us who was released from seg early. The more I saw of the way prison worked, the more I seethed.

Two months later, the anger I'd been holding in erupted big time. I had just returned to my unit after a painful visit with my older brother, Ricky, a Waterbury police officer. It had been Ricky's first visit to York. We talked about his kids, our parents, the food in prison—everything except the events that had led to my arrest and incarceration. Twenty minutes before our time was up, he'd stood up, making excuses about all the things he had to do. I knew the real reason why he had to leave: my brother the cop couldn't handle his baby sister being here. I had shamed Ricky with his fellow officers.

So I was in no mood when, back in the housing unit, a woman named Roz started giving me shit. We argued for several minutes, getting in each other's faces. "Look," I said. "You want to do something to me, then do it. And if not, then shut the hell up."

"You think I'm scared of you just 'cuz you're a murderer?" Roz said.

That did it. Roz became Provi, and those sheriffs up in Hartford, and every other person who'd used the word *murderer*. I lunged, slammed her against the wall, pummeled her with everything I had. By the time I regained control, I'd been pinned to the floor, shackled, and handcuffed. I was pulled to my feet and marched off to seg—this time for a reason.

At Niantic, minimum- and maximum-security prisoners interact. Staff keeps our security status straight by our color-coded ID cards. Low-risk inmates—levels one and two—wear green cards and are free to walk the grounds. Yellow cards go to level threes. Denied grounds privileges, a level three must be transported around the facility in a van, but she need not wear restraints. When I entered the compound, I was given level four status. The pink ID I wore meant transport by van *and* restraints whenever I left my housing unit and entered the compound. I had assumed that four was the highest level of security risk status, but when I was released from lockdown two weeks after my fight with Roz, I found out differently. "Congrats," the CO said as he handed me my level five orange card. "You're only the fourth inmate at this compound who's earned one of these."

"It's an honor," I said, smirking back. If they wanted to name me to the troublemakers' all-star team, I'd be happy to play the game.

Level fives are to be restrained even in the rec yard outside their unit, but there's freedom of choice: handcuffs or leg chains. To let everyone know what a badass I was, I always chose the more difficult option. First, I perfected walking in shackles, then running in them, and finally, dancing. One time, hoping to get under the skin of a CO who had gotten under mine, I inched slowly to the top of the picnic table, stood, and danced up a noise-making racket. I was doing the "cabbage patch" when the officer stormed over. "Get off of there before you fall!" she shouted.

"I *won't* fall!" I said. "Life is for dancing!"

"Get off now, Medina, or I'm writing you up!"

"Why? Because you're mad that I can dance with shackles?"

With my orange card clipped to my shirt pocket, I pulled out all the stops. When I felt angry, I let it show. When I saw something I didn't like, I let them know. I was carted back to Hotel Seg so frequently, they should have named a room after me. And, of course, my "badass" rep grew accordingly—with staff and inmates alike. "Hey, there, Ms. Respect," a CO named Shulman called to me one afternoon. I liked Shulman better than most; at least he had a sense of humor.

"What you call me that for?" I asked.

"Because of your orange card and your *baaad* attitude. The Godfather himself wouldn't mess with you, Ms. Respect." I rolled my eyes, unsure if he was complimenting me or making fun.

Five years into my bid, I was still stoking my "Ms. Respect" reputation and living down to my orange card expectations. Inmates came and went. Old staff retired, new staff replaced them. Fewer and fewer people understood that there was a frightened kid behind the tough girl mask.

My parents still knew me, though. During a visit I will never forget, my father let me have it. Mom and Dad had come the Sunday before but had been turned away at the gate because I'd been locked down. "I drive two hours here every Sunday just to be told you're in trouble again," Dad said, his voice raised in exasperation. "This happens over and over. Don't you know what it does to your mother when she can't see you and make sure you're all right? Look at her, Brenda. Why can't you just behave?"

Mom had been sitting there, holding my hand across the table and crying. She cried every visit. *"Brendita, por favor, porta te bien,"* she said. There was almost no trace of the woman I'd done battle with all my life.

I looked away from them both. "You just don't understand," I said. I'd been accusing them of not understanding for years. But it was *I* who didn't get it. No matter what I'd done, no matter how much I'd hurt and shamed them, they still loved me. Those two-hour rides every Sunday proved it—proved that their love was unconditional. Suddenly, in the middle of that visit, I understood that. And when it was time for them to go, it was harder than ever to watch them leave.

But *understanding* the price my parents were paying for my wild ways and *changing* those ways were two very different things. It wasn't until the middle of a counseling appointment a few weeks later that I made the decision to take the leap from one to the other.

I'd been seeing Ken for two and a half years' worth of mostly stormy sessions. Week after week he invited me to let down my guard and explore my feelings, and week after week I resisted. I always listened, though. In my bunk at night, I could admit to myself that many of Ken's observations about me were accurate. But in his office, I tried hard to let him know it was all a crock.

Ken was ignoring my dirty looks and bouncing a rubber ball against his wall the afternoon he hit me with a crucial question. "Brenda, why do you keep getting in trouble?" *Thunk, thunk, thunk,* that ball kept going. I thought *I* was supposed to be the rude one.

"Why? Because that's who I am."

He shook his head. "It's who you pretend to be. Big difference." I rolled my eyes, tried to tune him out. "Kid, I talk to a lot of people doing time in here. The way I see it, this place deals you two choices. Either you can roll over and die, or you can choose to live." *Thunk, thunk, thunk.*

"I'm not dying for nobody," I said. "No matter how many times they drag me over to seg."

He stopped bouncing and leaned forward. Looked me in the eye. "You got it backwards," he said. "That's exactly what you're doing. Every time you convince someone else what a hard case you are? Every time you earn yourself a ticket, or a lockdown? Your spirit dies a little more. They can make it pretty tough for you here, Brenda, but they can't kill your spirit. Only *you* have the power to do that."

I had never cried in front of him before.

From that day on, I have tried hard to stay out of trouble. Success was a zigzagging line at first, not a straight one, but whenever I did screw up, I refused to let my setbacks defeat me. I have not received a disciplinary ticket in the past three years. Just the other day, I bumped into Officer Shulman, whom I hadn't seen in a while. "Well, well, if it isn't Ms. Respect," he said.

"That was a long time ago, Mr. S.," I reminded him.

"Maybe so, but I *still* wouldn't mess with you." He could only see the wild girl I was, not the woman I had become.

Ineligible for parole, I have served the first nine years of my twenty-five-year sentence. I am twenty-seven. I'm kept afloat by my writing, by the friendships I've made, and, most of all, by my mother and father's enduring support. "Why *shouldn't* I see him!" I used to scream at my parents when they objected to my involvement with Manny. "What do *you two* know about love?" More than I thought, I guess. They recently celebrated their forty-fifth wedding anniversary. Dad's retired now. He and Mom still make the two-hour drive on Sundays. They wait for my release.

Hope and despair live side by side here at York prison. Goodness and evil live here, too. As for God, I retain my doubts about His existence, but search each day for evidence of His mercy and love.

Beyond the steel door, there's a mourning
Grief for misplaced innocence

Past the mourning, there's a darkness
Filled with fears that make no sense

Beyond the darkness, there's a bright light
Illuminating half the way

Past the bright light, there's a longing
One that will not go away

Beyond the longing, there is silence
Stillness that may save my soul

Beyond the stillness, there's salvation
Grace from God to make me whole

Incarcerated since 1993, Brendalis Medina is serving a twenty-five-year sentence without parole for a gang-related killing at which she was present. Ordered with three of her fellow gang members to accomplish the beating of a fifth woman, Medina contends that she was taken by surprise when one of her "sisters" stabbed and killed the victim during the fight. Each of the four teenagers was charged and ultimately convicted of first-degree homicide. Medina maintains that she participated in the violence but is innocent of felony murder.

While at York prison, Brenda Medina has obtained her high school general equivalency degree and has earned thirty-six credits toward an associate's degree. A bilingual tutor registered with Literacy Volunteers of America, she has taught fellow Hispanic inmates to read, speak, and write English. In addition, Medina serves as a reporter, photographer, and editor for the *York Voice*, an inmate newsletter. In 2002, she designed, organized, and implemented York prison's first-ever Latino Appreciation Week.

"I began writing about my life because it was the only way I knew how to keep my sanity in this place of confusion," Medina says. "My writing is a sanctuary in the middle of each day."

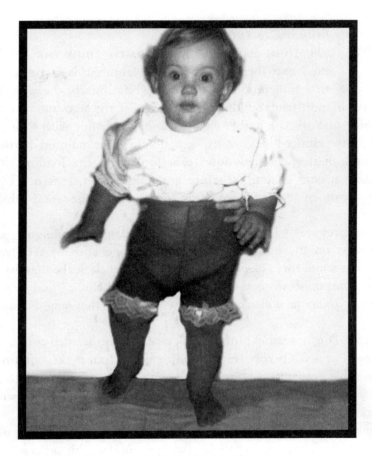

CHRISTMAS IN PRISON

ROBIN CULLEN

Born: 1962
Conviction: Second-degree
manslaughter with a motor vehicle
Sentence: 8 years
Entered prison: 1997
Status: Released

January 1, 2000

POPE JOHN PAUL HAS PROCLAIMED 2000 THE YEAR OF the Great Jubilee, and so we celebrate this first day of the new millennium in our makeshift church, the wide open hallway of Industrial Building No. 9. We of the maximum-security West Side of York C.I. gather each week in a corridor with white steel beams, raw cinder-block walls, a concrete floor painted battleship gray, and shatterproof windows that look onto the loading docks. Stackable plastic chairs, off-white and mint green, seat nearly two hundred women at this Saturday morning service. The Great Jubilee is upon us.

As he prepares to say Mass, Father Riordan, our bilingual priest, updates us on the battle between his waistline and his refrigerator. Dressed in white robe, black pants and shirt, and clerical collar, he nods to the dozen or so women of the "No Rehearsal Choir" and straps on his guitar. Today he will accompany the women as they sing the opening hymn.

Deacon Dugan readies himself, too, cinching the braided cord around the waist of his white robe. He's standing behind our makeshift altar—a sturdy table transformed each week with a wax-stained white altar cloth, a donation from an outside benefactor. He gives me a nod, my cue to begin the opening announcements.

Standing at the podium, I adjust the microphone and look out on the congregation. The women provide the only color at this otherwise gray gathering—a rainbow of skin tones, their chocolate, honey vanilla, and raspberry ripple–colored hair topped with crocheted red scrunchies that sit like cherries atop those ice cream–parlor hairdos. Hair ornaments were banned a while back, but now they're approved again. The prison giveth, taketh away, and giveth back.

I welcome those gathered and deliver the same announcements I've been reading each week for two years. "Only Catholics who have made their First Communion and are in a state of grace may receive the Holy Communion. All others may come forward with their arms crossed against their chests to receive God's blessings."

A woman in the fourth row looks to her right, her left, over her shoulder. From beneath her baggy gray sweatshirt she removes a "goodie bag" and passes it to the woman next to her. The recipient, in turn, tucks the package in her pants and rearranges her shirt over it. What's in the bag? Commissary. A few envelopes of instant soup maybe. A package of dried rice and beans, some Slim Jims, FireBalls, Jolly Ranchers. A stick of cocoa butter for her skin, a jar of grease for her hair, a bar of Irish Spring. If the seatmates have known each other on the streets or have done a bid together at York before, or if the receiver is being set up, there's probably a Butterfinger or Baby Ruth in there, too—candy to fortify the friendship or sweeten the romance.

"Sacramental preparation classes are held each Wednesday," I tell the faithful. "Bible study each Thursday afternoon."

There's a lot of silent negotiating during Mass; for friends and lovers who live in separate housing units, "church" can be more about a rendezvous than a religious experience. Con artists prey on the new girls. They play "Welcome Wagon" with some recent arrival who, the grapevine says, receives a fifty-dollar commissary allotment every week, or who is expecting "mad money" from her family or her man. Once the new girl's on the line, obligation-wise, the con has an arsenal of sob stories. For the small down payment of a goodie bag, she can cash in on commissary for weeks.

"The sacrament of reconciliation is available before Mass each Saturday. Let Father or Deacon know as soon as you arrive if you wish to confess."

Last week, the CO (corrections officer) on duty separated two women midservice. He had confiscated a "kite"—a love note folded into a tiny triangle for easy transport and smooth exchange. The women were segregated, their clip-on ID badges confiscated. They both received disciplines: *guilty of creating a disturbance and passing contraband.*

"Today's reading in English will be found on page 72 of your missalettes. The Spanish reading is on page 102."

A month ago, two women were thrown out for groping each other during Communion. The week after that, an argument erupted mid-Mass. Chicago didn't believe that Rayette, the stud she'd sat in church with a week earlier, was "just friends" with Monique, the woman Rayette was sitting beside *that* week. Their shouting drowned out Father Riordan and all three were removed. Too bad for Chicago. She'd just about convinced Rayette to buy her that $250 color TV from commissary.

"Please stand, and join in singing our opening hymn, 'Amazing Grace.' " The women rise, the music begins and, in spite of everything, the Light of the Mass embraces me.

After church, I walk chin up toward my housing unit. Nearly every inch of the world around me is gray: the sky, the ashen bark of bare trees, the concrete walkways, even the sweatshirt I'm wearing. I stretch my neck and hold my face to the sun. Nature is in a catering mood today—bright rays, above-freezing temperatures. I've been here two years now. Each day I battle against bad food, poor air circulation, and lack of exercise. My body has taken a beating, but my spirit is intact and healthy. I armor myself with white light to shield me from the endless gray of prison days.

At the entrance of my unit, I fill my lungs with crisp, fresh air. I know when the door to the outside locks behind me, it will be hours before I breathe good air again. Inside, the first-shift CO is hanging a sign in the window. In bold black letters, the message fills the entire sheet of paper:

INMATE MAIL IS NOW CAUGHT UP. HOWEVER THERE STILL REMAINS A WEEK BACKUP ON MONEY ORDERS. EXPECT M.O.'S WILL BE CAUGHT UP BY THURS./FRI.
—MAILROOM

A crowd gathers to read the new bulletin—long-faced women who look like children still waiting for a Santa who never showed. What the sign really means is: No Christmas presents delivered again this week.

Each Christmas in prison, the commissary sells overpriced holiday packages. These are the only "gifts" we are allowed to receive. Folks on the outside place their orders and send money to be deposited in our accounts. An inmate can order a holiday package as well—give herself a Christmas present if no one else has. The cost is deducted from the wages she's earned, between $0.75 and $2.25 per day for jobs ranging from food prep to janitorial to teacher's aide service.

Even if I'd saved three weeks' pay, I could only afford the lowest-priced holiday offering, the "Health Package," which sells for twenty-six dollars. It contains Smartfood popcorn, reduced-fat Oreos, Stella D'oro diet breadsticks, and a small box of herbal teas. Herbal tea is not available during the year and I would love to have some, but I'm not willing to spend all that money for the rest of that junk food marketed as "healthy." Last year, I lucked out. Other women who'd received the herb tea but wouldn't drink it gave me theirs. I made a dozen apple-cinnamon tea bags last from January through April.

Hundreds of Christmas packages are sold each year. The "Spicy Package," at twenty-nine dollars, has Goya seasonings, crackers, and beef jerky in two tangy flavors. The "Sweet Package," at thirty-one dollars, includes Pop-Tarts, Nips, Sno-Caps, Hershey's Nuggets, and regular-fat Oreos. The "Meat Package," at thirty-seven dollars, is top of the line: beef jerky, pickle in a pouch, sodium-loaded soup mixes, squeeze cheeses. *Bon appétit!*

The women who have been here longer than I share their stories of "back in the day" when inmates were allowed to receive packages from home. Boasting and teasing, they make us salivate to hear of homemade Christmas cookies, chocolate Santas, licorice ropes, boxes of roasted cashews and smoked almonds. "But no dried fruit." Gray-haired Lillian laughs. "One year, a few of the gals got creative and made hooch from dried figs and apricots. Staff caught them drunk off their asses!" My eyes well up from listening to these long-term inmates reminisce about their fond memories of Christmases past in prison, but they are not happy tears.

In 1997, the first of the three Christmases I've spent in jail, every woman on the maximum-security side of the compound found two bags of goodies outside her cell door on Christmas morning. Santa had left me a big blue bag of pretzel rings and a "party size" bag of salsa-flavored Doritos. Yuletide decorations at the shoreline prison were a little "thin" that year: two scrawny, artificial Christmas trees, absent of lights and presents. The one in the dining hall had faded decorations and foil limbs. It barely survived the women brushing by it on the way to the chow line. The tree in the visiting room was in worse shape—as defeated and sad as the seasonal "returnees," those emaciated women coming "home" to Niantic for the holidays, their faces ashen and drawn, their bodies decorated with old jailhouse tattoos. Names, signs, symbols, declarations of eternal love: the women here sometimes mark themselves and each other with sewing needles, shoe polish, and ink from the barrels of broken Bic pens. For Christmas dinner that year, we ate roast beef.

A year later, Christmas, 1998, there were no "secret Santa" bags of pretzels or tortilla chips outside our cell doors. But the trees were back, a little more debilitated than the year before. For Christmas dinner, we ate roast beef.

This past year, no junk food, no trees. We ate roast beef.

When the trumpet of the jubilee sounds on the day of atonement, the Old Testament promises, liberty will be proclaimed and every man shall be returned to his family. No man shall oppress another (Leviticus, chapter 25). When Jesus preached in the synagogue at Nazareth, He said no one belonged at the celebration more than the poor, the blind, and the imprisoned (Luke, chapter 4). Pope John Paul has proclaimed 2000 the Jubilee Year. At York C.I., however, no one's gotten the message. The trees have disappeared, the roast beef dinner's endangered, and the "presents" have been held up until the backup of money orders gets unclogged. We can't get out and Christmas is no longer allowed in. This is a maximum-security facility.

At age thirty-four, Robin Cullen was driving home from a wedding when she and her girlfriend, a passenger in Cullen's truck, changed destination. Cullen became disoriented, entered the wrong side of a divided road, and attempted unsuccessfully to correct her error. Her vehicle flipped over, killing her passenger. Cullen was subsequently convicted of "second-degree manslaughter with a motor vehicle, driving while intoxicated." She served three years of an eight-year sentence.

While incarcerated, Cullen served as a teacher's aide, a literacy volunteer, and a backup puppy trainer for the National Education of Assistance Dogs project. Additionally, she worked in data entry, coding accident reports for the Department of Transportation, served as lector for Catholic Mass, earned college credits, and painted walls throughout the prison school, including one classroom's four-sided mural of an enchanted garden. Upon release, Cullen became certified through the Amherst Writers and Artists Institute to teach therapeutic writing. Presently, she volunteers in weekly sessions at a halfway house, working with women just exiting prison. Now thirty-nine, Cullen is sole proprietor of her own painting company, Color Outside the Lines; she labors full-time throughout Connecticut, customizing homes inside and out.

"I never thought it would happen to me," Cullen says of the accident that sent her to prison. "I am grateful for all the love in my life, and for the truth that sets me free."

FAITH, POWER, AND PANTS

||||||||||||||||||||||||

BONNIE FORESHAW

Born: 1947
Conviction: Homicide
Sentence: 45 years without parole
Entered prison: 1986
Status: Incarcerated

I WAS BORN IN JAMAICA AND RAISED IN A BLACK NEIGH-borhood in South Florida, so I grew up with mainlanders and islanders alike and loved all kinds of music. R&B, gospel, Calypso, reggae. Up and down the street, the neighbors' music sang about life's joys and sufferations, God's goodness, and the highs and lows of love. You could tell by the selection and the volume when someone was "feeling" the music.

I always knew, for instance, how things were going between my aunt Mandy and uncle Raymond by the kind of blues coming through their windows. If the situation was rocky, Koko Taylor, B.B. King, or Big Maybelle would wail out Aunt Mandy's pain. When Bobby "Blue" Bland's velvet vocals serenaded you as you passed, that meant Uncle Raymond had redeemed himself and my aunt was in love again.

My laid-back cousin Stella listened to jazz. Ella Fitzgerald, Count Basie, Billy Ekstine, Duke Ellington. These musicians took up the subjects of love and pain, too, but they made it swing. Still, my old cous' had her "Lady Sings the Blues" days, too. When Billie Holiday was on the record player, Stella was apt to be stirring something on the stove, nursing a glass of White Label and milk, and working her way through the "good-morning-heartache" side of life.

Not everyone in the 'hood could afford a stereo and a stack of records, but nobody was without a radio. For us, Miami's main man was Fat Daddy, the nighttime DJ on WMBW. He played James Brown and Johnny Nash, took requests, and featured news and announcements of interest to blacks. On Saturdays, we tuned in to hear the winning daily number. Today you can check the daily lottery numbers in a dozen different ways, but back in sixties Florida, Fat Daddy had to slip his listeners the digits in code. "Speeder picked up by the police last night doing seventy-three miles an hour. Not sixteen, not thirty-four, but seventy-three miles an hour. Now here's Gladys Knight and the Pips, boarding that midnight train to Georgia." Today radio's different. I surf the airwaves looking for a good station, but in order to hear one decent song by Luther Vandross or Erykah Badu, I have to tolerate ten by rappers whose explicit lyrics defame women. Not all rap is negative, but when I hear it, I usually turn it off. For me, reggae and "old school" R&B is the music that's got heart and soul.

I raised my kids listening and grooving to music. At our house, there was no such thing as "Turn it off so I can go to sleep" or "Turn it down or you'll wake someone up." At night, my kids learned to go to sleep *to* the music, and in the morning, when it started up again, they knew it was time for *everyone* to get out of bed and get busy, not just their mother.

I cooked breakfast to Bob Marley's "Redemption Song," cleaned house to Aretha Franklin's "Respect," drove my car to the beat of the Temptations, Smokey Robinson, and Marvin Gaye. And please know that with the music came dancing. My babies could dance before they could walk because their entire family danced, even the old folks. When the grandparents' and great aunts' and uncles' feet got too old to cooperate, or their arthritis or corns were bothering them, they still swayed to the music, tapped their feet, clapped their hands, and bobbed their heads. Dancing's dancing, whether you're on your feet or in a chair. The music's in you, part of your culture, a chunk of who you are.

And hallelujah, God gave us noses and taste buds along with ears and feet. What would music be without the cooking and eating that went with it? At holiday times, my extended family knew whose house to come to when they wanted to eat, drink, and celebrate life. I'd start cooking two days ahead of time, knowing that, no matter what the recipe called for, the key ingredient was music. Reggae helped me season the food just right. I'd sway to the beat as I stirred the pot or cut up vegetables. Cooking's hard work, but cooking to music eases your fatigue and makes you lose track of time. Cook slowly and patiently for the best results, and let the beat of the music be the pulse of your soul.

Bear in mind, I did not cook breakfast on holiday mornings. I was too busy. My kids waited—or cheated, sneaking a hunk, a bite, a spoonful, a taste as they passed through my kitchen. By the time company came, I was ready. Onto the table would go turkey and dressing, curried goat, dumplings, gravy, rice and cabbage, smoked beef bones, okra, corn bread, potato salad, hard sour bread, yams, fried plantains, fish fritters, Ital stew, cakes, pies, custards, ginger beer, sorrel, carrot juice, and Irish mash. "Okay, everyone, come eat!" I'd announce. And eat they did, all day and into the night, stay over or come back the next day when more food was ready. And always, *always,* we ate to the soundtrack of laughter, talk, and music.

*   *   *

In my family, funerals are loving good-byes and celebrations of life, complete with music and food. I was twenty-seven, living up north, when my mother called to tell me the mourning wreath had been hung on Aunt Bertha's front door. I had no choice but to fly home to pay my respects to Mom's older sister.

Now, my mother was one of fourteen children. By the time I arrived in Miami, over two hundred family members were there, from Chicago, New York, New Jersey, Virginia, Georgia, Alabama, and Jamaica. So many, couldn't all of us stay at Aunt Bertha's, so the elders rented eight connected rooms at the Holiday Inn—four for showering, dressing, and sleeping; two for the kids; one for the "quiet folks" who didn't smoke or drink; and one for the bar where the "not so quiets" could relax and conversate. The kids swam in the pool, the teenagers baby-sat the little ones, and the Florida relatives shuttled out-of-staters to the malls and the movies. When my cousin Li'l Bert rumbled in from New York in her fully-equipped, sleeps-six RV, the Holiday Inn let her and her family set up camp in the parking lot. The following morning, Bert and I were up early, cooking and serving up muffins, eggs, and coffee inside the RV. Anyone looking for a little nourishment and caffeine, we had it covered. You see, for us a funeral is part grieving, part family reunion, and part vacation.

On Friday, the night of the wake, Aunt Bertha's house was headquarters. Cars lined the street for blocks and enough food was carted in to feed all of Dade County. The house and backyard came alive with remembering, rejoicing, and music—Mahalia Jackson, the Southernaires, and Blind Boys of Alabama at first, to sing our sorrow at Aunt Bertha's passing. Later, as the liquor flowed and tongues and limbs loosened, gospel gave way to good-time music: Jackie Wilson, Al Green, Etta James. I was in the midst of it all, of course. One of the younger cousins, I had my walk-on-the-wild-side reputation to keep up.

It was 8:00 A.M. the next morning by the time my sore dancing feet and I made it back to the motel. The funeral home was sending cars to pick us up for the 11:00 service. Now, three hours should have been plenty of time to get showered and dressed, but there was one small problem. In the midst of the dozens of sleeping, snoring, and hung-over relatives, I couldn't locate my luggage. And when I finally did find it, my funeral dress was missing.

Did I panic? Uh uh. I planned. Bear in mind, we were a family of jazzy dressers and, therefore, overpackers. There was no way all those women were going to wear everything they'd brought with them. With all those open suitcases in tight quarters, "borrowing" was inevitable. That was how *my* dress had disappeared. Now I'd just have to do a little borrowing of my own.

In my bathrobe, I moved from room to room, socializing with my aunts and cousins while they tried things on, changed their minds, tried on something else. At 10:30, folks started heading off for church. It was time for me to do my shopping.

I mixed and matched, blending what was chic in Chicago with what was hip in New York, Miami, and Kingston. I climbed into a pair of black dotted stockings and slipped on my Cousin Rethel's black designer dress. Cousin Stella's black leather pumps and matching handbag, Italian-made, looked good with Rethel's dress. I hitched a string of pearls around my neck, borrowed someone's silk handkerchief, and crowned my outfit with a black fedora with a polka dot band. I tilted it slightly for attitude and headed off to the funeral.

I was the best-dressed person at Aunt Bertha's service, and didn't I know it! The last to arrive, I strutted down the aisle like a fashion model on the runway, smiling, nodding, and waving my designer handkerchief at the approving glances and dirty looks I was getting. When Cousin Rethel recognized her dress, the look she gave me was lethal, and when my old cous' Stella saw *her* black pumps on *my* feet, she mouthed a word you don't hear too much in church. The undertaker would probably be fitting *me* for a casket once they got ahold of me, but my dressed-to-impress entrance had been worth it.

The minister, of course, got us refocused on the deceased. His inspired eulogy spoke of Aunt Bertha's life as a Christian woman of strong faith who took time to minister to the sick. And when the choir sang "Swing Low, Sweet Chariot," I looked around the overcrowded church, moved by my family's tribute to one of our own who had passed. Lord, I *felt* that music.

From the burial ground, we returned to Aunt Bertha's for more eating, drinking, and remembering. There was some reckoning for me, the fashion plate in borrowed threads. I pleaded my case to several relatives who still wanted to kill me. But after some shouting, arguing, explaining, and negotiating, I was forgiven. Cousin Rethel even let me keep her black dress. Good thing, because I never did find my own.

As the reunion drew to a close, there were hugs, tearful good-byes, and promises to stay in touch with people I have not seen or heard from since. Imprisoned these past sixteen years, I have missed all the family funerals since 1986. From what I hear, so have many of the others. Families change with the times, and as a generation dies off, its traditions are often buried with it. Last week, I got word that Aunt Matilda, my mother's last surviving sister, had passed on. Of those fourteen siblings, Mom is now the last one left. The Florida relatives gave Aunt Matilda a proper send-off, but none of the out-of-staters made the trip.

Still, for me, there are the memories. I'll hear a snatch of song on the radio and travel back to a time, a place, a person. Let the music mark our time, our living in this world and our leaving it.

Many lost women find their God after they come to prison, but I arrived at Niantic Correctional Institution already firm in my faith. It's true I had "walked on the wild side" during my twenties, but in my thirties, I underwent a transformation. Three abusive marriages had knocked much of the mischief out of me. When you live in fear that your husband may come at you again and crack your eardrum with a hard slap, cut you with a knife, or sink the teeth of an Afro pick into your neck, it alters your perspective. Makes you question and fear all kinds of things. By my early thirties, I felt beaten, tired, lonely, and lost. Rastafarianism showed me a way out of the maze.

Part of what had tangled me up was the rat race—the never-ending need for others' approval. Before coming to the teachings of Jah Rastafari, I had worked hard but lived desperately from paycheck to paycheck, buying the latest fashions and the slickest car, booking the best vacations for my kids. This instinct to fit in at all costs was, I suppose, a legacy from my parents, who had emigrated from Jamaica when I was a young child. Black islanders, you see, experience two kinds of bigotry when they move to the U.S. Besides the racism of whites, they also bear the prejudice of African Americans, who fear their Caribbean brothers and sisters will steal their jobs and hamper their own struggle to get ahead. So, the more quickly Jamaicans can assimilate—pass as *non*-islanders—the more quickly they'll be tolerated by other blacks. Born

Jamaican, I had become what islanders call, with a smile, "Jamerican." The teachings of Jah Rastafari made me realize that buying, wearing, and driving the symbols of success didn't make me successful. By assimilating, I had taken one step forward and two steps back.

Equality, simplicity, humility, and closeness to nature are the principles by which Rastafarians live. We believe, as the Old Testament tells us, that African people, enslaved and scattered to "the four corners of the world," are the Lost Tribes of Israel and that Haile Selassie, descendant of King Solomon and Emperor of Ethiopia from 1930 to 1975, was the promised messiah sent to reunite Africans the world over. "Ethiopianism" has deep roots in Jamaica. The island was birthplace both to Marcus Garvey, the "Black Moses" who called for Africans to reclaim their homeland, and musician Bob Marley, who set his inspirational lyrics to a reggae beat and spread the Rasta messages of nonviolence, love of nature, and racial equality throughout the world. During his historic pilgrimage to Kingston in 1966, His Imperial Majesty Haile Selassie declared, "Jamaicans and Ethiopians are brothers by blood."

As my faith deepened and my study of the Old Testament grew more serious, I stopped cutting my hair and began wearing it in dreadlocks as a sign of my humble obedience to God. This is as the Bible directs: *All the days of the vow of his separation there shall no razor come upon his head: until his days of dedication to the Lord are over, he shall be holy, and shall let the locks of the hair of his head grow* (Numbers, chapter 6, verse 5). I began visiting my homeland regularly and following more closely the orthodox Ital diet of fresh fruits and vegetables, untainted by preservatives. I readied myself to embrace my Divine Deity. At the age of thirty-two, I took my solemn vow and became a devoted Nazirite Rastafarian. Six years later, at the age of thirty-eight, I became a prisoner of the Niantic Correctional Institution, convicted on a charge of first-degree murder.*

Prison seemed unreal at first—like I had gotten lost in someone else's

On the night of March 26, 1986, Bonnie Foreshaw stopped for a beer at a Jamaican social club in Hartford. Recently separated from an abusive husband who continued to threaten and stalk her, she had begun carrying a .38-caliber handgun for protection. Hector Freeman, a fellow patron at the club whom Foreshaw did not know, offered to buy her a drink. When she refused, he became verbally abusive. Hoping to avoid trouble, Foreshaw left the club, but Freeman followed her outside, shouting insults and obscenities. Joyce Amos, a woman unknown to nightmare. One day I'm a machinist at a manufacturing company, a shop steward, a middle-class mom doing my best to provide a good life for my kids. Next day I'm a prisoner of the State of Connecticut, locked away in the mental health unit, confused, overtranquilized, and falling apart fast.

After four weeks in mental health, I was transferred to Thompson Hall, a sort of "Ellis Island" for new prisoners awaiting their housing assignments. Thompson Hall was wild and scary—a crowded zoo for women. I was the eighth inmate assigned to a single room. Each night, I'd lie on a mattress so filthy I couldn't sleep. In the morning, I could never shower myself clean enough. Privacy was nonexistent at Thompson Hall, and theft was common. Hollering went on all day long and arguments broke into fights that sent the COs running. Because I was a battered woman with emotional scars, these conditions were like triggers back to my worst days. Still, I never lost sight of the fact that I still had my life and Joyce Amos, the lady who had tried to help me that night, had lost hers. She had been someone's mother and someone's daughter, same as me. A powerful sadness was closing in. I began to ask myself how I could survive—or if I even wanted to. I was reassigned to

Foreshaw or Freeman, approached Freeman, trying to quell the disturbance. During this exchange, Foreshaw saw Freeman reach inside his pocket. Thinking she was about to be shot, she produced her own gun and fired a warning shot meant to scare off Freeman. When Freeman saw Foreshaw's gun, he pulled Joyce Amos against him as a shield. The bullet struck Amos and killed her. She was six months pregnant.

Foreshaw's arrest attracted the interest of abortion rights opponents, who demanded she be tried for the murders of both Joyce Amos and "Baby Amos." A Superior Court judge ruled that the shooting death of the fetus did not constitute homicide under state law and refused to grant the second murder warrant.

Prosecutor James Thomas opened his case against Foreshaw with the flourish of a handgun that was not the murder weapon but a prop signed out of the police evidence room. Thomas characterized Foreshaw as a "known drug seller," based on pending charges. (Acting on a "tip" that "Rastafarians with Jamaican accents and guns" had been spotted inside Foreshaw's home, local police had entered with a search warrant and found no drugs but "evidence of drug trafficking": two boxes of baking soda. Shortly after the murder trial concluded, all drug charges against Foreshaw were dropped.) Foreshaw's public defender chose not to acquaint judge and jury with his client's long history of physical and emotional abuse or Hector Freeman's criminal record, which included assault and battery convictions. Convicted of first-degree homicide, Bonnie Foreshaw was ordered by Judge Paul Vasington to serve a prison term of forty-five years.

the mental health unit, where I lived with the most disturbed women at the compound.

I was tranquilized three times a day with Elavil, an addictive drug that made me withdrawn, suicidal, and obese. I had entered Niantic at five feet nine and 110 pounds, down from my normal weight of 140 because of the tribulations I faced before and after my separation from my husband. Nine months after my incarceration, I weighed 240. How did I survive that first year at Niantic? The living conditions, the drugs and depression, the court runs, the hateful stares of protesters when I entered the courthouse, my public defender's indifference to my fate? *How* did I survive? Two ways. First, I made it through on the strength of my Rastafarian beliefs. I read my Bible—the Michael B. Scoffield translation, which purges the Old Testament of the Europeans' revisions and restores the truth. Second, the inmate elders stepped forward—my friend Miss Doris and other prisoners who befriended and mothered me back from the brink with cups of tea, comforting hugs, and a willingness to listen. I practiced as best I could the principles of simplicity, equality, and harmony with nature. I stopped trusting man-made medicines and freed myself as much as possible from the steady stream of processed junk food available at the commissary. I prayed. I accepted my new life. My dark depressions subsided.

Because I was the first Rastafarian ever incarcerated at Niantic, I was the object of many preconceptions among inmates and staff, especially the latter. I made no attempt to preach, but whenever the chance presented itself, I asked people to question their stereotypes of Rastas as jobless, reefer-smoking bums. Did I convince anyone to examine their prejudices? I don't know. What I do know is that I practiced my faith under a double standard. A fellow inmate who was an Orthodox Jew obtained permission to have kosher food brought in by an outside service. This woman's rabbi was granted the privilege of counseling her in the privacy of her room. My request for an untainted Ital diet was denied, and my religious counselor was restricted to the main visitors' room, where he was monitored by security. But a black woman raised in America knows all about the need to choose her battles, so I coped with these limitations and went on.

It was not all bad at Niantic. Some days my despair gave way to peace of mind and, occasionally, even moments of joy. In my early years at the prison, rehabilitation was the focus. Officers were stern when they had to be, but also humane enough to give a hug or a kind word when you were having a bad day, or to hand you a birthday card or a home-baked treat. These small acts of kindness helped me survive the bleakness.

Separation from her kids is always difficult for an incarcerated woman, but at holiday time it's brutal. In the "old days," staff understood that and did what they could to provide a familylike atmosphere. There were prizes for the best-decorated housing units and a special Christmas meal with table decorations and small gifts. We'd sit down, eat with our friends, and put aside our petty differences. In summertime, there was fishing at Bride Lake, a barbecue, and a staff-versus-inmate softball game, with the focus more on fun than winning. "Trailer visits" with family were possible for women with good behavior records. Overnight visitors could bring in music and food from home, and an inmate could wake up in the company of her loved ones. When I had *my* trailer visits, everyone at the compound knew it. You could smell Caribbean food cooking, hear reggae coming through the windows, see kids laughing and playing out in the yard. Staff and inmates would stop by to say hello and get a taste of conch salad, or some stewed peas and rice, or a banana fritter. These weren't "country club" conditions, the way some people have criticized. This was recognition that the women of Niantic are human beings first, prisoners second. This sharing and caring was love as I knew it—emotional survival.

Look, I understand how power works. Coming of age in the 1960s and '70s, I was in line with Bobby Seale's and Angela Davis's demands for equality for all Americans—such a radical idea! A decade later, I worked on voter registration, trying to get Democrats elected in my hometown. As a union steward, I defended workers' rights and urged people to "buy American." I am and always have been a political woman.

Politics outside of prison has a direct effect on the policies inside. In the sixteen years I've been here, governors have come and gone and prison administrations with them. At Niantic, the focus has shifted from rehabilitation to punishment. Stricter rules halted the holiday decorations, summer games, and other morale-building efforts by staff. Movement within the prison became more restricted and COs became more militarylike. Before, an inmate found breaking a rule might be given a verbal reprimand. Now, she received a disciplinary ticket, A, B, or C, depending on the seriousness of the charge. A ticket could result in loss of mail or commissary privileges, or confinement to "seg"—the segregation unit. A ticket could also extend an inmate's release date and affect the decision about her parole. A woman who felt she was innocent of an officer's charge could request a hearing and plead her case. (In a way, it was like going back to court again, after you'd already been convicted and sent to jail.) Wrongly accused or not, many women were reluctant to challenge an officer's word. It was a power thing. Keep in mind, the majority of us have histories of abuse. As Niantic became more harsh, our paranoia increased. And, of course, the rumor mill ran 24/7.

During my first years at Niantic, there was no dress code for prisoners or staff. Inmates could receive clothing packages from home. Once these were examined and approved, the inmate was free to wear her own clothes. My packages consisted of blouses, pullovers, and skirts that hung below the knee. In obedience to my religious vow, I wore no pants or shorts and contained my dreadlocks in a crocheted net.

I'd been hearing the dress code rumor since 1992. Most inmates were outraged at the idea of uniforms, but I saw both sides of the issue. In many ways, prison takes away a woman's identity along with her freedom. Having to wear a uniform would further limit her ability to be herself. But a dress code might also reduce some of the jealousy that existed among inmates, and between inmates and staff. Inside Niantic, a woman's clothing, shoes, and jewelry spoke without words about her status. The "elite" dressed to impress in Claiborne, Versace, and Victoria's Secret; the less fortunate covered their nakedness with "bargain bin" and prison issue. "Boosters" (shoplifters) or prostitutes with a sugar daddy or two flashed gold earrings, diamond rings, and expensive watches and bracelets. These items aroused envy and frequently got stolen, or were declared stolen. Arguments and fights resulted. And sometimes, inmates used dress to seduce staff and gain power and privileges. When the scam worked, the results included favoritism, personal relationships, transfers, and terminations. All in all, I was in favor of a dress code for reasons of safety and security.

But I was worried, too. I'd already been hassled by staff for wearing the net that covered my locks. "Hats aren't allowed," I'd been told. "Who knows what you could be hiding in there?" I would remind whoever objected that a net with an open weave wasn't a hat and that I had always cooperated and removed it when asked, and during strip searches. "All I'm asking is that you respect my religious practices and allow me to keep my vow," I'd say. When the harassment continued, I brought the problem to a deputy warden, who issued me a "permission card" to carry and show to objecting officers.

In 1996, my tenth year in prison, the dress code rumor was finally confirmed: inmates and Department of Correction officers would now wear uniforms and be restricted in their wearing of jewelry and cosmetics. I asked Lieutenant Jones, a staff member I trusted, to describe the uniforms. "Burgundy pullovers, gray sweatshirts, and blue denim jeans," she said. It was the jeans that worried me. Wearing trousers would violate my religious vow. I asked if it would be possible to substitute a blue denim skirt for the pants. Lieutenant Jones shrugged. "Write to Reverend Sanders," she said.

I wrote not only to Lisa Sanders, Niantic's religious liaison, but also to Warden O'Keefe, who would make the final decision regarding my request. In a detailed letter, I explained my vow and my dilemma, quoting from Deuteronomy, chapter 22, verse 5: *The woman shall not wear that which pertaineth unto a man, neither shall a man put on a woman's garment: for all that do so are an abomination unto the Lord thy God.*

I waited weeks for a response but none came. My worry was turning into preoccupation and panic. I asked the school librarian for help. She found and photocopied articles on the history and traditions of the Rastafarian faith. I sent duplicate packets to Reverend Sanders and Warden O'Keefe. Neither responded. The date for prison-issue uniforms was approaching fast.

In my lifetime, I had seen over and over that it was unwise to challenge authority unless it was absolutely necessary. But this *was* necessary. Practicing my religion was my constitutional right. My anxiety began to affect my classwork at the prison school and my job as a teacher's aide. Ironically, I'd been matched that year to Ms. Cash, a new employee, because I "knew the ropes" and had proven myself trustworthy and reliable. But now I was always arriving late for class or leaving early, running back and forth to the medical unit in an effort to control my growing sense of panic. Poor Ms. Cash didn't know *what* was going on.

Each day I would wait for the institutional mail to arrive, but nothing came. At night, I'd lie awake, sick with worry about what was going to happen once the uniforms arrived. Anyone who's ever suffered insomnia will understand how long and lonely a night can be. When you're the only person still awake in a building full of sleepers, it's as if you are the last person left alive. The sense of abandonment I'd suffered as a child returned with a vengeance, and with it all the long-buried memories. . . .

My father had been a construction worker and a weekend drunk. My earliest memories are of him smashing things and my mother, bloody and crying, snatching me from bed and escaping with me to a relative's home or to the "safe house"—a room she rented as a refuge from Daddy's rages. Mom would have Dad arrested on the worst nights. He'd spend a night or two in jail, then find us and threaten to *really* hurt Mom if she didn't get back home where she belonged. So we'd go back. Dad would work all week, get drunk on Friday, and beat her up again. The cycle continued until he left us and moved north to Orlando. When my parents divorced, I was four.

Mom wanted no part of welfare. She went to work as a maid, leaving me six days a week with her sisters, her cousins, strangers, and friends. One of my sitters, Aunt Tilly, ran a gambling parlor in the living room of her one-bedroom apartment. I had to stay put in that bedroom whenever the dice were rolling or the cards were in play, except if I had to use the toilet. I guess you could say my father was my first jailer and Aunt Tilly was my second.

I was at another aunt's house when I took a tumble from a bike, hurting my vagina on the crossbar. Mom took me to the clinic to have my injury examined. "Has someone been touching you down there?" the doctor asked.

"No," I said. I have held to that denial until now, but it was a lie. I'd been abused, but not penetrated, on separate occasions by two of my cousins—one a teenager, the other a grown man. Both had warned me they'd cause trouble if I told. I don't know which cousin gave me his venereal disease.

Mom took my denial at face value and went back to work. It was her sister, Aunt May, who brought me to the clinic for my follow-up visits. I hated going there and didn't understand why I had to. There were never any toys or books in the waiting area, no other children. Mostly, the room was filled with sick old men who smelled of alcohol. "Why can't *you* take me next time?" I'd ask Mom. Her answer was always the same. "I'm too busy. I have to work."

When I turned six, Mom put a key on a string and hung it around my neck. She told me I was now old enough to walk home after school, change out of my school clothes, and get myself to the baby-sitter's. If it was too noisy at Aunt Tilly's, or if I didn't like the folks at some other sitter's house, I'd change my clothes, then roam the neighborhood instead. I'd stare at other kids' play, or tease stray cats, or sit on strangers' porches. I didn't know these people's names, but I knew their schedules. I never sat on someone's porch steps when they were home. None of the baby-sitters ever seemed to tell my mother when I didn't show up. I guess they must have forgot I was coming.

Mom almost always got home late, and when she did, it was strictly business: eat supper, take my bath, go to bed. "I love you, Mom," I'd tell her when she said good night, and she'd look away and mumble a quick, "Me, too." My mother's awkward two-syllable "me, toos" have bothered me my whole life. She said the whole thing—"I love you, too"—only once that I can recall, over the phone during my third year in prison. It shocked me—her finally saying the word *love* to me. That was in 1989, the year I was forty-two.

My mother was a devoted Christian woman who never drank, smoked, or slept around. But she organized her life around her job, not me, her daughter. That might have been easier to take if I'd been a different kind of kid. But I was who I was: a nervous child, asthmatic, too shy to join teams or clubs, and quick to cry. I tried hard in school, but I was absent a lot. I often felt more lonely in class with others than I did alone in our apartment.

Mom met Mr. Fred on the bus going to work. They courted for a year, mostly away from home. When they got married, we moved from our apartment to a larger house. I liked Mr. Fred well enough at first. I was relieved to have a father again, and this one took Mom to the movies and didn't beat her up. Some nights when I cleared the supper dishes, I'd lift Mr. Fred's plate and find a half-dollar tip.

"Can I call Mr. Fred 'Daddy' now?" I asked Mom.

"Why you want to do that? He's not your father. Call him Mr. Fred."

After that conversation, I began noticing more and more that Mr.

Fred didn't want me around. "Don't she have any friends she can go play with?" he'd ask my mother. "Here," he'd say, handing me some change. "Go buy yourself some ice cream." I'd take my time walking to and from the ice cream store, because I knew that's what Mr. Fred wanted. When I got back, he'd usually be gone.

Mr. Fred liked to be the boss. He wanted *half* a chicken cooked for supper, not a whole chicken. (Only trouble was, he ate most of it.) He called home from work all day long because he had a *right* to know where his wife was and what she was doing. He didn't care what Mom wanted—no wife of *his* was going to work while she was pregnant. It wasn't right.

I was eight when my baby sister Shirley arrived. Mr. Fred, who was half-white, had fathered a curly-haired light-skinned sweetheart who was, without question, "Daddy's girl." Mom, too, was proud and possessive of Shirley. "Put her down, Bonnie. I don't want you picking her up." I loved my half-sister but couldn't get near her. Mom, Mr. Fred, and Shirley seemed like a family of three.

The year I was twelve, we moved to Liberty City, the project. My little brother had come into the world by then. Mr. Fred had bought a car and was home less and less. Mom hated being stranded with the babies. She went back to work over Mr. Fred's objections. She caught the bus early, five days a week. My job was to get my brother and sister ready and bring them to the baby-sitter before school. When school was over for the day, I had to hurry home to pick them up again. One time I stayed after with some friends and was an hour late. The sitter was mad as hell, and so was Mom.

My mother's second marriage was not a happy one. There were more pregnancies, abortions. Mom passed off the one that almost killed her as "food poisoning." The older I got, the more I was able to figure out. "What you keep going and getting yourself pregnant for?" I heard Mr. Fred scream once. "You know all I ever wanted was the one child!" True to his word, he doted on Shirley and ignored his only son.

By the time I reached puberty, I had become one of Mr. Fred's favorite targets. "Black bitch!" "Good-for-nothing whore!" "You the neighborhood tramp, that's what *you* are!" Mr. Fred was an equal-opportunity abuser, slinging the same ugly remarks at my mother and me. His children learned by example. After a while, my sister and brother were screaming those insults at us, too. But Mr. Fred taught *me* something: how to disconnect. How to disappear in plain sight while I was being screamed at. *I can't hear him because I'm not here,* I'd tell myself, standing there, blank-faced. *He's so stupid, he doesn't even know I'm gone.* It was a survival skill I used later on, with my own abusive husbands.

Problem was, disconnection only works when the abuse is verbal. You can detach from words but not from a surprise whack upside the head. Mom was seven months pregnant with my baby sister the afternoon Mr. Fred slapped the side of her face, hard as he could. Poor Mom never saw it coming and probably wouldn't have done anything if she had. A victim all her life, she didn't know how to defend herself. But *I* could defend her. While she stood there, holding her face and crying, I jumped Mr. Fred and started wailing away. He wailed back. Mom did her best to pull us apart and the younger kids stood there screaming bloody murder. When the police arrived, Mom downplayed the situation and chose not to have Mr. Fred arrested. Well, I figured, if everyone else was going to let him get away with it, I sure wasn't. I went outside, grabbed a rock, and busted out my stepfather's windshield. For the next few nights, I had to live at my aunt's.

In high school, I was usually the last one up because I liked late-night TV. I was at the kitchen sink, getting myself a drink of water before bed one night, when Mr. Fred entered the room and came up behind me. He and Mom had gone to bed hours ago. What was going on?

Without a word, he reached around and started groping my breast. With his free hand, he grabbed my face and tried to turn it toward him for a kiss. When he pressed his erection against my butt, I shoved backward, hard as I could, and twisted away from his grip. I got out of that kitchen fast. I was slumped in a living room chair, my heart thumping, when he came out of the kitchen a few minutes later and walked past me without a word. The bedroom door closed behind him. I knew Mr. Fred was capable of many things, but *this*?

I couldn't sleep that night, and the next day at school, I couldn't concentrate. What should I do? Tell my father? He hadn't been in the picture for years. I couldn't tell Mom either. She'd be devastated. The only thing I could think to do was keep my mouth shut and watch my back. The situation was confusing, but I understood one thing: Mr. Fred had done what he'd done because he hated me.

That weekend, I went with a friend to the football game at our school. When the game was over, two boys we knew walked us home. Mr. Fred started in before the others were out of earshot. "Filthy black whore! Four-legged bitch!" When Mom told him to stop cursing me like that, he started in on her. This was going nowhere good, I figured, and started to leave the room. "Don't you walk away when I'm talking to you!" he shouted. When I ignored his command, he charged me. Next thing I knew, our fists were flying again. I stopped Mr. Fred with a medium-sized flower pot to the head. He was gone by the time the police arrived.

I begged my mother to leave Mr. Fred and take us some place safe. She said she couldn't do that and I accepted her decision. But later, at suppertime, something clicked inside of me.

"What are *you* looking at, you no-good little whore?" he said.

"Oh, so now I'm a no-good whore?" I said. "Well, I sure wasn't one when you were pawing my bust and pressing your hard-on against me."

Mom sat there, shocked, saying nothing, and Mr. Fred made his case against me. "Why would I want an ugly black bitch like her? She's lying through her teeth, trying to break us up. Ain't no man gonna want *that* thing!"

Mom sent me to my aunt's that night. When I got home from school the next afternoon, she handed me the bag she'd packed. I moved from relative to relative for the rest of the school year and got shipped off to my grandmother's in Georgia for the summer. When September rolled around again, I returned to Florida. I was an eleventh grader now, a part-time orphan who could come home only when Mr. Fred was not going to be there. I had spent my whole life trying to please my mother—achieving at school, scrubbing and cleaning the house, caring for my younger siblings. I had only wanted her to be less cool and distant, to say "I love you, too." But now that she had made her choice, I gave up the cause. Shifted my focus. I was desperate to prove that Mr. Fred was wrong. To show them both that men *would* want a "thing" like me. It's like the song says: *Sometimes I feel like a motherless child, a long way from my home.*

This was my buried history. This was why I had crossed the street to walk on the wild side all those years ago, married men that hurt me, and then crossed back again. When I became a dedicated Rastafarian, it helped me deal with my past, but the bad memories came back to claim me during those long, sleepless nights while I waited to hear from the minister or the warden about whether or not my vow would be honored—whether or not I would be excused from wearing the pants.

One morning, I saw Reverend Sanders on the walkway and approached. "Oh, yes, I got your letter," she said. "I'm going to check it out for you. I've been so busy. You won't have a problem." I was less convinced than she was.

A few days later, I was summoned to the warden's office. Bear in mind, Warden O'Keefe was the *acting* warden—the just-passing-through head of the prison. "Have a seat," he said. "I've asked Lieutenant Miller to join us, too."

So there I was, seated across the desk from power itself: a six-two, 280-pound white warden and his white female lieutenant, standing beside him. I said a quick, silent prayer before beginning. *Jesus, my Savior, do not forsake me in my time of need.*

"I understand we have a problem with you concerning the uniform," the warden began. "Is that right?"

His blue eyes were severe and intimidating, but I forced myself to look right into them. "It doesn't have to be a problem," I said. "I will wear the uniform, but not the blue jeans, because doing so would break my religious vow. My family has offered to have blue denim skirts made for me instead, or to purchase them in any way the institution deems necessary. So if you'll let me substitute—"

"There will be no exceptions to the rules," he said.

I reminded him that forcing me to wear the pants denied me my constitutional and civil rights. "Did you read the information I sent you?" I asked. He didn't say whether he had or hadn't.

"Think of it this way, Warden O'Keefe," I said. "Would you force a Muslim or a Jew to eat pork?" He cleared his throat and looked up at his lieutenant.

"Bonnie, you're making a big mistake here," Lieutenant Miller told me.

I shook my head. "The mistake would be for me to break my vow."

The lieutenant began to pace. "Well, I just hope you realize that if you refuse to obey the order, you'll go to seg."

"Have you ever seen me in pants, Lieutenant?" I asked her. She shook her head no. "That's because I take my vow seriously."

"Well, as you'll find out, we're serious, too," the warden said. "I guess we're done." The two of them glared at me like God and his archangel.

On my way out, I stopped and turned to face the warden. "I will not forsake my Higher Power for man or woman," I said. "You are not my god."

I was scared to death of going to seg, now located at York, the new facility for maximum-security inmates. For a year, I had looked across the compound and watched that massive structure rise up from the dust like a monster. York was the last place I wanted to go. But there comes a time or two in everyone's life when a stand has to be taken, and this was mine.

I have been blessed with many strong friendships inside Niantic and had done for others in need. Now, my time of need had come, and inmates, COs, teachers, and counselors all knew it. They gathered around me to offer me support and good wishes. Most were worried about the repercussions I was about to face and advised me to give in and wear the pants. The friends who knew me best understood why I couldn't.

The following Monday, Officer Pratt, the CO on duty, called me to property. "Bonnie," he said, "I'm issuing you your uniform." He handed me the stack of clothing, which I took.

"Mr. Pratt, I'm not wearing the pants," I said. He nodded and looked away, mumbling something about just taking orders.

I returned to my room and removed the blouse I'd been wearing, replacing it with the burgundy pullover. I was already wearing my denim skirt. I was packing for the move to seg when my counselor, Ms. Doyle, appeared in the doorway. "I hate to do this, Bonnie, but it's a formality. I'm giving you a direct order to put on your uniform."

"Ms. Doyle, as you know, I can't put on the pants because it would violate my religious vow," I said.

"Then you're refusing a direct order." She disappeared.

Later, my friend Lieutenant Jones came by to wish me well. Lieutenant Jones was "old" Niantic. She was smiling, but there were tears in her eyes. "If there was anything I could do, I'd do it," she said. I gave her a hug and told her not to make me cry. I wouldn't be seeing Lieutenant Jones for a while, or Robin, or Patty, or any of my friends. My confinement in seg meant I couldn't go to school, or to the visiting room, or even to a medical appointment.

Just before the 11:00 P.M. count, Officer Walker appeared at my door. "Bonnie, it's time to go," she said. Ms. Walker had been one of the first COs I'd encountered at Niantic. One of the few black officers back then, she was a "token," I figured—hired to fill some quota and willing to sell out her race to appease her white co-workers. That had been a harsh judgment on my part, and an incorrect one. Over the years, I'd come to respect her fairness and willingness to help. She was kind that night. She didn't handcuff me. She transported me in the lieutenant's car rather than the prison van. She treated me with as much dignity as possible.

"I thought I was going to York," I said, when Officer Walker pulled unexpectedly in front of Thompson Hall. I'd be transferred to the new facility in a day or two, she said. For now, I'd been assigned to Thompson, one of the oldest and most depressing buildings at the compound— and the place where I had begun my prison term. It was like a demotion to my first, worst days at Niantic.

The room I had just evacuated back in Fenwick South had mini-blinds, family pictures, and colorful crocheted afghans on the beds. It was comfortable and homey, with a sparkling clean linoleum floor I kept waxed to a high shine. In contrast, my new "home" had an unmade bed, dirt and dust balls in the corners, and colorless walls. A quote from the Bible came to mind, a passage I couldn't quite place: *I came into this world with nothing, and I will leave this world with nothing.* I wanted to cry, but I prayed instead.

An hour later, the CO on duty opened my cell and handed me a shower robe and the special uniform prisoners in seg must wear—green scrubs, like the kind doctors wear in surgery. I kept the shirt and shower robe but gave him back the pants. After I'd changed he came back. I surrendered the clothes I'd arrived in—the burgundy pullover and my denim skirt. I felt strangely at peace. But when the lights went out a short time later, I lay in the dark and the old fears returned.

"Let's pray," Reverend Sanders suggested the next day. She had done nothing to defend my religious rights, but now she was there to counsel me. I said a silent prayer: *God, please grant me humility and the mental and spiritual strength to endure this trial I am facing.* I also prayed to be spared false prophets.

Later that day, I was transferred to the compound's West Side, York C.I., maximum security, and escorted to Lieutenant Jasper's office. I stood before him in my undergarments, socks, sneakers, my green scrub shirt, and my state-issued shower robe. "Have you changed your mind about wearing the pants?" he asked. I told him no. He nodded and dismissed me without a hassle.

Lieutenant Roper was a different story. I'd known him since his first days at Niantic and had never had a problem with him. But that day, he was all attitude and intimidation. "We can take 'good days' from you for disobeying a direct order.* What you're doing is biting your nose off to spite your face."

"What I'm doing is keeping my religious honor intact," I said.

When Lieutenant Jasper returned, he escorted me to 3 North, Seg. I felt the eerie chill as soon as I entered the building. Two uniformed staff members sat at a control panel—a series of electronic buttons that locked and opened cell doors, operated the intercom, turned the lights on and off. Seated at that panel, the officers could control a prisoner's life without ever having to make direct contact. I was issued two sheets and a blanket and assigned cell 6A on the top tier. I climbed the stairs, stood before the door, and waited. The door opened with a click. I entered. It closed behind me and clicked again.

Four gray walls, a door, a window, toilet and sink, and the hum of recycled air from the vent—a prison inside a prison. I felt alone and afraid, but determined, too. Hadn't Jesus been persecuted? Hadn't Martin Luther King, Nelson Mandela, Mahatma Gandhi, and Steven Biko all seen the inside of a prison cell? Thinking about those great men gave me strength. With God's grace and guidance, I would endure whatever toll segregation was going to take on my mind, heart, body, and soul.

But it was hard. Isolation can make the weak weaker. Push an unstable mind over the edge. Make prisoners of war cooperate with their captors. How was this going to end? Who would I be when it was all over?

"Pop 6A," someone called. *Click.* A CO opened the door, handed me a lunch tray, and backed out again. *Click.*

An hour or two later, while I was staring out through the slit of glass in my cell door, I spotted a staff member I recognized. "Ms. Ray! Ms. Ray, it's me! Bonnie!" She stopped and looked in at me. Ms. Ray and I

---

*"Good days" accumulate for women whose records remain clean. They are subtracted from her sentence as she nears the end of her term and thus can shorten her prison stay.

had known each other a long time. We respected each other. She had sometimes come to me for advice about how to deal with the youthful offenders she supervised. "I didn't do anything wrong, Ms. Ray!" I shouted out. She stared back like I was a creature at the Bronx Zoo. Then she walked away.

The next several days were filled with silence, Bible reading, and prayer. My old, familiar enemy—the feeling of abandonment—had crept into the cell with me, but people came and went. The officers with my food trays, Reverend Sanders, a deacon I had never met before, "bad cop" and "good cop" lieutenants trying to convince me to obey the rules. I told them all the same thing: that I had done everything I could to try to prevent this situation but would not break my religious vow. "Even when I'm right, people say I'm wrong," I told them. "But I am at peace with my decision."

It was a bluff. I was not at peace. I prayed to God for the strength to endure this tribulation but was haunted by a swirl of fears, demons, and memories. I saw my mother's bruised face and those old drunks at the VD clinic . . . I heard my husbands' and Hector Freeman's taunts and jeers . . . I felt my cousin's hot breath on my face, Mr. Fred's hand on my breast, and the blows of the metal bat as my husband pinned me against the bed and beat the dignity out of me. In that cell, I was a woman fighting for her religious freedom, but I was also a woman cut off from her family—a little girl no one had ever really wanted. "Help me, Jesus," I whispered. "Take this fear from me. Jah Rastafari, please don't forsake me in my time of need."

Deputy Warden Levy appeared the following morning. I had never worked with him before—had never even seen him. He was a little guy, five-five or five-six, medium build. He had thick, choppy hair, gentle brown eyes, and an aura of inner peace that I noticed immediately. He entered my cell almost like an angel of mercy.

"Bonnie, I've come to reason with you," he said.

I told him my obedience was to God, not to man or woman. He nodded and said he understood. His use of the word *reason* was a comfort.

"What religion do you profess to?" I asked.

"I'm a Jew, but not a practicing one." Well, I thought, practicing or not, here is a man who knows about religious persecution.

"Bonnie, you have every right to practice your faith. By right, you shouldn't even be here in seg. But a line's been drawn and the uniform issue is beyond my control. I'm not here to force or intimidate you in any way, and I don't expect you to disobey your vow. But I think I know a way out of this. Would you like to hear my idea?"

I nodded.

"Suppose I go get the pants and come back here. Suppose *I* put them on you. That way, come Judgment Day, it would be me who'd have to account for the disavowal, not you. If I put the pants on you, would you resist?"

Confused and exhausted, I began to cry. Was this a way out or a hypocrisy? Was this man's intervention proof that God had not forsaken me or proof that He had? A hundred arguments rushed through my head.

"I won't resist you," I finally said.

When Deputy Warden Levy returned with the green scrub pants, he knelt at my feet and gently slipped them on. "Could you stand, please, Bonnie?" he asked. When I did, he tied the drawstring around my waist. I fell back on the bed and began to wail. "Bonnie, you did nothing wrong," he said. "Thank you for letting me help you. Please take care of yourself."

After he left, I cried a river. I cried until there were no tears left. For the rest of that long day, I couldn't get off the bed.

When I left seg the following day wearing pants, it was hard to walk back into the general population. Clutching my Bible, I kept my eyes cast down to avoid people's stares, sympathetic or otherwise. I had traveled a long, long way from that sassy young woman in the black fedora and borrowed clothes who'd sashayed down the church aisle. Now I was a broken, bitter woman in prison blue jeans.

For the next several days, I couldn't eat, sleep, or even move much. I was not interested in talking to anyone either. I was ordered to the mental health unit for an examination.

"Are you hearing voices?" the doctor asked me.

"No."

"Do you feel like you want to hurt yourself?"

"No."

"Maybe you'd like to tell me what's bothering you?"

I shook my head. "What's done is done and can't be *un*done," I said.

He nodded and left the room. A minute later, he returned and said I could leave.

I was despondent for weeks. I had no appetite. I couldn't smile. Staff whom I'd come to trust no longer seemed trustworthy. I wanted only to stay in my room, read my Bible, and have people leave me alone. Each morning, with shame in my heart, I rose from bed and put on my pants.

But God is merciful. Little by little, He guided me away from my despair and made me want to live again. I came to understand that bitterness and animosity would eat my soul like a cancer. Only forgiveness would set me free.

I came to see, too, that actions speak louder than pants. When I arrived in Niantic back in 1986, confused and scared, I was cradled in the arms of the elders who comforted me and helped me survive. Today I serve as a mentor and substitute mom to other frightened women, and as "Grandma" to several youthful offenders, those tough, scared babies whose innocence I can see beneath their masks of defiance.

I am a better and wiser person because of all I've endured. I no longer bury my painful memories, but I try not to dwell on them either. It's like I told that psychologist, "What's done is done and can't be undone." My focus is on the here and now, and on my future. It's like the song says: *Any day now, any day now, I shall be released.* I can smell the home cooking already.

Bonnie Jean Foreshaw was the first person ever tried in Connecticut for the murder of a pregnant woman. Convicted of first-degree homicide, she was ordered to serve a prison term of forty-five years, the lengthiest sentence ever given an inmate at the facility. To date, Foreshaw has been imprisoned longer than any other woman serving time at York prison.

Legal experts familiar with the Foreshaw case maintain that her public defender failed to meet the minimum standard of competency provided by the Constitution and that, given the circumstances surrounding the shooting, Foreshaw should have been charged with manslaughter, not first-degree murder. Attorney Mary Werblin, who has done pro bono legal work for Foreshaw in an effort to get her case reexamined, contends that Foreshaw's trial exposes the court's gender and class bias.

Bonnie Foreshaw has four children and four grandchildren and serves unofficially as a surrogate "mom" to many of the women and teenage girls at York. Dedicated to the cause of helping women less fortunate than herself, Foreshaw is active in York prison's chapter of Literacy Volunteers of America and support groups such as Alternatives to Violence.

"Writing has given me a voice I never had before," she says. "It has become an important part of my healing, which continues to this very day. What I hope is that people reading this book will bear in mind that we are human beings first, inmates second."

In October 2002, prison officials reversed their earlier decision and allowed Bonnie Foreshaw to wear a skirt.

P U Z Z L E   P I E C E S

B A R B A R A   P A R S O N S   L A N E

Born: 1948

Conviction: Manslaughter, due to
emotional duress

Sentence: 25 years, to be suspended
after 10

Entered prison: 1996

Status: Incarcerated

1. THE VISIT

I'm seated at a long metal table on the maximum-security side of the York visiting room, waiting. My hands fidget. Someone's laughter makes me jump. Since I came here ten days ago, I've been troubled by surprise noises: a raised voice, the slam of a cell door, the slap of playing cards on a tabletop. I'm on high alert. Who's standing near me? Will she invade my space? Am I safe?

Whoever's come to see me will be my first visitor. I have no comb, no makeup. My bangs droop down in my face because the delousing shampoo neutralized my perm. Until now, I haven't even thought about my appearance. I haven't been able to face myself in a mirror anyway.

The visiting room door opens. Four faces appear—my four beautiful children: Andrea, twenty-eight, tall and willowy; Arthur, twenty-six, responsible beyond his years; his brother, Adam, twenty, the most fun-loving of my four; and Amanda, seventeen, my baby in her baggy jeans, ripped at the knees. Oh, my God, what have I done? How am I going to live without them?

There are rules: prisoner on one side of the table, visitors on the other; no lingering embraces or body-to-body hugs. Because the table that separates us is three feet wide, I can hardly reach my children. I give each a kiss on the cheek, a brief, awkward embrace. "I can't talk about what happened," I tell them. "I don't want you to say anything bad about Mark."

Andrea takes charge, keeping the conversation neutral: her husband has stayed in Georgia with the kids; Arthur sent her the money for her flight to Connecticut. "Thank you, Arthur," I tell my son. "That means a lot to me." He nods, smiles back. Eye contact is an effort for both of us.

"Mom, I *hate* what's happened to you!" Adam blurts out. "Isn't there *anything* we can do to get you home?" There isn't.

We have two hours together, but the time goes by too fast. We cry, console each other, make plans for what's dreaded but necessary: rerouting the mail, notifying the creditors, packing up the home I'm about to lose. As the rules dictate, I remain seated when my children stand to leave. Watching them walk back into their lives makes me feel like I'm losing parts of my own body. Back in my cell, I curl up on my bunk and rock for hours.

* * *

"This one is mines," the tall black girl says. She's pregnant, in her twenties. When she drapes her arm around my shoulder, I shrug away from her.

"Please don't touch me," I say.

But she's persistent. "You want an apple?"

"No thanks."

"That's right, baby," Bertha advises. "Don't take anything from Big Bird. She'll think you owe her if you do. Big Bird uses kindness to prey on new faces." A tall, powerfully built black woman, Bertha is fifteen or sixteen years younger than I am, but she's taken me under her wing, coaching me through the official rules of the prison and the unofficial rules of the twenty-four women on our tier.

I'm a mess. I speak slowly, and seldom. When people talk to me, it takes a long time for my brain to register what they said. I don't know why these girls act like we're at a pajama party. No one seems to understand the seriousness of our situation. I feel like I've been stranded on a foreign island where the native speech is street talk, Spanish, and jailhouse slang.

During recreation time, I risk the TV room. Moving to a chair, I sit with my feet tucked under me, trying to curl up in a ball. I'm pretending to watch television, but I can't hear it. Everyone's talking at once; no one's listening. The clamor hurts my ears. When it's too loud, my mind shuts down and the room goes silent. Abrupt noises, loud music, shouted words: all of these trigger flashbacks to my crime. I keep going back and going back there. "Don't talk to *anyone* about that night," my lawyers have warned me. "The walls have ears." But what more could I reveal? By the time a lawyer arrived at the Litchfield Barracks to represent me, I had confessed to whatever I could think of—every sin I'd committed in a lifetime of forty-eight years.

"Here, baby," Bertha says. "Make yourself a cup of tea." She unfolds my hand and places a teabag and several Sugar Twins on my palm. I close my hand around them and begin to cry. "You'll be okay," Bertha whispers.

The next day, Bertha's hollering. Someone's thrown used, unwrapped sanitary pads in the shower trash can and she's not having it. "Nothing but a bunch of dirty 'hos! Clean up after yourselves! No one wants to look at *that*!" Her shouting bounces off the walls of the tier.

I'm scared. I don't want to make Bertha any madder than she is, but I don't know what a dirty 'ho is. When I ask her in a whisper, she whispers back. "It's okay, Miss Barbara. This isn't meant for you." Then she resumes her ranting. "Place looks like a bunch of pigs live here! Well, let me tell *you* something. This ain't Hotel York and I ain't your maid!"

Bertha's sidekick is Twink, a football tackle of a woman who looks like a man. At night, they sit side by side, rocking as one. Twink sucks her thumb, the right one. With her left hand, she rubs Bertha's earlobe. I have never seen grown women do this before: suck their thumbs and rock together like children. How can they be so tough yet so afraid?

I'm leery of everyone here, but afraid only of myself. I have so many emotions bottled inside. What if I lose control and erupt? The others tell me there's a prison inside the prison called segregation. "You don't want to go to seg, baby," Bertha warns. So I use whatever's left of my mind to stay in control.

My counselor, Mr. Planky, calls me to his office and says I've been ordered to work. I begin to shake. I tell him about my flashbacks, my inability to focus. "I just don't think I can handle a job assignment yet."

"Well, you *have* to. If you refuse a direct order, you'll go to seg."

The paperwork he hands me says I don't have to work if I'm unsentenced, but I'm afraid to mention it. If I make trouble, I might end up in seg no matter what it says. "You've been assigned to Food Prep," Mr. Planky says. "Security has cleared you to work in the kitchen."

I've just killed someone. What kind of security do they have here? I say nothing and sign.

Court runs are the worst of the nightmare I'm living now. Whenever I'm scheduled to appear before the judge, I rise at five A.M., pack all my belongings, and drag them to Admittance & Departure. Along with the other women who have court that day, I'm strip-searched, locked in a communal holding cell, and given cereal, milk, and a piece of fruit. At seven, we're herded onto the prison bus in handcuffs, shackles, and belly chains. A locked black box secures our hands close to our waists. In Bridgeport, I'm transferred from the bus to a paddy wagon—an "ice cream truck" in prison lingo—which will take me to the courthouse where I'm due to appear. I share the ride with other prisoners, most of them men. We few women huddle opposite them on bench seats. The men leer, ridicule, and make sexual comments about us as we ride.

I arrive at the courthouse at about ten A.M. Because of postponements and legal maneuverings, I sometimes never even make it before the judge, and so have made the grueling trip for nothing. I spend the day in chains, waiting to return to Niantic. When court closes at five, I'm loaded back onto the ice cream truck. I face a commute of several hours, slowed by pickups of other Niantic inmates at court lockups across the state.

I arrive back at York at nine P.M. I'm strip-searched for reentry and my belongings are returned. I drag them back to my housing unit. By now, the headache I've been nursing all day is pounding so badly that it would be easier for me to *crawl* back to my cell than walk there. Sometimes, after these endless court days, a friend gets me a cup of hot water. I mix it with the coffee crystals they sell at the commissary and swallow my first caffeine of the day. I take two Tylenol and fall into bed, waiting for the throbbing in my head to subside and the day's images to fade.

After a number of these trips, I'm ready to surrender—to take any sentence just to be done with court runs. My lawyer files a request for expediency. Nine months after I committed my crime, I am tried, convicted, and sentenced to twenty-five years in prison, suspended after ten.

In therapy, I'm asked if my husband's talk of killing me made me afraid.

"No," I answer firmly.

Did his threats impair my ability to function in daily life?

"No. I functioned fine."

But had I? How could I *not* have been afraid? Why do I feel safer here in prison than I felt at home?

My brain won't work the way it used to. My attention span is shorter and I have difficulty retaining what I've read. A good speller all my life, I now struggle to remember how to spell common words. The doctors call my preoccupation with my surroundings "hypervigilance." Loud noises trigger nausea, moments of emotional blankness, and flashbacks to my scariest memories. About my crime, I have what's called "dissociative amnesia." I can't remember shooting Mark but can still see the look of hatred on his face the moment before. That look haunts me. The flashbacks make me feel as if my nerves are exposed, as if electricity is crackling along the surface of my skin.

In Food Prep, we cook for inmates here and at other state facilities. Sometimes I work two shifts. I don't mind. Being busy leaves me less time to think. After work, I play Scrabble to improve my spelling and concentration. I still don't talk much, but writing letters helps me retrieve some of the memories that had gone blank. In the fall, I enroll in evening classes at the prison school. The coursework overwhelms me, but I'm trying to coax my brain back to functioning the way it once did.

I know I am in prison because I took a life and must be punished. I take full responsibility for my crime. My greatest punishment is not the loss of my freedom, or the bleakness of my new "home," or the fears I face. Far worse than these is the separation from my children's lives—the lost opportunity to watch my grandchildren grow, the inability to make sure my family is safe. I used to tell my kids, "You're going to get curious about trying things, and I may not always agree with the choices you make along the way, but I always need to know where you are. If I know you're safe, I can deal with the rest."

Because of my crime, I have forfeited that reassurance. It's hard to mother my children from prison and right now they need me as much as they ever have. What I've done has devastated them.

2. PUZZLE PIECES

Childhood memories are like an old puzzle taken down from a shelf. You open the box, finger the pieces. But old puzzles can be frustrating. Some pieces that looked like matches refuse to fit. Others are bent or misplaced. Some pieces are lost forever. My earliest memories begin at age four.

Aunt Eleanor's the baby-sitter this afternoon while Mommy's over at Grandma's. I'm supposed to take a nap, but I'm not sleepy. It's hot in here and I can't get comfortable. I miss my mother.

My room's at the front of the house. I get up from bed to watch the cars drive by. The window screen has millions of little tic-tac-toes. I've watched Mommy take out this screen when she washes the windows. I flip the latch and it comes out. Maybe I'll surprise my mother with a visit.

I swing my leg over the ledge, hike my dress to my waist, and pull myself up. *Jump!* I tell myself. After I land, I pick the little pebbles out of my hands and wipe the dirt on the sides of my dress. Grandma lives near the center of town. I know how to get there. I start walking.

A car slows down behind me. Follows me. The man pulls up beside me and rolls down his window. "Hello, Barbara," he says. "Where you headed?" I know this man. He's called the Constable. He and my father are friends.

"Grandma's house. I know the way."

"Well, that's about a mile and a half down the road. I'm going that way. Why don't I just make sure you get there safely?" Daddy says that's the Constable's job: to make sure everyone's safe.

I shake my head. "I want to walk."

"Tell you what, then. I'll drive behind you real slow, and if you get tired, you just let me know."

As I walk, I kick stones, pick dandelions, sing to myself. Whenever I look back, I see the shiny grille of the Constable's car. My grandparents' house is farther away than I thought, but the closer I get, the more excited I feel, and the faster I walk. Then, yippee, I'm *there*. The car pulls into Grandma's driveway. I run inside and slam the door.

Grandma stands there, staring at me. "What are you doing here?" she says. "Who brought you?" Before I can answer, she calls my mother's name.

Their faces are red; their hands are flying. I tell them about my walk, and the car in the driveway. Grandma runs outside. Mommy runs to the ringing telephone. "Calm down," she keeps saying. "She's okay. She's *here*." Was it bad for me to want to be with Mom? Am I in trouble?

Grandma comes back from her talk with the Constable. Everyone's glad I'm safe, but Mom says she'll spank me next time. "But you're never going to do *that* again. Right, Barbara?"

I've been taught not to lie, so I don't answer her. Maybe I *will* do it again. Why were they scared? The Constable was following right behind me. And anyway, I knew the way.

Later that same year, we have another visitor. Grandpa's handsome. He has thick black wavy hair and brown eyes. He talks Southern.

When Grandpa visits, he and I take walks, either into town or down

Route 7 to the store that sells gas and newspapers. I like going there because it has a soda fountain, a pinball machine, and a shelf of gifts like miniature tea sets and dishes. Grandpa's friends with the owner of the store, a red-haired man who loves to talk and has a million freckles.

Today the owner says he has to go somewhere in a hurry. Can we stay until he gets back? "Sure," my grandfather says. "Take your time."

After he leaves, Grandpa lifts me onto a stool at the soda fountain. I'm dressed in my white dress covered with flowers and my straw hat. Grandpa brings me a soda in a tall glass. I have to sit on my knees to reach the straw.

Grandpa walks over to a funny doorway that has cloth hanging down instead of a door. He pulls the cloth to the side and looks in. I peek, too. It's dark. There's a little bed in there, and newspapers over the windows. "Want to see what's in this room?" Grandpa asks.

Inside the room, he picks me up and rushes me to the bed. He puts his hand over my mouth and tugs at my underpants. He's breathing fast. I don't know what's happening. I close my eyes tight and push my legs together, make them as stiff as I can, but Grandpa keeps pulling them apart.

On the walk back, Grandpa's lips move but I can't hear him. I don't like him anymore. When he goes home the next morning, I'm glad.

It takes me a while to tell my mother what Grandpa did, and when I do, she looks me in the eye. "Don't ever mention this to anyone," she says. "Don't you ever say a word."

And I don't. I become a quiet girl. "Barbara's so quiet, I forget she's here," people say. I'm quiet, but I'm angry, too. Lots of things make me mad, and when they do, I bite. Adults, other kids, even animals. If you cross me when I'm boiling inside, I will bite you as hard as I can.

Many years later, in 1990, my mother committed suicide by hurling herself from the twelfth floor of an apartment building. In the months that followed, I grieved and struggled with my feelings about her life and death. It was to my aunt Ruth, Mom's oldest sister, that I broke my promise of silence. My aunt revealed a secret of her own. Grandpa had molested Mommy, too.

That's the puzzle piece that's lost for good—the one buried with my mother. She had known who he was, what he was capable of. She'd been his victim, too. How could Mom have stood at the window and watched me walk hand in hand with Grandpa down Route 7?

I am tired now, sick of puzzles and memories. My grandfather is long dead, and my mother, now, too. And I'm in prison for having taken the life of my husband, the man who molested my granddaughter, the child of my child.

3. CELL DOOR WINDOW

Walking up the stairs to my twelve-cell tier, I spot an inmate standing at her window, staring out at nothing. The faraway look on her face makes me nervous and I hurry past.

I'm impatient as I stand in front of my locked cell door, waiting for the guard to see me and trigger the switch. *Click.* I enter the dim cell, nodding to my roommate, Sherry. The door closes behind me. *Click.*

Our cell has two windows. One looks onto the compound. The other, a three-by-eighteen-inch strip of glass built into the cell door, gives a narrow view of the corridor. I lie on my bed—the lower bunk because I'm over forty. In her boredom, Sherry stands at our skinny strip of window and broadcasts bulletins about what she sees. "Tara's in the common area, moving her bags. Wonder where she's going. . . . The counselor's talking to Remmy. Maybe she's moving, too." Tara's a skinny black girl with a scarred face she's constantly picking at. Remmy wears her pants low, hip-hop style, and swaggers like a boy. I roll onto my side and face the wall, hoping to discourage Sherry's chatter. *Who cares?* I want to scream. *Do you know what you look like from the other side of that door? A caged animal, that's what!*

Suddenly, I'm seventeen again, walking the corridor of Fairfield Hills Psychiatric Hospital to my mother's room and ignoring, as best I can, the stares of her peers, the other caged mental patients.

The drive from Kent to Fairfield Hills took over an hour in fast-moving traffic, a nerve-racking commute for a beginning driver. The travel drained me, and the visits were worse, but I kept my feelings in check, pretending I was stronger than I was. I went every day. Mom needed the company and no one else would visit her.

Her first hospitalization began in August and stretched two months into the school year. Dad had trouble accepting Mom's condition. He'd work late at the garage, then stop by the firehouse to visit his buddies. When he came home, there was usually liquor on his breath. My brother Steve was fifteen that summer and my sister, Joanne, was twelve. The few times I managed to shame my brother and sister into going with me, Mom and I did all the talking. Joanne and Steve just sat there, scared to death, gaping at the other patients.

Mom believed it was the responsibility of the eldest daughter to assist with household chores and put little stock in the idea that Steve and Joanne should pitch in, too. While she was hospitalized, I cooked, cleaned, did the laundry, and drove to Fairfield Hills. At night, I'd fall asleep doing homework. Joanne's unwillingness to help was particularly galling. "You don't do anything around here, you spoiled baby! When I was your age, I was doing half the housework!"

"Ask me if I care!"

"Baby!"

With my brother, I took on the role of nagging parent. "You'd better stay out of trouble. Mom would be in *worse* shape if she knew you were staying out late and doing things you shouldn't. And you *know* how mad Dad can get." There was a fist-size hole in Steve's bedroom wall, a leftover from a "discussion" with Dad. As mad as my brother could make me, I dreaded the thought of one of those punches connecting.

Rather than stay home, my siblings fled. Joanne practically *lived* at her friend's house. Steve packed his things and moved into the bunkhouse at the dairy farm where he worked part-time. I resented the irony of it: Mom's illness had freed my brother and sister and made me a slave.

If you spared the rod, you would spoil the child, my mother believed, and I was the daughter she was least interested in spoiling. She threatened, hit, threw things: once, a pot of peas, boiling away on the stove; another time a plastic hairbrush that hit so hard, it broke in two against my arm.

At Fairfield Hills, however, Mom was peaceful and composed. Walking down the corridors to the visiting room, I'd pass other patients peering out of their rooms, their faces emotionless masks. Some men had food caked in their beard stubble. Some women wore limply tied housecoats that exposed their bare chests. One toothless, drooling patient seemed unaware of the wet mark on the front of his T-shirt, as big as a dinner plate.

So as not to excite my mother, I kept my voice low and my conversation neutral. "Steve's working at the farm today. . . . Joanne's sure lucky. Her friend Patty invited her to the beach." I'd pass along Dad's excuse of the day. "He *wanted* to come tonight, Mom, but the fire truck needed repairing."

Mom would shake her head and sigh. "I had to sit all by myself next to your brother's hospital bed and watch him die while your father was at work."

"I know, Mom. That was hard for you."

Just before his second birthday, my brother David had developed bronchial pneumonia and gone to the hospital, where his condition worsened. Powerless to fix his son, Dad had left his bedside for a few hours and gone to work. When David died later that night, both of my parents were with him, but Mom had never forgiven her husband the hours he'd left.

"*I* was the one who stayed with David. Not him."

"David's death was tough on all of us, Mom. Dad included."

"*I* stayed with David."

She looked so pitiful, hunched in her chair, wearing her white dress with the little tan flowers and green leaves, the print faded from too many washings. "Not to change the subject, Mom, but I'm making your spaghetti sauce tonight. Should I put the Italian sausage right in while it's simmering?"

"Or you could stick in hamburger meat." For the rest of that visit, we stayed safely on the subject of recipes.

On another visit, my mother introduced me to her new friend, a fellow patient who halted my attempt at conversation to inform me that she was a worm who lived in coffee grounds. I was wearing pigtails that day. Mom's friend advised me that I was much too old for a style like that. "Who do you think you are?" she asked. "Pollyanna?" Of course, *her* hair looked like a fright wig and she'd buttoned the wrong buttons all the way up the front of her dress. I thanked her politely and promised I'd try a different style the next day. She nodded, pleased with herself for having straightened me out. Driving home, I fumed and muttered to myself. Now I had to take fashion advice from a *worm*?

From visit to visit, Mom's moods were unpredictable and subject to abrupt change. Sometimes, my getting up to leave at the end of visiting hours would trigger hysteria. "Mom, I *can't* take you home with me," I cried during one such incident. "They won't *let* me." She howled so loudly, resisted my exit so strenuously, that the attendants had to restrain her. "Okay, we got her," they told me. *"Go!"* On the long drive home, I made myself a list of reasons why this hospital stay was *good* for her. But my heart wasn't in it. I kept seeing her being straitjacketed and strong-armed back to her room.

Back at home, I vacuumed, cooked, and scoured, fighting back a jumble of conflicting feelings: my fear for Mom, my embarrassment of her, my resentment of all the responsibilities her illness had dumped on me. Mom's mental condition was a *private* shame. There was no one to talk to outside the family, and my father, brother, and sister were never home. It was up to me to stay strong and do what needed to be done, for Mom and for the rest of them.

I will *not* go to my cell window and stare out without a purpose. *Get away from that window!* I want to scream at Sherry. *Don't let this place swallow you up! Don't become a caged animal!* But I'm silent, self-preserving. I no longer have the strength to carry the others, too.

4. THE THREAT

I come home from work to a backyard of dead birds. They'd been shot, picked off one by one at the bird feeder. The sunflowers growing around our well had been decapitated. Mark had used the flowers and birds for target practice.

Lately, he's become intolerant of my body hair and has ordered me to keep my pubic area shaved. It embarrasses me to do this, but I obey him in the name of what I still call "love." It's best not to question Mark's demands or to criticize his new habits: drinking and smoking with a younger crowd, following me to check on my whereabouts. In our eleven years together, I've never given him cause to suspect me of cheating. It's his own infidelity that makes him imagine I've been unfaithful, too.

Each evening he floods our yard with light to prevent burglaries. This preoccupation with thieves has caused him to chain his snowmobile to a tree, his three-wheeler to the truck bumper. "No one's going to steal *my* shit," he insists. His possessions are tethered and cinched, bathed in light.

It's strange, really. They say a woman ends up married to a version of her father, but Mark is more like Mom. Two years into our marriage, he was diagnosed with the same disease she'd suffered: paranoid schizophrenia. Many of Mark's behaviors are like hers. But unlike Mom, Mark refuses to take his prescriptions, medicating himself with alcohol instead.

Mark had tried to win my heart for months before I noticed. I'd divorced my children's father a few years earlier, when my oldest was sixteen and my youngest was six. Between work and single motherhood, I was too busy for romance. I was skeptical of the difference in our ages, too; Mark was closer in age to my teenagers than to me. But he persisted, offering me an intoxicating blend of excitement and romance. Roses, teddy bears, amusement parks, motorcycle rides. After a lifetime of serving others, suddenly *I* was the one being indulged—and by a younger man. We became friends first, then inseparable companions. I came to love Mark more than the breath I drew.

We were married in 1988, at a pondside service in early fall. The next year, we moved to a bigger house with a backyard that sloped down to the river. I recall these as happy times, Mark and my sons fishing and biking, Amanda and I working in the garden and cooking big family meals. Andrea, who'd been living in Germany with her husband, came home to await the end of his duty overseas and to prepare for the birth of their baby. Alesha, my first grandchild, was born in January 1990.

But happy times were hard to hold on to. My mother took her life. My son-in-law was ordered to Operation Desert Storm. Problems had begun to surface in my marriage, too. Mark had joined a dart team that competed at local taverns, and he insisted I meet him after work at these bars. It was hard to watch his flirtations with younger women. He began drinking more heavily and lying about his whereabouts. Upset about his behavior, and still working through my grief over my mother, I saw my family doctor, then a therapist, and finally a lawyer. Mark and I traveled to his father's home in Montana for Thanksgiving. It was on that trip that Mark first threatened to harm me if I ever tried to leave him.

For a while, things improved. On New Year's Day, 1992, we rented a five-bedroom house, bought furniture, and fixed up the kids' rooms. In April, I threw an all-day "open house" party in honor of Mark's birthday. He beamed throughout the day and was on his best behavior. This was the first birthday party he had ever had.

Walking home from work on the afternoon of May 5, 1992, I had no idea that the wailing sirens I heard were rushing toward my husband. Typically, when I arrived home, I'd be greeted by the sounds of a basketball game in the driveway, or music blasting from inside. But that afternoon, all was quiet. In the kitchen, the message machine was blinking. "Barbara?" the voice said. "Mark's had an accident. It's bad."

Three years after Mark's nearly fatal collision, the insurance company's lawyers would seek to convince the jury that my husband had been riding his motorcycle in excess of ninety miles an hour. But accident reconstruction experts on both sides had concluded his actual speed was between forty and forty-five miles per hour when a motorist pulled out of his driveway into oncoming traffic, realized his mistake, and stopped dead. The collision that followed changed our lives.

In the days and weeks Mark lay in intensive care fighting for his life, I was at his side almost constantly. "Bumps in the road" his doctor called each new setback. Somehow, Mark survived risky surgeries, infections, pneumonia, and the violent coughing that went with it. Through it all, his hand clung to mine as if he was drawing survival from my grip. It came to seem as if we were one person rather than two—that a single heart beat for us both.

Nine weeks after his accident, I brought home a husband who seemed like a stranger. Mark had become angry at the world, and those of us closest to him bore the brunt of his bitterness. "Inconvenience" became his favorite word. Anyone interfering with "what I want to do, when I want to do it, whoever I want to do it with" was an inconvenience, and people who inconvenienced him, he warned me, had better watch their backs. Even though he was warned not to drink because of the danger of seizures, he used alcohol to blunt his depression and pain.

Before our marriage, Mark and I had pledged to be faithful to each other. "I couldn't cheat on you anyway," he told me. "I'm a lousy liar." He was right; it was easy to figure out when his affair with Lisa began. Arriving home later and later, Mark used the excuse that he was helping his friend Dave restore a car. In truth, he was spending most of that time with Dave's younger sister, a girl of fifteen. "I'll be home at nine tonight," he'd promise. I'd still be awake when he pulled in at one in the morning.

Although Mark is back to work again, he calls in sick as often as he goes. He keeps his paychecks now, refusing to contribute toward the household expenses. Our debts increase each month. He's having blackouts, mood swings. Some days he drinks from noon until late at night. If I challenge him or question him, I'm told I'm an "inconvenience"—his code for: watch out.

Last week, the paper ran a public service ad from the women's shelter. "If you're reading this and suspect you might be a victim of abuse," it said, "then you *are*." I know it's true, but I keep hoping we'll round some corner and things will be better. The article calls this "denial." Sometimes when he's drunk, Mark rapes me anally. The pain during and after these encounters dulls my brain and rips at my soul. I'm left hurt and humiliated, and worry that people can tell what he does by looking at me. In my life, pain has always accompanied love. Whenever things are going well, I hold my breath and wait.

One afternoon, I come home to a note on the dining room table. Mark has canceled our dinner plans, claiming some part for Dave's car has come in and they want to get right to the job. When he comes home at midnight, he's drunk and reeking of campfire smoke. I confront him about Lisa. "Has your relationship with her become sexual?"

"Don't worry, I wear a condom," he says. "And anyway, she's inexperienced. Sex with you is much better."

A few days later, when I call Lisa's house, it's her mother I confront. "Where are my husband and your daughter?" She claims she's not sure—maybe they went to get something to eat. "Any idea which way they went?"

"Nope." She's lying, I know it. How can a mother possibly condone her child's involvement with an older married man?

Later that night, Mark charges into the house. "Lisa's mom says you called the state police!" he shouts. "How could you do that when you know I have things in my car that could get me arrested?"

"I have no idea what you have in your car," I shout back.

Amanda and Arthur are both home. Our fight sends them scattering to their rooms. I try to cool down—to talk seriously to Mark about the damage he's doing to both our lives. Drunk, he stands there, hands in his pockets, fondling himself. It's hopeless. In the morning, he won't remember any of this.

Mark calls from work the next day to tell me he's taking a two-week vacation. Dave's family has invited him to go with them to some car races in Delaware. From there, he'll fly out to his dad's in Montana. His father is moving back east and Mark's agreed to help him drive the U-haul.

"Who's going to these races?" I ask.

"The whole family."

"Lisa, too?"

"The whole family," he repeats. I tell him I think his "vacation" means that our marriage is over.

On the morning of his trip, I stay in bed, pretending to be asleep. "You awake?" he asks. "We're leaving at noon. I'll call you from work before we take off." He leaves the house, the car starts, he drives away.

I lie in bed, thinking about the toll this marriage has taken. I feel ugly and old. I can't laugh anymore, can't concentrate, can't go out because Mark's affair has gone humiliatingly public. A dependable worker all my life, I've had to leave my job as a nursing-home aide. I liked the patients and the facility; it was my *own* home that was the problem. I worked second shift. Sometimes, Mark would give me a ride to work because it was "on his way." To where, he wouldn't say. At the end of my shift, he'd pick me up late, often *very* late, and sometimes not at all. On the nights I took my own car to work, he'd drive to the facility in the middle of my shift, leave his car locked in the parking lot, and take off in mine without leaving me his keys. At the end of my shift, I'd go out-side and realize I was stranded. I'd become frantic and disoriented, for-getting for a few moments where I was, particularly on the nights when I knew he was out with Lisa. I'm obsessed with Mark's whereabouts, constantly on guard against his lies. In the middle of conversations, I lose track of the subject. I've lost track of good friends. Lost thirty pounds. Lately, I've thought about ending my life rather than going on like this. But my mother's suicide has been so hard on our family. I can't put my own children through that.

The divorce lawyer has bushy hair that reminds me of Gene Wilder's. Oh, great. My attorney is Young Frankenstein. I tell him about Mark's instability since the accident, his anger. With difficulty, I admit that I am twenty years older than my husband and that, at the age of twenty-eight, he has involved himself with a girl of fifteen. Because Mark has threatened me, the lawyer says it's safest to have the divorce papers served to him at work when he returns from his trip.

While Mark's away, I function like a robot. In the daytime, I go to my per diem home-health-care jobs. In the evening, I return bill collectors' calls. I take long baths, catch up on sleep. Each day Mark is gone, I feel a little stronger.

I'm in the kitchen peeling vegetables when he pulls in. "Sweetie? Where are you?" A wave of nausea passes through me. Whatever courage I've gathered disappears with the sound of his voice.

"I'm in the kitchen."

He comes up behind me and wraps his arms around my waist. "You have a good time?" I ask. It comes out as a whisper.

"It was okay. Come see what I brought back for you." I put down the peeler, turn off the water, and follow him. I'm trying to anticipate his next move. In the bedroom, he's all over me, covering my face with kisses, unbuttoning his shirt and pulling it from his jeans. "I've been thinking," he says. "I want to stay and work on this marriage. I missed you so much."

I tell him I missed him, too. But I can't relax enough to even pretend I'm a part of this lovemaking. I'm frightened about what's coming: the divorce papers, his reaction. When he's finished, I roll away from him, get up, get dressed. It's been so long since I've been able to respond to him sexually.

At dinner, Mark's the devoted husband and I'm the dutiful wife. Later, we watch a video, *Natural Born Killers*. Mark's watched this film many times and likes to compare himself to Mickey Knox, the character played by Woody Harrelson. He turns from the TV screen to me. "I'm a natural born killer," he says. "You're just a *Thelma and Louise*."

This is an insult; he means I'm weak. When "inconveniences" get in Mickey Knox's way, he kills them, but when Thelma and Louise reach the point of no return, they take their *own* lives. Mark often talks about terminating people who get in his way. The person whose name comes up most often is the driver who, four years earlier, caused his accident and ruined his life. "You're right," I say. "I probably *would* take my own life instead of someone else's."

As usual, watching *Natural Born Killers* arouses Mark. He wants us to shower together and I obey. As we rub soap over each other, Mark becomes so turned on that he pulls me from the water. We dry off quickly and have sex again. Exhausted, he wraps his arms around me and falls asleep. I'm awake all night, thinking, worrying. I decide I'd better call the lawyer in the morning and tell him I've changed my mind.

When the alarm goes off, I stay in bed, listening to his morning rituals: showering, coffee-making, dressing. Before he leaves for work, he bends and kisses the back of my head. After he's gone, I get up, go to the kitchen. Check the clock. I have to stop those papers. I watch the birds at the feeder, watch the *Today* show. It's 7:10. An hour and fifty minutes before I can call the lawyer's office. I wait.

"You're too late," the secretary says. "The sheriff's already picked up the documents." When she hears the panic in my voice, she promises she'll try to locate him and stop the delivery. Later, she calls back. "The sheriff wasn't in, but I left a message. I'll call you as soon as I hear from him."

A few minutes later, the phone rings again. "I just received your little surprise," Mark says.

After work, he returns home with friends, so the showdown I've been dreading all day doesn't happen. It doesn't happen the next night either. But on the third night, when I arrive home from work, he's drunk. At six-two, Mark is nine inches taller than I am. He screams. His fist sends me flying backward. He takes a sip of his Molson. "You know something? I was *lying* when I said I wanted to stay with you. Soon as I get things set up, I'm moving to Virginia."

"Just go then, Mark! I can't stand living like this."

"I'll go when I'm ready!"

I storm into our bedroom and send his stuff flying. His golf trophy, his model of Dale Earnhardt's car, the water globe I gave him for a wedding present. Why *shouldn't* I destroy this crap? I bought most of it. All *his* money goes toward alcohol and guns and Lisa.

Mark watches my outburst from the doorway, then turns and leaves. The door bangs, the car drives off. I have no idea if he's ever coming back.

Late that night, he crawls into bed beside me. In the morning, he kisses the back of my head, and goes to work. It's as if the night before didn't happen.

When he comes home from work that afternoon, he eyes the envelopes and letters I've laid out on the table. "What's all this?"

"My résumé. I'm looking for a full-time job." I remind him that he's moving to Virginia and that I need to make plans of my own.

"Don't think you're going *anywhere*," he says. "You're staying put in case things don't work out for me. And don't think you can have anyone else in your life either. That's okay for me but not for you."

I stand there, amazed. Is he kidding?

"What's yours is mine, and what's mine is mine," he reminds me. He says this often, always with that stupid, self-satisfied grin. "Oh, and by the way, we're driving up to see my dad this weekend. The Catskills should have a lot of color this time of year. It'll be a nice ride. I'm going to go work on the truck for a while. Call me when dinner's ready."

We leave for New York State early Saturday morning. The silence between us is unsettling. Mark's wanted nothing to do with me for weeks. Why this sudden invitation to be together?

Thirty minutes into the trip, he puts a CD in the player. "Killing Me Softly with His Song," the Fugees' remake of the old Roberta Flack song, begins. It's one of "our" songs, but today the lyrics are a bitter reminder of all that's gone wrong. "Gotta watch my speed today," Mark says. "Lot of cops on the thruway and I don't want to get stopped. I brought a couple of guns."

Guns? It dawns on me that I haven't mentioned this trip to anyone.

"Gonna look for that little hunting cabin my father used to take me to," he says a few minutes later. "Thought I'd get in some target practice."

Is he planning to kill me? Am I being paranoid? I don't trust Mark, but I don't trust my emotional state either.

The trip takes two hours. Mark drives up a mountain road, in search of a trail he remembers at the edge of some woods. He finds it an hour later. We ride through woods and pastures until the trail becomes too narrow for a vehicle to pass. "Let's walk the rest of the way," he says. "We're close. That cabin's around here somewhere." He gets out of the car and reaches under the driver's seat. When he stands again, he's holding his Colt .45.

"I can't believe you're driving around with that thing under there," I say.

"I put it there after I had a few words with Lisa's stepdad," he says. "In case he felt like giving me any trouble." He opens the trunk and removes a rifle.

We slog through mud and briers. Mark finds the cabin. It's built atop a rock formation. We climb the rocks. Inside, there are four bunks, a few chairs, a woodstove. A window faces onto the woods.

"I'm going out and set up some targets," Mark tells me.

"You came all this way just to target shoot?" I ask.

"No, I came all this way to show you how easy it would be to make you disappear."

I sit facing the window. I can *feel,* as well as hear, the vibration as his bullets bounce off the mountain. An hour later, he comes back. "Ready to go?"

"Yes."

"See how easy it would be to get rid of you?"

"I get the message." It comes out in a whisper.

On the ride home, Mark plays "Killing Me Softly with His Song" repeatedly for two hours. My nerves are shot. I'm exhausted but keenly alert. And I've been warned.

What's his is his, and what's mine is his, too.

He does not want a divorce.

He can make me disappear whenever he wants to.

5. ADAM

Dark clouds close in on the prison compound tonight. Even a nonmeteorologist could predict that we're in for a hell of a storm.

My roommate, Jackie, has left for her 7:00 meeting, and I'm spending a quiet evening in my cell, working on my accounting homework. The TV's on, the volume turned low. In the corner of the screen, a postage stamp–size map of Connecticut shows the storm's movement. It's bearing down on my hometown, heading this way. Three of my four children live in the area. Are they home tonight, safe and dry?

Every hour on the hour, our cell door opens to allow us a five-minute break. When the lock clicks, I walk out onto the tier where there are couches, a phone to use for preapproved collect calls, an electric urn that holds hot water. I make myself a cup of tea and return to my cell before "unlock" is over. I put away my homework; I'm too unsettled to work on accounting tonight. Even through these reinforced concrete walls, I can hear and feel the storm.

Jackie returns at nine, soaked to the bone. "Can you believe how hard it's coming down out there, Mom?" she says. Cellmates for several months now, Jackie and I have established a mother-daughter connection. Many of the younger inmates here, streetwise or not, seek out surrogate moms. Separated from my own children, I'm happy to fill that need for Jackie.

"There are storm warnings all over the state," I tell her. "You should get into some dry clothes before you get sick."

"Did you see the hailstones, Mom? They were *huge*!"

That night I dream about my own mother. In the eight years since her suicide, Mom has visited me often in my dreams. But this one's different. In this dream, she's dead. I approach her coffin. Beneath the thick makeup, I can see the bruises from her twelve-story fall, the nylon thread that sews her lips together. I awake shaken. What does this dream mean?

I work first shift in Food Prep, slicing cold cuts. I've been in this department for most of my two years in prison, not unhappily. Because it's always busy here, I have less time to brood.

It's about 8:30 when Ms. Hagen, a counselor from my unit, arrives. She gives me a quick glance and enters the office. I've just finished packaging a large tray of meat and am heading for the sink to wash my hands. As Ms. Hagen speaks to the supervisors, one of them keeps glancing at me. We make eye contact. I've never seen this look of compassion on his face before and I don't like it. What's wrong?

When I look up again, Ms. Hagen is approaching. She's young, blond, soft-spoken. She floats so gracefully toward me, she could be an angel. "Barbara, I need to meet with you," she says. "Would you follow me?" I ask her if I'm coming back. If I'm not, I'll need to get my sweatshirt and my Chapstick. "Get your things," she says.

We leave. "Am I going back to the unit?"

"No, we're going to Mental Health. Someone's meeting us there."

"Oh, my God. Has something happened to my father?" Dad's age and failing health prevent him from visiting me here in prison. One of my fears is that he'll die before I'm released and I'll never see him again.

"Your father's all right," Ms. Hagen says.

Suddenly, I'm gasping for air. "Please don't say it's one of my children!"

Inside the mental health unit, I'm introduced to Ms. Egan, a social worker whose specialty is crisis management. "Barbara, your son Adam was killed last night," Ms. Hagen says. "He was out in the storm. His truck hydroplaned and flipped over onto its roof. I was told he didn't suffer."

I shake my head. They must be wrong. How can Adam, so full of life, be dead? What about his wife? His little girls? He can't be dead because they *need* him. I can't catch my breath. Ms. Hagen and Ms. Egan watch me and wait.

I'd been taking birth control pills when Adam was conceived, so the pregnancy came as a surprise. Andrea was nine. Arthur, at six, had just started school. I'd recently made the decision to return to college and had just started my coursework. Did I really want this baby? I thought hard and decided I did.

He was so small: five pounds, ten ounces, nineteen inches long. When the nurse placed him against my chest, I loved him immediately. That wispy blond hair, those crinkly eyes searching but unable, yet, to focus. "Born on December 25," the nurse noted. "Have you considered naming him Christopher?" But from the start, he was Adam.

He was a happy, fun-loving boy—the most mischievous of my children and the most active. A daredevil by nature, he gave me more than a few gray hairs when I caught him jumping his bike off a forbidden dirt mound or riding his skateboard down the middle of the highway.

He was no saint. As a teenager, he got in a few minor scrapes with the law. He had talents for both causing trouble and sweet-talking his way out of it. In high school, he joined the hockey team and enrolled in Alternative Education; with its mix of academics, life skills, and outdoor activities, this program was a better fit for him than the traditional classroom. I wasn't surprised when Adam chose to make his living as an excavator. At six feet, he was slim and muscular from his physical labor.

I remember so vividly the day Adam brought home his high school sweetheart to meet me. "Mom, this is Laura," he said. "I finally met someone who's just like you." The expression on his face told me he was in love. I saw that same joyous look the day Adam handed me his and Laura's baby girl. From the start, Ashley was "Daddy's girl." I loved baby-sitting for her, rocking her and watching her drift off to sleep. Before my arrest, I had seen my granddaughter almost every day and, in those awful first weeks at York, I felt Ashley's absence as physical aching.

"Okay if I hold your new baby sister?" I asked Ashley the day I first saw Ann. She nodded, staring at my tears. I was crying because Ann looked so much like Adam had as an infant, and because this introduction was taking place in prison. But what a comfort it was to hold a newborn again, to cradle that small, warm bundle of hope. "Please bring the girls as often as you can," I said. "I don't want to be shut out of their lives."

"We will, Mom," Adam assured me.

On one of his later visits, I was in lockdown because one of the officers had smelled cigarette smoke on our tier. Adam was upset when he learned he could neither see me nor find out if I was okay. His talent for sweet-talking must have come in handy that day. Atypically, the officer in charge of visits investigated and reported back to my son about the suspicion of smoking—*and* that I was safe. "Thanks," Adam told the officer. "And by the way, whoever did it, it wasn't *my* mom. She doesn't even smoke."

Ms. Hagen walks me back to my unit and informs the CO that I've had a death in the family. This information is shared not for the purpose of eliciting sympathy, but so that the officer can be alert for signs of suicide. Alone in my cell, I try bargaining with God. *Please take me instead.*

"Oh, Mom, I just heard," Jackie says when she enters the cell. She sits on my bed, tries to comfort me. Her kindness makes me sob.

My sister Joanne visits later that afternoon. The wake is in Canaan, she says. The warden has all the information and arrangements are being made for me to attend. Joanne doesn't know if the casket will be open or closed.

"I have to see him, Jo," I tell her. "I need to know this is real."

The next day, my intercom beeps. "Lane? Your transport's here." As

I'm being signed out, I look around to see who's escorting me. My counselor had promised to put in a special request for a compassionate staff person, but the man approaching me is one of the most insensitive officers on staff. On our way to Discharge, he keeps stopping to joke with inmates and other COs. He orders me to stand with my back against the office building so he can run to the snack room and grab himself some sodas for the trip. It's as if we're going for some routine medical appointment instead of my son's wake. The second escort meets us at the van. I'm shackled, handcuffed, wrapped in belly chains, and lifted into the vehicle.

On the two-hour trip to Canaan, the shackles dig into my ankles and wrists. The officers chat with each other but neither says a word to me.

Family and friends are forbidden to be in the funeral parlor when I'm there, so it's just the officers, the undertaker, my son, and me. The casket is open. I walk toward Adam, kneel before his body. He looks peaceful—asleep, not dead. His hands have been placed across his chest. "Your daughter-in-law felt his injuries were sufficiently covered," the funeral director explains. "But it would be best if you didn't touch him below the hands."

He's wearing his jeans, a T-shirt he bought during a visit to Andrea's in Georgia, his favorite green plaid button-up summer shirt over it. Pictures of Laura and the girls poke out from the pocket. Adam's well-worn John Deere hat and sunglasses have been placed in the coffin with him. There's a scar in his right eyebrow; some of the hair is missing. A gash on his forehead has been stitched in a circle. His bruises are thick with makeup.

I can't touch him because my chains are too tight. "Would you please help me?" I ask one of the escorts. "I can't reach him." He comes forward and unlocks the cuffs. I bend toward Adam, kiss his forehead, caress his hands.

Later, I walk around the room. It's been so long since I've seen flowers, and they're beautiful: a heart covered with red roses, to Adam from me; a spray of sunflowers from my lawyers. Hometown friends of mine are the florists who've done most of these arrangements. In the midst of this unbearable pain, I'm comforted by their efforts to include me in Adam's farewell.

There are pictures everywhere: on tabletops, walls, in oversized collages resting against easels. Adam's whole life is here in photographs. I pause to read a poem he wrote to Laura four years earlier. Titled "Eternal Love," it speaks of hearts locked together forever, of good things never ending. *I'll be the angel looking over you till you die,* he promised her. How did he know?

I'm supposed to have an hour; it's what was agreed upon and arranged. But after thirty minutes, the officers tell me we're heading back. It's a long trip, they say; there'll be traffic. There's no arguing with them and there'll be no objection raised when I return. It would be my word against theirs, and an inmate's word is never as good as an officer's. So I'm recuffed, chained, and lifted back into the transport van. Neither man speaks to me on the way back.

Back at York, I'm escorted to Mental Health and interviewed by the social worker on duty. Once again, this is not compassion; it's procedure. The mental state of a returning inmate allowed off grounds because of a death must be assessed. Back in my cell, Jackie is gentle and comforting. "Were the guards good to you, Mom?"

"They made me leave early. They took away the last half-hour I could have had with him." The emotions I've kept in check all day come pouring out. There's no stopping them. I wail harder than I ever have before.

The next morning, I get up, go back to work. I've convinced myself that staying busy will lessen the pain. The funeral is this afternoon, but I'm unsure of the time. For hours, I stand, slice meat, try not to think about Adam's burial.

In the early afternoon, my superviser calls to me, phone in hand. The prison minister wants to speak to me. But there's a problem. I can't seem to move. I ask if I can please talk to her some other time. My boss tells me the minister will call to reschedule. Thirty minutes go by, an hour, an hour and a half. I can slice the meat, but I can't move my legs. The others work around me. No one stares or speaks to me. They let me slice in silence.

Adam's body lies in a town north of ours—in a cemetery I've never seen. It's hard not to be able to picture this place or to visit his grave—to feel beneath my feet the ground that cradles him. I long to touch his stone, the carved letters of his name. Until I'm released from prison and able to do this, there'll be no closure for me, no relief from this grief.

The questions that haunt me are these: Am I responsible? Was my son's life taken because I took the life of another woman's son? Is God merciful or vengeful?

6. REHABILITATION

Maizy, my newest roommate on maximum-side, gives me a big smile. "I was hoping I'd get someone with a TV," she says. "If you's not here in the afternoon, you won't mind if I watch mines soaps?" I tell her I *do* mind because my TV has to last for the ten years I'm here. The smile drops off her face.

Of course, each afternoon when I return from school to our cell, my TV is warm to the touch. Rather than confront Maizy, I start locking up my headphones. Now I have to worry about sabotage inside our eight-by-ten-foot cell. Cutting power cords with toenail clippers and pouring water or Kool-Aid into the back of a TV set are common revenge tactics here. The set will work again once the water's dry, but sticky Kool-Aid does permanent damage. I'm especially alert to any news that Maizy might be transferring. Vengeful roommates strike most often just before they exit.

An earlier roommate, Carrie, had serious health issues. I returned from breakfast one morning to find her bloody underwear and thermals on the counter and in our sink. She was not in the room and I needed to get ready for work. I approached the CO's desk and asked for a pair of rubber gloves.

"For what?" the officer snapped.

"My roommate's left some nasty stuff in our sink and I need to brush my teeth for work." He followed me back to my cell and was mortified by what he saw. I was told to get to work and promised that the room would be scrubbed down by the time I returned. "I came in here disease-free," I grumbled as I left my cell. "I sure hope I go home that way."

In addition to her medical problems, Carrie had mental health issues and few life management skills. I sometimes tried to help her with commissary purchases—small snacks, hygiene items. She liked these so much that she stole mine, too. Many of the women at York ignore the boundaries of personal property. They don't think twice about stealing from you, or borrowing your hair dryer or Walkman and breaking it, or hitting you if you object.

Women like me don't hit back. We put up with renegade roommates and follow the rules because breaking them can mean loss of institutional privileges—school and therapy group attendance, family visits, access to the telephone and our mail. These are the lifelines to our sanity, so we obey.

Still, respectful obedience exacts a cost. We are the overlooked inmates. Staff shuffles our requests to the bottom of the paperwork pile because they know we won't cause trouble if our needs aren't met. Ironically, if a troublesome inmate decides to start playing by the rules, staff goes out of their way to accommodate her. A public relations sweetheart, she is touted as a model citizen of the prison community—a woman whose soul they've saved.

In 1996, I joined the sisterhood of society's misfits. I live surrounded by chaos, raw language, masterful manipulation, and ambiguous sexuality. Wives and mothers in the free world become lesbians in prison. Many become "boys," latching on to feminine inmates willing to support them with commissary in exchange for sex. This is what we prisoners call "bulldagging." I've discovered that women sentenced for murder or manslaughter—women who reached their emotional limit and snapped—are the safest people to befriend in prison. Addicts are the most dangerous. Trapped in the revolving door of the justice system, the majority have become immune to rehabilitation and hope. To survive, they lie, steal, betray, manipulate staff, and incite chaos. Substance abusers with charismatic personalities are particularly powerful. They draw others into the excitement and anarchy and end up ruining lives.

Changing yourself for the better—understanding and then breaking vicious cycles—is hard work. *Too* hard for many women. Seventy-five percent of the women at York do not take advantage of school or counseling programs. Instead of changing self-destructive habits, they adapt them to their new environment. Separated from violent spouses, their codependency rages on in the form of volatile relationships with other women. Commissary substitutes for drugs. I've seen some of my peers triple in size as they feed their addiction to junk food. A "commissary 'ho" will study how other women shop and choose a victim, usually a new arrival. She'll cozy up, become a friend at first, begin to flirt. Shared secrets and compliments will become sweet nothings whispered into the needy woman's ear. The jailhouse mating ritual has begun in earnest.

Some inmates are magnets to jailhouse bulldagging. They get hooked on the attention they receive and, in return, hand over to their commissary 'ho a fortune in squeeze cheese, cinnamon rolls, pork rinds, and peanut butter cups.

"My money didn't hit the books this week. You got a couple soups and Honey Buns I can borrow?" (The day before, I've seen this same woman leave commissary with two big grocery bags.) . . . "If y'all buy some extra cheese and pepperoni, I'll cook for us both this week." (Notice she's not kicking in any of her stash; turning on the hot plate is *her* contribution.) "I took some cream cheese and butter from work. You buy any bagels or Dunkin' Sticks this week?" (In other words: hand over the thing *you* paid for so that *I* can enjoy it with the stuff I just swiped.) "Got any coffee?" is a favorite question on the tier. The woman naive or generous enough to donate a tea-spoon of crystals gets hit up for more. "Got any sugar to go with this? Any extra creamer?"

For some, religion is woven into the con. *Jesus, save me! Show me the light!* Many women attend services to pray for the miracle of a reduced sentence. Others go for the sex. Recently, a church service was halted when a "kite"—a love note folded in the shape of a small triangle for inconspicuous delivery—was found and turned over to the minister. Inside the note was a promise of true love, and a request: please wear your special pants with the hole in the crotch next Sunday and I'll take you to Heaven. At the end of a service, you're apt to hear, "Fuckin' bitch couldn't get her ass to church today. Wait'll I get my hands on that 'ho. I'll beat the shit out of her." Alleluia.

Still, it is possible for a woman at York C.I. to stay spiritually con-nected and to rehabilitate herself with the help of staff and programs. Locked within the confines of the institution for six years now, I have become better educated and more self-aware. Remorse no longer threat-ens to eat me alive. I have also undergone some changes that I do not consider positive or rehabilitative. I am more suspicious now—untrust-ing, disillusioned, and bitter. My eyes are wide open and I don't like much of what I see around me.

Who am I, then? I am Barbara Lane, who *was* a health-care worker, business manager, wife, mother, homemaker, gardener, and killer—and who *is* an inmate. Good-bye to the trusting daughter, sister, wife, and mother I once was. In June, I will have one grandson and five grand-daughters. I live in fear that I will again hear the words that one of them has been made a victim. I don't care who you are—I am sure you have a dark side, especially if you are a man. You cannot convince me otherwise.

7. SIX YEARS AND COUNTING

Long-term incarceration is a strange mix of sadness, sameness, and explosiveness. I have now passed my two-thousandth day in prison. There are brighter moments for me now: shared smiles with friends, watching the antics of the dogs I train for the prison's Puppy Program. Staff has nicknamed me "the mail lady" because of all the letters and cards I still receive from faithful supporters. For my fifty-second birthday, my best friend, Elle, surprised me with a video she'd worked on for weeks. The tape included a "tour" of our hometown and the good wishes of thirty friends and family members who'd stood before Elle's camera to send me their love. It was one of the best gifts I have ever received.

If life is a pile of puzzle pieces, my most precious ones remain out of reach. Except for phone calls and visits here at York, I have been absent from the lives of my children and grandchildren these past two thousand days.

Andrea makes the trip north to Connecticut twice a year. When she visits, we make no mention of Mark, no reference to the act that brought me here or the events and disclosures that preceded it.

Arthur manages a visit once a month, less often when he's swamped with work. Although he never complains, these trips are hard on him. My son's long-term relationships with several wonderful young women have ended in breakups. "How come you can't make a commitment?" I asked him once. He told me he didn't want to have to go through the things I did. In that response, I heard how deeply his life had been scarred by mine.

Adam's widow, Laura, has moved on. Over the past years, I've seen less and less of my granddaughters Ashley and Ann. I hope and pray I'll be able to reestablish my connection with Adam's children after I'm released.

Amanda visits infrequently. She no longer cries during entire visits, but she hardly ever smiles. A chain-smoker, Amanda cites the prison's "no smoking" policy as the reason why she can't stay the two hours we're allotted. My youngest child is floundering, reaching for the wrong things, and I am powerless to do anything but pray for God's mercy. I pray for His forgiveness, too. My failure to escape an abusive marriage, my crime, my incarceration—for all of this I bear the guilt of having let go of my baby.

In the middle of writing this essay, I asked my three surviving children to write, from their own perspectives, about the "then and now" of my crime and punishment.

Amanda wrote:

> I'd been feeling a pain in my heart for hours before I heard the actual news. How could my mother have forgotten everything she'd ever taught me? . . . Arthur and I went to the funeral. It was painful to be in a room with Mark's family and friends. I felt as if everyone was staring at me—as if I was guilty of my mother's crime. Mark looked peaceful, almost happy. Maybe he wasn't thinking about his death but about the things we had shared as a family. . . . I haven't really been the same since. There have been threats on my mother's life. Because of these, I have a fear of standing in front of windows. I'm afraid I might be seen and shot. Many nights, I can't sleep. I stare up at the ceiling, listening for night sounds, afraid of the unknown. But it's hard for me to say if my mother's crime made the other things happen—my brother's death, my drinking problem, the cars I crashed, even the happy things like the birth of my daughter. Things like that just happen, right?

Andrea wrote:

> We had moved to Georgia that year and Mom came to see us in October. She was preoccupied about Mark, wondering about his whereabouts and calling home constantly to check. She wasn't herself. . . . Two weeks after her visit, Aunt Joanne called to tell me the news. I didn't know how to react. How could something like this have happened to our family? The first words out of my mouth were angry ones. "I'm going to kill her," I said. . . . When I visited Mom in prison that first

time, I reached across the table to hold her hands. They felt so tiny and cold. She was thirsty but forbidden to use the drinking fountain. She had no winter coat, but we weren't allowed to bring her one. I was powerless to fix things for her. It ate me up inside. . . . Looking back on the past six years, I can't really tell how all this has affected me. I've become a harder person, I think. Someone's first impression is likely to be "She's a bitch." I don't smile much anymore. A while back, I participated in a line dance competition. We were encouraged to engage the audience—to look them in the eye and smile as much as possible. I thought I did great, smiling and making eye contact, working as hard as ever to please. After the competition, my husband asked me why I hadn't smiled. On the inside, I'd been smiling up a storm. On the outside, nobody could see.

Arthur wrote:

I'd just broken up with my girlfriend of five and a half years. I'd been attending college at night but decided to make a full-time effort. I applied to Rochester Institute of Technology and the University of Connecticut with my eye on a mechanical engineering degree and was accepted at both. At the age of twenty-five, I was finally going to fulfill my dream. Mom suggested I move back in with her and Mark to save money toward tuition and expenses. . . . I knew immediately that there were serious problems. They were deeply in debt. Mark was cheating on Mom and treating her like crap. At about three A.M. on the morning of November 4, I awoke to the sound of arguing. Then I heard a bang. Was it a gunshot? Was I next? Mom burst into my room with a blaze in her eyes that I'd never seen before. She wanted me to get dressed and go to the end of our driveway because she had shot Mark and called 911. An ambulance was on its way. As soon as the police arrived, my mother confessed. They put me through nine hours of interrogation, anyway. . . . The next year was a drunken blur for me. I'd never been much of a drinker, but alcohol seemed to ease the pain. I had no place to live, so I drove around with my belongings in my car, sleeping wherever. My family and friends tried to help me, but we were all confused. . . . The psychological fallout stuck with me. Even simple tasks seemed like huge chores. I drowned myself in my work because I wanted to hide from society and myself. I was constantly worrying about what people were saying and thinking about my mother, and me. . . . To this day and until it is over, every visit with Mom, every telephone call from her, is a painful reminder of what happened. She is not the same wonderful, caring, and giving person she was before her ordeal. She never will be. The "system" has seen to that.

In the fall of 2000, Barbara Lane earned an associate of science degree in general studies from Three Rivers Community–Technical College, graduating with honors. A certified tutor for Literacy Volunteers of America, Lane also assists math students preparing for their high school equivalency diplomas. As she has pursued her education, Barbara Lane has also maintained active membership in such support groups as Survivors of Abuse and Struggles, a writing- and reading-based group for victims of battering. Currently, she is studying microcomputers, journalism, meditation, and yoga. Additionally, she is deeply involved in York C.I.'s Prison PUP Partnership, a program through which inmates train Labrador retrievers to assist adults and children with special needs. Lane is "mom" to two retrievers, Webster and Durham, who accompany her wherever she goes.

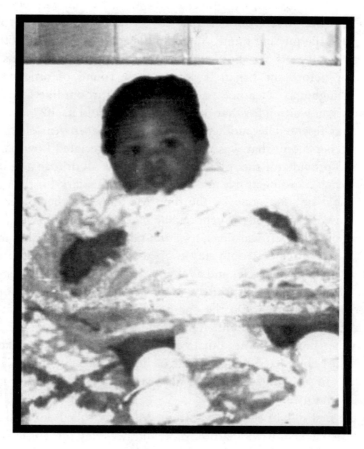

MOTHERLOVE

MICHELLE JESSAMY

Born: 1967
Conviction: Manslaughter
Sentence: 20 years
Entered prison: 1994
Status: Incarcerated

ACH EVENING, SHIRLEY SHAMBLY WOULD RETURN HOME dog-tired from her long day of caring for the old folks at the nursing home. Sometimes she wouldn't even bother to take off her shoes or get out of her coat before she started supper, or before she began barking a new round of orders to her teenage daughters. "Heather, you clean that bathroom like I told you? Mo'Shay, you waiting for that pile of laundry to fold itself?"

Mo'Shay resented her mother the way most fourteen-year-old girls do. She loved her mom; that wasn't it. And she appreciated how hard she worked to provide for them. But the woman was all drudge and no joy. She rose each morning at five and headed off in the dark for the nursing home. She'd be long gone by the time Mo'Shay and her older sister, Heather, awoke to the lists of chores she had left them: *do this, do that*. Mo'Shay's mother left warnings, too: *don't* do this or that. If her mother had her way, Mo'Shay would stay cooped up in the house all day long, toiling away like Cinderella and avoiding the temptations of the street.

Yes, Ma. No, Ma. Right away, Ma. Mo'Shay felt mixed about her mother—and confused. On the one hand, she still wanted what she'd always craved from her mom: attention, reassurance that she was loved, more of her mother's time. But lately, Mo'Shay wanted distance, too. She had just completed her first year of high school. She had places to go, friends to see. She was an adult now, whether or not her mother had bothered to notice.

On the first day of summer vacation, Mo'Shay rolled out of bed and entered the kitchen. It was Saturday, her mother's day off. Shirley looked up from her floor mopping, skipped "good morning," and got right down to business. "I need you to get dressed and run to the store, Mo'Shay." She handed her daughter a grocery list. "And don't you be batting your big eyes at those boys out on the street either. Come on, now. Git!"

Although it was not Mo'Shay's style to "bat her big eyes" at boys, her mother's telling her not to wouldn't stop her from doing it if she felt like it. More and more, she had boys' attention; she had a growing awareness of that. On her way out the door, Shay checked herself in the mirror: medium build, caramel complexion, hazel brown eyes. Her friends Tammy and Tarshia had assured her that her eyes were her best feature and she guessed she agreed. Tammy and Tarshia had boyfriends now and had begun experimenting with some of the things on Shay's mother's "don't do" list. But Shay had resisted Tammy's attempts to fix her up. It wasn't that she wasn't interested—or that she didn't have crushes, small flirtations. But she'd been comfortable keeping things at that. "And I'm *never* gonna have sex," she had declared to her two friends. But her vow was a personal, private decision; it had nothing to do with obedience. Her mother didn't own her; Mo'Shay owned herself.

Turning the corner that day on her way to the store, Mo'Shay noticed him immediately. She had lived on Center Street for over six years and knew just about everyone in the neighborhood—the older folks, their kids, their grandkids. But she had never seen *this* guy before. It was if he had suddenly popped out of her fantasy life and onto the street. Tall and lean, with hazelnut skin, he sat straddling a purring motorcycle parked at the curb on the other side of the street. He wore a white shirt and black jeans, white Adidas, and a black baseball cap tilted to the side. He looked about sixteen or seventeen. When he noticed her, she averted her eyes and kept walking. Who *was* he?

At the store, Shay wandered through the aisles, thinking more about the guy on the bike than the items on her mother's list. Maybe Tammy or Tarshia knew who he was. The crushes she'd had on other guys suddenly seemed like child's play. Maybe this was just what happened to you when you turned fourteen, she thought. Maybe it was time.

Toting the shopping bags, Mo'Shay hurried back onto the street, hoping he hadn't left yet—hadn't been a mirage. But when she turned the corner, there he was. Shay felt both relieved and shaken. He'd gotten off his bike and was standing beside it now. He was watching her, too. Feeling suddenly bold, she took a longer look, and when she did, it was he who turned away.

Mo'Shay rushed into her building, plunked down the groceries, and raced back outside, taking the stairs two at a time. "Hey, girl!" someone called. She looked around. There was Tarshia, just the person she wanted to talk to.

"Hey, yourself," Shay called back. "You think Tammy's home? You wanna go over to Tammy's?" She made her voice as casual as she could. To get to Tammy's, they'd have to walk right past the boy.

"I guess so," Tarshia said.

As they approached him, Mo'Shay felt as if someone had just turned up the thermostat. She kept reminding herself to act relaxed and nonchalant, but just as they were passing him, Tarshia stopped dead on the sidewalk, turned abruptly, and faced her friend. "Girl, what's wrong with you?" she demanded. Mo'Shay felt the hot blood rush to her face. Grunting a response, she kept walking, hoping her knees wouldn't buckle and cause her to fall on her face.

The two girls walked past him. He followed them.

"Hey," he called. "Your name Hazel?"

When she turned around, he was gazing directly at her.

"Yeah," Mo'Shay said, but she was shaking her head. "Well, no. That's my nickname, not my real name."

"Well, what *is* your real name?"

"Mo'Shay," she said.

"What they call you Hazel for?"

"Because of my eyes," she said. She blinked, smiled. *His* eyes were as dark as the night sky. And those lips of his looked as soft and succulent as a just-ripe peach. "And this is, uh . . . this is Tarshia," she said, nearly forgetting who her best friend was. "What's *your* name?" she asked.

"Reese," he said. "But my friends call me Ree."

Mo'Shay nodded, staring stupidly. It didn't occur to her that the introductions were over. "Well, see you around," Tarshia said. Half-hypnotized, Shay followed Tarshia up the stairs and into Tammy's building.

"Mmm mmm mmm mmm mmm," Tarshia teased when they were inside. "You see the way that guy was looking at you?"

"Yeah, ain't he fine?" Mo'Shay said. "And how'd he know I'm Hazel?"

"Don't know," her friend said. "He musta been doin' some research."

Tammy was stretched across her bed, gossiping on the phone as usual. They motioned her to get off quick—they had some urgent business.

"What's up?" Tammy said. "I was just talking to—"

"Never mind that," Mo'Shay interrupted. "There's this guy down in the street named Reese. He has a motorcycle. You seen him yet?"

"Only from a distance," Tammy said. "His family just moved into the apartment downstairs. There's a bunch of kids."

"How old you think he is?" Shay asked. "Must be at least sixteen if he's driving a motorcycle, right?"

"Uh uh," her friend said. "That bike ain't his. It's his brother-in-law's. He our age."

Well, Shay thought, so what? She moved to the window to get another look. Now Reese was talking to another guy, older than him. The brother-in-law? They both hopped onto the bike, Reese behind the older guy, and the two of them roared away. Where had he moved *from*? she wondered. Did he have a girlfriend? Could someone as cool as this possibly be interested in her? Mo'Shay could hear her friends yakking in the background, but she had no idea what they were saying. In the daydream she was having, she was back at school. The pile of books she was carrying slipped out of her hands. And when she bent to pick them up, Reese was suddenly there, bending, too, to help her. Looking into each other's eyes, they both knew that this was love.

"Tammy, you gotta help me!" she blurted out, cutting into her friends' conversation. "I gotta get to know that guy."

"Okay, come on then," Tammy said.

"Where we going?"

"Outside to chill."

They sat out on the wall for an hour, but Reese never came back.

She watched him for the next several days, her heart revving as loudly as that motorcycle whenever she spotted him. Meanwhile, Tammy planned her matchmaking strategy. She favored the direct approach, she said. She would simply tell Reese that Mo'Shay was interested in him and grill him about his feelings, too.

It was the last day of June when Tammy finally made her move. The three girls had been walking up and down Center Street all afternoon when Reese came out of his building and into the sun. He was wearing jean shorts and a tanktop—looking finer than ever. Leaving Mo'Shay and Tarshia on one side of the street, Tammy crossed to the other. She was a woman on a mission.

As Shay waited and watched this conference between her friend and the guy of her dreams, she felt sick to her stomach. They nodded, talked. She could read neither their faces nor their gestures. She wished she could read lips. She wished, too, that she had never even asked Tammy for this favor. Why was Reese's "No, thanks, I'm not interested" taking so long?

Tammy walked back across the street toward Mo'Shay, her expression blank. "He wanna ask you something, Hazel," Tammy said.

Shay crossed the street, her face as hot as a flat iron, her feet as heavy as if someone had strapped bricks to them. She looked Reese in the eye, ready to take the rejection she was about to be handed.

"Do you have a boyfriend?" Reese asked her.

She shook her head, lost eye contact. "I'm single," she said. When she looked up again, she saw his half-smile.

"You doing anything tonight?"

Shay shrugged, smiled a little herself. "Not really."

"You wanna go out later on, then?"

"Where to?"

"I don't know. How 'bout pizza and video games?"

"I'd like that," she said.

As June turned into July, Mo'Shay and Reese saw more and more of each other. They went to the movies, to the park, out to eat. Slowly but steadily, Shay began to share personal feelings and private details about herself and her family. She had never trusted a guy like this before, but she found that she could open up to this boy. She felt that Ree trusted her, too. By midsummer, they had become inseparable.

Shirley Shambly knew about her daughter's blossoming relationship with this boy Reese and let her know that she disapproved. "You're both too young to be getting this close," she cautioned Mo'Shay. Shay knew that her mother only wanted the best for her, but she dismissed these warnings. Work was all that woman ever had time for. She never smiled, never had time for romance, never even took a moment in front of the mirror to make herself look pretty. What did her mother know about love?

One hot midsummer night, Shay was at Reese's house. No one else was home. They were in Ree's bedroom, lounging on his bed and listening to music as usual. The fan in the window was blowing hot, thick air. They talked, kissed a little. Ree's touch made Mo'Shay happy— took away some of the loneliness she often felt. She was where she wanted to be.

"Mo'Shay, I really care about you," Ree whispered.

"I care about you, too," she said.

"And I was wondering . . ." He massaged her arm and shoulder; he was struggling to say something. "Shay, we've been together for a while now," he said. "And, well, I was just wondering . . . if you think you'd be ready to take our relationship further."

Mo'Shay took a deep breath before answering him. Somehow, she felt frightened and calm at the same time. She trusted Ree; that wasn't it. He always took his time and made sure she was happy. He was patient and respectful of her, even at those times when his hormones seemed to be trying to take control. And she *wanted* to take it further. She had desired him from that very first day. It was just that she'd never been with a man in this serious and willing way before. *Was* she ready? She didn't know. She needed time to think.

Shay took Reese's hand and squeezed it gently. "I want to, Ree," she said. "But I think we still need time to get to know each other. I'm just not sure yet. What if we wait until the end of the summer?"

Reese covered his disappointment with a smile. "Okay," he said. "I understand. Whenever you're ready."

The days passed, a heat wave came and went, a hurricane scare blew out to sea. Soon it was late August, almost time to head back to school. Time, too, for Mo'Shay to make her decision. True to his word, Reese had waited patiently without pressuring her. But Shay knew that no guy would sit around forever.

Still, she was afraid. She had been battling that fear for weeks now, trying to push her mind away from the secret—the ugly memory she had struggled for years to avoid. But each time Shay thought about giving herself to the guy she trusted and loved, her mind wandered back to the one man she hated—the "friend of the family" who had betrayed her trust. . . .

It had happened one Saturday morning when Shay was eleven. As usual, her mother was out of the house and, as usual, she had left instructions that Mo'Shay and Heather were to stay put safely inside. The two sisters had finished their chores and were squeezed together in front of their little thirteen-inch TV, watching cartoons. The family's bigger floor-model television had been on the blink for weeks, its back off and leaning against the wall, its insides sitting on top of the cabinet. Fred, a friend of her mother's, had begun to fix the television weeks earlier but had stopped to order a part. They'd been squinting at their little TV ever since.

There was a knock on the door. Mo'Shay and Heather looked at each other, puzzled. They knew it couldn't be Ma wanting to be let back in;

she'd left for work early that morning and wasn't expected back until nighttime. And they knew the drill about letting strangers in.

Heather went to the door. "Who is it?" Mo'Shay heard her sister say. Then she heard the lock click, the door open. Hearing a man's voice in the other room, Shay got up to take a peek. It was only Fred.

"That tube I been waiting for finally come in," he said. Mo'Shay and Heather hadn't expected him—their mother hadn't left a note—but still, there was no problem letting Fred in the apartment. Fred and his wife, Ruth, had known Shay's mother for years. At last, the big TV would be fixed.

Heather wandered off into her room, but Mo'Shay stayed to watch Fred. A curious child, she enjoyed studying the way things worked and how they got fixed. Fred tinkered with the set for half an hour or so, occasionally asking Mo'Shay to hand him something out of his reach. "There, that should do it," he finally said. "Let's check and see." He plugged in the TV and turned it on. Mo'Shay grinned and clapped her hands. Picture and sound had been restored.

"Hey, you wanna do me a favor?" Fred asked her when he was packed up and ready to go. "Help me carry these tools down to my car, okay?"

"Sure," she said. "What do you want me to take?"

"That little box there. That's light enough for you, isn't it?"

Mo'Shay nodded. A second-grader could have carried that little box.

Going down the stairs, she didn't know why Fred was walking so closely behind her. He bumped her from the back once, and then again. The third bump caused her to drop the little box she was carrying. Nuts, bolts, and screws rolled everywhere. "I'm sorry," she said. "It slipped out of my hand."

"That's all right," he said. "We just have to pick them all up now, right?" He was staring strangely at her. Shay looked away. She bent to pick up the bolts and nuts by her feet.

"Look over there," Fred told her. "Don't forget that one in the corner. See it?" When she reached over to get it, he took a step closer, boxing her in between the wall and himself.

"What are you doing?" Shay asked.

"Helping you," he said.

"I don't need help. I already got it."

He moved closer still, then reached down and grabbed her by the arm. She was jerked to her feet. Frightened and confused, Shay didn't know what he was doing. Whatever this was, she didn't like it one bit.

"Let me go!" she demanded.

Instead, he shoved her against the wall with a force so sudden and angry that she bumped her head. It hurt. He leaned his weight against her and pressed his ugly lips against her mouth. She felt his big, rough hand slide up her shirt. Jerking her head first one way, and then the other, she managed to scream.

"Stop it! Please! What are you *doing*?"

He clamped his other hand over her mouth. "You're a sweet little girl," he whispered. "What you want to give your uncle Fred a hard time for?"

He *wasn't* her uncle; he was her mother's friend Ruth's husband. She pushed against him, but it was no use. He was too heavy, too strong. Mo'Shay began to cry. She felt his hand move down her pants. "Been watching you for a long time, little girl," he said. He was touching her, rubbing her, "down there."

"This gonna make you feel real good," he said. "Or who knows? Maybe I'll stop if you give me a little kiss back."

She knew about rape. Was that what this was? Was Fred going to rape and kill her? Was she about to die?

Then she felt something she had never felt before down there—a pressure pushing against her. It hurt her, scared her. She shuddered when his finger went up inside of her.

Downstairs, the front door opened. A look of panic flashed across Fred's face. He jerked his hand out of her pants and stood up straight, releasing her from his crushing weight. He grabbed his tools and hurried down the stairs.

For a minute or more, she couldn't move. She just stood there, trembling, staring at the wide-open door below. She had never felt this alone before—this detached from herself or her surroundings. Then she heard her sister calling her. The sound of her name brought her back to herself again. She hurried to straighten her clothes before anyone saw her. She forced a smile onto her face, ordered herself to take deep breaths—to relax and walk back up the stairs as if nothing at all had happened. She would tell Heather nothing about what he'd done. She would not tell her mother or anyone else. She would keep this dirty secret to herself forever.

Mo'Shay and Reese had made plans to be together for the last day before school started—the last day of summer. On her way to Reese's house that morning, her usual conflicting feelings of excitement and fear were heightened. When she saw Ree's building, she took deeper breaths, smaller steps. Had Ree even remembered the significance of this day? The promise she had tentatively made? Should she keep that promise? Could she?

The door to his apartment was open. She stuck her head inside. "Hello?"

Reese was in the living room, playing a video game. His brothers and sisters were all out, enjoying their last day of freedom. They were alone.

She sat down beside him, her eyes moving from the game on the screen to his fingers working the controls. If they were going to go through with this, she wanted to get it over with and behind her. She hoped it wouldn't take forever.

"If you're gonna play for a while, I guess I'll go outside," she said.

"Yeah? You feel all right?"

"Uh huh. I just need some air."

"Open the window, then."

Feeling fidgety, she did what he said. She stuck her head out and breathed in, filling her lungs with the sweet late August air. She reminded herself that Reese was not Fred, that she was no longer that frightened little girl on the front stairs.

"Hazel?"

She jumped, looked around. "Hmm?"

"You want something to drink?"

He stood at the doorway, waiting for her response. She felt impatient with him, resentful of this childish game they were playing. Why had she ever suggested this stupid wait-until-the-end-of-summer thing anyway? And why did he have to stand there looking so sweet and good?

"Sure," she said. Reese disappeared into the kitchen.

She flopped down on the couch, unpaused the game he'd been playing, played a little herself. This foolish midget Mario: what did *she* care if he fell off the mountain or got swallowed up by a dragon? Matter of fact, she hoped he *did*. Reese walked back into the room with two glasses of iced tea.

For a few minutes, they were both quiet. They held hands, sipped their tea. Reese began to stroke her arm, caress the spaces between her fingers. He smiled, leaned forward and kissed her. She kissed him back. The kissing felt good. She tried not to think about Fred, the spilled bolts on the stairs, the sinking feeling she'd had as she struggled helplessly against his crushing weight.

Reese sat back. He put his arm around her. "You want to go in the other room?" he asked. "Watch some TV or put a movie on or just relax?"

She shrugged. "What movie?" she said.

"I don't know. If there's nothing good, maybe we can make our own movie." He smiled when he said it and she smiled back, nervously. Then she got up and followed him into the bedroom.

He put a cassette in the VCR. They cuddled up together. He touched her wrists, her hair. A few minutes into the movie, he reached past her, grabbed the remote, and turned it off. "You comfortable?" he whispered. She nodded.

The deeper he kissed her, the more she felt the warm sensations take over her body, her soul. She felt hungry for his kisses, his touch—and then hungry to touch him back. She wanted him. She was ready.

"Make love to me, Reese," she whispered.

"Are you sure?" he whispered back.

She nodded.

He was gentle, undressing her, touching her, exploring her in ways that made her feel safe and secure. He was taking nothing from her that she wasn't ready to give. And she explored him, too, this man she loved. She felt in control of what was happening to her, no longer alone. And when their bodies came together, there was a kind of harmony, a music in their mutual touch.

When they were finished, they lay quietly in each other's arms, their breathing regulating. Mo'Shay placed her hand on Ree's chest to feel the beat of his heart. She had banished her fears, cleansed herself of her earlier bad experience—the way those memories had always made her feel dirty, ashamed, and alone. What had happened that day on the stairs no longer mattered. She was fine, no longer by herself. She had just made beautiful love to a guy who, two months earlier, she had thought existed only in her private dreams.

Someone knocked on the door!

Mo'Shay and Reese jumped from the bed and scrambled for their clothes. Dressing as quickly as they could, they kept bumping into each other. "Be right back," Reese mumbled, zipping and buttoning as he rushed out of the bedroom and toward the front door.

When Shay walked into Ree's living room, her sister Heather narrowed her eyes and stared at her. "You ain't heard Ma calling for you?" she asked.

Did Heather know what they had just done? Could she read in Shay's eyes that she'd just had the most satisfying experience of her life? That everything was different now?

"Calling me for what?" Shay asked.

"How should I know? Just go see."

Shay was in no mood for her sister's snotty attitude, but if her mother had sent Heather to find her, she knew she'd better get home. "I have to go," she told Reese. "I'll be back later."

She followed her sister's clomping steps down the stairs. "What was you guys doin' up there anyway?" Heather asked her.

"Nothin', that's what," Shay snapped back. "Gosh, you so nosy."

When they opened the door to their building, Mo'Shay pushed past her sister and ran up the stairs to the apartment. Her mother was in the kitchen, but Shay wasn't up to meeting her face-to-face. "Hi, Ma! I'm home!" she called, moving toward the safety of her bedroom. "Did you want something?"

"Stop yelling and get in here!" her mother called back. "And don't be running up the stairs like that, making all that racket."

"Sorry, Ma," Mo'Shay said. She took a breath and entered the kitchen.

"Here," her mother said, handing Shay a grocery list and a ten-dollar bill. "Go pick up these things." Her mother hardly looked at her; she didn't appear to suspect a thing. It made Shay feel both relieved and a little resentful, too. That woman wouldn't recognize what love looked like if it hit her in the face.

"What you waitin' for, Mo'Shay?" she said. "Come on. I'm in a hurry."

Ten minutes earlier, Shay had been a woman in the arms of the man she loved. Now, here she was again: her mama's errand girl. "Heather was right here, Ma. Why you ain't ask *her* to go?"

"Cause I'm asking *you* instead! Now git. I gotta start cooking."

"Can I keep the change?" Shay asked. If she was going to be demoted to errand girl, she might as well enjoy a few of the benefits.

Her mother rolled her eyes and shook her head. "I guess so," she mumbled. "Now go!"

On her way to the store, Shay wondered if her mother had suspected something after all. If she was in such a big hurry, why *hadn't* she sent Heather to the store instead of over to Reese's apartment? Well, if she suspected something, so what? Shay was a woman now, not a child. Her mother was going to have to accept that fact, whether she wanted to or not.

Mo'Shay saw Tammy and Tarshia sitting on the brick wall, watching the world go by as usual. Probably gossiping as usual, too, Shay thought. Well, she had a news flash for them—one that might make them both fall off that wall in shock. Mo'Shay had told her friends more than once that she wasn't interested in sex and never would be. Although the three girls knew almost everything about one another's lives, Shay had never told Tarshia and Tammy the reason *why* she'd taken her stand against sex. She'd kept her promise to herself—had told no one her shameful secret about Fred. Some things were better left unspoken, even to friends, and that was one of them. But now, thanks to Reese, what Fred had done to her no longer mattered.

"Hey, girl, what's happening?" Tarshia called when she spotted Shay. She approached them. They would grill her about the particulars when she gave them her news—she was sure of that. She decided she'd share a few of the details, but keep most of them for herself and Ree.

Labor Day came and went. Mo'Shay settled into the familiar school year routines: going to classes, doing her chores at home, hanging with her friends when there was time. Reese went to the same school now, too. They had none of the same classes but saw each other in the hallways, sat together some days at lunch. On weekends, they were together as much as possible. Shay liked school well enough, but it tired her out more than it had the year before. She groaned when her alarm clock rattled her out of her sleep and struggled, most days, to get out of bed.

Some mornings, she felt sick. But it was nothing much. She'd be fine once she caught up on her rest. She was just so tired.

One evening after supper, Mo'Shay was at the sink washing dishes. She heard the front door open. Her mother was home from work, late as usual. She came in, sat at the table, and put her feet up on the chair. Mo'Shay had been keeping her supper warm. She placed the meal before her.

"How was work?" she asked.

"Same as usual," her mother grumbled.

Mo'Shay stole glances at her mother as she ate. Her slouchy jaw moved listlessly as she chewed her food; her tired eyes looked out at nothing. Her mother's whole body seemed slumped in defeat. The nursing home had used her up—had kept her exhausted and unavailable to her children's needs. As usual, Shay felt conflicted, sympathetic and angry at the same time.

As she dried the dishes and put them away, something began to make Shay feel self-conscious. She *felt* her mother's eyes upon her before she turned and saw her staring.

"Mo'Shay?" her mother said. "Are you pregnant?"

Afraid to look her in the eye, Shay turned her back to her mother instead. Close to tears, she wiped down the same counters she had wiped five minutes earlier. A few weeks before, her mother had confronted Mo'Shay with her suspicion that she and "that boyfriend of yours" were messing around. Center Street was a close-knit neighborhood; the older people kept one another informed about the comings and goings of the kids. But Shay had denied the accusation and her mother had let it drop. And Shay wasn't totally naive. The thought *had* occurred to her a few times that she might be pregnant. Were her nausea and fatigue signs? She couldn't remember if she'd had her period the month before or not. She'd done her best to dismiss the possibility of pregnancy, convincing herself that these were coincidences, not symptoms. Until that night in the kitchen—until her mother actually spoke the word *pregnant*—Shay had managed to convince herself that that was not the case.

She scrubbed the counter harder. "No, Ma, I'm not pregnant," she said. Then she stopped what she was doing. For several seconds, neither of them moved or spoke.

"Could you at least face me when I'm talking to you?" her mother said.

When Shay turned around, she saw the tears rolling down her mother's face. Shirley Shambly never cried in front of her children; she was the strongest woman in the world. But now, there she sat, broken-hearted and weak and suffering terribly. Oh, god. Was it possible? *Was* she pregnant?

"I'm going to make an appointment for you," her mother said. "Okay?"

Shay nodded in agreement. She looked away again. For three years, she had kept from her mother the secret about Fred. She had assumed she could keep her intimacy with Reese a secret, too. But now some doctor would examine her, inform her mother that she was sexually active, and, possibly, that she was going to have a child.

Without another word, Shirley stood up and walked to her room, shutting the door behind her. Shay stood there, listening to her mother's muffled sobs.

The possibility that her fourteen-year-old daughter was pregnant seemed to crush Shirley Shambly, but it thrilled Reese. He beamed when Shay gave him the news, only half-listening as Mo'Shay described how sick she'd been feeling lately, and how hard her mother was taking it. Shay tried to warn Reese that if there *was* a baby on the way, their lives were about to become very complicated. But Ree just grinned and nodded at the prospect of fatherhood.

"Ma's taking me to the clinic to find out for sure," Mo'Shay told him. "You don't have to go. I'll call you when we get back."

"Oh, I'll go," Reese said. "I want to go."

Shay thought back to that first time she'd seen him out in the street at the beginning of the summer. Reese had looked so handsome and mature. Now he sat there, jumping around in his chair, as excited as a little kid about to be let loose in a candy store. This was just what she needed, Shay thought: *two* children to raise.

On the morning of her daughter's appointment at the medical clinic, Mo'Shay's mom stayed home from work. She, Reese, and Mo'Shay walked uneasily together to the bus stop. As they waited, none of them said a word. The bus was running late, of course. And when at last it chugged to the stop, Mo'Shay and Reese climbed the steps and hurried to the back seats. Shay's mother fell into a seat up front behind the driver and leaned her head against the window.

In the waiting room at the clinic, Shay sat between her mother and Reese. Her mom looked like she had aged ten years in one week. Reese, on the other hand, looked annoyingly juvenile. Shay felt uncomfortable about everything: the seating arrangement, the examination she was about to endure, the weeks and months to come. She turned abruptly to Reese. "Stop pumping that leg up and down," she snapped. "It's making me nervous."

"Sorry, Hazel," he said. "I'm excited."

"Hmph."

She tried to spark a little conversation with her mother, but her mother wasn't saying much. It was almost a relief when the nurse appeared in the doorway and smiled at her. "Right through here, please," she said.

The door closed behind them. Mo'Shay was handed a blue-and-white-striped examination gown. "You'll need to undress from the waist down," the nurse said. "I'll be back in a minute with the doctor."

Shay stood there for a second, alone and scared. Then she undressed quickly, worried that the doctor might come in before she was finished. When her pants and underwear were off and the gown was in place, she sat on the examining table. She began to cry softly to herself, her hands over her face to hide the tears. It was as if she was that eleven-year-old girl on the stairs again, alone and waiting for the worst to happen.

"Miss Shambly?" a man's voice said. It startled her. The doctor, a middle-aged man with gray hair, entered the examining room. The nurse from before was behind him. "I'm Dr. Bridges," he said. "How are we doing today?"

"All right, I guess." Shay's voice was hardly audible.

She was told to lie back and relax. She felt him press his hands on her lower abdomen as he asked his questions: Did she feel that? Did it hurt? When was the last time she had her period? The doctor ignored her shaking.

She answered as best she could, fighting off the sense of panic that engulfed her. She was trying very hard not to cry. As he examined her, Dr. Bridges gave information to the nurse and she wrote down what he said on a yellow notepad.

"Okay, I need you to put your legs up and spread them apart," the doctor said. Her trembling had subsided but now it started up again. "Don't worry," the nurse said. "This isn't going to hurt."

Feeling ashamed and humiliated, Mo'Shay did as she was told.

"Well, you're definitely pregnant, my dear," the doctor said. "Still in your first trimester, though. Do you want to keep this baby or have an abortion?"

She blurted out her answer without having to think: "I wanna keep the baby."

"Okay, then. You can sit up and get dressed." She rose from the table, quickly dressing herself. She watched the nurse prepare the table for the next patient, watched the doctor jot down notes about her.

"Miss Shambly, are you ready for your mom to come in so we can talk?"

Not really, Shay thought to herself. But to the doctor, she nodded yes.

Sitting in a chair with her head bowed low, Mo'Shay saw her mother's shoes as she walked into the room. She looked up into her mother's eyes. Those hurt and worried eyes said it all: this pregnancy had stuck a knife through her mother's heart.

"Sit down, please," the doctor told her mom.

She sat. As soon as Dr. Bridges began to speak, her mother began to cry. The more he said, the more she lost control of her emotions. Then, Shay was crying, too. "Miss Shambly, could I ask you to step out of the room for a moment?" the doctor said. "I'd like to speak to your mother alone."

As Shay sat out in the waiting room beside Reese, she tried to explain everything that had happened. "I'm pregnant for sure," she said. His face lit up like a Christmas tree. There was no turning back from any of this now. She knew that when she got home, her mother was going to kill her.

"Your mom's upset because she's still getting used to the idea," Reese said. "You need to give her some time."

"You don't know my mother," Shay sobbed.

When she was called back into the examining room, Reese rose to go with her, but the nurse asked him to wait outside.

Shay and her mother exchanged glances, neither one smiling. Her mom sniffled, wiped her eyes with a balled-up tissue. There was a whole box of tissues in her lap.

Dr. Bridges talked business. Shay had to make sure she ate healthy foods and got plenty of exercise. She should start taking vitamins. They needed to make another appointment to see him for two weeks from that day. All these instructions made her pregnancy—her baby—seem suddenly real. The doctor handed Shay some instruction sheets and sample packs of vitamins and wished the two women good luck.

Her mother stood and held out her hand to the doctor. The two shook hands. "Thank you for your time and your support," Shay's mom said.

On the long bus ride home, Shay, her mother, and Reese sat as silently as strangers, each of them lost in a private world. Only once did her mother speak, and it was Reese, not Mo'Shay, whom she addressed. "I just got one thing to say to *you* . . ." she began. Then she stopped, unable or unwilling to continue. Her mother had never really taken to Reese, and now that it had been verified that he'd gotten her daughter pregnant, she had no use for him at all.

At the front door of her building, Mo'Shay told Reese that she would see him later. She lingered a while on the staircase. Her mother had already gone upstairs. Shay dreaded the showdown that was coming.

When she got inside the apartment, she headed straight for her room. She closed the door, flopped onto her bed. It was quiet out there in the kitchen—no radio playing, no water running or pots being banged in preparation for supper. Her mother must just be sitting there.

"Mo'Shay!"

Shay awoke with a start. She hadn't realized she'd been dozing. "Yes, Ma?" Half asleep and half awake, she rose and headed for the kitchen, bracing for their delayed encounter.

"It's time we had a talk," her mother said. Her voice was calm. She motioned for Shay to sit down at the table.

"Is this something you want for yourself, Mo'Shay?" her mother asked.

Shay bowed her head, spoke in a low voice. "Yes, Ma." The room filled up with silence.

"All right, then. Here's what we're going to do. I'm sending you to live with your grandmother in New York and—"

Shay's bowed head jerked up. "But why?"

"Because I feel it would be better to get you away from here. You can come back after the baby is born."

"But, Mama, I don't wanna go! I wanna stay here with you!"

Was her mother embarrassed to have her around once her condition became obvious? Was she being punished for what she'd done? Shay *couldn't* leave. Her family, her friends, and Reese were all she had. She needed them now more than ever.

"Ma, I'm sorry I'm a disappointment to you," Shay pleaded. "But I can't take back what I did. The only thing I can do is try and make things right. I promise you, Ma, I'll take good care of this baby. And I'll do it by myself. I won't ask you for nothing. Please, please don't send me away."

Her mother looked upset. "I don't know, Mo'Shay," she said. "I need time to think things through."

The days got shorter, the leaves changed color, and word about Mo'Shay's condition got around. Most of her friends turned their backs on Shay. It was Tammy and Tarshia's rejection that hurt her the most. "I thought we were friends," she said, confronting them one afternoon at school.

"We are," Tarshia said. "But you went and got yourself pregnant. My mother doesn't want me hanging with you anymore."

Shay turned to Tammy. "Mine either," she said, averting her eyes.

Mo'Shay felt lonely, scared, and unwanted. Everything around her was changing, along with her body. And still there was the burden of her mother's decision hanging over her head. Was she going to be sent off to her grandmother's? Cut off from the few things about her life that still seemed the same? Whenever she asked her mom about it, she got the same answer: "I haven't decided yet."

Only Reese remained loyal. He was always around now, more and more excited about the baby each day. Reese's family had not been any happier than Shay's about the news of the pregnancy. But the young couple worked hard to demonstrate to both their families that they were responsible enough to raise this child. They stayed in school, did the best they could about attendance and grades. Reese tended to Shay's needs and her comforts. He accompanied her to her doctor's appointments and provided whatever he could for the child's prenatal care. Shay was thankful for his support, grateful for all of his efforts. But the person she most needed was the one whose support she felt least sure about: her mother.

Mo'Shay had never meant to bring her mother this much pain. Hadn't she held her tongue about missing her all those long, lonely hours while she was away at work? Hadn't she spared her mother the disturbing secret about what Fred had done to her? But Shay *wanted* this child growing inside of her—this unborn baby who would always be there for her and love her and need her as much as she needed *her* mother. Mo'Shay had never been as close to her mother as her sister Heather was. Now she understood why. The love between a mother and her first-born was the strongest bond in the world. But still, Shay longed for her mother's acceptance of her situation, and with it, her unconditional love.

Doing the supper dishes one evening, Shay looked up to see her mother coming in from work. Shay was almost into her second trimester now. She was still nervous about being shipped off to New York to have the baby.

Shirley placed a couple of bags on the table and flopped onto a kitchen chair. She sighed, hooking her feet around the legs of another chair and pulling it closer. She put her feet up and sighed again.

"You tired, Ma?" Shay asked her.

"I'm always tired," her mother said. And she was, too. Her mother was the hardest-working woman Shay knew.

She smiled, nodded toward her mother's purchases. "Been shopping, I see." Sometimes her mother stopped at the downtown stores after work. She liked to buy inexpensive knickknacks to pretty up the house. It cheered her up.

"I've decided," her mother said.

Mo'Shay knew immediately what her mother meant. She turned from her housework and faced her. Waited. "I'm going to let you stay at home."

Shay nodded, smiled sadly, but said nothing. She went back to her dishes, feeling the relief that flooded through her body. She willed her-self not to cry.

"It's not going to be easy, though," her mother continued. "Things are going to change around here with a small baby in the house. We're going to have to work together."

Shay nodded, keeping her back to her mother. Her tears fell into the dishwater.

"Mo'Shay, come here a minute," her mother said.

When she turned around, her mother was taking something out of one of the bags. She laid it on top of the table: the cutest little baby set, a yellow sweater with matching bonnet and booties. Shay looked up from the baby clothes to her mother's face. She smiled. Her mother smiled back.

"I love you, Ma," Shay said. "With all my heart."

"I love you, too, Mo'Shay," her mother whispered. "All I ever wanted was what's best for you. I'm going to take care of you and the baby when it comes along. I'm still not sure how we're going to manage it all, but we will."

She got up and walked to her daughter, her arms extended.

Mo'Shay fell into those arms. Her mother held her, cuddled her, rocking her back and forth as if she were a baby.

———◆———

Michelle Jessamy was born in London, England. A mother of four, she is serving a twenty-year sentence for manslaughter, the result of her violent response to an unwanted advance by a family friend. Both during her trial and today, Jessamy maintains that hers was an act of self-defense during a situation that went rapidly out of control.

At York prison, Jessamy has completed the requirements for her high school equivalency certificate and has gone on to study algebra, computer technology, and writing. She has also worked in the counseling program for York's youthful offenders and served as a teacher's aide. "The prison environment causes you to shut down and distrust other people, but writing has the opposite effect," Jessamy says. "By exploring my past through autobiographical fiction and sharing it with others, I am learning how to come to terms with the 'whys' of my past actions and how to release my spirit from *its* prison. Writing gives me a sense of peace."

SNAPSHOTS OF MY EARLY LIFE
DIANE BARTHOLOMEW

Born: 1946
Conviction: Homicide in the first degree
Sentence: 25 years
Entered prison: 1990
Deceased

1. SUPPERTIME

Mother worries all the time that I'm not eating enough. "You're too bony, Diane," she'll say. The spoon hovers toward me and the daily dose of Geritol is spilled down my throat. Then she hurries off to work.

Mom works second shift at the U.S. Rubber Shop, and when she's not home, Daddy's in charge. I often hear Mother explaining my bruises to other people. "Oh, Diane's double-jointed and she falls a lot." But my bruises don't come from accidents like she wants to believe. They come from suppertime.

"Supper!" Grammy calls. "Come on, get up to the table! Supper's ready!" Grammy unties her blue ruffled bib apron and pulls it over her head, neatly placing it on the counter. She smooths a few loose strands of her graying auburn hair back into her tightly twisted bun. Pouring our milk, she calls over her shoulder, "Did you girls wash your hands?"

"Yeah, Grammy, we did," Katie replies.

We climb onto our assigned chairs, me sitting on my knees so I can see what I'm going to have to force myself to eat. I have to be extra careful that the metal buckles on my red Buster Brown sandals don't puncture the speckly gray Naugahyde chairs. If that happens, I'll get cuffed even before the food's on the table.

Please, God, I pray, let it be something I like. I hate vegetables and Grammy's always making vegetable dishes from the garden. Sometimes I wonder if she does it deliberately. I know Grammy likes Katie better than me. And I know that before supper's over, Daddy's going to whip me for being a bad girl and not eating everything on my plate.

Oh, God, it's eggplant. "Yuck," I protest. "I ain't eatin' that stuff."

"You're too darn fussy, young lady!"

Our nightly ritual has begun.

I sit there hoping that the food will magically disappear off my plate, but I know it won't. Sometimes I get lucky and slip Queeny, our black wavy-haired mongrel, a handful or two of the yucky stuff. Queeny's a picky eater, too, but she comes to my rescue when she can. She even eats my vegetables, the ones I know she doesn't like. I swear that Queeny knows that she's saving my life. But tonight, she's outside, not under the table, so I'm sunk.

An hour into it, we're still at a standstill, Daddy and me. "You ain't getting up from that table until you eat what's in front of you!" he warns. I figure I'll sit here all night if I have to—not go to sleep until Mother gets home. But as soon as I tell myself that, I start to doze. When I nod off, Daddy shakes me awake again. He grabs me by the arm and pulls me off the kitchen chair, pulls off his belt. *Whack! Whack!* After a while it doesn't even matter where the belt lands. It's become so normal that nobody notices. Grammy wipes up around me, doing as much cleanup as she can without disturbing me. Katie's excused herself long ago. A nontroublemaker, she gets to sit in the living room and watch TV.

I wish Grammy would holler at Daddy for hitting me. She's his mother; maybe she could make him stop. Can't she see he's really hurting me bad? Even if Grammy *does* like Katie better, she should help me.

Eventually, I learn how to swallow things whole. I use my left hand to pinch my nose shut and my right hand to shovel the food down my throat. I know it's either eat or be beaten.

If it's not too late when I've finally finished eating, Daddy takes us to Carvel. The creamy chocolate ice cream is cold and smooth on my tongue and throat. It slides down easy, not like the homemade stuff with all those chunks of ice. I think maybe Daddy feels bad about having beat the tar out of me and this ice cream is his way of saying he's sorry he hit me so hard. As I swallow the last bite of my soggy cone, I wonder what yucky vegetable Grammy will cook tomorrow night, what trouble we'll bring to the table.

2. WILDWOOD

It's an odd kind of day—Labor Day, 1953, the last full day of our seashore vacation in Wildwood, New Jersey. The air is hot and clammy, the sky overcast. In the other room of our cramped vacation apartment, Mother and Katie are gearing up.

"Katie, I want you to put on your white cotton dress with the pink flowers," Mother says. "And remember, you can't go in the water today."

"But, Ma! Only old ladies like Grammy wear dresses to the beach, with those ugly, heavier-than-sin roll-up socks."

"You hush about Grammy. You can't expect someone her age to be seen in public in a bathing suit. It wouldn't be proper."

"But it's proper for *me,* Ma! I don't want to wear no dress on the beach!"

"Well, you're going to have to!" Mother snaps back, her tone reminding my sister which of the two of them is in charge.

I'm puzzled about why Mother is making Katie wear a dress. Is my sister's pale skin the problem? Mother's always worrying that Katie will get sunburned. Not me, though. "Diane never burns," Mother boasts. "Must be all that oil I used on her when she was a baby."

"Nah, it's that guinea blood of hers keeps her from getting burnt," Daddy teases back. I can never understand, exactly, what it is about my "guinea blood" that Daddy doesn't like, but I know his comments are intended as insults. I guess Dad considers me defective, not entirely of his making, because before I was born, during a postwar blood short-age, Mother received a transfusion. She has an uncommon blood type; the only person whose blood matched hers was an Italian shoemaker from New Haven. Dad's teasing always makes me feel mad—like I'm not as pure as my brothers and sister. But if "guinea blood" saved Mother's life and saves me from sunburns, then I guess I can live with being different.

We have a beach-packing ritual at Wildwood, Katie and me. Even though she's eleven, four years older than I, when it's time to head for the beach, we always race each other for the sand toys piled neatly by the outside shower. Then we run to the car, where Daddy's packing the trunk. Katie almost always beats me, but today I win. Katie doesn't even try. As we hand our stuff to Daddy to be placed, packed, and wedged into the trunk of our black Buick, Katie sighs.

"What's the matter with you?" I ask her.

"Oh, nothing," she says. "I was just thinking about poor Marvin—how he had to stay home and work and miss all the fun." Katie's always worrying about our older brothers.

"Marvin didn't even *want* to come on vacation with us," I remind her.

Daddy places our pails and shovels in the trunk. "Don't worry about Marvin," Daddy scowls. "He didn't stay home to work. He stayed home to be with that new little chippy of his. He wasn't fooling anyone but you two."

Daddy angles our beach umbrella into the trunk. Carl Jr. comes out carrying the beach chairs, and Dora, his fiancée, puts the blankets and towels in Carl's '46 Chevy. Mom and Grammy join the caravan. Like a parade of ants carrying food to their nest, the family marches back and forth from the house, loading up the two cars. And if the rest of us seem restless, impatient to get to the beach, Carl and Dora don't even seem to notice. They're gazing cow-eyed at each other, acting all mushy. I can tell by the way they touch each other's hands that they want to kiss. But they know Mother won't approve of that kind of behavior in public.

Before our trip, I listened in on Mother's telephone conversation with Mrs. Gardner, Dora's mother. Mother had a difficult time convincing her to let Dora come with us on vacation. She had to promise that she wouldn't let Carl and Dora out of her sight. "They can't do anything at Wildwood that they haven't had an opportunity to do already," Mother pointed out. After she got off the phone, I asked, "What can't Carl and Dora do?"

Sharply, Mother reminded me that she hadn't been talking to me, so I put that little mystery on hold, figuring I'd get to the bottom of it later. All during our stay at the beach, I've been watching Dora and Carl like a hawk.

Dora is always nice to me, but I know it's Carl Jr. she likes the most. She isn't fooling me. I can't blame her. Carl Jr.'s handsome and tall and he has blond hair and hazel eyes. I can see that Carl really likes Dora, too, but I don't mind sharing him because I'm sure he loves me more. And besides, I have Dad.

Daddy jams the last of the stuff in the trunk and slams the door. "Diane," he says, "go tell your mother and Grammy to get a move on."

As I approach the porch, I hear Grammy and Mother whispering with Mommy Cannon, the old lady who owns the house where we rent our apartment. Daddy told me Mommy Cannon and her dead husband were vaudeville dancers, but, honestly, this old lady can just barely struggle out of her Adirondack chair and onto her feet. With my mother and grandmother, whispering usually means secrets revealed, so I tiptoe closer and listen. "It's just happened to Katie, during the night," Mother confides. "Diane doesn't know, of course. She's—"

"My my my," Mommy Cannon interrupts when she notices me. "Little pitchers sure do have big ears."

Diane doesn't know *what*? I wonder. What's wrong with Katie? She looks okay to me. I promise myself I'll find out once we get to where we're going—that I will yank the information out of someone.

*   *   *

The beach is hot and hazy today and there's a gray mist around the sun. The ocean looks more powerful than usual.

"Ma, it's wicked hot," Katie complains, as we step from the board-walk onto the beach.

"Ouch!" I cry. "This sand's burning my feet!"

Having spent money at the beginning of our vacation for yellow shovels, red buckets, and blue plastic brick makers, Mother isn't eager to buy more equipment on our last day here. But she feels sorry for Katie and me, so she takes us to a little open-air store on the boardwalk and buys us terrycloth beach shoes with rubber soles.

As soon as Daddy has the umbrella set up and we've put the chairs in place and the blankets down, I start nagging Mother. "Mother, what don't I know about Katie?"

"I'll tell you when you're older."

"I'm old enough now."

"Later, Diane. Go down to the shore and play."

Instead, I scoot over to Carl Jr., who's busy rubbing sun tan lotion all over Dora's back. "Hey, Carl, what don't I know about Katie?" I ask.

Dora blushes and giggles and shares a knowing smile with Carl Jr. He smiles back at her the same way and gives her googly eyes. Finally, he turns his attention to me. "Hey, Diane," he says. "What kind of Good Humor bar did you say you wanted?"

But my big brother's attempt to distract me with ice cream doesn't work. I'm not giving up that easily. I've made up my mind that I'm going to find out something from someone or else drive them all nuts trying.

"Answer me about Katie, Carl," I say. "Come on!"

"Where we going?" Carl Jr. quips back.

"Cut it out."

"Okay. Where's the scissors?"

"I mean it, Carl. What don't I know about Katie?"

It's Grammy who comes to his rescue, flapping her wrist to shoo me away. "Go on now, Diane. You leave Carl and Dora alone. Go play." My brother Carl Jr. and my sister Katie are Grammy's favorites. I'm not sure which of the two she's protecting. I decide to let the mystery drop for a few minutes, but I'm not about to give up.

Katie's standing at the water's edge in her dress, letting the little waves lap at her bare feet. I run down to her. "Wanna build a castle?" I ask. Usually Katie likes making sandcastles with me, but today she says she doesn't feel like it. "You go ahead and I'll watch," she says.

"Katie, what the heck is—"

"Diane!" Mother shouts.

I look back up at the blanket. "What?"

"Leave your sister alone."

I plop down and start digging, muttering to myself. Every time I look over at Katie, she's staring off into space instead of watching me, like she said. I'm halfway done with Sleeping Beauty's sandcastle when, out of the corner of my eye, I spot maroon trunks pass by headed for the water.

"Daddy!" I shout. "Wait for me!"

But he just keeps going. *Splash!*

I toss my new beach shoes into the air and follow him in.

The icy water makes goose bumps on my skin. I wade in, jumping the little waves, trying to catch up to Daddy. A little farther out, the bigger waves push me back toward shore. The moving water eats the sand out from under my feet.

From the beach, Mother hollers, "Carl! Keep an eye on Diane!"

Daddy pauses for a minute and turns back slightly. "Come on," he says, reaching for me. He takes me by both hands and pulls me to him. "Turn sideways when you see a big one coming," he says. "Makes it easier to break the wave." He inches us out to deeper water. The waves are up to Daddy's chin and I'm way, way over my head. "You scared?" Daddy asks.

"Nope." And I'm not either. I know Daddy will keep me safe. I grab onto his neck and wrap my legs around his waist.

We go out farther—so far that now Daddy's over his head, too. We float above the waves, waiting and waiting for the most powerful one to ride back in to shore. "Not this one," Daddy keeps saying. "Nope, not yet."

As we wait, I lean close and whisper into his ear. "Daddy?"

"Hmm?"

"What don't I know about Katie?"

A puny wave rolls toward us. We have let waves twice the size of this one go past. "Okay, this is the one," Daddy says. "Get ready!" And he tosses me into the crest.

I stretch my arms out stiff, like Daddy's taught me, and make my body straight as a board. Everything's going fine until halfway in. The wave forces me below the surface, the momentum tossing me around like I have no bones. By the time I reach the shore, I'm spitting up water, gasping for air, and scared to death. I'm careful not to let Daddy know, though. Daddy hates crybabies. If he sees my fear, he will leave the water and be mad.

I wade back out to him. We give up waiting for the best waves and ride in whatever rolls toward us. Again and again we ride the waves, Daddy and me. Finally, Dad says, "That's it. I'm pooped," and we walk out of the water and back onto the beach.

When evening comes and we return to the apartment, everyone but me is miserable. Dora's eyes are almost swollen shut. Carl Jr.'s and Daddy's backs are roast-beef red. Mother has to cut Katie's dress off her. "Look at this!" Grammy grumbles. "My legs got burned under my cotton socks."

As for me, I'm tan. For once, being a "little guinea" has paid off. All those other big dodos have gotten sunburned, but not me. In the mirror, I trace the white edge where my bathing cap ends. My face is a brown mask. I am so fascinated that I nearly forget about the mysterious thing that has happened to Katie.

But then I remember and start over, moving from one red and blistering family member to the next, strutting my bronze self around the apartment. "All I want to know is," I announce, "what in the world is wrong with Katie!"

It's Mother who breaks. She grasps my wrist and leads me into the bathroom. "Please, Diane, stop annoying everyone," she pleads. "We're all sick and cranky and we're not up to being badgered. Today was a special day for Katie, that's all."

"Special why?"

"Because she got her friend."

Huh?

"What friend?" I say. "I didn't see anyone."

Mother hits me with the gruesome details. "You bleed, and sometimes you feel cramps. You have to wear a pad and a belt for a few days so that the blood doesn't soak through. After you've had your friend the first time, it comes back and visits you every month."

"Yuck!" I say. "I won't be getting this friend, will I?"

"Well, no, not for now," Mother says.

I don't really understand, but I decide I've heard enough. It doesn't sound like a friend to me. Katie can have this friend that makes her so special. I'll skip it and ride the waves with Daddy instead, tossing and tanning forever.

3. COFFEE GROUNDS

"It's real pretty," I tell Carl Jr. I am holding the ruby ring between my thumb and index finger, twisting my wrist back and forth so that the sun catches the red stone just right. "Did you buy it for one of your girl-friends?"

"Nope," he says. "Didn't buy it at all. I found it."

I look up at him in disbelief. "Where?"

"In the parking lot at work. It's not any cheap tin ring that bends easy either. It's the real thing."

I nod, eyes still on the ring. "Who you giving it to?" I ask Carl. "Dora?"

"Uh-uh," he says. "It's a birthstone ring and she wasn't born in July. You don't know anyone who was born in that month, do you?"

I know Carl Jr. is teasing me. "July's *my* birthday month," I remind him.

He gives me a goofy smile. "Oh, yeah, so it is," he says. "Guess you better try it on then. If a girl wears a ring with her birthstone in it, it brings her good luck."

I slip the ring on my finger. It fits perfectly.

I need some good luck right about then. We all do. Daddy's been planning for months to move our family to Pennsylvania—planning for us to strike it rich once he and Mother take over the combination lun-cheonette and filling station he's leased. We're close to our leaving date when Grammy gets sicker. She's been coughing for weeks, and Mother finally finds the time to take her to the hospital. They take tests and say it's tuberculosis, so Grammy goes straight from the hospital to a sanato-rium, and they can't say how long she'll need to stay there. That puts us in a pickle. Mother works the evening shift at U.S. Rubber and Grammy's been our family's cook. Now Katie has to pick up the slack and I have to help her. On top of that, we're tiptoeing on eggshells. Daddy's mother's TB has put the brakes on his get-rich-in-Pennsylvania plan. He feels frustrated, and when Dad feels frustrated, watch out. So I shut my mouth and behave for a change, and wear my birthstone ring as much as possible.

"Katie, you're to make meatloaf for your dad tonight," Mother says, hurrying into her coat. If she punches in late at the rubber shop, they dock her pay. "Diane, you make sure you listen to your sister and help her with the cleanup. Remember to take off that pretty ring of yours if you're working around the sink." I nod, wave her good-bye. She runs out the door. A second or two later, it opens again. "Please, girls," Mother pleads. "I need you to be extra, extra good while I'm gone."

Katie and I play for a bit and then get on our bikes to deliver our newspapers. We split the job. Katie takes the papers for Buckley Lane and I load up the ones for our road. I speed down Rek Lane as fast as I can, hurling papers onto customers' porches so that I can buy a little playtime before Katie finishes her route and starts supper. But once the kitchen chores begin, I am planning to be extra, extra good.

Katie's never made meatloaf before, but she rummages around as if she knows what she's doing. She plops the meat Mother's defrosted into Grammy's favorite sage-colored bowl and adds breadcrumbs, ketchup, onions, and eggs. Then she sticks her hands into the whole mess and starts squishing. Yuck, I think to myself. I'll have to eat *this*? But I know Daddy will kill me if I don't. And besides, I promised Mother.

I'm extra good at supper. I pinch my nose and eat my whole piece of Katie's salty meatloaf. I'm disappointed when Daddy doesn't even notice. Gee whiz, I know the rule is that no one talks at the table, but I thought he'd be so happy I ate that, for a change, he'd say *something*.

Now it's time for us to clean up the kitchen. I take off my ring like Mother told me and put it on the windowsill over the sink. Katie clears the dishes and washes the glasses. She reaches for the coffeepot next.

"Diane, take the core out of this pot," Katie orders. "Clean out the coffee grounds." Just what I need, I think to myself: someone else in this house to boss me around. And besides, I'm not touching that slimy stuff.

"No!" I say. "I don't want to."

"Then I'll tell Dad," she warns. She jerks her sudsy hands from the dishwater and heads for the living room.

"Come on, Katie," I beg her. "I'll do anything else. I just don't want to put my hands in those nasty, slimy grounds."

"Hey, Dad!" Katie yells. "Diane won't clean the grounds out of the coffeepot!"

"Don't you make me come in there, Diane!" he hollers back from the living room. When he yells like that—when one of our standoffs is about to start—I can feel the trouble start to shake my body.

"Why should I?" I holler back. "If she doesn't want to, then why—"

I haven't even finished my sentence when he thunders around the corner like an angry bull, his belt in hand. He whacks me a couple across my legs. Breathes like he's out of breath. Whacks me again.

I look Dad in the eye, which, I know, will infuriate him. "What are *you* looking at?" he screams. *Pow! Pow!* The belt cuts across my flesh, the sting almost unbearable. When it comes to eye contact at these moments, you can't win with Dad. If you look away, he screams at you for not paying attention and hits you some more. If you face him, he reads it as sass.

Dad lifts me off the ground, then slams me onto the kitchen floor. He beats me some more with the belt. I can feel the blood coming to the surface, the welts rising on my legs, my back, my butt. Trying to ease the sting of each blow, I roll back and forth across our new black and white rubber-tile kitchen floor.

Dad stops to catch his breath. He looms over me, glaring, and I look up, look away, look up at him again. "You have enough yet?" he barks.

But I can be as stubborn as Daddy is mean. "Nope."

This makes him madder than he's ever been. When he lets loose a new round of blows, I can feel my bones rattle. "Had enough?" he asks again.

"Nope."

We maintain our positions, me on the floor, Dad over me. The beating continues for another fifteen or twenty minutes, stopping every few so that Dad can ask me the same question, and then starting up again when I give the same answer. Finally, Dad gets down on his hands and knees and whispers in my face, "For the last time, have . . . you . . . had . . . enough?"

I hurt all over. I can't take any more pain. He's won. "Yes," I say. "Yes *what*? Say it."

I scream out what he wants to hear. "Yes! Yes! I've had enough!"

The screaming renews his anger. He can't stop hitting me. He's out of control. I roll around the floor, hoping to dodge as many blows as possible until he tires enough to stop. But when he doesn't stop, I manage to stand and run to the bathroom.

"Unlock that goddamn door!" he screams, pounding from the other side. Unlock it? I want to slam it so hard, it will come off its hinges.

"Okay, Diane," Dad shouts in at me. "You wanna play that way? I'll fix *your* wagon!"

Later that night, when it's safe to come out again, I see my expensive birthstone ring mangled on the kitchen floor. I pick it up, go into my room, and cry and cry.

I can forgive Daddy all the beatings he gives me, but it takes a long, long time before I forgive him for ruining the ring Carl Jr. gave me. But, finally, I do. Mother always taught us to work as hard as we could at forgiving people because it's always the right thing to do.

4. TROUT RUN

Mother has finished unpacking and putting away our belongings in this new place. The March wind is whipping down the valley. Pennsylvania is colder than Connecticut.

This will be my first day at my new school, and I'm shaking inside because the wind's cold and because I'm scared. The bus stop is right behind the small Gulf gas station and luncheonette that Dad found and my family's going to run. I hear the bus before I see it, the lumbering sound of the engine. Then it appears on the horizon, crossing over the bridge.

Urrrch. The brakes groan, the bus comes to a stop, the door slaps open. As I board, I see it's practically empty, except for a few kids horsing around in the back. I sit up front. I want to be back on my old bus with kids I know, going to my old school in Prospect.

The bus rolls on. I stare out at the little cottages and houses we pass. The countryside here is different from Connecticut. The mountains surround green fields and there're little brooks and streams everywhere. Finally, a small town appears out of nowhere. It's not much: an old run-down country store, a gas station, a few two-family houses. At a distance, there's an old gristmill tucked into a grove of oak trees alongside a creek. This has to be Trout Run.

The bus eases over the railroad tracks. Just beyond, a redbrick two-room school sits all by itself in the middle of a field. It reminds me of all those hick schools I've seen on TV westerns. I'm scared as I walk up the front steps and enter the foyer. Inside, I can see the whole layout of the school. To the right, stairs lead down to the girls' room, and to the left, there are identical stairs and a bathroom for the boys. I walk up the five wide center steps to the main hallway. A bulky frayed rope hangs from the ceiling like a noose. My eyes follow it up to the large, tarnished black bell suspended high above my head. It's all alone up there in its square steeple. I think I'm going to hate this school.

Straight ahead at the far end of the hall is the cloakroom: coats, hats, and scarves hanging on rows of metal hooks. I peek inside the noisy classroom on the left. It's filled with little kids—first-, second-, and third-graders. So I walk to the doorway of the other classroom. Inside are the kids closer to my age: fourth-, fifth-, sixth-graders. I stand at the threshold. I'm in fifth.

The classroom has sooty yellow walls and a beat-up picture of George Washington hanging above the blackboard. The teacher's desk sits in the front left corner; the kids' rickety wooden desks are bolted to the floor in rows. Large, drafty windows let in plenty of sunlight and air. Even from here, I can feel the cold draft on my bare legs. The floor's dirty and stinks of oil. What a crummy, disgusting school this is, I think to myself.

I enter the classroom and walk toward the front. I'm wearing my flowered lilac dress, ruffled ankle socks, and black dress shoes. I can feel them all gaping at me. I'm not looking anyone in the eye, but I can see that all of them, boys and girls, are wearing blue jeans.

"I'm Mr. Peterson," the teacher says. "And who do we have here?"

"My name is Diane Hiller," I say in a shy and tiny voice.

"Well, hello, Diane Hiller," he says, standing up. He's about six-foot-three or -four and has a large, wide frame. His hair's slicked back with grease. Even though his voice is gentle, he reminds me of the picture of that scary Jack-in-the-beanstalk giant in the book Mother used to read to Katie and me—the one who grinds men's bones to make his bread. He tells me to take the second seat near the window.

My desktop's dingy and scarred with the names and smart remarks of all the kids who sat here before. A dark, dirty hole peers out of the right upper corner. Once it must have held a bottle of ink, but it reminds me of an open mouth that's screaming. I wish these dumb Trout Run kids would stop turning in their seats to look at me.

All day long I listen to Mr. Peterson's and the class's twangy accents. Although I'm the only one speaking right, they tell me that *I* talk odd. They laugh when I say "aunt," not "ant" and "Mother," not "Mom." I sense they dislike me because they think I'm uppity.

For the rest of that school year, I try to fit in, but I get nowhere. They don't like anything I do. Mr. Peterson says my penmanship's unacceptable and that I have to learn how to write all over again. All the other kids write like they're composing the Declaration of Independence or something—all these flairs and swirls and curlicues in every sentence. It makes me dizzy to try to write like that and gives my hand cramps. They all read better than I do, too. They study science, history, geography, and subjects I never even heard of out of textbooks much fatter than the ones at my old school. I feel like a jerky Connecticut school kindergartener at the University of Trout Run. And so, of course, I stay back.

It's a long, hot, and boring summer. Katie and I help out at the luncheonette, but there's not too much to do because there aren't many customers. But things are a little better the following school year. I have begged Mother all summer long to buy me some blue jeans and she finally agreed. So on the first day I don't feel like such a stranger.

The boys let me play baseball with them; Sandra Campbell and I are the only girls they will allow on their team. So I turn myself into a rough-and-tumble tomboy to make friends. One day, I get hit in the eye with a hardball. It knocks the wind out of me and my left eye looks Chinese. I walk around with a shiner for about a week, but that doesn't stop me from playing ball.

After I make friends with the boys, some of the girls start speaking to me, too. Sharon Shea's the first girl to make friends with me. She's fun to be with because she's crazy and wild. One day she gets the bright idea to wipe poison ivy all over her body so she won't have to go to school.

It works, all right. The poison gets into her bloodstream and she has to go to the hospital instead.

Another time Sharon says something that Mr. Peterson doesn't like. He goes to his closet and brings out his paddle. It's about three inches wide and almost three feet long and has a fancy carved handle. Mr. Peterson approaches Sharon. This is the first time I've seen him get angry. Size-wise, he's scary enough without the paddle, but he's much spookier with it. He uses one hand to grab onto Sharon's upper arm. With his other hand, he delivers powerful blows to Sharon's rear end. With each whack, she jumps and sways, trying to avoid the next one. It looks like she's doing some strange war dance. Later on, when Sharon's parents see the bruises on her butt and hands, they come to school and yell at Mr. Peterson. Sharon had put her hands back there to protect her fanny; that's how her fingers got black and blue.

Dad's not around as much as he was in Connecticut. Business at the gas station and restaurant is lousy; Mother handles what there is of it. Dad's found places to go and things to do that have nothing to do with us. This is good, in a way. If Dad's not there, he can't "supervise" me during supper. And besides, Mother is always nearby now to intervene if necessary. But the restaurant takes most of Mother's time. And because it's not making any money, she's fretful and distracted, even when she's home with us. So I'm lonely—invisible, in a way. At least when Dad hit me, I got noticed.

At school, I campaign for Mr. Peterson's attention. I try harder on my papers. I volunteer for the classroom chores that no one else wants to do. I raise my hand even when I don't know the answer, just to get him to notice me and say my name. But nothing works. Mr. Peterson barely gives me a second look. And then an idea dawns on me. Mr. Peterson always notices the bad kids like Sharon and Ace Hodges and Leon Combs. If I do something I'm not supposed to, maybe I won't be invisible. Won't be empty anymore. It always worked with Dad, and it would work with Mr. Peterson, too.

That afternoon, out at recess, I challenge the roughest boys in our class to a wrestling match. We knock each other down, roll around on the ground, try to pin each other. When the bell rings, we go back inside. Our clothes are dirty and my blue-and-white-striped blouse is ripped at the seam.

I was right. Mr. Peterson notices us, and he's mad.

"I'll give you four a choice," Mr. Peterson informs Ace and Leon and Freddie Grissom and me. The rest of the class has gone home for the day; we wrestlers have been detained. "You can either write a thousand times each the following sentence—*I will not wrestle on the ground at school*—or else you can get a licking here and now with the paddle. Which do you choose?"

"Write the sentences," the three boys answer, in unison.

Mr. Peterson turns to me, and so do the others. I like having everyone's attention. I keep them waiting.

"Diane?" Mr. Peterson says.

"I'll write the sentences."

The next day the boys hand in their three thousand sentences. "Do you have your sentences ready?" Mr. Peterson inquires.

"No, sir," I tell him. "I haven't finished them yet. I'll have them tomorrow." But I have no intention of finishing them. He will ask again the next day, and when I tell him they're not ready, he will have to paddle me.

But that doesn't happen. Several days go by. Mr. Peterson fails to paddle me or even mention the sentences. Why not? Doesn't he care enough about me to teach me a lesson? Am I not worth the bother? Am I invisible?

The weeks pass. The weather warms. First it's baseball season, then it's May Day, and then summer vacation is only a week away. I've long since swallowed my disappointment about not being important enough to be punished by Mr. Peterson. I've gone on to other worries. But on the second to last day of school, Mr. Peterson walks up my row and stops at my desk. "Diane, do you have those sentences yet?" he asks.

I am frozen in my seat, trembling and thrilled. I look away from his gaze. He hasn't forgotten after all. "I'll bring them tomorrow," I promise.

I mean that promise when I make it, but the next day I still don't have the sentences. I wait all day, but Mr. Peterson doesn't ask for them. At three o'clock, the bell rings, kids cheer, and we are let out for the long summer.

Mr. Peterson hasn't paddled me. He doesn't love me—doesn't care one little bit about teaching me a lesson.

I haven't mattered to him all year long.

5. I LEARN TO HUNT

Fastening the last button of an old hand-me-down hunting coat, I stumble groggily into the kitchen where Dad sits. He is slugging down the last of his morning mug of coffee, taking a last long drag on his Winston.

"You ready?" he asks. I give him a nod in response. Now that I am ten, the legal age, we are going hunting.

Dad grabs the sixteen-gauge shotgun for himself and tells me to take the twenty-two. "That's what your brothers learned on," he says. "It's light. You should be able to handle it all right."

We cross the busy highway and reach the base of the mountain, then start to climb. It's steep and hard to get good footing on the slippery slate shale that's scattered loosely all over the ground, some of it covered up with newly fallen leaves. Now I know why Dad wanted me to carry the lighter rifle; ten minutes into our hunting trip, my skinny arms are already tired from the gun's weight. I step carefully, trying to keep my balance and not fall, but also trying to keep up with Dad. I'm slipping and sliding, barely managing to hang on to that damn twenty-two.

We get to the first shelf and start climbing down the other side of the mountain. When we're deep enough into the woods, we cross the stream. Now we're trespassing on Mrs. McIntyre's land, heading for a large pine grove nestled near the valley floor. Dad's seen deer there. We haven't spotted game of any kind yet, but I know we're not going home until I kill something. It's more important to Dad than it is to me that I bring home a kill.

When we reach the grove, the walking becomes quieter, easier, because the rain's waterlogged the pine needles and softened our crunching footsteps. The density of the trees shuts out what little sunlight there is. The light rain falls like a veil. Inside the grove, it's as dark as a cave and sopping wet. Then, out of the darkness, I hear something move high up in the trees.

I know what I'm supposed to do because I've watched my brother, Carl Jr., when he used to hunt in the woods behind our house on Rek

Lane. I raise my rifle, aim it in the direction of the noise, and wait for the next move.

"There!" Dad whispers, pointing to an area to the left of where I've been looking. I wait. Then there he is, a soaked gray squirrel.

He jumps to another branch. I switch off the safety lock. Take aim. He blends in with the dark backdrop of the black, saturated needles and branches and I can barely see him. I point the rifle skyward. My arm aches. A hunter's adrenaline rushes through my veins.

"Shoot him!" Dad whispers excitedly. "Shoot!"

I aim, squeeze the trigger. The squirrel keeps moving.

I grab the bolt, expel the casing, and shove it back into position for the next shot. Seconds later, I shoot again. I repeat the process until, like Chicken Little, the little squirrel drops out of the sky.

Of course, the poor thing's dead. He has enough lead in him to plug a hole and save a sinking battleship. Dad and I approach and examine him. I've shot off his tail, a front leg, and a back one before finally firing the fatal blow.

"You got him, Diane!" Dad hoots. "You got him!"

Well, sure I did. What creature could have survived the rain of bullets I'd just fired off? That poor little thing didn't have a chance. But Dad's excitement pleases me. I'm proud that he's proud of me.

Eating the squirrel is out of the question because of all the metal I pumped into him, but Dad insists we gut him anyway. I don't have the heart to stick a knife point into him after everything else I've put him through, so Dad does it. "You know, sooner or later you'll have to learn to clean 'em, too," Dad says. He sticks the tip of his hunting knife into the squirrel's creamy gray stomach. Blood caresses the edge of the blade as he pushes up, splitting open the skin. When he reaches the chest, Dad pulls the wound open wide and leans the squirrel forward so his guts fall out.

Dad hands me the bloody squirrel and I stuff it inside my hunting vest like he tells me. We begin the long trek home.

I'm not happy about killing the squirrel, but I'm not sad either. I'm just glad to spend the day with Dad. The squirrel feels warm against my chest at first, but within minutes he turns cold and stiff.

Today I pleased my father with a kill.

6. HOBO

Mother's crying. "Look, it's not my fault business is bad. I work every day at that place until I drop. There's just not enough money to pay the mortgage."

"And whose fault is that supposed to be?" Dad snaps back. "Mine?"

"Well, it was your idea to move to Pennsylvania in the first place," Mom reminds him. "Look, if you *don't* go back to the factory and bring some money in, we're going to lose everything we've worked for all our lives."

"No! Forget it!" Dad shouts. "You know how much I hate that place."

It's temporary, Mom tells him—just until business picks up and they can get back on their feet. Dad can work in the factory back in Connecticut during the week, bunk in at my brother Carl's place, and drive back to Pennsylvania on weekends. Dad resists the idea for a while, but then finally gives in because he knows Mom's right. There's just no other way.

One evening while Dad's working up north and Mother's away for the day, Grammy, Katie, and I spot a hobo through the window. He's across the road, in front of the gas station, jabbing his thumb in the air whenever cars pass. He's wearing filthy, tattered clothes and shabby shoes so caked with dirt that you can't even make out what color they are. That bum tries all afternoon to hitch a ride, but no one will stop.

"He's scary-looking," Katie says. Grammy and I nod in agreement. "Who'd ever be crazy enough to give *him* a ride?" I add.

We look away for a minute, no more, and the next minute the hobo's gone. Now we're really scared. What if he's snuck down under the bridge? What if he's planning to come back here to rob us once it gets dark?

That night Katie and I dread more than ever the chore of locking up the gas station and storage sheds. Katie grabs the ring of keys and the chrome five-cell flashlight and I load the sixteen-gauge shotgun. "You girls be careful now," Grammy warns. Neither of us wants to go out there in the dark, but we have to. I sure wish Dad wasn't all the way back up in Connecticut.

When everything else has been secured, we inch our way to the edge of the pine grove where the station and picnic area meet. The farthest shed lies beyond there, past the spotlight beams and out in the pitch-black country darkness.

My heart thumps crazily. I am shaking hard and hoping I won't have to fire this gun. I'm afraid for that hobo if he tries to harm us, and also for what Dad's rifle will do to me if I have to use it. It's too powerful a firearm for an eleven-year-old girl, but I know what to do. My big brother Marvin tried using this gun once when he was sixteen and its impact thrust him backward and onto the ground. His shoulder was bruised for weeks.

So, I'm afraid for all of us.

Please, Mr. Hobo, don't be out there.

7. BALLERINA

It's summertime. I'm fourteen. Dad's living back in Pennsylvania with us again. He's found work delivering house trailers for the Nashua Trailer Company in Montoursville. Mom feels better because this new job pays well. I enjoy accompanying Dad on his deliveries, traveling with him from state to state. The drives are long hauls usually, and Dad likes the company.

It's a hot June day, late afternoon. We've picked up Dad's paycheck and stopped by the company's yard to prepare the trailer we're delivering the next day. Dad wants to get an early start because the traffic's better first thing in the morning. We've made sure all the kitchen and dresser drawers are taped shut and secured anything else that might shift during transit and get damaged. We're all set for our morning run now, and Dad's speeding home with his paycheck in his shirt pocket. We make good time because the traffic's light and there're no state cops to slow us down.

We're about to turn into our driveway when Dad passes Mavis, our neighbor, who's planting irises in her front garden. He brakes, backs up, smiles. I don't like Mavis much. She acts uppity, for no good reason that I can see. As usual, she's got on that elastic strapless halter-top of hers that flattens her bust and emphasizes her protruding belly. Her mustardy-gray hair's frizzier than a French poodle and her nose is stuck up in the air as usual. Put a tutu on her, I think to myself, and she'd make a perfect Henrietta the Hippo.

"Looks like you're working pretty hard planting those flowers," Dad says.

"Nah, they're easy. And they spread fast, too."

"We're just getting back from Montoursville," Dad volunteers. "Had to get my trailer ready for tomorrow's transport. Boy, I sure am making good money hauling those house trailers."

"Gee, that's great," Mavis gushes. When she stops in at the luncheonette for milk or a loaf of bread, she acts like the Queen of Sheba just barely tolerating her lowly subjects. But for Dad, she goes all sugary sweet.

"Looky here," Dad says. He takes out his paycheck and holds it out to her. Mavis approaches the truck and squints.

"Five hundred and fifty bucks," she coos. "Wow."

Dad nods, grins goofily. "There's no one around here makes *this* kind of money," he crows.

Abruptly, Mavis changes her standing position like she's got a cramp in her leg or something. She points her toe straight out like a ballerina dancer. It suddenly dawns on me that this is supposed to be sexy, but she's missed her mark by a mile and a half.

Mavis bats her eyes, rakes her fingers through her ugly French poodle hair. Dad acting like a spell's come over him.

"Come on, Dad," I snap. "I'm hungry and I gotta pee. Let's go!"

8. WHAT DAD DID

The late-afternoon sun beats down on Dad's sky blue and white snubnosed truck as we cross the Mason-Dixon Line heading toward Chattanooga. Dad maneuvers the trailer in and out of heavy vacation traffic. The stink of asphalt and exhaust fumes hangs in the cab, but it's the humidity that's killing me. All summer long, our mobile home deliveries have taken us *up* the coast, but now, this last week of July, there's a heat wave on and we're headed south.

Trying to get comfortable, I lay my head down on Dad's lap and stretch myself across the seat, dangling my feet out the passenger's window. Dad strokes my hair as he drives. "Your hair's pretty," he says. "So soft and shiny." The breeze coming in the window is hot and heavy on me. I can't get cool or comfortable.

We stop to eat and gas up at a small filling station–restaurant where other tractor trailers are parked. When we enter and make our way over to a booth, the other drivers follow us with their eyes. We sit. One of the men smiles at me. Another winks. Dad's busy reading the menu and doesn't see.

There's a burly guy with a white T-shirt seated by himself in the booth across from ours, both hands on a cheeseburger. He gives me the once-over, then turns to Dad. "What direction you folks coming from?" he asks.

"Up north," Dad says. "We're heading to Chattanooga."

"How's the road up ahead? Any construction?"

"No, it's pretty smooth sailing."

The guy turns toward me and smiles. "And who's your lovely companion?"

I'm embarrassed but a little pleased. "She's my daughter," Dad says.

I've just had my fifteenth birthday, but everyone always thinks I'm much older. Men at these roadside places have been smiling and looking at me like this all summer. I can tell by their smirks that some of them think I'm Dad's girlfriend. I like the attention and the fact that they're so wrong. It's fun. It's like a game. I just don't get why these men act so stupid and smiley around me.

After we fuel up and pull back onto the highway, Dad and I joke about the gas station attendant, who drawled to Dad, "It's mighty *sultry* today, ain't it?"

Dad mimics him for my benefit. "It's so durn hot and ahm so tahhred."

"Yep, it sho' nuff is *mahty sultry*," I answer. We laugh some more and sing a twangy, hillbilly version of that Hank Williams song, "Your Cheatin' Heart." The minutes pass, the miles drag on, the traffic's slower than we'd expected. At this rate, we probably won't make it into Chattanooga until after ten.

I'm half dozing when Dad says, "Hey, what do you say we stop early tonight and finish the run tomorrow? We can sleep in the trailer and get up right at sunrise."

"Okay," I tell him. "Sounds good to me."

We search for a long time to find a spot big enough to park the truck and trailer. The few spaces I point out aren't good enough for Dad. "Here we go," he finally says. "Right there, under those trees." It seems to me that the other spaces he rejected for being too small were bigger than this, but Dad's wicked pleased with his discovery.

"You sure you can get in there?" I ask.

"Sure I'm sure," he says. "I'll *make* it fit."

When Dad unlocks and opens the trailer door, heat blasts us in the face like a hot oven. We enter the living room. The trailer reeks from the sterile smell of never having been used. Protective plastic covers the cheap new furniture. New or not, it's junk—as cheesy as the rest of our life in Pennsylvania. The pathetic thing is, it's better than the stuff *we* own. If we still lived in Connecticut, I think to myself, we'd have nicer furniture, a better life all around. But I've learned to keep my mouth shut rather than make comparisons like that in front of Dad.

Something's weird. When we readied the trailer for the trip this morning, the double mattress was on the bed where it belonged. Now it's on the living room floor. How did that happen?

"It's hot as heck in here," I complain.

"So, open a window," Dad snaps. I yank up the avocado-green curtain with its insulated rubbery backing, then crank open the jalousie window. "Leave the curtains shut," Dad says.

I don't want to argue with him because he's acting a little cranky, but I wonder how we're going to get any air in here with the curtain closed. I open the opposite window, too, careful not to disturb the curtain. Despite how sweltering it is in here, I guess I can forget about getting any cross-ventilation.

The sun is setting, daylight fading fast. "We'll sleep here on the mattress," Dad says. "Might as well get comfortable. Why don't you take off your bra?"

Huh? I'm shocked that Dad even knows I have breasts, much less that I'm wearing something to hold them in. "Nah," I mumble. "I'm okay." I recognize the odd sense of doom descending, the uneasy quiet before one of Dad's storms. But something's different this time, too.

"I said, take off your bra." Now it's an order, not a suggestion. Then his voice softens again. "What do you care? You don't have anything anyway."

I don't want to, but I know I'd better listen. Something's about to happen. I don't know what exactly, but I know it's not going to be nice and there's no one here to stop him.

With my short-sleeve shirt still on, I reach in and start unhooking my bra. Dad's hand creeps under the back of my shirt and up my back. I jerk away, finish the unfastening, work the straps down without taking off my shirt. I'm trying hard to fight back tears.

"Oh, for cryin' out loud," Dad scolds. "Don't be such a baby."

He flops down, pats the mattress. "Come on," he says. "Lie down." I kneel, lowering myself onto the makeshift bed. Turning onto my side, I face the wall with my back to him. Everything's still, but I can feel his overwhelming presence. I'm confused. Dad's hurt my feelings. I'm *not* a baby, but I'm scared. I stare and stare at the blond wood paneling in front of my face, waiting for Daddy to say he's sorry, or to wish me good-night, or something. Instead, I feel him move up close behind me. I move away. He moves closer.

"If you keep this up, you'll fall right off the mattress." His voice is gentle now. Something's moving across the back of my neck. I flinch, jerk around to see what it is. Dad's tickling me with a handful of my own hair. He motions for me to lie on my back. "Move over next to me," he says. "Get comfortable."

I feel his arm cross over my chest, his fingers on the first button of my blouse. I am staring hard at the little white flower decorative insert around one of the screws that hold up the ceiling. I count the six little sculptured petals, over and over. I shut my eyes, hoping he'll stop. But he doesn't. I feel his feathery fingertips on my nipple. His touch stuns me. I lie still, too afraid to move. I feel my nipple harden like it's caught a chill. I'm terrified.

"Please, Daddy, don't," I plead, softly, hoping that my quiet voice will trigger some kind of compassion. It doesn't. I feel his wet mouth on my breast. I feel dizzy. The decorative flowers turn gray. It's getting darker and darker and then everything goes black.

When I wake in the morning, Dad's outside checking the trailer. My clothes are wrinkled. My zipper's down. I'm sticky. I want to believe I've had a bad dream, but I know it was real. I can smell Dad's sweat on me, mingled with my own. I feel so dirty, so ashamed. I want to scrub myself clean, but there's no water. I want Dad to stay away from me.

"Hey, there," he says, poking his head in the trailer. "You want to get cleaned up, have some breakfast? I'm starved." He's acting pleasant, like nothing's wrong. Like none of it happened. Maybe I *was* dreaming. Now I'm not sure.

"So what do you think? You hungry?"

I can't look at him. I can't reply.

We arrive in Chattanooga at about ten. The distributor examines the truck, signs the paperwork. We're on our way back home.

Usually our return trips are speedy. We make quick stops, order sandwiches to go so that Dad can eat and drive, save time. But this return trip takes forever. Minutes pass like hours. We hardly talk.

"It's another *mahty sultry* one today, ain't it?" Dad jokes, but I don't smile or answer him and he doesn't push it. I think Dad senses that he'd better leave me alone or I'll cry. I don't want to be a baby, but this hurts so bad deep down inside. For my whole childhood, I have known how to defy Dad, call his bluff, withstand his beatings. But this is different. I keep trying to convince myself that this is just a bad dream—that Dad wouldn't hurt me like this. I just can't shake the feeling of being dirty, of my skin almost screaming to get clean. I keep asking myself why he did something so wrong to me. I keep wondering if it's my fault.

Once we reach home, I make the bath water as hot as I can stand it and scrub until my skin is red and sore. Out of the bathroom I escape to whatever room is farthest away from Dad. If he moves, I move.

That was the last trailer trip I ever took with Dad. For the rest of that summer, whenever he asked me to go with him on a haul, I'd find some excuse. He didn't push it. Not long after that Dad hired Katie to drive the flag car for wide trailers. Then he left.

9. WATCH OUT FOR DAD!

"Watch out for Dad!" Mom keeps cautioning Katie and me. "No telling what he might do to us. You know how mean he can get."

Katie groans and tries again. "Mother, for the last time, Dad's not next door at Mavis's or anyplace else in Trout Run. He's *gone.*"

Mother shakes her head. "He's next door."

Poor Mother. Dad's departure has left her normally warm brown eyes jumpy and unfocused with dark circles beneath. Crow's-feet fan out toward her temples. Her hair's limp and uncombed, its inky blackness startling still. Mom's been gray-haired for years, but she dyed it a while ago in desperate response to Dad's new look. Dad had had his old hairstyle forever: combed back, with an old-fashioned part down the middle. Then one day he stepped into the kitchen with a crewcut and a cocky smirk to match. He looked great, years younger, but Mother's dye job backfired pathetically. Raven hair frames her old, tired face, accentuating the toll taken by her years with Dad. "I *know* he's over there," she insists. "He's hiding out with her."

"Her" is Mavis, the hussy who lives across from us and always used to flirt with Dad. Mother's suspicion that Mavis is mixed up in Dad's leaving stems back to the rare visit she made to our place of business a while back.

"Guess who came into the luncheonette today?" Mom asked one evening while we were finishing up the dishes.

"Who?" I said. "President Kennedy? Elvis?"

She didn't smile. "Mavis," she said.

"That old cat? What did *she* want?"

"She came over to buy a loaf of bread. She was showing off this new hunter green coat of hers with a mink collar. She made a point of asking me if I liked her new coat. I told her yes, it was very nice. Now doesn't it seem odd that Mavis would make a special trip across the road? She always sends her son, Charlie, when she needs something. And what was she making such a big deal about that coat for? You don't think your father bought it for her, do you?" I told Mom I didn't, but she hadn't let it rest. We heard over and over about "the old cat" flaunting that coat in front of Mom's face. And when Dad packed his bags, despite all evidence to the contrary, Mom kept insisting that he had dropped them no farther than across the road.

"Mother, Dad's moved away from Trout Run," Katie reminds her now. "He's living in that apartment over in Williamsport." Tears come to Mother's eyes. She shakes her head. "He's across the road," she says. "Watch out."

Are all these warnings that Dad's lurking nearby signs that she simply can't accept the fact he's gone? Is Mother coming unglued? I'm worried for her and angrier than ever at Dad for having brought this down upon her. "Mom, please, you have to stop this," I tell her. "You're driving the rest of us crazy." But reasoning with Mother does little to squelch her bizarre suspicions, so Katie and I try ignoring her instead. Grammy's keeping her mouth shut, too. She knows her son's a louse for leaving us, and if Mother, who's not even her flesh and blood, ever decided to give her the boot, Grammy would have no other place to go.

Late one Friday afternoon we hear a racket coming from the direction of Mavis's house across the road. There's banging on the walls, the tap-tap-tapping of nails, the singsong hum of a saw. Of course, the noise stirs our curiosity. I look out the window to see what I can see. Our houses are close, separated only by our driveway and the old road. "What are you up to over there, you old cat?" I say out loud. Mother, Grammy, and Katie hunch behind me and look out. They're wondering, too.

Whatever Mavis's "home improvement" project is, it's going on in her garage. At first, we can't tell what she's doing out there, but when the garage door swings open, I realize that she's building a doorway. Why, after all these years, does the old cat suddenly need a new private entryway to her kitchen? Mom swears that this is evidence and starts up again. "See! He's over there. We better watch out."

Mother's at it all weekend. Then, on Sunday night, she announces her plan. "Tomorrow morning, we're getting up at 4:30 while it's still dark," she says. "She's got to open up that garage door and back her car out to get to work. And when she does, we'll see who's coming and going with her."

"Come on, Mom," I moan. "Give us a break. He's not *over* there!"

Katie strokes Mother's wrinkled cheek, her dyed black hair. "Please, Mother," Katie says. "You've got to stop thinking about Dad and get on with your life. You're making yourself sick." But Mother crosses her arms against her chest and looks away.

And sure enough, before dawn the next morning, Mom shakes Katie and me awake. "Be absolutely quiet," she whispers. "Don't turn on any lights."

We dress in the dark. When I head for the bathroom to relieve myself, a hand clamps onto my shoulder. It's Mom. "Don't flush," she warns in a conspirator's whisper. "They'll hear us."

As quietly as cat burglars, we undo the chain lock, the bolt lock, and the regular lock. We open the back door a crack and lay in wait for Mavis. Fifteen minutes later the garage door yawns open and her car starts.

It will only take a minute for the old cat to back out her pint-size Nash and close the door again. Mom hands me the five-cell chrome flashlight. Of the three of us, I'm the fastest, the sneakiest, and the one most able to protect myself in case there's trouble. Mom knows I'll pro-

tect her, Katie, and Grammy, too, if I have to. It doesn't matter that I'm
the youngest. If Dad *was* over there—which I'm sure he isn't—he'd have
to kill me before I'd let him harm them.

I slip out the back door. Hunching down, I run across our driveway
without making a sound. The moon's full. I stick the big, clunky flashlight under my jersey and advance across the road to Mavis's driveway.
She's out of the car. In seconds, she'll have that garage door closed and
be headed back to her purring Nash. I have to move fast, make sure the
car's empty, or else we'll be hearing Mother's laments all day.

I run to the passenger's side and lift the heavy flashlight, aiming it at
the back window. The switch is stuck. I jostle it so hard, I practically rip
the damn thing off. It gives.

The beam illuminates Dad's face.

I'm shaking badly. I can't speak. He's cowering on Mavis's backseat
like the cornered rat he is—his new, younger, crewcut self. The flashlight's ray reflects off his glasses, but beneath the lenses I can see those
beady, black eyes. At first Dad's face looks surprised, even a little scared,
but then he puts his hands behind his back and gives me a shitty smirk.
That slight upward curl at the end of his lip is meanness itself. I suddenly
understand who he really is. I want to kill the bastard because I hate him.

But I love him, too.

Why is he doing this to us? Is it my fault? Would he have stayed if I
kept going on the road with him? Maybe I could have learned to please
him, for Mom's and Katie's and Grammy's sake. Despite everything, we
still love him—all of us.

In a split second, Mavis is back. "Get out of here right now!" she
screams. She lunges toward me and I run.

I'm halfway between our two houses when I stop cold. I'm suddenly
unafraid of her and I'm not even sure why. I stand there, on the old
road, and look her right in the eye.

"If I get ahold of you, I'll . . ." Mavis takes a few steps toward me,
then stops. Her threat hangs in the air, empty and unfinished.

You'll do *what*, I think. I *want* this old cat to keep coming at me
because I'm ready for her. If she hits me, I'll strike back with all the
hatred that lives inside of me from Dad's having beaten me, betrayed me
and the others. Just try it, Mavis, I think. You'll be on the losing end of
this battle because I sure do not love *you*.

She does an about-face and heads back to her car. Lucky for *her,* I think. I stand there, seething, breathing heavily, filling up with a hurt too big to bear. When Dad's girlfriend started toward me, he made no move to stop her, to save me. He didn't care if she hurt me or not. He doesn't give a damn about any of us.

I hurry back across our driveway and into the house. We lock the locks, then gawk out the window at the two of them. Dad moves to the front passenger seat and lights a cigarette. Mavis gets behind the wheel and backs her car onto the road. Before taking off, they hesitate for several seconds, glaring back at us. I can see the tip of Dad's cigarette as he inhales. Now that his little secret's out, he's rubbing it in our faces.

After they've driven off, I begin to shake so badly that I have to sit. Pee seeps out of me and wets my panties, but I'm unable to move. My stomach starts spasming with the dry heaves.

That dirty, rotten bastard! He's been hiding over there, just like poor Mother said. And all this time we've been pronouncing her crazy!

10. I LEARN TO DRIVE

Some days Dad flaunts his new life at Mavis's house and some days he merely goes about his business. There are all kinds of emotional hardships for me to face, the most confusing being that Dad is, simultaneously, gone from our lives and just across the road. There are some practical drawbacks to Dad's betrayal, too. Now that I'm certain he isn't coming back home again, I have no one to teach me how to drive.

No one, that is, except Katie.

She's my only chance, I figure. Grammy doesn't drive and Mother's too busy. Katie took driver's ed lessons at Williamsport High, and Dad took her out several times to get her familiar with both our car and the road. She passed her test and got her license, so she must know *something.* It's May now, two short months until my sixteenth birthday. It's my turn.

Begging Katie doesn't work, so I try nagging. That's equally unsuccessful. I try a combination of begging *and* nagging, and she finally surrenders, driving me to the Motor Vehicle Department so I can get my learner's permit.

I'm a burden on her spare time, so Katie's not too thrilled about teaching me. On day number one, she shuffles across the driveway and opens

the driver's door of our tank-size '49 Ford, the crappy old clunker that
Dad has abandoned along with his wife and daughters. She fluffs the
purple pillow and hoists herself onto it. I jump into the passenger's seat.

"Now, listen carefully," she says as if she's lecturing an entire class of
driving students instead of just me. "The first thing you have to do is
cock the mirrors into positions that will allow you to see both the sides
of the car and what's behind it." She demonstrates this, adjusting the
mirror to her liking. Then she tells me we're going to switch seats.

Katie slides over and I get out of the car, walk around, and take the
driver's seat. Now I can see why it's necessary to sit on the purple pillow.
Even with it, I can just barely see past the hood and onto the road. And
she expects me to see out the sides and in the back, too. She's got to be
kidding.

"The first thing you've got to do is learn the shift pattern," Katie
instructs. Her know-it-all tone is already getting on my nerves a little.

"The second thing," I say.

"What?"

"Cocking the mirrors is the first thing. The shift pattern's the second."

Katie gives me a dirty look and goes on. "You've got to get the big *H*
pattern down pat. First gear goes down, up for second, over and back
down for third, and over and up for reverse. See? When you do them
one after the other, it makes a letter *H*. Now you try it."

The shift handle seems stiff and stubborn, and I have a heck of a time
figuring out the stupid "big *H*" business. I tell Katie that I just can't get
this shifting stuff. "Well, you'd *better* get it," she warns. "Because if you
learn on an automatic transmission, the state puts 'automatic only' right
on your license. And it costs extra to buy a car with automatic, so I
guess if you don't learn standard shifting, you'll be sitting home a lot."
She smiles annoyingly and continues. "Okay, now, give it the gas and
ease off the clutch *gently*."

How am I ever going to shift, let up on the clutch, and give it gas all
at the same time, I wonder. I try it and the car stalls out. I try again and
we buck along the driveway until Katie yells "Stop! Stop!" as if there's a
fire engine in our path or some other big emergency. Every time I give it
another try, we stall or buck and Katie screams at me. After about fifteen minutes of this, I'm pretty sure I know what riding a bucking

bronco at the rodeo must feel like, but we have jerked and lurched our way across the driveway. "Okay," Katie says, mopping the sweat off her face. "That's the end of your first lesson."

"How'd I do?" I ask her.

"No comment."

My stubbornness pays off. A week later I can drive the Ford across the driveway without bucking. "Thank God you finally got it," Katie groans. "Now tomorrow when I get home from work, we'll practice on the back road."

Look out, world, I think. Diane's graduated from the driveway and she's going cruising! Tomorrow seems a million years away.

The following day I wait by the door for an hour until Katie comes home. I accost her the second she steps inside. "Ready when you are, Katie."

"Geez," she snaps. "I just got home. Can't you even wait a minute?"

She takes her sweet time in the bathroom. Then she has to lounge around for a while. Then she decides she's hungry and needs something to eat. Good Lord, I want to scream at her. That road is *calling* to me. Hurry *up*!

I pace around the kitchen while I wait, trying hard not to make her mad. If our pattern holds, she'll be yelling at me soon enough when I take the wheel. Meanwhile, Katie pokes around here, meanders there. She thumbs through the Sears catalog, decides her nails need filing. Then she decides to make herself a sandwich. She slops about a quart of mayonnaise on two slices of bread. In what seems like slow motion, she applies lettuce, tomato, two slices of ham. She's taking so much loving care with that sandwich, you'd think she was working on an art project. She nibbles the thing instead of devouring it, chewing more sluggishly than a cow chews its cud. Katie's got all the time in the world. At last, she turns to me, noticing my existence.

"Are you ready yet?" she asks.

Am *I* ready? "Katie," I say, "if *I* were any more ready, I'd be too *old* to drive." My wise remark will probably cost me when we're out on the road.

I get behind the wheel, impatient to go cruising, but Katie makes me take a driveway refresher course. I review the big *H*, practice the clutch thing. I tell her I'll wait to practice the clutch-and-gas-together maneuver because I don't want to flood the engine while we're just sitting here. We buck a few times across the driveway and Katie pronounces me ready for the back road.

Nervous, I floor the gas pedal and we fly out of the driveway and down the back road. "Slow down!" Katie hollers. "You're going too fast!" I take a quick glance at her. The wind's gushing in the window, tossing her short black hair. She gets that same look she had that time at the carnival on the Tilt-a-Whirl. I hit the brake. "Now you're going too slow!" Katie scolds. "Shift!"

"Now?"

"Yes, now!" My hand moves to the shifting handle. "No! Not yet!" I ask myself if driving's really worth this much hassle. *Yes!* Another part of me answers. It *is!*

My first day on the road doesn't go much better than my first day in the driveway did. "It's a miracle *anyone* ever learns to drive a standard shift," I grumble, getting out of the car when the lesson's over.

"Next time maybe I'd better teach a chimpanzee," Katie mumbles.

A couple of days' worth of practicing later, I feel like I'm ready for the Indy 500. I'm zipping up and down the back road like a pro, shifting so smoothly that even Katie is proud of me. She sits closer to the passenger door, no longer anticipating, I guess, that she might have to take emergency control of the wheel. She leans her left arm on the window frame. Her whole body looks relaxed.

A week later we're cruising on the creek road, not far from the swinging footbridge. My ego's so big by now that my last name might as well be Andretti. "Make a left here," Katie says.

"Why here?" I question. This dirt road goes over the mountain to some farms.

"Because you're going to learn to stop on a hill and start again without rolling backward." Okay, I think. She's the boss. And how hard can stopping on some stupid hill be, anyway? I slow, signal, make the turn. Halfway up the hill, Katie hollers, wicked dramatic, "Stop the car!" I roll my eyes and do what she says. This driving teacher thing has really gone to her head.

"Now give it gas and ease off the clutch," she orders.

The dust and gravel fly. I roll backward. Three attempts later, my

Andretti status is gone for good. Katie's still screaming at me, but now she's laughing, too. "Jeepers creepers, Diane! Not so much gas!" That afternoon I carve ruts the size of wading pools into that hilly dirt road. But in the end, I can stop and restart on a hill without rolling back. I have emerged victorious!

"Okay," Katie says on our way back home. "You're ready for your driving test."

First thing in the morning, I call the Pennsylvania State Police barracks to make my appointment. And guess what? They have an opening for the very next day!

On the way to the test, my inner engine's revving fast and I'm a nervous wreck. "Wow, you're sweating bullets," Katie observes. "I wasn't anywhere near this nervous when I was going for *my* test. Stop biting your nails."

The officer's a big, scowling lollapalooza—six-foot-six or so with a chest that looks like it's part of a suit of armor. I'm too spooked to make eye contact. He asks me eight questions and I give him eight correct answers. "Okay," he says, "let's go on out to the bullpen and finish the test."

I get in the driver's side; King Kong takes Katie's place. I remember to plump up the pillow, adjust the mirrors, disengage the emergency brake. So far, so good. On the test road, I stop when I'm supposed to, yield at the proper places, observe the speed limit, and shift as smoothly as butter on their little artificial hill. Everything's fine. I'm going to walk away with a driving license.

"Okay, now let's see you park," Kong says. "Pull up there and back her in between those two white lines. In order to pass, you have to get into the spot without turning your wheel more than three times."

What? Katie never made me do this. He's crazy.

I nod, smile sweetly, pull up. I turn the wheel once, twice, a third time. I've missed that tiny space by about a yard and a half.

"Try again," he says.

I do. I turn that wheel a million times. My arms are sore. I'm holding back tears. All I want to do is tell that officer to park the damn car himself and get out of there. And I can't wait to get ahold of that jackass Katie. How could she have forgotten to teach me how to parallel park?

Of course, I fail the test.

But I don't give up, and the next time I take it, I pass. Three swipes and I'm parked. Bingo!

11. DAD TAKES AIM

Late one afternoon Katie and I return from the Acme Grocery Store in Garden View. We park the car in the driveway to unload the groceries, same as usual. Only this time I forget to pop the hood and remove the rotor from under the distributor cap so that Dad can't steal our car. I know enough not to trust Dad further than I can throw him, but the divorce war hasn't heated up yet, so I don't know just how bad things are going to get. Back then, I was under the illusion that I could, from time to time, let down my guard.

Two apiece, Katie and I tote the heavy sacks to the kitchen counter and go back out for the rest. We're halfway between the house and the car when, suddenly, Dad appears out of nowhere. He jumps into the car and starts it up.

"Hey, that's our car!" Katie shouts at him. "Get out of there!"

"Yeah, you leave that car alone!" I scream.

He ignores us, throws her into gear, and begins to back out of the driveway. Katie runs after him. The trunk's still open because of the groceries and she reaches in and grabs the four-pronged lug wrench. She lifts it over her head, threatening to throw it hard at Dad. I'm shocked. I've never seen Katie act this brave before. She's actually going to hurt Dad to defend what's ours.

When Dad sees Katie raise the wrench, he turns the wheel and points the car directly at us. He guns it. He's going to kill us.

"Throw it, Katie!" I scream. "Get him!"

But she doesn't. Her arms drop, we jump out of the way, and the car whizzes past, missing us by inches. He's almost killed us, that jerk! Our own father!

Frozen in fear, not even able to cry yet, we watch helplessly as he parks our car in Mavis's driveway and gets out. He saunters, more than walks, toward the door, smirking back at us. He knows full well that we can't step onto her property and reclaim our car without trespassing. He's just tried to run us over on *our own* property. What would he do if we went over *there*?

I turn toward Katie, glaring. "For cryin' out loud," I bark. "Why didn't you throw the damn wrench at him when you had the chance?" But I'm angrier with myself than I am with Katie. It was *me* who got careless, let down my guard. It's *me* who's supposed to protect the others. Poor Katie's just standing there, ghastly white. Her eyes are unfocused, as if she's in a state of shock, and she's still holding on to the wrench. I grab hold of the damn thing, shake it, and she lets go. For a couple more seconds, Katie doesn't seem to register much of anything. Then, she blinks—sees me. She's back.

We go into the house, both of us shaking uncontrollably. Mom's shift at the ribbon mill will be over soon and she'll be home. What's she going to do when she finds out what happened? Can she get our car back?

Goddamn that Dad! It's twenty-five miles to Williamsport, the nearest town. Without a car, we're stranded. Just before he decided to abandon us for Mavis, Dad convinced Mother to buy that 1960 Fairlane he drives around in. Why did he need to hijack our old clunker, too? For spite, that's why—just for the meanness of it.

Later, when we hear a car in the driveway, we run to the window. It's Mom; the guy she rides in with is dropping her off. We don't even wait for her to open the front door. "Mom! Mom!" we both chime in. "Dad stole the car! He tried to run us over!"

As she listens to the details, Mom looks terrified but unsurprised. Then, uncharacteristically, she's angry enough to act. She goes to the telephone and dials the state police. As she explains what happened, her voice is firm and insistent. "No, we can't wait until tomorrow," she says. "We need someone to come out here tonight."

We wait for nearly an hour before our "rescuer" arrives. Mother keeps reassuring us that she's going to see to it that we're protected. It's nice to see her showing some backbone for a change, but how can we be safe as long as Dad's across the road? In a showdown with Dad, Mom wouldn't stand a chance.

The cruiser slows, looking for our house. We run out waving, making sure he knows he's found the right place. When he pulls into the driveway, I push past Katie and Mom. "Dad tried to run us over!" I blurt. "He missed us by *this much*!" I stick my hand in front of the policeman's face, indicating our close call by the gap between my thumb and index finger.

"Diane, please," Mom says, and I shut up. Mother repeats to the officer everything we've told her. Katie and I stand alongside the cruiser, listening to Mom's version, nodding, correcting it here and there. All the while, we keep taking nervous glances across the road.

The officer just listens. Isn't he supposed to take notes? Ask questions? When we finish, he asks only one thing: "Whose name is on the registration?"

Mom's been trying hard, but I can see defeat creeping back into her facial expression, her posture. "His name," she says.

The cop shrugs, holds open his hands in defeat.

"But, Officer," Mother says, "he tried to run down his own daughters with that car. Can't you do something about *that*?"

"I'm sorry, but you'll have to wait for him to do something else. If there's a second incident, maybe we can get a restraining order."

As he explains how restraining orders work, I listen hard for some sign of comfort or reassurance in his voice, but I hear none. All my life, I've been promised that if someone's in danger, the police will help. But this cop says he can't or won't protect us. And what "something else" do we have to wait for Dad to do: kill one of us? How are the police going to help us then? Dial the coroner's number for us? Go over there and cart Dad away after it's too late?

After the officer leaves, Mom's really agitated—beside herself with worry. "A restraining order's nothing more than a piece of paper," she says. "It'll only make him *more* violent." She begins to cry. "His own daughters. How could he *do* such a thing?"

"Maybe he's gone crazy," Katie offers.

Something dawns on Mother's face. "Or maybe it's not his fault at all," she says. "Maybe that old cat's drugging him."

12. SWEET TALK AND SURVEILLANCE

Dad's attempt to run down Katie and me makes Mom paranoid. Worse than a record overplayed on the radio, her spooky refrain plays over and over and over: "Watch out! Keep your eyes open! With her drugging him over there, there's no telling what he might pull next!"

Mom quits the ribbon factory and takes a job as a cook at Summit Lodge, which is quicker to get home from in case of an emergency. A week later, the lodge hires Katie, too. That leaves just Grammy and me at home. Our job is to take turns watching Mavis's house so that we can report anything suspicious to Mother. Mom's theory is that we'll all be safer if we can just stay one step ahead of Dad. Safer, too, if we load the sixteen-gauge shotgun, which Dad left behind and which I know how to use if I have to. We keep it propped against the corner of the inner bedroom, just in case.

Although I'm scared all day long, surveillance of the old cat's house is boring. I keep getting up from the chair by the window, taking longer and longer breaks. But Grammy remains dead serious about her daily vigil at the window. The things Dad's been pulling have taken their toll on her, made her more sickly. Grammy and I have never been each other's favorite—it's obvious to everyone that she prefers Katie—but lately I feel sorry for her. All day long, she sits there, spying on her own son.

Meanwhile, Mother's campaign continues, intensifying whenever the lodge makes her work nights. "Don't talk loudly or anywhere near the windows," she warns Grammy and me before she leaves for Summit Lodge. "He and the old cat probably sneak over here after dark and listen." We live in uneasy fear by day and in pure terror each night. We're afraid to fall asleep, afraid we may be killed if we stop listening.

Late one afternoon I hear a gooey-sweet voice calling from outside. "Mother? . . . Mother?"

I've been watching out for Dad all summer, but at first it doesn't even register that this strange voice belongs to him. For one thing, Dad's never sounded sweet in his life. For another, I have never once heard him refer to Grammy as "Mother." He calls her "Grammy," same as everybody else. But then, abruptly, I realize it's Dad out there.

"Mother? Are you in there?"

Who does Mr. Sweetie Pie think he's kidding? Certainly not me. And if he's assumed I'm not home, he has a little surprise in store.

I go to the inner bedroom and grab the gun. I'm scared but ready to use it if I have to. No matter what Dad's up to, Grammy and I are safe behind locked doors with this shotgun.

"Mother? Are you home?" He's at the back door.

I undo two of the safety locks but leave the chain lock in place. Surprise, surprise, Dad, I think. I open the door a crack. In the meanest, nastiest voice I can manage, I snarl, "What do *you* want?"

He's surprised, all right. He stands there with his jaw hanging open because it's not his weak, frightened mother who's answering the door. It's me. And I'm holding his shotgun. And he knows I know how to use it. Where's that smirk of yours now, Dad?

Without saying a word, he pivots on one heel and creeps back across the road. He doesn't look back. When he's inside Mavis's house again, I close the door and relock the locks.

Although I feel safe, I'm shivering thinking about what he might have done to Grammy if I wasn't home. And come to think of it, where *is* Grammy? She had to have heard him calling her. She must have been hiding from him, pretending she wasn't home.

Her door squeaks open and she steps into the kitchen. Even from across the room, I can see that she's trembling wildly. At this moment, it dawns on me that Grammy is as terrified of her own son as we are.

13. LAST RESPECTS

About six months after Dad's sneaky trip across the old road to woo Grammy, I begin a part-time waitress job at Summit Lodge where Mom and Katie work as cooks. But I'm at home, not at work, the night Mother comes home from her shift close to hysteria. Grammy and I sit her down at the kitchen table. "What is it, Mom?" I ask. "Tell us what's wrong."

"It's your dad," she says. "He's been in a bad accident in upstate New York. He's hurt pretty badly." Grammy's eyes fill up with tears and she sits down, too. As usual, she's listening but not saying anything. "That good-for-nothing old cat's behind this, you mark my words!" Mom sobs. "Drugged him so bad that he almost killed himself out there on the road. I've got *her* number. She's after his life insurance!"

It's become increasingly clear to me that, in spite of everything, Mom has never stopped loving Dad. No matter what he's done, it's not his fault. When I was little, my bruises had come from my double-jointedness, not from Dad's beating the tar out of me. When he cheated on Mother with Mavis, it was because Mother had let herself go and Mavis had hypnotized him with her whorish wiles. When Dad tried to kill us with the car, he'd been made crazy with drugs, courtesy of Mavis. Mother clings tightly to her "Dad's-been-drugged" theory because she doesn't want to see him as the rat he is.

Grammy excuses herself to go and pray. Later, when I go to bed, I can hear her in her room, weeping. In the middle of the night, I wake up and hear her crying in there, still.

The next day Mom calls my brother Marvin to see what we can do for Dad. "And that's *all* you can think of?" she says into the phone. Whatever his suggestion is, she's disappointed. When she hangs up, she announces, "Marvin's going to send flowers from us all."

During the next several days, Mom tries to get information about Dad's condition, but she's unsuccessful. "I'll bet he never even got our flowers," she snips. "Either that or the old cat threw away the card and told him they were from her." Marvin's over at our house for a family powwow. He tries to make her listen to reason.

"Oh, Mom, I doubt if she'd do——"

"We need to go visit him, Marvin," Mom interrupts. "We won't know how he is until we see him. And besides, at a time like this, a man needs to see his family." She's working herself into a lather over this.

Trying to calm her down, Marvin suggests we wait and see.

"We've waited long enough!" Mom declares. "We're driving up to that hospital in New York this weekend to make sure your dad's all right. And don't try to talk me out of it because my mind's made up."

Grammy has planned to take the trip with us, but by Saturday she's good and sick and has to stay home. The ride from Pennsylvania to upstate New York is hours longer than we've calculated. In the car, no one says too much because we feel pretty mixed about our mission. Finally, after a zillion wrong turns, we find the hospital.

"Do you have a Carl Hiller here?" Marvin asks the receptionist.

She flips through her files. "Why, yes, we do. Are you a relative?"

My brother nods. "His son. My name's Marvin Hiller."

She flips some more. "I'm sorry, but you're not listed, so I can't——"

"But he's my *father*," Marvin persists.

"I'm sorry, but I'm only authorized to allow visits from family members on the list."

"Well, who made up this list of yours?" Marvin asks her.

Mother turns away, heading for the exit. "Who do you think?" she says.

Because there's nothing else we can do, we leave. The trip home seems even longer than the trip there. Mom's quiet, mostly. Sullen. Every once in a while, she punctures the silence with some comment about the old cat.

Halfway back to Trout Run, we stop to eat at a roadside café. Mom only drinks alcohol on special occasions, and even then she usually pours most of it down the sink. So I'm shocked when the waitress comes for our order and Mom tells her she'll have a beer. Marvin orders the same. The waitress turns to me next. "And how about you?" she asks.

It's been a long and difficult day. For years now, people have remarked about how much older than my age I look. I decide to take advantage for once.

"I'll have a shot," I tell her.

The waitress smiles patiently. "Can I see some ID?"

"Oh, yeah, that's right," I tell her. "I'll have a Coke."

Several months later Dad is released from the hospital and returns to the old cat's house to convalesce. I'm not thrilled to have him back in range, but now that he's injured, I'm not as fearful about him harming any of us. Grammy's grown more and more frail. She seems to be wasting away before our eyes. But sick or not, she rarely misses a day at the window.

One afternoon Mom bursts in after work. "Grammy!" she hollers. "Dad's downtown in the Williamsport Hospital. One of the customers at the restaurant just told me."

Grammy's worried about Dad. She won't risk going over to Mavis's, but Williamsport Hospital is neutral ground. Every day she asks me the same question. "Diane, can you take me to the hospital to see your dad?"

By this time, any love I felt for my father has pretty much eroded away, leaving only the hate. Grammy knows how I feel about Dad—that seeing the bastard over there in his hospital bed is about the last thing I want to do. But she's his mother. I feel guilty saying no. And I'm sick of her always asking. So one night I finally cave in. "Okay, go get ready," I tell her. "I'll take you."

I see the shock in her eyes. Through her open bedroom door, I watch her struggle into a clean dress, comb her hair. When she's ready, I help her down the stairs and into the car.

It takes all the strength Grammy's got to walk from the parking lot into the hospital, then down the long corridor, then into the visitors' elevator. Dad's at the far end of the east wing on the third floor. All the way, I've had to hold Grammy by the arm, supporting her as she takes her little half-steps. We haven't even got to Dad's room yet, and already this trip seems like it's been too much for her.

The door to Dad's room is wide open. The old cat's in there, flopped on a chair with her fat gut sticking out in front of her. Dad's the first to spot us. A look of contempt comes over his face, and before Grammy or I can say a word, he growls, "What do you two want?"

How dare he talk to his mother like that! I'm furious. I hate him more than ever. "It was my idea to come," I tell him. "So that I could tell you that you got exactly what you deserved."

In my anger, I spin Grammy around faster than I should and she almost falls. She regains her balance and I grab onto her more tightly. We leave.

The walk back down the corridor, the ride back down the elevator, the trip back to the parking lot: it takes forever. Grammy keeps giving me quick glances and, just as quickly, looking away again. She knows she might as well save her breath; there's nothing she can say to me that will make me change my mind about her son of a bitch of a son. But the deep sadness and pain in her eyes do not go unseen.

We're both stone silent on the way home, each of us alone with her thoughts and feelings, and I have to grip the steering wheel as tight as I can to control my trembling hands. When we reach the house, I tell Mom about the way Dad treated us, my voice shaking as I speak.

"He *had* to act nasty to you two because the old cat was there," Mom says. "He's afraid of her, Diane. Just look what she's done to him. He'd have never talked to you that way if *she* wasn't there." But I'm not buying it. I've long since accepted that Dad is Dad.

Several days later Grammy sits at her post in the window and watches the old cat help Dad back into her house. Our hospital encounter has been a major blow to Grammy. She's grown weaker, sadder. Her will to live seems to be slipping away, but I deny the evidence. She has good days and bad days now, I tell myself. That's all. I have enough on my mind without having to worry about Grammy.

One afternoon when I get home, Grammy's not there. Katie's crying. "Where is she?" I ask.

"Mom had to take her to Williamsport Hospital. She's bad, Diane."

But I'm not scared. I'm tired of being scared by every little thing. Take Dad, for instance. I'm no longer afraid of him at all.

Katie wants to see Grammy, so we go together to the hospital. My body's there, in those corridors, but my mind is elsewhere. I'm more worried about Katie than Grammy. What's she so upset about? She has such a gentle heart and an oversensitive disposition that she gets herself worked up over nothing.

But I'm shocked by how bad Grammy looks. I don't want to see her like this. Her face is ash gray; her body seems almost bloodless. It's as if she's died already. She sleeps most of our visit, and my sister cries. "You ready yet?" I keep asking Katie. "Come on. Let's get out of here. You ready?"

We get the bad news a few days later, the week after Easter, 1962. Grammy's passing doesn't seem real—doesn't penetrate. I feel guilty because Katie keeps crying and crying and I jut sit there, dry-eyed and numb. Well, I reason, Grammy was always good to Katie, but she was never that nice to me. She never helped me when Dad was giving me those suppertime beatings. That must be why I can't feel the deep pain that Katie's feeling. I love her, though, more than ever the past couple of years when she became our ally against the old cat and Dad. Mom's strong; she cries a little over Grammy's death, but not like Katie. Maybe I'm strong, too. Maybe that's why I can't cry.

The undertaker's clean and well dressed, but he smells like death. I don't like being here, helping Mom make the arrangements, but she's asked me and so here I am. "Keep in mind that her second husband was a veteran," the undertaker says. "So there's a seventy-five-dollar burial benefit from the V.A." Her second husband: Dad's stepfather, the guy who used to beat him silly. Dad's real father died when he was ten days old.

"I promised her a vault," Mom says. "She doesn't have to have an expensive coffin, but I have to make sure there's enough money left for a vault. That's what she wanted most."

The undertaker leads us to the coffin room. The nice ones are up on stands underneath little spotlights. The cheap ones are on the floor in back, in the shadows. "If you want a vault, these are about all you can afford," the undertaker says. Mom picks the cheapest casket, which is also the shabbiest-looking: gray velvety material glued onto some kind of glorified cardboard. I'm not sure how that undertaker knows so much about Grammy's family history and our finances. Grammy never talked to us much about either of her husbands. It was Mom who told me once about those beatings Dad got.

Back in the office the calling hours are set and Mom signs some paperwork. "Now, did you remember to bring the burial dress?" the undertaker asks. Mom nods and pulls Grammy's best black dress out of the bag she's brought. The undertaker hangs it on a hook. Next, Mother takes Grammy's Bible out of the bag. It's Katie's and my idea that Grammy should be buried with her Bible. She read it daily, sometimes following me around the house reading from Revelations when she figured I need a sermon. Grammy liked best the Bible passages where whores were punished, where the children and grandchildren of whores were banned from Heaven. According to Grammy, there wasn't anything worse in this world you could be than a whore. Whores went straight to Hell.

The day of the funeral I'm numb. When the family's dressed and ready to leave for the funeral parlor, Mom says what's been swirling around in everyone's mind for the past few days. "I wonder if your dad's going to come to say good-bye to his mother." It comes out in a soft whisper.

All along I've felt edgy about Dad's showing up. Marvin's a big marshmallow when it comes to dealing with Dad, but Carl Jr. isn't. Until yesterday, I've been dreading a showdown between him and Dad. But now Carl's called to say he can't come because of his daughter's meningitis. So even if Dad does show, there probably won't be a fight. Lucky for him. If Carl Jr. had come and seen Dad, he'd probably have raised the roof.

Hardly anyone comes to Grammy's funeral. Dad never shows. Now I hate him even more, something I didn't think was possible. If she was *my* mother, I would have gotten myself there no matter how sick I was.

Katie's torn up about Grammy. I stay by her side to help keep her strong, something that I have done for my older sister since I was a little girl. The family is shown to the limousine. On the long ride out to the Baptist church on Beauty's Run Road, we weep silently. No one speaks. I am thinking about how, during these last few years, Grammy has given me all her rings and trinkets. Why me? I wonder. Why not Katie, whom she loved so much more? I pray to God that, in the end, Grammy forgave me for all the times I smart-mouthed her and for that time at Williamsport Hospital when my anger got the best of me and I yanked her away from her reunion with Dad. All those times he beat me, she never stepped in or intervened, but I had failed her, too.

Grammy's grave is up on the hill. The wind whips through the cemetery. Even in our winter coats, we're shivering. After the service is over, Katie can't seem to leave the gravesite. At first the workers are respectful, but after a while they get impatient and start to fill the grave. "Can we please go now?" the undertaker asks impatiently. But it's as if Katie's frozen to the ground, hypnotized by that hole that's swallowing up Grammy. At first, the shovelfuls of dirt thud against the vault. But as the grave fills up, the sound gets softer. On our way back, Mother says, "I promise you girls that I will save some money for a headstone as quickly as I can."

After that day we rarely speak about Grammy. We're too busy going about our regular routine, struggling to make ends meet, trying hard as we can to get ahead a little.

14. SKYLINE DRIVE

They're hiring over at the brand-new Howard Johnson's in Williamsport, so Katie decides to quit her cook's job at Summit Lodge and waitress at HoJo's. For a week or so, I listen to Katie's stories about how Howard Johnson's is so modern and efficient and how their customers tip so much better than the folks who come to the lodge. Next thing you know, I'm working there, too. Mother decides to stay put, but there's a buzz among the Summit Lodge's female crew and they decide they want to check out the new place. Work schedules are checked and a "girls' night out" at HoJo's is planned.

On the big night, I get dressed up in my bright red two-piece suit with the fake mink mandarin collar, my patent leather three-inch heels with the matching purse, and white dress gloves. I drive over to Williamsport in the new '64 black Volkswagen I've purchased with money I've saved from my pay and tips. Mom and the rest of the Summit Lodge crew are waiting, wide-eyed, in the Howard Johnson's foyer. Eileen and Charlotte go on about how my outfit makes me look like Jackie Kennedy. They mean it as a compliment, but I'm not too thrilled. I'm probably the only person in America who thinks Jackie's homely.

The hostess, Mrs. Mock, gives us special treatment. Stepping out from behind the register, she leads our large party to a long table that's been set up at the center of the restaurant. We all sit down and get comfortable. Everyone but Mother starts studying the menu.

"Diane, you know what's good. You can order for me," Mom whispers. Whenever our family went to a restaurant during summer vacations at Wildwood, Mom always left her menu closed and ordered the simplest thing: toast. As a kid, I'd assumed she did it to save money. But here in Howard Johnson's, I suddenly realize that menus overwhelm Mother. She's illiterate; she can only read the things she has to. But for a woman of modest means and limited experience, restaurant formality and decision-making between dozens of choices is intimidating. "No problem, Mother," I tell her. "Leave it to me."

Our waitress approaches. It's cheerful Mrs. Bartholomew, with her bouncy blond hair. "Hello, ladies. Can I take your orders? Diane, why don't we start with you?"

"I'll have the beef burgundy and a large HoJo Cola," I tell her. "And for my mother the Summer Delight salad and a cup of coffee."

"Very good," Mrs. Bartholomew says and moves on to the others.

I've chosen this salad for Mom because I want her to have something creative and colorful—a culinary work of art that's different from the humdrum dishes she serves up over at the Summit Lodge. The Summer Delight salad comes with three different flavors of sherbet and a dome of cottage cheese in the middle. Sliced peaches, pears, and prunes are arranged between the scoops in an attractive way. It's a fancy, sophisticated entrée—something Jackie Kennedy herself might order in that soft and whispery voice of hers. Most of the rest of our party get burgers and clam plates.

Mrs. Bartholomew places our orders and returns with our drinks, rolls, and condiments. The Summit Lodge gals are impressed with both the restaurant itself and my status as an insider. This outing was a good idea.

When our food arrives, Mrs. Bartholomew places the festive Summer Delight salad in front of my mother. Mom turns to me, a disgusted look on her face. "Diane, why'd you order me *this*?"

The other women eat and talk and laugh. I pick a little at my beef burgundy, but I've lost my appetite. I'm so ashamed that my selection

for Mom has backfired—disappointing Mom instead of pleasing her—
When Mrs. Bartholomew takes away her platter, I can't even look to see
if Mom's eaten any of her salad.

Later, when our desserts come, Mrs. Bartholomew says to me, out of
the blue, "Diane, you know my son, Buzz, don't you?"

Buzz Bartholomew started at HoJo's as a busboy a few weeks earlier.
He's built like a bull: wide shoulders, broad chest, curly blond hair. But
in my opinion there's a silly kid trapped inside that man's body. The
week before, during our shift, Buzz was horsing around with Jim Sleigh,
another busboy, and he ripped the pocket off of Jim's uniform shirt and
yanked Jim's pants down to his ankles. I know Buzz, all right, but I'm
not too impressed.

"Yes, I know him," I tell his mother.

"Well, how come you don't go out with him?"

Because he's shorter than I am and I'm only five-four, I think to
myself. Because I'm looking for a mature man, not a childish boy. "He's
never asked me, Mrs. Bartholomew" is what I actually say.

Two weeks later Buzz asks me out and I accept.

On our date, Buzz drives me up to Skyline Drive and starts kissing
me. My body likes it well enough, but in the middle of things I get
scared without really understanding why. I tell him to stop and he does.

Second date, same thing. And the third date, too. No matter where
Buzz takes me, we always end up on Skyline Drive. Sex isn't something
I have ever talked about with Mother or Katie, and I've buried deeply
that incident in the trailer with Dad—have long since shoveled confusion and denial over our trip to Chattanooga. So I'm naive. I don't even
realize, for instance, that kissing stimulates the body. Gets you ready for
other things. But each time we're necking up there on the mountain, the
fear comes over me, and I tell Buzz to stop, and he does.

On our fourth date, he *won't* stop. He holds my wrists when I try to
push him away and uses his body weight to prevent me from struggling
out from under him. He yanks down my nylons and rips my panties and
forces himself inside of me. He's rough. Mad almost. He's got my face
squashed between the seat and the side door. I can feel my flesh tear, the
oozing of blood and mucus. I don't know what else to do, so I stare out
the window and wait. Buzz thrusts himself in and out of me as if he's

riding a bull at the rodeo. At first, he doesn't even seem to notice he's hurting me; it's like I'm not even really there. But I begin to wonder if hurting me is part of what he's enjoying. A minute later he grunts and collapses against me.

He gets off me and starts tucking and putting himself back together. "Oh, damn," he moans. "I broke the zipper on my good pants. My mom's going to have a fit."

The shooting pains have stopped, but I'm sore as anything and the crotch of my panties is soggy, stuck to my private area. Buzz starts the car, heads back down the mountain. He loves me, I remind myself. He's always telling me he does while he's kissing and groping me. If he loves me, he wouldn't hurt me, so I'm not hurt. Still, I feel dirty, ashamed, and sad. And more than anything else, I'm confused. I trusted Buzz. I thought he would stop and he didn't.

Later, after I was well into my life with Buzz, I came to believe that he knew from our very first date what he wanted from me and had calculated how to get it. Later still, my suspicions were confirmed when I learned that Buzz had bet Mr. Lugan, the assistant manager at Howard Johnson's, twenty dollars that he could "get into Diane Hiller's pants." But driving back down the mountain that night, I'm still a stupid sixteen-year-old who doesn't even realize she's just been raped—who doesn't even understand what "rape" really means. Because I'm sure I told Buzz "no" in no uncertain terms, I must still be a virgin. After all, I have never even seen him, or any man, naked. What girl who had lost her virginity could claim *that*?

By the time we get back to Buzz's house, I'm too sick to drive my own car home. I call my sister and she comes and gets me. I don't tell her what has happened. I don't want her hollering at me or running home and telling Mom. I wish I could tell her, though. I feel so dirty and ashamed. This has to have been my fault. Katie looks momentarily away from the road and at me. "What happened to you anyway?" she asks.

"Nothing," I tell her. "I just feel so sick."

When we get home, the first thing I do is wash myself. The mucus and blood have spotted my skirt and I pray that, if Katie has seen the stains, she will assume I just started my period.

15. CENTRIFUGAL FORCE

Buzz gives me his signet ring to wear around my neck. Our intimacy proves that Buzz loves me and this ring shows everyone at school and work that we're a steady item. We're having sex regularly now, in the backseat of the car up on Skyline Drive. It doesn't usually hurt like it did in the beginning, and when it does, I don't really mind because pain is part of love.

One Saturday night, Buzz drives me over the bridge to downtown Williamsport. "Where are we going?" I ask, but he won't say. Buzz pulls in front of the bus station and stops, motor idling. Are we getting on a bus? Going on some romantic mystery trip?

"Slide over and take the wheel," Buzz says.

"Why? Where are *you* going?"

"Men's room. There's a machine in there sells rubbers."

I grab the wheel and drive around the block. I don't know why he needs those things all the time. I'm not even sure what they're for, but I'm too embarrassed to ask. I hate when Buzz teases me about not knowing stuff.

When I drive back around, he's waiting in front of the station. "Shit," he says, hopping into the passenger's side. "Got all the way in there and realized I didn't have any change."

It's fun being with Buzz. His practical jokes at HoJo's used to annoy me, but now I enjoy them. Growing up in our house, Buzz's kind of playfulness was discouraged. "Diane, stop acting fresh!" Mother would order if, for some reason, I was in a silly mood. It made me quiet and shy when I got out with other people; I was never sure what was appropriate behavior and what wasn't. But it's fun watching Buzz do all kinds of stupid stuff I would never do. His playful behavior's a kind of freedom. I've never laughed this much in my life.

One night, at the end of our shift, Buzz says, "Come on over to my house, Diane. You can follow me home." He's grinning ear to ear as he strolls across the parking lot and climbs into his '58 red-and-white Pontiac convertible. Getting into my Volkswagen, I know something's up. Buzz sidles up alongside my Bug and revs his engine. "Let's say you and me were going to have a race," he says. "Who do you think could get to my house first?"

"Let me put it this way," I say. "You tell me what kind of soda pop you want and I'll have it opened and ready for you by the time you get there."

We peel out of HoJo's. Up the double-striped road we race, looking out for city cops as we zigzag through traffic. Crossing the Market Street Bridge, I'm on Buzz's bumper. I whip the wheel to the right and put the pedal to the metal. I know one thing: if Buzz thinks I'm letting him win, he's crazy.

Neck and neck, side by side, we roar through downtown South Williamsport. Then I take the lead. I'm doing great until we come to a hairpin turn I hadn't planned on. Driving over fifty on the inside lane, I start to lose control. Centrifugal force lifts my outside tires off the ground, and I skid along on two wheels, racetrack style. I hit the shoulder, then veer off and into the dirt, barely missing a roadside telephone booth. When I ease off the gas, my airborne tires flop back down onto the ground and I steer her back onto the road. Whatever problems Buzz has had with the turn, by some miracle, he's still behind me.

I jerk the wheel, making the left onto Buzz's road. Approaching his house, I slam on the brakes, fishtailing up his driveway. The Beetle's just barely stopped when I hop out on rubbery legs. A few seconds later, Buzz comes to a brake-screeching halt behind me. He just sits there in his Pontiac, blank-faced, like he's in shock. "What took you so long?" I ask him. I don't think it occurred to him back at Hojo's that I might have the nerve to accept his challenge and then the guts and driving skills to beat him.

We sit around at Buzz's for a while, but it's no fun. He's in a sulky mood. He snaps out of it later, up on Skyline Drive, but he's rougher than usual.

After Buzz and I have been dating for a couple of months, Mrs. Bartholomew declares that her son no longer has permission to drive up the creek road to my house. If I want to see him, she says, I have to drive over to *her* house and visit him there. Buzz's younger brother, Frank, on the other hand, can drive twice as far to *his* girlfriend's house whenever he wants. It seems to me that Frank is his mother's favorite and Buzz isn't.

Mary Bartholomew confuses me. She acts sweet and lovable one minute, distant and cold the next. It's painful to see the way she seems to favor Frank over Buzz, and then to see Buzz pretend it doesn't bother him when I know it does. But although I resent Mrs. Bartholomew, I admire her, too, and want very much to win her favor. Maybe it's because I've seen her sarcastic side and don't want to be on the receiving end of it. Or maybe it's because she's the exact opposite of my own mother. In a room full of people, Mother would want only to fade into the woodwork and go unnoticed. Mary Bartholomew, on the other hand, would call for a drum roll and spotlights. With her bleached blond hair and china doll complexion, her big laugh and outgoing disposition, she's larger than life.

When Mrs. Bartholomew issues her order about Buzz not visiting me at home, I start spending most of my spare time at his house. Mother and Katie are both working double shifts, and I hate going home to our lonely, empty house. At Buzz's, there's always a swirl of activity, much of it centering around Mary. Worried that Buzz's mom might peg me as a "moocher," I always politely refuse when she asks me to stay for supper. Mother has raised us to be considerate of others and not take advantage. Besides that, I don't want to accept Mrs. Bartholomew's dinner invitation and then hear some sarcastic remark about an added mouth to feed. So every night, I make some excuse and leave as soon as she starts setting the table. I drive around, killing time and trying as best I can to guess when they'll be finished eating. Then I go back there. Other than home, I have no place else to go.

On the subject of me, Buzz's mom runs hot and cold. One time when I'm over there, she tells me "Mrs. Bartholomew" is too formal and invites me to call her Mary. I'm thrilled because I want her to like me, and calling her by her first name almost makes us girlfriends. But the next time I visit, she's critical of me and rude. With Mary, it's always: take two steps forward and three steps back and try as best you can to keep your balance.

One afternoon when I'm over there, Mary sends Buzz and Frank out to the department store over in New Berry because Frank needs new sneakers. I stand, start to go with them, but Mary says, "Diane, you're welcome to wait for the boys here with me."

"Oh, okay, Mary," I say. "Sure." I figure maybe Mary wants to have a talk with me or something, but that's not it. I sit there for an hour, bored out of my mind from some stupid thing on TV. When the phone rings, Mary answers it. "Uh-huh," she keeps saying. "Yes, I see." I know from watching her face go beet red that something's up. When she hangs up, she asks me if my two brothers ever gave my mother trouble.

I shrug. "They'd play hooky once in a while. That's about all."

A police cruiser pulls into the Bartholomews' driveway and Mary hurries outside to meet the officers. Whatever's going on, I figure it's best if I stay put in the living room. A few minutes later Buzz and Frank come into the house, looking hangdog. "What's the matter?" I ask, but they pass right by me like I'm a ghost and go to their bedroom, slamming the door behind them.

After the cops leave, Mary comes back inside and starts screaming at the bedroom door. "I gave you *money* for those sneakers! You didn't have to *steal* them!" When Buzz comes out, Mary hauls off and slugs him on the arm.

"What are you hitting *me* for?" Buzz protests. "*I* didn't do it. He did."

"Did any of the neighbors see you when you pulled in here in that police car? You should have known better! How could you have been so stupid?"

"I *told* you. I didn't steal the sneakers. I was waiting out in the car."

"You're grounded!"

"I wasn't even in the *store*!"

"You're older. You should have never let him steal."

Buzz groans and goes back to his room, slamming the door again. It doesn't take a genius to realize that this visit's shot. "Tell Buzz I'll see him tomorrow," I say, getting out of there as quickly as I can.

Driving home, I feel angry at Mary. Why did she have to hit Buzz? How was *he* supposed to stop her little angel from stealing? Frank's only a year younger than Buzz. He's old enough to know the difference between right and wrong and then some.

The next time I see Buzz is at work, a few days later. He's still grounded. "Don't worry," he tells me. "I'll just get Frank to sweet-talk the keys away from Mom." Buzz doesn't even seem to mind the way Mary plays favorites. But I do.

Something's the matter with me. I'm queasy, off and on, all day long and I can't keep anything in my stomach. I don't even *want* to put anything in there. It doesn't feel like a cold. I'm tired, too. Maybe I'm just run-down from too many late nights out with Buzz. Whatever's wrong with me, I can't shake it. "Make yourself an appointment with a doctor," Mother finally says. She's having fits because I keep missing school.

I keep dragging myself to work, but I can't stand the smell of all that food, or the look of all those HoJo's customers always moving their jaws, feeding their faces. And I feel like *burning* that stupid uniform they make us wear: aqua and white print dress, frilly apron, seamed nylons, double hairnet plopped onto my head like I'm an old lady. The nylons are held up with garters that hook onto my girdle. That's the part I hate the most these days: that stupid regulation girdle I have to squeeze into before every shift.

I do as Mother says: make the appointment. The doctor I've picked out of the phone book is in New Derry. When I get there, the waiting room's empty, except for me. There are six or seven straight-back wooden chairs lined up against the wall and a bunch of shabby magazines on a beat-up coffee table. In the corner there's an end table with an ugly orange teardrop-base lamp. The shade looks like no one's dusted it for a decade. There's a small glass window where the receptionist's supposed to check you in, but no one's there either.

I sit there for fifteen minutes or so. I've got better things to do than wait *here* all day. But just as I stand to leave, a door opens. "Miss Hiller?" a short, elderly woman in a white uniform asks.

"Yes." Who else was she expecting? Rebecca of Sunnybrook Farm?

"Come in. The doctor will be examining you in just a few minutes."

Who said anything about *examining* me? All's I've got is a weird cold or something. The nurse leads me to a small room that's got two more of those straight-back chairs, some medical equipment, and a table that looks like a slab from the morgue. Nursie covers the table with a long sheet of white paper and the doctor comes in. He's as old as she is. What is this: a husband-and-wife deal? Dr. and Mrs. Frankenstein?

He asks the questions; she writes down my answers. "Have you been having fever or chills?"

"No."

"Stomach cramps?"

"Uh-uh."

"Headaches?"

"Nope."

"Have you been having sexual relations, Miss Hiller?"

I feel my face catch fire. I can't look at him, of course, and when I look over at her, she's waiting, pen in hand, without looking up.

"Yes." It's come out so quietly, I'm not even sure I've spoken aloud.

"Well, then," the doctor says. He stands. "Better take her temperature, Mildred, and have her slip into an examination gown. I'll be back."

I'm handed a worn green gown that smells like Clorox and looks like it's been worn by thousands of patients before I got here. The nurse tells me she'll be right back. At the doorway, she stops, her hand on the knob. "Are you all right?" she asks me.

"Yup."

I undress, put on the gown, and sit up on the table, crinkling the white paper strip. I suddenly know beyond a doubt that this isn't a cold or fatigue from staying out late with Buzz. I'm pregnant.

When the nurse returns, she smiles patiently. "Dearie," she says, "the gown goes on with the opening in the *back*."

"Oh, yeah." I try sliding it around by the tie at my neck, but I'm so nervous, I practically choke myself. The nurse has to help me untie it and get it right. I was in the hospital once when I was a kid. I should have remembered how these gowns go. I feel like such a stupid jerk.

"Okay, now," she says. "Lie back and put your feet up in the stirrups."

What? If I do that, that doctor will see everything. But I guess that's the point. My feet hit the stirrups. They're ice cold and I jerk my feet off. Try again. That damn doctor better hurry up and get in here, because I definitely don't like this position one little bit.

The door opens. "Are we ready?" he asks.

Yeah, *we're* ready, I feel like answering. I didn't know he had *his* feet up in stirrups, too. I swallow and nod, trying to smile.

Lying there, I have nowhere to look but up at the ceiling. Tears creep out of the corners of my eyes and I can't stop shaking. I try to tell myself that he's not groping and prodding me down there—that he isn't even in the room. I know what he must be thinking: that because I'm pregnant and unmarried, I'm dirty and bad—one of those whores Grammy used to read aloud about from her Bible.

"This will be cold," the doctor says. "Try not to jump."

But the word *jump* makes me jumpy, and I can't help lurching as he inserts the cold metal object into me. "Relax, relax," he says. When it's all the way inside, it expands. It hurts, but Buzz hurt me worse that first time. I can feel the doctor's finger poking around inside of me. You're not here, I keep telling myself. You're someplace else. This isn't happening.

"Looks like you may be pregnant," he says. I look at him, then look away again. "We won't know for sure until the urine tests come back. Meet me in my office after you get dressed and we'll chat."

A few minutes later I'm standing at the entrance of his dark, walnut-paneled office, waiting for him to notice me. He's at his desk, bent over whatever it is he's writing. When he looks up, he tells me to come in and sit.

He says he's 95 percent sure I'm pregnant and that I should come back in a week for the test results. But I don't need them. I'm 100 percent sure that those trips up the mountain to Skyline Drive have put Buzz's baby inside of me.

Leaving the doctor's office, I'm dazed by the bright sunlight and the news I've just received. I concentrate hard on my Volkswagen, parked at the curb. Nauseous and light-headed, I put one foot forward, then the other. Keep going, I tell myself. Keep going. Keep going. . . .

On the drive home, I keep wondering where I'll go now, what I'll do. Mother doesn't have much more tolerance for whores than Grammy did. At worst, she'll murder me. At best, she'll put me out of the house and I'll never see my family again.

I wait all afternoon, both wanting and dreading to see my mother. When she gets home from work that night, I open my mouth to tell her we have to talk, but she rushes past me and into the bathroom. When she comes out again, I've lost my nerve. I sit there, watching her put water on for her coffee. "Diane," she says, "you're white as a sheet. Are you sick again?"

"Nah, I'm okay," I tell her. She has no idea that I've gone to the doctor's, as she had urged, and I can't seem to tell her. I stand, walk to the fridge, look inside. It's empty except for a Pepsi. I grab the can with my trembling hand, rustle through the junk drawer and find the opener. My hands are shaking so badly that the point of the can opener keeps skidding across the tin surface. Tears roll down my cheeks. I want so badly *not* to give Mother this news.

"Mom?" She turns and faces me. "I'm pregnant."

She doesn't shout, like I figured she would. Without a word, she sits down on our old gray Naugahyde chair, the one we carted down from Connecticut years back, when she was still Dad's wife and they were chasing their Pennsylvania dream of striking it rich. Mom reaches for her saddlebag pocketbook, takes out her Winstons, and lights one. The sulphur smell from the match wafts over to where I'm standing. Waiting. For several minutes, Mom just smokes, staring out the picture window into the night. Cars whiz by on the highway out front, the reflections from their oncoming headlights moving across the window.

I study my mother. Her white poplin cook's uniform is puckered at the snaps, spattered with grease stains from the grill. Her wavy black hair's matted down from the net she's required to wear and hasn't even bothered to take off yet. A few strands of gray poke out from under the hairnet. When she dyes it that inky black color, she always misses the hair at her temples.

She turns and faces me. "You're sure?"

I nod. "I went to the doctor's today."

She nods back, offers me a sad half-smile. In her warm brown eyes, I see not the anger I've expected, only sadness and disappointment. Her unexpected gentleness heightens my sense of shame.

"Well, you don't have to marry him if you don't want to. I'll help you raise the baby. What do you want to do, Diane?"

Mother has raised Katie and me to be proper ladies. Why is she saying this? Of course I have to marry Buzz. I'm carrying his baby. Anyway, I *want* to marry him. And when Buzz finds out, he'll want to marry me, too.

That night in bed I'm exhausted but too edgy to sleep. Another life is growing inside of me. By the end of the year, I'll be a married woman. I lie in the dark, reviewing the spinning sensations that have brought me to the brink of this unclear future: my awkward first date with Buzz, made at the urging of his mother; his rough, insistent plunging in and out of me during sex; the fun he's introduced to my dreary life. I fall asleep thinking about that crazy car race Buzz and I had a while back—the frightening thrill of entering that unexpected turn and feeling my wheels lift off the ground, my car begin its scary two-wheel skid. Already, this pregnancy has a centrifugal force all its own, and I lie there, skidding toward a future I can neither predict nor control.

16. THE WEDDING

"Buzz, there's something I've got to tell you," I begin. He doesn't answer. The radio's blaring so loudly, he probably hasn't even heard me.

We are in my Volkswagen, driving back down the mountain from Skyline Drive. He's quiet, the way he usually is after he's gotten what he wants up there. Sometimes after we have sex, I feel like talking, but Buzz prefers to play the radio, the louder the better.

I reach over and turn off the music. "Hey!" he protests.

"Buzz, I got something important to tell you."

"Yeah? So?" He turns the radio back on.

When I reach again for the knob, he swats my hand away. So I have to announce it over the music. "I'm pregnant, Buzz."

Now *he* kills the radio. "Did you go to . . . are you *sure*?"

"Yes, I went, and yes, I'm sure."

Neither of us says another word until we get to his house. When I pull into the Bartholomews' driveway and cut the engine, I look over at him. He smiles. "Maybe if you jump off Dad's garage roof, you'll lose it," he says.

I'm not thrilled with his humor, but I smile anyway.

"Well?" he says. "What do you say?"

Is he serious? Is he nuts? "You love me, don't you, Buzz?" I ask him. When he doesn't answer my question, I feel dizzy—knocked off my feet.

"Guess we're going to have to get married, huh?" Buzz says. He laughs in that way people do when they don't think anything's funny. "You sure you don't want to jump off the garage? How about if I push you?"

"You're crazy if you think I'm jumping *or* being pushed," I snap back.

"Oh, man," he says. "My mother's going to kill me." He gets out and slams the door. Without bothering to turn back, he calls over his shoulder that he'll see me at work. Driving home, I think about Mom's promise that she'll help me. Even if Buzz abandons me, Mom won't.

The next day at the restaurant, Buzz doesn't say much until we're on our break. "Well, did you tell her?" I ask him.

He nods.

"And?"

"She had a fit."

I figured that much. "What did she say?"

"That she's not thrilled about having you become her daughter-in-law, but she doesn't have much of a choice."

Well, I don't have much of a choice about Mary either, because I *need* her support. Mother's already had such a hard-luck life. She's promised to help Buzz and me, but I don't have the heart to saddle her with *all* the extra burdens of this surprise pregnancy. The best I can do is to keep going over there to see Buzz, hoping that Mary will like me again, and maybe even come to love me.

Instead, Mary manipulates the situation. She's been campaigning for months to get Buzz on the full-time schedule at Howard Johnson's. "If Buzz doesn't get more hours, he's not going to be able to marry you," she tells me with a sigh one afternoon. I know what she's up to. She's hoping I run home and repeat what she's just said to Katie. Now that Katie's been made a manager, she has some pull with the big boss. But even though a fatter paycheck from Buzz would help, I resent Mary's attempt to push around my sister through me. When I get home that night, I tell Katie what Mary's said, not to pressure her but to warn her about what she's up to.

"Don't worry," Katie says. "I've got Mary's number."

When the new schedules come out and Mary sees that she hasn't gotten what she wanted, she gives me the silent treatment. When I call, she hands someone else the phone without saying hello. When I go over there, she goes into her bedroom and shuts the door.

"Your mother's like a little kid when she doesn't get what she wants," I complain to Buzz.

He gives me a dismissive wave. "She's just going through menopause."

"Listen, Buzz. My mother went through menopause, too, and I don't remember her acting like a little spoiled brat!"

Mom shows no interest in my coming wedding. She keeps suggesting that Buzz and I marry in the chapel—a small, quiet service like she and Dad had, no frills. She's afraid of the expense, I think. Even working two jobs, Mom struggles to make ends meet. Plus, all this wedding talk makes her dwell on Dad again. A couple of years have gone by now since he moved out, but Mom's never really gotten over his abrupt departure and the way he rubbed her face in his new "relationship." And, of course, she's disappointed that I *have* to get married. A big wedding's the *last* thing Mother wants to contend with.

One evening, I stop by the Bartholomews' to see Buzz. "He's not home," Mary tells me. "But come in! Come in! I want to show you what I bought for you to wear to the altar." She's over her pouting now, and in a joyful mood. When it comes to Mary's emotions, it's best to wear your seatbelt because the ride's bound to be unpredictable.

In her bedroom, she holds up the most elegant white sheath dress I've ever seen. It's made of a beautiful brocade fabric and trimmed with white fur. I put my hands over my mouth. "Oh, my goodness!" I shriek.

"And look!" From the hatbox on her bed, Mary removes a sequined pillbox with a mesh veil, a perfect match for the dress. "And I'll lend you my long, off-white coat and beige heels, and a pair of my earrings," she says. "You're going to be a beautiful bride."

I'm knocked dizzy by her kindness. But I'm immediately worried, too. I've been putting off making arrangements for a ceremony because I don't belong to any church. Now I've got the bridal outfit but no place to be a bride. When I confide my concern to Mary, she suggests I call *their* pastor and make an appointment for me and Buzz. So I do.

Three days later, Buzz and I cross over the Susquehanna River on the Market Street Bridge on our way to the Faith Tabernacle Church in downtown Williamsport. The pastor tells us we're in luck: he's got one small spot left in the middle of his busy holiday schedule. He can marry us on the afternoon of December 22. "And what a beautiful gift it will be to give yourselves to each other for Christmas," he says. I nod, looking down at my hands in my lap instead of into the eyes of this pastor who assumes I'm pure.

In the car on the way back, Buzz chuckles about how, on the twenty-second, the two of us can finally "give" ourselves to each other. He looks over at me. "What are you all teary-eyed over?" he asks.

"Nothing," I tell him. In truth, I am thinking about a quarrel I had with Grammy not long before she died—a painful buried memory that's just poked unavoidably out of the ground. She'd been sitting at the table, reading aloud from her Bible and spouting off, as usual, about the evil ways of whores. I was fed up with Grammy's constant warnings about depravity, and sick of her hypocrisy, too. Not long before that, I had learned a secret about Grammy: that, as an unmarried girl, she'd had a daughter whom she gave up to her parents to raise as theirs. So I turned to her, hoping to hurt her badly enough to shut her up: "Who do you think you're kidding?" I screamed. "*You're* a whore!"

Grammy knew exactly what I meant. She shut up, all right. She choked back her tears and stood to leave the room. "Someday you'll be sorry," she mumbled. I was sorry immediately, of course. I felt guilty as anything. But on this day, I am sorrier still, because I am both a whore and a hypocrite—a bride-to-be with a church date, a pretty white dress to wear, and a baby inside of me.

Carl Jr. can't come to the wedding and Dad, of course, hasn't been invited. My brother Marvin's giving me away. He's nervous, too. Before the ceremony he insists on practice-escorting me down the aisle, like it's a real big affair and so we have to get things right.

The music starts. With my brother by my side, I walk down the aisle in my white dress, carrying the flowers the Bartholomews have provided for the ceremony. On the groom's side, Buzz's father stands there, handsome in his off-white suit. Mary's next to him, short and solid, fashionably dressed in two-tone beige that sets off her blond hair and china doll skin. Mom's across the aisle from Buzz's parents. She's wearing her navy-blue sailor dress, the one she wore to the court when she got her divorce. It's nothing more than a housedress, really. Katie, on the other hand, is dressed to the nines in the same royal-blue satin bridesmaid's dress she wore in Marvin's wedding. Buzz is waiting for me at the altar, smiling nervously, poking his hands in and out of his suit pants. They're the same pants with the repaired zipper from that first time he forced himself on me.

I weep while I say my vows, because our wedding's beautiful but tainted by our sin. "I do," I say, and Buzz says it, too, and it's done.

After the church service, we return to my mother's house. No one's planned a reception. It's what I thought I wanted—get the wedding over with and go on from there—but now it makes me feel sad not to have any kind of celebration.

Mother assigns us the inner bedroom and Buzz totes in his stuff. The only thing he's brought to our marriage is an oval turquoise laundry basket filled with his socks, briefs, pants, and shirts. The four of us sit down to supper—Mother, Katie, Buzz, and me. No one says much, and the food's bland as usual. Because it's my big day, Mother excuses me from doing the dishes.

At night, I go into the bathroom to freshen up and put on my new white negligee. I study her shyly: this woman in the mirror whose wedding night it is. I pretend that Buzz and I are the couple that preacher thought we were and that I am about to go out there so that we can consummate our marriage.

Buzz is in bed, naked under the covers, his thing poking up between his legs. I slip in beside him and he kisses me hard on the lips. I realize I've forgotten to turn off the light. "Can you get it?" I ask. Buzz doesn't move.

I sugar up my voice and try again. "Please, Buzz?"

"Oh, all right," he says. He throws off the covers and crawls over me, poking me with his thing as he climbs out of bed. Pregnant or not, I have never seen Buzz or any man naked before this moment, and as Buzz bobs his way to the wall switch, I gasp. *That's* what it looks like? *That* pink, hard thing with its bald, shiny top and hanging giblets is the critter that hurt me so bad that first time? It's so ridiculous-looking, I want to laugh, but God help me if I do.

"What's the matter with *you?*" Buzz asks. He's got one hand on the wall switch and he's using the other to scratch himself. Buzz Jr.'s standing there at attention.

"Nothing," I say. "Nothing at all. Come back to bed."

In the dark, he presses his lips against mine again, then mounts me like a wild bronco that needs breaking. Sex is rodeo-style, as usual, only this time we're not in the backseat of the car but in bed.

And he's wild, all right. The bed rocks and creaks, the headboard banging against the wall. I'm still more or less invisible to Buzz, but on his way to getting where he intends to go, the frame cracks and we go crashing to the floor. Somehow, Buzz manages to stay on the mattress, but I've bounced off with a thump and rolled onto the floor. It's me who asks *him* if he's all right.

He responds with a laugh. "Shit," he says. "How are we going to explain *this* to your mother?" He doesn't ask if I'm okay or bother to help me up. My being two months pregnant seems to have slipped his mind.

On our second night of married life, I can't wait for Buzz to get home. He's worked the day shift at the restaurant, so I'm expecting him back by late afternoon. Mother and Katie are both working tonight. That means Buzz and I have the house to ourselves.

I wait, watch the clock. It gets later and later. At eight o'clock, I start making phone calls, but no one's seen Buzz. He finally shows up after eleven. And as soon as I see he's okay, I'm ripping mad.

"Where *were* you?" I demand.

He tells me it's none of my business.

"It certainly *is* my business!" I shout. "In case you forgot, I'm your *wife*! Now, are you going to tell me where you've been or am I—"

"Awright, awright," he blurts out. "I was with Penny."

That shuts me up, but only for a second. "*Penny?* Who the hell is *Penny?*"

"My other girlfriend. I had to go tell her I got married."

"You couldn't have just picked up the phone? You had to spend the whole night telling her?"

I stomp into our bedroom and grab his stuff—five pairs of socks, five changes of underwear, five T-shirts, five pairs of pants. I slam each item as hard as I can into his stupid laundry basket. "Here's your stuff!" I scream, shoving the basket at him. "Now get out!" And out he marches, slamming the door behind him.

When Katie and Mother return from work, I stay in my bedroom so that I won't have to deal with them—admit to them that my marriage has already flopped. But after my mother and sister are asleep, I get up again. I pace from one room to the next, cry, vomit, toss and turn back in our broken bed. I want so much for Buzz to love me. I am having his baby. How am I supposed to raise a child alone?

Somewhere in the middle of the night, my anger turns to cold fear. Ever since Grammy died and Mom and Katie started working all those extra hours, I've been so lonely. And now, the day after my wedding, here I am all alone again. I shouldn't have been so hard on Buzz. He may not be perfect, but he's somebody. Another person to take away my loneliness.

In the morning, I drive over to the Bartholomews to hear what Buzz has to say for himself. Mary, my new mother-in-law, answers the door.

"What's going on with you two?" she asks me.

I'm only too glad to tell her about Buzz's late night, and his girlfriend, Penny.

"Let me go talk to him," she says.

She leaves me in their pink kitchen and goes into Buzz's bedroom. I can hear their voices behind the closed door, but can't make out any of the words. Minutes later, they come out again, Buzz first and Mary right behind him. Buzz looks both pissed and guilty.

"Come on," he says to me, then walks out their back door. I jump up and follow him like a loyal little puppy.

On the ride back to Mother's, the only thing he says to me is that he doesn't appreciate the fact that I squealed to his mother about Penny. Rather than start everything up again, I keep my mouth shut. But God, doesn't he *get* it? He's married now. We're having a baby. The rest of the ride home is silent.

Before we get out of the car, I touch his sleeve and he turns and looks at me. "I'm sorry I yelled at you," I say.

Whatever emotion he's feeling, I can't read it on Buzz's face. He gets out of the car without a word.

That argument of ours turns out to be the first of many fights. We clash about Buzz not getting himself up for work in the morning and about his taking off without telling me where he's going or where he's been. We fight about whether to save our money or spend it. We're living free at Mother's so that we can build up a nest egg and get our own apartment, maybe buy a few of the zillion things we're going to need once the baby arrives. But Buzz is always trying to crack open that nest egg for what he *wants*, not what we *need*.

And, of course, there's Penny. Buzz insists that he's broken it off with her, but if so, what are these disappearing acts of his all about? And what does this Penny look like anyway? Is she some scrawny little thing? A hippopotamus with a big pot belly, like Dad's girlfriend, Mavis? Is her name even Penny? Is there only one of her? Now that I know about Penny, I just can't trust Buzz.

And as if all these things aren't enough to keep us newlyweds battling, my mother-in-law's constantly manipulating and criticizing and dragging Buzz and me into the Bartholomew family soap opera. Buzz's brother Frank is in trouble again. His sister Jolene's shitty husband up and left her for the third time. Jolene needs money to help her get away from Roy. Roy needs someone to go over there and pound some sense into him. Half the time our phone rings, it's Mary calling to stir up the pot.

But, as usual, my mother-in-law swings back and forth between sour and sweet. Every time I get fed up and ready to put my foot down, she does something generous and nice and I lose my nerve. And I *need* Mary's help. When Buzz mistreats me, the ace I'm still holding in my hand is his fear of his mother. So I keep going over to Buzz's family's house in hopes that Mary's in one of her good moods, that it's not me who's coming in for criticism, that Mary's still my ally and not my enemy.

One afternoon, Buzz gets off the phone with his mother and groans. "Come on, Diane," he says. "Mom wants us over at the house."

"Well, too bad for her," I snap back at him. "I'm not going any place until I'm done with my cleaning." Like most days lately, I'm exhausted and sick to my stomach. I'm in my third month now, and just plum miserable. When that woman wants something, she expects the whole family to just drop everything and run.

"You better get ready," Buzz warns me a few minutes later. "She sounded like she means business." So I slap my cleaning rag into the sink and wash my hands and face. "Come on, come on," Buzz keeps bellyaching, pushing me toward the door, so I give up on the idea of changing.

When I walk into Mary's kitchen, everyone yells, "Surprise!" All of Buzz's aunts and uncles are there, a bunch of his cousins. They're all standing there, staring at me, and here I am, looking like a rat that's just crawled out of the sewer. I'm wearing my ripped white blouse and my filthy black clam diggers that I always wear when I do the housecleaning. My hair's sticking out in every direction. I could kill Buzz. I turn from one relative's face to the next, smiling as hard as I can. Under my breath, I hiss, "You're in for it, Buzz."

When I've regained my composure, I notice the large sheet cake sitting on the table. A little bride and groom stand in a field of whipped cream frosting. There are wedding bells in each of the four corners.

Next to the cake is a big frosted glass bowl filled with punch and float-ing strawberries. "Come on into the living room, everyone," Mary com-mands.

Someone's stuck a big white paper bell at the center of the ceiling and strung twisted crepe paper from it to the corners of the small living room. I'm pleased with all the fuss they've gone to but still embarrassed because I look so shabby. "Come on, Diane," Mary says. "Sit down next to Buzz and open your presents."

We've never been big gift-givers at our house; we could never afford the extra expense. So I'm extra careful about opening the first present, loosening the bow as gently as I can and taking care not to rip the paper. Inside is a set of drinking glasses decorated with orange and yellow rings. They must have cost all of ninety-nine cents, but I'm grateful to get them. I ooh and ahh like they're Waterford crystal. I open the next gift, thinking that the more careful I am, the more wrapping paper I'll have to use when I'm done. Then someone yells, "Just tear the paper off!" and everyone else chimes in, in agreement. So I rip open the pack-age and there's a shaggy beige bath mat. "We can *really* use this!" I announce.

The third gift, a sea foam green baby sweater, floods me with shame. I look up in disbelief at the smiling faces. Has Mary told the whole world that I'm pregnant? My face must show I'm upset, and one of Buzz's aunts tries to soften the moment. "This is both a wedding shower and a baby shower!" she says, cheerily. "Two for the price of one."

Each time I open another baby gift, I cover my embarrassment with a grateful smile. If I'm uncomfortable about getting them, I'm also relieved, because we need things for the baby and I've worried about how we were going to afford them.

By the end of the evening, I'm flooded with love and gratitude for Mary for having thrown us this surprise shower. Buzz and his dad fill up the car with the gifts for our baby and our home. I give Mary a hug and whisper a thank-you in her ear. I'm not sure if I'm going to laugh or cry.

Mary doesn't know this, and I can't bring myself to tell her, but this is the first party I have ever had.

17. DAD'S DEAD

I'm in the living room over at the Bartholomews' when the phone rings. From where I'm sitting, I can see through the archway into the kitchen. Mary reaches for the pink wall phone. She's doing more listening than speaking. Her face has become pale and serious. She keeps looking in at me.

When she hangs up, she comes into the living room and sits down beside me. "Diane, that was your mother. I have bad news. Your father died."

My first thought is this: Well, the good-for-nothing bum finally got what he deserved. But, of course, I don't say that aloud.

For some reason, I begin to sob. I hate Dad for having beaten me and molested me—for having nearly killed Katie and me with the car. More than all that, I hate him for what he did to Mom—the way he just tossed her away like an old shoe after thirty-two years. And for *what*? For that big, mean hippopotamus next door. He *did* get what he deserved: the accident, a life of slowly wasting away. So why am I sad? Why aren't I celebrating and shouting with glee?

Another wave of nausea comes over me. Part of it's the pregnancy, I guess. I'm sick so much of the time lately. But I'm also stomach-sick from uneasiness about hearing the news while over here. Mary knows a little of the story about Dad, but not much. I've learned not to trust her with my family secrets because she betrays confidences.

"Mary, I better go," I say.

"Are you sure you're all right? You can always wait for Buzz to drive you home. Or someone else can give you a ride." There's genuine concern on her face, for the baby *and* for me. She must think I love my father.

"No, I'm all right," I tell her. "I'll be fine." I'm going to heave if I don't get out of there.

Mom meets me at the door. "The old cat's having Dad's funeral over at her house," she says. "She thinks we won't go, but we're going." Her jaw is set and there's a determined look in her eye. She will fight, if she has to, for her own and her family's right to see Dad one last time.

On the afternoon of the funeral, we gather in the kitchen: Mother, Marvin, his wife Judy, Katie, and me. "Now, Mom, you know you can't say anything to her when you get there," Marvin warns. "You have to remember that it's her house."

"Yes, yes, I know," Mom snaps back. "Believe me, I don't need any of my children to tell me the proper way to act." And with that, we open the door and walk together across the road.

Marvin knocks. When the old cat opens the front door, she looks surprised but not shocked. There's no guilt in her eyes, no shame.

She says nothing, but steps back and lets us enter. In silence, she leads us through her knotty pine dining room. Steppy and a few of my father's other friends are seated at the table, drinking coffee. We nod terse hellos and follow Mavis into the living room.

The casket's been set up in front of the picture window, facing our house. The others approach the body, but I stand where I am a minute more, wondering if Dad's ever stood over here at this window and watched our comings and goings—wondering if, after he left, he ever wished he hadn't made himself an outsider, an onlooker at our lives, if, even once, the son of a bitch ever felt regret.

I walk up to him. He's a skeleton with sagging skin that's mushroom-pale. There's nothing left of the bully who wielded those powerful blows at suppertime, the dad who tumbled with me in the waves at Wildwood and taught me to hunt. Who is this corpse, so cold and still?

Hello, Dad, and good-bye. Good riddance. The others are sad, sobbing. Why? Have they forgotten all the things you did to us? I stand here, feeling nothing, unless you count relief.

Then, without warning, tears spill from my eyes, too. But don't misunderstand, Dad. I'm weeping not from sadness but from relief. You bastard, Dad. I wish I'd brought a hat pin to jab you with—to make sure you're really, truly dead.

Then I'll know you can't hurt us anymore, Dad.

Then I'll know I'm safe.

Diane Bartholomew, a Waterbury, Connecticut, native, was the youngest of four children. After the great flood of 1955, her family relocated to Trout Run, Pennsylvania, to escape factory work and to open a filling station/luncheonette. Bartholomew returned to Connecticut ten years later, settling with her husband in Naugatuck and taking a job at the Peter Paul Candy Company, where she was employed for twenty-two years. A mother of three daughters, Bartholomew was physically, emotionally, and sexually abused throughout her twenty-four-year marriage. Living in denial of her circumstances, she eventually experienced a psychotic break, during which she shot and killed her husband. Unsuccessful in her attempt to prove her condition of temporary insanity, she entered Niantic Correctional Institution in June 1990.

While incarcerated, Bartholomew battled breast cancer and underwent rigorous self-reflection through counseling and self-help groups. A high school dropout, she earned an associate's degree and went on to pursue a bachelor's degree in social work. Her goal: to become a mental health counselor for victims of domestic abuse.

"I entered prison in a state of confusion," Bartholomew said. "How could I have done something so horribly out of character? I couldn't undo my crime, but my unbearable pain and guilt motivated me to find out what had gone wrong with my mind and how I might learn healthy behaviors. Today I am able to process the chain of events that led to the killing of my husband and to explore these in my writing. I'm going public with my story—facing my past in print—in hopes of raising awareness about violence within the home and helping to bring change to an American justice system still in its primitive stage of understanding the issues surrounding abuse. Whether or not I achieve my personal and professional goals, mine should not be misunderstood as a story of triumph. My husband lost his life. I lost my freedom. When my children visit me, the rules dictate that they can embrace me only across a table four feet in width. In situations of domestic violence, there simply are no winners."

At the halfway point of her twenty-five-year sentence, Bartholomew's cancer returned. For several months, she was misdiagnosed. An unexpected parole followed. Bartholomew died in November 2001, five months after she had regained her freedom.

BAD GIRLS

DALE GRIFFITH

The writer has taught at York School
since 1994.

Y FIRST MEMORY OF NIANTIC STATE FARM FOR Women reaches back to August 1957, the year I was six. My big brother Tommy and I were in the backseat of our old green Dodge and Mom was at the wheel. I was minding my own business, leafing through the Sears catalog, when, without warning, Tommy reached over and yanked it away. "Hey!" I shouted, yanking back. A tug-of-war followed, complete with pinching, slapping, and flying catalog pages. "Stop!" Mom ordered, and when we didn't, she hit the brakes and bumped the car to the shoulder of Route 156. "Knock it off right now," she said. "Or when you're older, you'll end up in there."

"Where?" I said.

"There!" I followed Mom's pointing finger to a series of brick buildings at the edge of a lush green lawn. Shrouded in veils of the road dust we'd just kicked up, it looked mysterious and enchanting—nothing like that *other* place where bad people went. The scary prison we passed on the way to our relatives' in Fall River had barbed wire and barred windows, and guards with guns in the towers. I was confused.

"What did the bad people inside this place do?" I asked Mom.

"All kinds of terrible things. You wouldn't want to end up *there*."

I sat up straight and folded my hands in my lap. As Mom pulled back onto the road, Tom poked me and pointed to the entrance sign we were passing. In his infinite eight-year-old wisdom, my big brother could read, even blurry words at accelerating speeds. "Only bad GIRLS go there," he said.

The idea that I might be locked away for naughtiness helped me to behave myself, for the rest of that day and beyond. Whenever I rode past the prison farm, I'd think about those bad girls stuck inside and wonder what "terrible things" they'd done. I was more curious than worried, though. If you were a *bad* girl, you went there; if you were good, you didn't. Back in 1957, justice had a simple and logical design.

Not so in 1994. The ink on my college diploma was barely dry when I'd applied for the teaching position at Niantic Correctional Institution, and since I'd spent most of my twenty-plus working years in a waitress uniform, I wasn't exactly sure *how* to dress for a "professional" job interview. I stood before the mirror, sucked in my stomach, and tried to

view myself objectively: streaky blond pageboy, long flowered skirt, peri-
winkle T-shirt, beige flats. Did I look like a teacher or a plump middle-
aged hippie? I pulled at the elastic waistband of my skirt, hoping a little
stretching might make the fit less snug. Having quit smoking the previous
fall, I'd gained twelve pounds, but that morning, it felt like a hundred on
my small frame. I pivoted, practiced my professional smile. With three
kids to support and student loans to repay, I needed the job. Now.

Niantic Prison seemed virtually unchanged from the place I recalled
from childhood drive-bys: stately brick buildings, a quaint chapel, tree-
lined roads. An oblivious stranger might assume she'd driven onto the
campus of a small New England college.

Marcia Wade, Niantic's school principal, had a smile that balanced
self-confidence with warmth and a handshake that communicated
authority. In her tailored red linen suit and pinstriped shirt, she could
have graced the cover of *Working Woman* magazine. Marcia led me
toward a chain-link fence, behind which prisoners of varying shapes,
shades, and personal styles were going about their business. She produced a ring of keys, opened a padlock, and swung open the gate. "Go
on in," she said.

I hesitated for a second, held back by my mother's old rule about who
belonged in there and who did not. But at forty, I was in dire need of a
regular salary and the kind of benefits package the State of Connecticut
offered. Besides, I'd worked heart and soul to become a teacher. So I
took a first step toward the open gate, then a second, and before I could
chicken out, I was "inside."

When the inmates spotted Marcia, they swarmed her, reporting a
cacophony of news from home, court, and their housing units. They fired
questions like bullets. "Miz Wade, when's that computer class starting?"
a tall black woman in a shiny purple jogging suit wanted to know.

"Next week, Jasmine. Just like the flyer said." Principal Wade placed
a hand on her hip in mock indignation. "You *did* read the flyer, didn't
you?"

"I'm on it, Miz Wade," Jasmine said. "Read more *carefully*, right?"
Her broad grin revealed several missing teeth.

Marcia addressed each woman by name, listening and responding to
her concern. One by one, the crowd dispersed with the exception of a
small cluster of inmates who'd hung back, eyeing me as if I'd dropped in

from Mars. Was it my outfit? Something caught in my teeth? Why were they staring at me?

A tiny Latina with a shaved head and a fierce look in her eye marched toward Marcia. "Who's *she*?" she asked.

"This is Ms. Griffith, Carmen. She's a teacher and she wants to work here. Anything special you think she should know?"

"Yeah. Tell her to watch her back. These people ain't no joke."

That much I'd figured out already. Half the women looked like giants, some with wrestlers' muscles. Carmen shoved her thumbs into the belt loops of her Wranglers, as if readying herself for a Dodge City showdown. She looked me straight in the eye. "And don't be no trick," she said. As I watched Carmen saunter across the asphalt yard, I swallowed hard.

A "trick," Marcia explained, was a staff member whom the inmates manipulated into doing favors. "Carmen's right," she said. "Some of the women here are professional cons. Just remember, a staff member who gets played and violates the rules can lose her job." Noting my apprehension, she added. "But don't worry. If you're hired, your training and your instincts will tell you what to do."

"And you *BELIEVE* that bitch?" someone shouted. "Well, fuck *YOU* then, 'cuz I never said *NOTHIN'* about you to that bitch!"

My eyes jumped to a scrawny, rat-faced woman who was poking her index finger into the breastbone of a stocky brunette. The brunette bellowed back and two uniformed guards rushed from nowhere to separate them. The combatants were handcuffed and escorted away.

Okay, I thought, I've seen enough. Teaching at a women's prison may have seemed like a good idea, but a decent wage and a classroom of my own would hardly compensate for the stress of working with these thugs. Maybe I'd pack up my teaching dreams and pursue Career Plan B: grocery bagger.

But throughout that first day inside Niantic Prison, my fear of the place engaged in a tug-of-war with my feeling that, in some inexplicable way, I belonged there. My friend Nancy, who'd worked for the Department of Correction for many years, had said, "I promise you this much: you'll never be bored. And mostly, the women are a hoot." Nancy had started at the jail in the early seventies, when inmates still had fishing privileges at Bride Lake and could fry up their catch and host a feed for

the other women in their housing unit. Back then, the units were operated like group homes—makeshift families with staff members functioning as surrogate parents. "The place has changed a lot since those days,"
Nancy had said. "But the women haven't. Most have been through hell
and back. You'll relate."

From the start, I loved my job at Niantic. Because school was volun-
tary, most of the students were motivated, polite, and hopeful. Many
had quit school in eighth or ninth grade as other forces invaded their
lives and spun them in different directions. A third- or fourth-grade
reading level was not unusual; often, my students could neither read nor
write. At the prison school, our mission was to help these women fill in
the lost years of their education, and I felt a strong sense of purpose
immediately.

In 1994, inmates still wore their own clothes, and with the exception
of uniformed corrections officers, it was sometimes a challenge to distinguish prisoners from staff. Residents in good standing roamed the
grounds with relative freedom, heading for school or to their jobs in the
kitchen, the laundry, or the maintenance department. It would have
been easy for an inmate to simply walk off the property to freedom, but
escape attempts were rare.

Change was in the air at Niantic, however, and with it the sound of
drilling, hammering, and construction workers' banter. Two years earlier, ground had been broken for a new maximum-security facility.
Designed to relieve overcrowding and address a new breed of more violent female inmate, the new state-of-the-art structure would be up and
running by year's end.

"State of the art" hardly described my first official classroom, which
was located in Thompson Hall, a housing unit in "old" Niantic.
Thompson Hall residents were mostly women waiting to be sentenced
or high-security inmates forbidden to walk the grounds unescorted and
required to wear handcuffs and leg irons when venturing outside their
residence hall. Because it was difficult to accommodate this population
at the main school, the school came to them. *Someone* had to teach at
Thompson Hall, lugging books and supplies in and out of the trunk of
her car because there were no locking cabinets to discourage itchy fingers. As the newest hire, that dubious honor went to me.

Spacious and sunny, my classroom was wedged between the laundry room and the main hallway, which was lined on both sides with cells. The classroom windows allowed a view of the fenced recreation yard where inmates sat on broken chairs, smoking, laughing, and shouting. Unseen but most definitely heard, the women locked above us in Thompson Hall's second story called down from their windows to the women below.

"Hey, baby, what you doin' here? Thought you was going home."

"Tomorrow. They messed up my papers. Can't wait for some *real* food."

"I hear you, baby! Tell Sookie I love her, okay?"

"You know I will. Tell my sister I'll miss her."

The women in the yard waved, called, and blew kisses not only to one another and to the women on the second floor, but to my students as well—some of whom had no qualms about interrupting instruction to respond in kind. From the hallway, there'd be more commotion. Officer Marsan, a gray-haired CO with a boom-box voice, enforced order with stand-up comedy. "Hey, Jackie! You've got a visitor. Mel Gibson, I think. . . . Get ready for transport, Cinderella. Your carriage awaits! . . . Hey, Miss Campbell Soup. I want this spill cleaned up NOW!" Thompson Hall residents shuffled past, indifferent to my lesson plans. "Anybody seen my fucking toothbrush?" "That your popcorn burning?" "Don't go in that bathroom, y'all; it's *nasty!*"

Inside the classroom, a door on the left led into the laundry room, a tiny, unventilated cubicle where a pretty Chilean inmate who spoke almost no English laundered the entire building's soiled belongings, bag by bag by bag. When she'd finish a load, Estelle would pack the clean, folded items into the inmate's bag and place it inside my classroom. By lunchtime, laundry bags awaiting pickup would line an entire wall. One by one, women would clomp in for their clean clothes while I scrawled notes on the cracked blackboard, covering everything from fractions to fiction for a motley assortment of twenty students of diverse abilities. Occasionally, an inmate would return moments later, dragging her bag behind her and barging into the laundry room to chew out Estelle. "Goddammit Estelle! Where's my pink underwear? The ones my mother just freakin' sent me?" And poor Estelle would unpack the bag, discover the missing item glued to a sock or hidden in a sleeve, and send the complainer on her way.

Because the staff bathroom was located inside the office of Bob Carini, Thompson Hall's overworked unit manager, he and I saw each other frequently. Part of Mr. Carini's job was to listen to the endless demands of the inmates, many of which I overheard during my lavatory visits. "That bitch stole my coffee. I know she did!" Tasha insisted. "You gotta do something about her, Mr. C., or else *I'll* do something."

"Was the coffee locked in your box, Tasha?"

"I left it on my bed while I went to the john. Come back and it's gone."

"Then it's possible someone other than Stacy took it. Right?"

"She was right there! I know she took it!"

"Stacy told me she was across the hall, talking to Yolie. Isn't it possible someone else took it while she was out? Isn't it *possible* she's telling the truth?"

I marveled at Bob Carini's calm, caring tone as he processed the dozens of crises and complaints. "How do you stand it?" I asked him one afternoon.

He pointed to the framed poster of the "Serenity Prayer" on his wall: *God, grant me the Serenity to accept the things I cannot change, the Courage to change the things I can, and the Wisdom to know the difference.* "One day at a time," he said. "Sometimes one minute at a time. And what really helps is knowing I'm not doing this job alone." Every morning, Bob said, he asked God to help him help the women—and if helping them wasn't possible, at least to avoid doing them harm. I've borrowed Mr. Carini's prayer many times since that day, comforted by its reminder of the limitations of my power to fix all of the world's injustices, and the fact that I am not working alone.

I nicknamed my next Niantic classroom "the Gingerbread House." Located down the road from the main school, this tiny two-room structure came equipped with its own bathroom and an attached greenhouse. For years the building had been used for maintenance storage, but because the school was short on space, the warden had okayed a renovation for the school's use. After a good cleaning, a couple of coats of paint, and some decorative touches, my students and I were ready to roll.

The Gingerbread House operated as a writing center, from which I instructed writers of all levels, both individually and in groups. From the center, we launched Niantic's first personal essay contest, "Acts of Courage." Posted flyers promised that the women's stories would be read by a panel of judges, the winners' names announced, and small prizes awarded, including publication of all entries in a booklet to be distributed around the compound. Twenty-seven women responded, and at a school assembly, three winners read their essays aloud. After the program ended, I was surrounded. "When's the *next* contest?" "What's the deadline?" "Can anyone enter?"

As the Gingerbread House was separated from the rest of the institution, I enjoyed a degree of flexibility not available to instructors at the main school. With permission from my supervisor, I held afternoon classes outdoors, reading and discussing poetry. One fall day, we planted daffodil bulbs, something most of my city-raised students had never experienced. A few months later, a sudden cold snap burst the pipes of the Gingerbread House and the administration opted not to make repairs. What had been our haven was now off-limits to the students, and when the daffodils bloomed the following spring, no one was there to notice.

"Homeless" in the wake of the Gingerbread House's burst pipes and emergency closing, I was one of the first teachers transferred to the compound's new super-facility. Each living unit was a replica of the next and each cell conformed to a standard intolerant of deviation. Unlike "old" Niantic, where inmates could add their own small touches—a crocheted pillow, an embroidered picture frame—expressions of individuality were now taboo. All personal clothing was surrendered, replaced by inmate uniforms. Inmates were now addressed by their last names only.

Concrete and steel may wall away much of outside life for Connecticut's incarcerated citizens, but inmates feel shifts in the political wind. Indeed, most are directly affected. Reflecting the national trends of the early 1990s, Connecticut's justice system had begun handing out tougher sentences for drug-related crimes and withholding early parole. Prisoners now had to serve a mandatory 50 percent of their sentences before such mitigating factors as good behavior or successful completion of treatment programs could be factored into the parole equation. As a result, the inmate population soared and crowded conditions taxed prisoners and staff alike. Niantic's new facility would, by all reports, alleviate the problem.

The reinvented compound was renamed the Janet S. York Correctional Institution. Janet York, who had served as Niantic's highly regarded warden from 1960 through 1975, had first set foot on the prison grounds in 1948 as a volunteer—a college student majoring in social work. Impressed by the facility's progressive policies and its emphasis on treatment and rehabilitation, she was hired as a counselor, ascending to the position of deputy warden, then warden. Throughout her fifteen-year tenure as the prison's chief administrator, York focused her efforts on education, vocational training, and addiction counseling. Under her direction, the compound became a model for success—a prison that "cures by kindness," according to one national publication, and one whose policies were studied and emulated by reformers and penologists around the country.

The new compound, which bore Janet York's name, was a decidedly different facility. Now, *all* inmates lived under tightly enforced maximum-security regulation. Many of the small, incentive-building privileges and humanizing gestures extended to low-risk inmates were surrendered during this transition. Ms. York's ideals, however, remain intact at the prison school, where standards are high, personal responsibility is a must, and rehabilitation is the reason for existence.

Sadly, some inmates have known nothing but violence and domestic chaos since birth. A visit to any psychiatric facility for abused children will reveal the wounded throwaways who are prime candidates for future criminal activity and incarceration. It's tempting to slap a label on an inmate and lock her up, rather than look beneath the surface of her conviction to the complexities that shaped her for prison. More often than not, the label drives the woman's treatment while she is "inside." By the time she reaches my classroom, school is the least of her troubles. Yet her troubles probably began in elementary school, or even earlier.

According to current research, girls between the ages of twelve and sixteen who are convicted of violent crimes were, in most cases, physically and/or sexually abused by the age of *two*. By the time these victims reach puberty, problems have proliferated and labels have been affixed. Our future inmate has attention deficit disorder, or she is "socially and emotionally maladjusted," or she exhibits "at risk"

behavior. She has poor attendance, poor nutrition, and family problems: her mom may be addicted, her dad may be long gone, and there
may have been evidence of neglect or violence and Department of Children and Families involvement. She may have moved four or five times
in as many years.

These are *my* students—the ones who fell through the cracks in public school. They looked unusual or smelled bad and were frequently the
targets of other children. Their mothers signed the parent-teacher conference form but never showed. These are the girls who learned slowly
or differently—the ones who sat at the back of the room hoping to
remain invisible (and largely succeeding), or the ones who sat right next
to the teacher's desk because they had to be seen and heard constantly
by *everyone*. My students' treasures are buried under piles of emotional
and institutional rubble—yet the treasures are there, waiting to be
unearthed and discovered.

It's the individuals, not the place, that make my work more a calling
than a job. Mary, thirty-two, a Latino mother of five, moved from Puerto
Rico to Hartford when she was eleven. Instead of going to school, she
cared for her siblings while her mother worked at a factory, screwing lids
on jars of face cream. Meanwhile, on a daily basis, Mom's boyfriend,
Willy (the father of Mary's youngest siblings), forced her to have sex.
"Don't tell your mother," Willy warned. "You know how jealous she is.
She might not understand." When Mary became pregnant at thirteen,
she had no choice but to tell. And Willy was right: Mom didn't under-
stand. "You steal my man in my own house? Get out, you filthy whore!"
Mary was evicted; Willy stayed. Believing she had wronged her family,
Mary lived with an aunt until the baby was born and a new man took an
interest. She and her infant son moved in with him.

By the age of sixteen, Mary had two children by two fathers. The
father of her second beat her and taught her how to shoot heroin, and
later, how to peddle it. Mary had seen the inside of prison before she
was eighteen. The cycle of crime had begun in earnest and, if the statistics bear out, will likely have repercussions for her children, her grandchildren, and the rest of us.

When Mary came to school at York, she could read and write no English and had mastered only the rudiments of Spanish. Yet she was
bright and eager to learn. Within a year, she could read English at the

eighth-grade level. One day she handed me a two-page letter. "To my children," she said with a grin. "Before school, my roommate used to write my letters. This one *I* wrote, all by myself. It's good?"

I wanted to shout hallelujah—to grab Mary and dance her around the classroom. But we had a full house and I didn't want to risk embarrassing her. "It's *very* good," I whispered. "Give yourself a hug."

Loretta, a black woman in her late forties, was born at Niantic Prison to an alcoholic mom, back in the days when incarcerated women were allowed to keep their children with them for the first year after birth. Like her mother, Loretta had been returning to jail since she was sixteen, the result of convictions for shoplifting, prostitution, and possession and sale of narcotics, and for numerous failures to appear in court. Until her most recent bid, Loretta had assumed herself "too cool for school," but at last she was ready for a change. She had lost custody of her three children and tested positive for HIV. "I gotta do *something*," she told me. "Street life is killing me."

One day, Loretta returned a book to me, Toni Morrison's *The Bluest Eye*. "This is the first book I ever finished," she said, her eyes working hard to stay fixed on mine. "You know what I'm saying?"

"Did you like it?" I asked. Talking about literature is often a way for my students and me to get beyond surface exchanges, and Morrison's book is a favorite of mine.

"Yeah. I mean, that little girl had it hard," Loretta said. She stopped to survey the room for spies and eavesdroppers, then whispered the rest. "Some of the same stuff that happened to Pecola happened to me. The rape and all. I could've written *that* story."

"Well, why don't you write your own?" I said. "Don't worry about spelling or punctuation or any of that stuff. Just write from the heart."

Her eyes widened. "You think I could do that? Huh. Maybe I will."

A week later, Loretta handed me her manuscript—a wad of crumpled papers. "How'd it go?" I asked.

"At first, I couldn't get going, know what I'm saying? But then I remembered you said just write down anything, so I wrote, 'I don't have nothing to say.' I kept writing that until something else came out. It's not too good, but it's something. And I feel good now, like I got a load off my chest."

That night, when I read Loretta's words, chills ran through me as though God herself was breathing against my neck. In the midst of the scratch-outs, misspellings, and bad grammar, the beauty of Loretta's voice moved me as only spiritual Truth can.

Acclaimed authors from Charles Dickens to Virginia Woolf to Tim O'Brien have transformed personal suffering into art, but the benefits of a writing life are available to the lay writer as well as the literary genius. Scientific researchers such as James Pennebaker (*Opening Up: The Healing Power of Expressing Emotions*) and Louise DeSalvo (*Writing as a Way of Healing: How Telling Our Stories Transforms Our Lives*) have measured and testified to the emotional and physical benefits of the written word. Cancer and AIDs patients live longer when they keep daily journals. Sufferers of asthma and hypertension can lessen their symptoms with a regimen of autobiographical writing. Scripting their memories increases the odds that recovery program participants will succeed and move on to more productive lives.

By my seventh year of teaching at York, I had gathered, edited, and "published" four booklets of my students' writing—stories describing worlds where love and hate blur and where sexual abuse, violence, and drug addiction are both commonplace and epidemic. I'd long known the statistical connection between childhood brutality and incarceration. Now I knew the writers, too. Each of those alarming statistics has a name, a face, a history. And if editing and publishing the women's testimonies was time-consuming and emotionally draining, it was worthwhile work in that it seemed to have a positive effect on the writers involved. The women whose work appeared in print reported feeling proud of their accomplishments and pleased with the responses they received from others. "Storytelling teaches or reteaches us empathy," Louise DeSalvo observes in *Writing as a Way of Healing*. "Because the capacity for empathy is often lost in extreme situations, restoring empathy in survivors is essential. Writing is one important way to accomplish this."

Once an inmate is released, I usually lose track of her, especially if she is doing well; department restrictions limit outside contact with ex-offenders. However, I sometimes hear news through the grapevine or bump into a former student "outside." Of course, many women *do* return to prison, often within months of their release. Recidivism is high at York and in other prisons, about 70 percent.

It's hard not to be disappointed when a woman resurfaces, having "messed up" and lost her freedom once again. I've come to realize, however, that for many, prison is a step up from life on the streets—a safe harbor of sorts. Rehabilitation, like other forms of recovery, is a process. Healing for the women at York is painfully slow, often fraught with setbacks; it sometimes requires far more support than the institution—and the society whose priorities it reflects—is prepared to give. Alternatives to incarceration do exist, and there's evidence that such programs are more effective than prison in reducing re-arrest rates, but our knee-jerk tendency is to bypass these alternative solutions and re-incarcerate. It's particularly difficult to find safe housing for women between the ages of sixteen and twenty-one. Trapped between childhood and womanhood, these unfortunates often wind up back on the streets, where they fall prey to all kinds of trouble. Often, by the time a woman returns to prison, she's desperately ill, physically *and* mentally.

In the spring of 1999, two suicides and a number of thwarted attempts by other inmates rattled the foundation of York C.I. One of the victims was a thirty-three-year-old woman who'd been coming to Niantic since her teens. She killed herself within a week of her reentry, a critical time when many recidivists are overwhelmed by feelings of hopelessness and vulnerable to their self-destructive impulses. The other victim, a student at our school, was only nineteen. A fight with her girl-friend had triggered a final act of self-violence. In the wake of these tragedies, an epidemic of angry defeat infected the population.

The York School staff called to the outside community for help in combating despair. We brainstormed, networked, made inquiries, and made pleas. The school broadened its curriculum to include year-round workshops on women's health and healing, and volunteers stepped forward: poets and journalists, dancers and musicians, humorists and businesswomen and Buddhist monks. One of the volunteers who came to us when we cast our nets was the award-winning author and teacher Wally Lamb.

Lamb had committed to a two-hour workshop on the use of writing as a coping tool, and I was assigned as the program's faculty coordinator. Something an inmate said that day must have moved Wally, because at the end of the session, he agreed to return two weeks later, *if* the women agreed to write. Wally moved the women, too. By our third session, inmates who "didn't trust anyone" were sharing intimate life experiences with him.

Now in our third year as a writing group, alternate Thursdays have become "Wally days" for twenty or so of our students. Within the prison, however, nothing is certain except uncertainty. We may have an emergency lockdown, a fight may break out in the chow hall, or a medical code may be called. While our custody staff is efficient and responsive, with over twelve hundred inmates, crises large and small do occur at York. Wally knows that on any given Thursday, he may be refused entry into the institution without explanation.

As the months have rolled into years, Wally has lost his celebrity status and become part of the York School family, sharing his expertise in the craft, his stories, and his heart. Within the group, we've had our share of bumps and triumphs, tears and laughter. Laughter is a precious gift among the incarcerated. During one particularly silly session, the group dubbed themselves The Lambettes. "We oughta get black satin jackets with our names in hot pink across the back, like those girls in *Grease*," someone suggested.

"Or lamb suits," I said. "Fleecy hats, little tails. Man, we'd look baaaa-d." The Lambettes groaned in unison.

"Come on, now," Nancy said. "Do I *look* like the lamb-suit type?" Attractive and vain, Nancy prides herself on her ability to look sexy even in prison sweats. "A *bunny* suit maybe. With fishnet stockings and spiked heels."

"Yeah, no offense, Ms. G., but I'm not wearing a lamb suit either," Brenda added. "I like the jackets idea, though—with tight black leather pants."

Humor is in short supply at York; prison life is not a joke. Yet once a woman is able to laugh, especially at her own foibles, she's on the right road. The Lambettes (the name stuck) laugh often—*at* themselves and *with* one another. Writing, laughter, and deep conversation have worked magic on their lives. And because the Lambettes are committed to revision, their stories push deeper and deeper beneath the surface with each subsequent draft. Revision does more than improve the writer's work; it teaches patience as well, a quality that's especially useful in prison. The women learn over time that good writing, like a good life, requires effort and forbearance. It requires courage, too, but yields rewards as well. Writing seems to provide a means of self-forgiveness, and when the writer grants herself such a reprieve, healing begins. It's hard to tell the truth—almost as hard as holding it in.

Today, when I consider my life's work at York prison, I can hardly believe my good fortune. Who would have thought I'd find my calling at the place with which my mother had tried to scare me back in 1957? "That's where *bad* people go," she'd said. "You sure wouldn't want to end up *there*."

My mom was wrong on both counts. The women I know at York have done some bad things, but they are not bad people. Like you and me and the rest of us, they need a little kindness, a little forgiveness. I know that, but for the grace of God, I might not be the one who gets to leave the compound at the end of the day and drive home to the people I love. This knowledge keeps me both humble and grateful.

Within the walls of York Correctional Institution, physical freedom is removed and, all too often, residents receive the message that they are society's subhuman throwaways. Writing, especially deep recorded recollections of specific events and the feelings these memories engender, is a means of fighting back—a way to take control and preserve one's dignity in the face of adversity. "Writing's helped me figure out who I am and who I want to be," a Lambette told me recently. "My body's still in prison, but my spirit's finally free."

Dale Griffith returned to college and earned undergraduate and master's degrees from Wesleyan University. She lives in her childhood home on the Connecticut shore with her children and her cats. Griffith has taught English classes at Middlesex Community College and has taught writing and a variety of other courses at York C.I. since 1994.

"Writing and the teaching of writing have helped me to heal and define myself," Griffith says.

SOURCES AND SUGGESTED READING

The following works were instructive to the writers of the York prison writers' group and may prove useful to readers of this book who write:

Brande, Dorothea. *Becoming a Writer*. New York: Putnam, 1981.

Cameron, Julia. *The Artist's Way: A Spiritual Path to Higher Creativity*. New York: Tarcher/Putnam, 1992.

DeSalvo, Louise. *Writing as a Way of Healing: How Telling Our Stories Transforms Our Lives*. San Francisco: HarperCollins, 1999.

Gardner, John. *On Becoming a Novelist*. New York: HarperCollins, 1983.

Goldberg, Natalie. *Writing Down the Bones: Freeing the Writer Within*. Boston: Shambhala, 1986.

Henderson, Bill, ed. *The Pushcart Prize: Best of the Small Presses*, volumes xx–xxvi. Wainscott, N.Y.: Pushcart Press, 1996–2002.

Lamott, Anne. *Bird by Bird: Some Instructions on Writing and Life*. New York: Anchor/Doubleday, 1994.

McKee, Robert. *Story: Substance, Style, and the Principles of Screenwriting*. New York: ReganBooks, 1997.

Murray, Donald. *Crafting a Life in Essay, Story, and Poem*. Portsmouth, N.H.: Boynton/Cook, 1996.

Pennebaker, James. *Opening Up: The Healing Power of Expressing Emotions*. New York: Guilford Press, 1997.

The editor consulted the following sources:

Rierdan, Andi. *The Farm: Life Inside a Women's Prison*. Amherst: University of Massachusetts Press, 1977.

Timoner, Ondi (dir.). *The Nature of the Beast: The Life of Bonnie Jean Foreshaw* (film). Inside Time Productions.

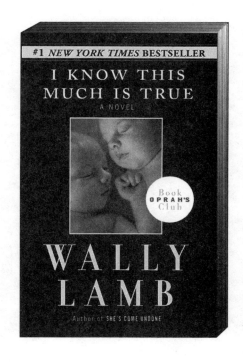